CAMBRIDGE

Brighter Thinking

A Level Further Mathematics for OCR A
Pure Core Student Book 1 (AS/Year 1)
Vesna Kadelburg, Ben Woolley, Paul Fannon and Stephen Ward

CAMBRIDGE
UNIVERSITY PRESS

University Printing House, Cambridge CB2 8BS, United Kingdom

One Liberty Plaza, 20th Floor, New York, NY 10006, USA

477 Williamstown Road, Port Melbourne, VIC 3207, Australia

4843/24, 2nd Floor, Ansari Road, Daryaganj, Delhi – 110002, India

79 Anson Road, #06-04/06, Singapore 079906

Cambridge University Press is part of the University of Cambridge.

It furthers the University's mission by disseminating knowledge in the pursuit of education, learning and research at the highest international levels of excellence.

www.cambridge.org
Information on this title: www.cambridge.org/9781316644386 (Paperback)
www.cambridge.org/9781316644232 (Paperback with Cambridge Elevate edition)

© Cambridge University Press 2017

This publication is in copyright. Subject to statutory exception
and to the provisions of relevant collective licensing agreements,
no reproduction of any part may take place without the written
permission of Cambridge University Press.

First published 2017

20 19 18 17 16 15 14 13 12 11 10 9 8 7 6 5 4 3 2 1

Printed in the United Kingdom by Latimer Trend

A catalogue record for this publication is available from the British Library

ISBN 978-1-316-64438-6 Paperback
ISBN 978-1-316-64423-2 Paperback with Cambridge Elevate edition

Additional resources for this publication at www.cambridge.org/education

Cambridge University Press has no responsibility for the persistence or accuracy of URLs for external or third-party internet websites referred to in this publication, and does not guarantee that any content on such websites is, or will remain, accurate or appropriate.

....

NOTICE TO TEACHERS IN THE UK

It is illegal to reproduce any part of this work in material form (including photocopying and electronic storage) except under the following circumstances:
(i)   where you are abiding by a licence granted to your school or institution by the Copyright Licensing Agency;
(ii) where no such licence exists, or where you wish to exceed the terms of a licence, and you have gained the written permission of Cambridge University Press;
(iii) where you are allowed to reproduce without permission under the provisions of Chapter 3 of the Copyright, Designs and Patents Act 1988, which covers, for example, the reproduction of short passages within certain types of educational anthology and reproduction for the purposes of setting examination questions.

....

This resource is endorsed by OCR for use with specification AS Further Mathematics A (H235) and specification A Level Further Mathematics A (H245). In order to gain OCR endorsement, this resource has undergone an independent quality check. Any references to assessment and/or assessment preparation are the publisher's interpretation of the specification requirements and are not endorsed by OCR. OCR recommends that a range of teaching and learning resources are used in preparing learners for assessment. OCR has not paid for the production of this resource, nor does OCR receive any royalties from its sale. For more information about the endorsement process, please visit the OCR website, **www.ocr.org.uk**.

Contents

Introduction iv
How to use this book v

1 Matrices 1

Section 1: Addition, subtraction and scalar
multiplication of matrices 1
Section 2: Matrix multiplication 7
Section 3: Determinants and inverses
of 2 × 2 matrices 13
Section 4: Determinants and inverses
of 3 × 3 matrices 23
Mixed practice 1 30

2 Further vectors 32

Section 1: Vector equation of a line 33
Section 2: Cartesian equation of a line 39
Section 3: Intersections of lines 45
Section 4: Angles and the scalar product 48
Section 5: The vector product 56
Mixed practice 2 62

3 Applications of matrices 64

Section 1: Linear simultaneous equations 65
Section 2: Matrices as linear transformations ... 70
Section 3: Further transformations in 2-D 78
Section 4: Invariant points and invariant lines ... 83
Section 5: Transformations in 3-D 88
Mixed practice 3 95

Focus on … Proof 1 98
Focus on … Problem-solving 1 100
Focus on … Modelling 1 103
Cross-topic review exercise 1 106

4 Complex numbers 109

Section 1: Definition and basic arithmetic of i ... 110
Section 2: Division and complex conjugates 115
Section 3: Geometric representation 119
Section 4: Modulus and argument 121
Section 5: Loci in the complex plane 129
Section 6: Operations in modulus–argument
form 134
Mixed practice 4 139

5 Roots of polynomials 141

Section 1: Factorising polynomials 141
Section 2: Complex solutions to polynomial
equations 144
Section 3: Roots and coefficients 148
Section 4: Finding an equation with
given roots 154
Section 5: Transforming equations 160
Mixed practice 5 165

6 Mathematical induction 167

Section 1: The principle of mathematical
induction 168
Section 2: Induction and matrices 169
Section 3: Induction and divisibility 171
Section 4: Induction and inequalities 174
Mixed practice 6 177

Focus on … Proof 2 178
Focus on … Problem-solving 2 180
Focus on … Modelling 2 182
Cross-topic review exercise 2 184

Practice paper 187
Formulae 188
Answers 189
Glossary 212
Index 214
Acknowledgements 217

Introduction

You have probably been told that mathematics is very useful, yet it can often seem like a lot of techniques that just have to be learnt to answer examination questions. You are now getting to the point where you will start to see where some of these techniques can be applied in solving real problems. However, as well as seeing how maths can be useful we hope that anyone working through this book will realise that it can also be incredibly frustrating, surprising and ultimately beautiful.

The book is woven around three key themes from the new curriculum:

Proof
Maths is valued because it trains you to think logically and communicate precisely. At a high level, maths is far less concerned about answers and more about the clear communication of ideas. It is not about being neat – although that might help! It is about creating a coherent argument that other people can easily follow but find difficult to refute. Have you ever tried looking at your own work? If you cannot follow it yourself it is unlikely anybody else will be able to understand it. In maths we communicate using a variety of means – feel free to use combinations of diagrams, words and algebra to aid your argument. And once you have attempted a proof, try presenting it to your peers. Look critically (but positively) at some other people's attempts. It is only through having your own attempts evaluated and trying to find flaws in other proofs that you will develop sophisticated mathematical thinking. This is why we have included lots of common errors in our 'work it out' boxes – just in case your friends don't make any mistakes!

Problem-solving
Maths is valued because it trains you to look at situations in unusual, creative ways, to persevere and to evaluate solutions along the way. We have been heavily influenced by a great mathematician and maths educator, George Polya, who believed that students were not born with problem-solving skills – such skills were developed by seeing problems being solved and reflecting on their solutions before trying similar problems. You may not realise it but good mathematicians spend most of their time being stuck.

You need to spend some time on problems you can't do, trying out different possibilities. If after a while you have not cracked it then look at the solution and try a similar problem. Don't be disheartened if you cannot get it immediately – in fact, the longer you spend puzzling over a problem the more you will learn from the solution. You may never need to integrate a rational function in future, but we firmly believe that the problem-solving skills you will develop by trying it can be applied to many other situations.

Modelling
Maths is valued because it helps us solve real-world problems. However, maths describes ideal situations and the real world is messy! Modelling is about deciding on the important features needed to describe the essence of a situation and turning that into a mathematical form, then using it to make predictions, compare to reality and possibly improve the model. In many situations the technical maths is actually the easy part – especially with modern technology. Deciding which features of reality to include or ignore and anticipating the consequences of these decisions is the hard part. Yet it is amazing how some fairly drastic assumptions – such as pretending a car is a single point or that people's votes are independent – can result in models that are surprisingly accurate.

More than anything else, this book is about making links. Links between the different chapters, the topics covered and the themes above, links to other subjects and links to the real world. We hope that you will grow to see maths as one great complex but beautiful web of interlinking ideas.

Maths is about so much more than examinations, but we hope that if you take on board these ideas (and do plenty of practice!) you will find maths examinations a much more approachable and possibly even enjoyable experience. However, always remember that the result of what you write down in a few hours by yourself in silence under exam conditions is not the only measure you should consider when judging your mathematical ability – it is only one variable in a much more complicated mathematical model!

How to use this book

Throughout this book you will notice particular features that are designed to aid your learning. This section provides a brief overview of these features.

> **In this chapter you will learn:**
> - how to add, subtract and perform scalar multiplication with conformable matrices
> - about zero and identity matrices and their significance

Learning objectives
A short summary of the content that you will learn in each chapter.

> **Before you start...**
>
> | A Level Mathematics Student Book 1, Chapter 12 | You should know how to add, subtract and perform scalar multiplication of vectors. | 1 Calculate $\begin{pmatrix} 2 \\ 3 \\ -1 \end{pmatrix}$ |
> | --- | --- | --- |

Before you start
Points you should know from your previous learning and questions to check that you're ready to start the chapter.

> **WORKED EXAMPLE**
>
> The left-hand side shows you how to set out your working. The right-hand side explains the more difficult steps and helps you understand why a particular method was chosen.

> **Key point**
>
> A summary of the most important methods, facts and formulae.

> **PROOF**
>
> Step-by-step walkthroughs of standard proofs and methods of proof.

> **Explore**
>
> Ideas for activities and investigations to extend your understanding of the topic.

> **WORK IT OUT**
>
> Can you identify the correct solution and find the mistakes in the two incorrect solutions?

> **Tip**
>
> Useful guidance, including on ways of calculating or checking and use of technology.

Each chapter ends with a **Checklist of learning and understanding** and a **Mixed practice exercise**, which includes **past paper questions** marked with the icon.

In between chapters, you will find extra sections that bring together topics in a more synoptic way.

> **Focus on …**
>
> Unique sections relating to the preceding chapters that develop your skills in proof, problem solving and modelling.

> **CROSS-TOPIC REVIEW EXERCISE**
>
> Questions covering topics from across the preceding chapters, testing your ability to apply what you have learnt.

You will find **Paper 1 and Paper 2 practice questions** towards the end of the book, as well as a glossary of key terms (picked out in colour within the chapters), and **answers** to all questions. Full **worked solutions** can be found on the Cambridge Elevate digital platform, along with a **digital version** of this Student Book.

A Level Further Mathematics for OCR A Pure Core Student Book 1

Maths is all about making links, which is why throughout this book you will find signposts emphasising connections between different topics, applications and suggestions for further research.

▶ Rewind
Reminders of where to find useful information from earlier in your study.

⏭ Fast forward
Links to topics that you may cover in greater detail later in your study.

📷 Focus on...
Links to problem-solving, modelling or proof exercises that relate to the topic currently being studied.

ⓘ Did you know?
Interesting or historical information and links with other subjects to improve your awareness about how mathematics contributes to society.

Colour-coding of exercises
The questions in the exercises are designed to provide careful progression, ranging from basic fluency to practice questions. They are uniquely colour-coded, as shown below.

1 A sequence is defined by $u_n = 2 \times 3^{n-1}$. Use the principle of mathematical induction to prove that $u_1 + u_2 + \ldots + u_n = 3^n - 1$.

2 Show that $1^2 + 2^2 + \ldots + n^2 = \dfrac{n(n+1)(2n+1)}{6}$.

3 Show that $1^3 + 2^3 + \ldots + n^3 = \dfrac{n^2(n+1)^2}{4}$.

4 Prove by induction that $\dfrac{1}{1 \times 2} + \dfrac{1}{2 \times 3} + \dfrac{1}{3 \times 4} + \ldots + \dfrac{1}{n(n+1)} = \dfrac{n}{n+1}$.

5 Prove by induction that $\dfrac{1}{1 \times 3} + \dfrac{1}{3 \times 5} + \dfrac{1}{5 \times 7} + \ldots + \dfrac{1}{(2n-1) \times (2n+1)} = \dfrac{n}{2n+1}$.

6 Prove that $1 \times 1! + 2 \times 2! + 3 \times 3! \ldots + n \times n! = (n+1)! - 1$

7 Use the principle of mathematical induction to show that $1^2 - 2^2 + 3^2 - 4^2 + \ldots + (-1)^{n-1} n^2 = (-1)^{n-1} \dfrac{n(n+1)}{2}$.

8 Prove that $(n+1) + (n+2) + (n+3) + \ldots + (2n) = \dfrac{1}{2}n(3n+1)$

9 Prove using induction that $\sin\theta + \sin 3\theta + \ldots + \sin(2n-1)\theta = \dfrac{\sin^2 n\theta}{\sin\theta}$, $n \in \mathbb{Z}^+$

10 Prove that $\sum_{k=1}^{n} k\, 2^k = (n-1) 2^{n+1} + 2$

Black – drill questions. These come in several parts, each with subparts i and ii. You only need attempt subpart i at first; subpart ii is essentially the same question, which you can use for further practice if you got part i wrong, for homework, or when you revisit the exercise during revision.

Green – practice questions at a basic level.

Blue – practice questions at an intermediate level.

Red – practice questions at an advanced level.

Purple – challenging questions that apply the concept of the current chapter across other areas of maths.

Yellow – designed to encourage reflection and discussion.

Ⓐ – indicates content that is for A Level students only

ⒶⓈ – indicates content that is for AS Level students only

1 Matrices

In this chapter you will learn:

- how to add, subtract and perform scalar multiplication with conformable matrices
- about zero and identity matrices and their significance
- how to calculate the determinant of a 2×2 or 3×3 matrix
- how to find and interpret the inverse of a 2×2 or 3×3 matrix, where one exists.

Before you start…

A Level Mathematics Student Book 1, Chapter 12	You should know how to add, subtract and perform scalar multiplication of vectors.	1 Calculate $\begin{pmatrix} 2 \\ 3 \\ -1 \end{pmatrix} - 2 \begin{pmatrix} 1 \\ -4 \\ -3 \end{pmatrix}$.

What is a matrix?

In both pure and applied mathematics it is often convenient to structure information in a rectangular array of numbers. For example, connections in a network can be represented in this way. A rectangular array of numbers is called a matrix.

You have already worked with vectors, which are a special type of matrix. The rules for manipulating vectors can be extended to other rectangular arrays. Although some of those rules may seem abstract at first, they can in fact represent many practical situations. For example, in Chapter 3 you will see how matrix multiplication can be used to combine geometrical transformations and to count the number of paths in a network. You will also learn that you can use matrices to solve simultaneous equations.

Section 1: Addition, subtraction and scalar multiplication of matrices

A matrix (plural: matrices) is a rectangular array of elements, which may be numerical or algebraic. For example,

$$\mathbf{A} = \begin{pmatrix} 1 & -3 & x \\ 2.5 & a^2 - \pi & 4 \end{pmatrix}$$

is a matrix with two rows and three columns, with a total of six elements.

Key point 1.1

An $m \times n$ matrix is a rectangular array of elements with m rows and n columns, written within parentheses (also called brackets). A matrix that has the same number of rows and columns is called a **square matrix**.

Matrices are generally designated by a bold or underlined upper-case letter (**A** in print and either $\underline{A}$ or A when handwritten).

There are two special matrices with which you will need to be familiar.

Key point 1.2

- A **zero matrix**, denoted by **Z** (also called the **null matrix**), has every element equal to zero.
- An **identity matrix**, denoted by **I**, is a square matrix with 1 on each element of the lead diagonal (upper left to lower right) and a zero everywhere else.

For example, the 2×2 identity matrix is $\begin{pmatrix} 1 & 0 \\ 0 & 1 \end{pmatrix}$, the 3×3 identity matrix is $\begin{pmatrix} 1 & 0 & 0 \\ 0 & 1 & 0 \\ 0 & 0 & 1 \end{pmatrix}$, etc.

> **▶▶ Fast forward**
>
> You will discover one use of the identity matrix in Section 3.

WORKED EXAMPLE 1.1

Matrices **A**, **B** and **C** are given by $\mathbf{A} = \begin{pmatrix} 1 & 3 & 2 \\ 6 & 3 & -4 \end{pmatrix}$, $\mathbf{B} = \begin{pmatrix} 2 \\ 4 \end{pmatrix}$, $\mathbf{C} = \begin{pmatrix} -6 & 2 \end{pmatrix}$.

Write down the dimensions of **A**, **B** and **C**.

$\underline{A}$ is a 2×3 matrix.	There are 2 rows and 3 columns.
$\underline{B}$ is a 2×1 matrix.	There are 2 rows and 1 column.
$\underline{C}$ is a 1×2 matrix.	There is 1 row and 2 columns.

Notice that a matrix with just one column, such as **B** in Worked example 1.1, is a column vector.

In some circumstances you need to flip a matrix around its lead diagonal, exchanging rows for columns. This is called transposing a matrix. The **transpose** of matrix **A** is denoted $\mathbf{A}^T$.

Key point 1.3

The transpose of a matrix **A** is a new matrix, $\mathbf{A}^T$, such that the rows of $\mathbf{A}^T$ are the columns of **A**.

1 Matrices

WORKED EXAMPLE 1.2

Matrices **A**, **B** and **C** are given by $\mathbf{A} = \begin{pmatrix} 1 & 3 & 2 \\ 6 & 3 & -4 \end{pmatrix}$, $\mathbf{B} = \begin{pmatrix} 2 & -8 \\ 4 & 3 \end{pmatrix}$, $\mathbf{C} = (-6 \quad 2)$.

Write down the transpose matrices $\mathbf{A}^T$, $\mathbf{B}^T$ and $\mathbf{C}^T$.

$\mathbf{A}^T = \begin{pmatrix} 1 & 6 \\ 3 & 3 \\ 2 & -4 \end{pmatrix}$ .... **A** is a 2×3 matrix so $\mathbf{A}^T$ is a 3×2 matrix, where the ith row of $\mathbf{A}^T$ is the ith column of **A**.

$\mathbf{B}^T = \begin{pmatrix} 2 & 4 \\ -8 & 3 \end{pmatrix}$ .... **B** is a 2×2 matrix so $\mathbf{B}^T$ is a 2×2 matrix, where the ith row of $\mathbf{B}^T$ is the ith column of **B**.

$\mathbf{C}^T = \begin{pmatrix} -6 \\ 2 \end{pmatrix}$ .... **C** is a 1×2 matrix so $\mathbf{C}^T$ is a 2×1 matrix.

Addition and subtraction of matrices

The rules for matrix addition and subtraction are equivalent to the rules for vector addition and subtraction.

> **Rewind**
>
> You learnt how to add and subtract vectors in A Level Mathematics Student Book 1, Chapter 12.

> **Key point 1.4**
>
> You can only add (or subtract) two matrices with the same dimensions.
>
> Take each position in the matrix in turn and add (or subtract) the elements for that position.

Matrices that have the appropriate dimensions for an operation are said to be **conformable**. For addition and subtraction, two matrices are conformable only if they have identical dimensions.

WORKED EXAMPLE 1.3

The 2×2 matrix **A** is given by $\mathbf{A} = \begin{pmatrix} 1 & 3 \\ 2 & -5 \end{pmatrix}$.

For each of the following, determine $\mathbf{A} + \mathbf{B}$ and $\mathbf{A} - \mathbf{B}$ or explain why they do not exist.

a $\mathbf{B}_1 = \begin{pmatrix} 3 & -4 \\ 1 & 2 \end{pmatrix}$

b $\mathbf{B}_2 = \begin{pmatrix} 4 & 5 & -3 \\ 2 & 22 & -1 \end{pmatrix}$

Continues on next page ...

c $B_3 = \begin{pmatrix} 2 & 1 \\ 2 & -3 \\ 2 & 3 \end{pmatrix}$

d $B_4 = \begin{pmatrix} x & 2x \\ -2 & x^2+1 \end{pmatrix}$

a $\underline{A}+\underline{B}_1 = \begin{pmatrix} 1 & 3 \\ 2 & -5 \end{pmatrix} + \begin{pmatrix} 3 & -4 \\ 1 & 2 \end{pmatrix}$ .... Dimensions match so you can perform the addition.

$= \begin{pmatrix} 1+3 & 3-4 \\ 2+1 & -5+2 \end{pmatrix}$ For each position in the matrix take the element in **A** and add the element in B_1.

$= \begin{pmatrix} 4 & -1 \\ 3 & -3 \end{pmatrix}$

$\underline{A}-\underline{B}_1 = \begin{pmatrix} 1 & 3 \\ 2 & -5 \end{pmatrix} - \begin{pmatrix} 3 & -4 \\ 1 & 2 \end{pmatrix}$ .... Dimensions match so you can perform the subtraction.

$= \begin{pmatrix} 1-3 & 3-(-4) \\ 2-1 & -5-2 \end{pmatrix}$ For each position in the matrix take the element in **A** and subtract the element in B_1.

$= \begin{pmatrix} -2 & 7 \\ 1 & -7 \end{pmatrix}$

b Cannot add or subtract a 2×2 matrix and a 2×3 matrix. .... Dimensions do not match. You cannot add or subtract.

c Cannot add or subtract a 2×2 matrix and a 3×2 matrix. .... Dimensions do not match. You cannot add or subtract.

d $\underline{A}+\underline{B}_4 = \begin{pmatrix} 1 & 3 \\ 2 & -5 \end{pmatrix} + \begin{pmatrix} x & 2x \\ -2 & x^2+1 \end{pmatrix}$ .... Dimensions match so you can perform the addition.

$= \begin{pmatrix} 1+x & 3+2x \\ 2-2 & -5+x^2+1 \end{pmatrix}$ For each position in the matrix take the element in **A** and add the element in B_4.

$= \begin{pmatrix} 1+x & 3+2x \\ 0 & x^2-4 \end{pmatrix}$

$\underline{A}-\underline{B}_4 = \begin{pmatrix} 1 & 3 \\ 2 & -5 \end{pmatrix} - \begin{pmatrix} x & 2x \\ -2 & x^2+1 \end{pmatrix}$ .... Dimensions match so you can perform the subtraction.

$= \begin{pmatrix} 1-x & 3-2x \\ 2-(-2) & -5-(x^2+1) \end{pmatrix}$ For each position in the matrix take the element in **A** and subtract the element in B_4.

$= \begin{pmatrix} 1-x & 3-2x \\ 4 & -6-x^2 \end{pmatrix}$

1 Matrices

Just as with vectors, you can multiply a matrix by a scalar value.

> **Key point 1.5**
>
> When a matrix is multiplied by a scalar, each element is multiplied by that scalar.

WORKED EXAMPLE 1.4

Matrix $\mathbf{A} = \begin{pmatrix} 1 & a \\ 2 & 2 \end{pmatrix}$, matrix $\mathbf{B} = \begin{pmatrix} b & 3 \\ -4 & -5 \end{pmatrix}$ and matrix $\mathbf{C} = \begin{pmatrix} 2 & 2 \\ 4 & 0 \end{pmatrix}$.

a Write down $\frac{1}{2}\mathbf{C}$.

b p and q are scalar constants. Write down $p\mathbf{A}$ and $q\mathbf{B}$.

c Given $\frac{1}{2}\mathbf{C} = p\mathbf{A} + q\mathbf{B}$, find the values of a, b, p and q.

a $\frac{1}{2}\mathbf{C} = \frac{1}{2}\begin{pmatrix} 2 & 2 \\ 4 & 0 \end{pmatrix} = \begin{pmatrix} 1 & 1 \\ 2 & 0 \end{pmatrix}$
 — Scalar multiplication: multiply each element of the matrix by the scalar quantity.

b $p\mathbf{A} = \begin{pmatrix} p & ap \\ 2p & 2p \end{pmatrix}$, $q\mathbf{B} = \begin{pmatrix} bq & 3q \\ -4q & -5q \end{pmatrix}$
 — Scalar multiplication: multiply each element of the matrix by the scalar quantity.

c $p\mathbf{A} + q\mathbf{B} = \begin{pmatrix} p+bq & ap+3q \\ 2p-4q & 2p-5q \end{pmatrix}$
 — For each position in the matrix take the element in $p\mathbf{A}$ and add the element in $q\mathbf{B}$.

$= \begin{pmatrix} 1 & 1 \\ 2 & 0 \end{pmatrix}$
 — This should equal the matrix $\frac{1}{2}\mathbf{C}$ you found in part **a**.

$\begin{cases} p+bq=1 & (1) \\ ap+3q=1 & (2) \\ 2p-4q=2 & (3) \\ 2p-5q=0 & (4) \end{cases}$
 — Comparing each element gives a set of simultaneous equations.

(3) − (4): $q = 2$
 — (3) and (4) involve only unknowns p and q. Solve these, and then substitute into (1) and (2) to solve for a and b.

(3): $2p - 8 = 2$

$p = 5$

$\begin{cases} 5+2b=1 & (1) \\ 5a+6=1 & (2) \end{cases}$

(1): $b = -2$

(2): $a = -1$

$a = -1, b = -2, p = 5, q = 2$

EXERCISE 1A

1 **a** State the dimensions of each matrix.

i $\begin{pmatrix} 1 & 2 \\ 1 & 3 \end{pmatrix}$ ii $\begin{pmatrix} 1 & 5 \\ 2 & 3 \\ 1 & -3 \end{pmatrix}$ iii $\begin{pmatrix} 2 & 6 & 0 \\ 4 & 1 & 0 \end{pmatrix}$ iv $\begin{pmatrix} 1 & 2 & -4 \\ 8 & -3 & 3 \\ -1 & 7 & 22 \\ -5 & -2 & 0 \end{pmatrix}$

b For each matrix in part **a**, write down its transpose matrix.

2 $\mathbf{A} = \begin{pmatrix} 1 & 2 \\ 1 & 3 \end{pmatrix}$, $\mathbf{B} = \begin{pmatrix} 4 & 2 \\ 6 & -8 \end{pmatrix}$, $\mathbf{C} = \begin{pmatrix} 3 & 3 \\ 0 & -2 \end{pmatrix}$, $\mathbf{D} = \begin{pmatrix} 2 & 1 \\ 3 & -4 \end{pmatrix}$, $\mathbf{E} = \begin{pmatrix} 1 & 5 \\ 2 & 3 \\ 1 & -3 \end{pmatrix}$, $\mathbf{F} = \begin{pmatrix} -4 & 0 \\ 2 & 1 \\ 3 & 1 \end{pmatrix}$

Calculate, or state that the calculation is not possible:

a i A + B   ii C + D   iii E + F

b i B − C   ii D − E   iii A − C

c i 2A   ii −3C   iii 4E

d i 2A − 3C   ii B − 2D   iii 3E − F

3 Add the two given matrices where possible.

a i $\begin{pmatrix} 3 & -1 \\ 4 & 5 \end{pmatrix}$ and $\begin{pmatrix} -2 & 5 \\ 1 & 1 \end{pmatrix}$ ii $\begin{pmatrix} -1 \\ 2 \end{pmatrix}$ and $\begin{pmatrix} 3 & 3 \\ 1 & 2 \end{pmatrix}$

b i $\begin{pmatrix} -4 \\ 2 \end{pmatrix}$ and $(1 \;\; -3)$ ii $\begin{pmatrix} 4 & -1 \\ 3 & 3 \end{pmatrix}$ and $\begin{pmatrix} 1 & 1 \\ -2 & 4 \end{pmatrix}$

c i $\begin{pmatrix} 3 & -1 & 2 \\ 0 & 4 & 2 \end{pmatrix}$ and $\begin{pmatrix} 1 & 1 \\ -2 & 3 \end{pmatrix}$ ii $\begin{pmatrix} 6 & 0 & 1 \\ 1 & 2 & 1 \\ 7 & 1 & 5 \end{pmatrix}$ and $\begin{pmatrix} 4 & -2 & 3 \\ -1 & 0 & 0 \\ 1 & 0 & 2 \end{pmatrix}$

4 Given that $\mathbf{A} = \begin{pmatrix} 1 & -1 \\ 3 & 2 \end{pmatrix}$, $\mathbf{B} = \begin{pmatrix} 1 & 0 \\ 2 & -2 \end{pmatrix}$ and $\mathbf{C} = \begin{pmatrix} 3 & -1 \\ 0 & 5 \end{pmatrix}$, calculate the following:

a i A + 2B   ii 3A − 2I

b i 3C − B + 2I   ii A − B + 2C

5 Find the values of x and y to satisfy the following matrix equations, or state that there is no solution.

a i $\begin{pmatrix} 1 & x \\ -1 & 5 \end{pmatrix} + \begin{pmatrix} 2 & 2 \\ y & 7 \end{pmatrix} = \begin{pmatrix} 3 & 5 \\ 7 & 12 \end{pmatrix}$ ii $\begin{pmatrix} x & 2 \\ 3 & 5 \end{pmatrix} + \begin{pmatrix} 3 & y \\ 7 & 3 \end{pmatrix} = \begin{pmatrix} 5 & 7 \\ 10 & 8 \end{pmatrix}$

b i $\begin{pmatrix} 2x & 3 \\ 5 & y \end{pmatrix} + \begin{pmatrix} -y & -5 \\ 3 & 3x \end{pmatrix} = \begin{pmatrix} 7 & -2 \\ 8 & 8 \end{pmatrix}$ ii $\begin{pmatrix} 3 & 2x \\ -1 & y \end{pmatrix} + \begin{pmatrix} -1 & y \\ 5 & 2x \end{pmatrix} = \begin{pmatrix} 2 & 7 \\ 4 & 5 \end{pmatrix}$

6 Given that $\mathbf{A} = \begin{pmatrix} 4 & -1 \\ 3 & 3 \end{pmatrix}$ and $\mathbf{B} = \begin{pmatrix} 3 & -5 \\ 1 & 7 \end{pmatrix}$, find the matrix $\mathbf{X}$.

    a   **i** $2\mathbf{A} + \mathbf{X} = \mathbf{B}$ **ii** $3\mathbf{X} - 4\mathbf{A} = \mathbf{B}$

    b   **i** $\mathbf{X} - 3\mathbf{I} = 5\mathbf{A}$ **ii** $2\mathbf{I} - 3\mathbf{X} = \mathbf{B}$

7 Matrices $\mathbf{A} = \begin{pmatrix} a & 3 \\ -2 & 1 \end{pmatrix}$ and $\mathbf{B} = \begin{pmatrix} 2 & b \\ 1 & 3 \end{pmatrix}$ are such that $\mathbf{A} + s\mathbf{B} = t\mathbf{I}$. Find values a, b, s and t.

8 Matrices $\mathbf{A} = \begin{pmatrix} 2x^2 & x \\ -x^2 & -3 \end{pmatrix}$ and $\mathbf{B} = \begin{pmatrix} 6 & -1 \\ x & x+2 \end{pmatrix}$ are such that $\mathbf{A} + x\mathbf{B} = y\mathbf{I}$. Find all possible values of x and y.

9 Matrices $\mathbf{A} = \begin{pmatrix} 1 & 2a \\ -a & 3 \end{pmatrix}$ and $\mathbf{B} = \begin{pmatrix} 4 & b+1 \\ 3b & 1 \end{pmatrix}$ satisfy $c\mathbf{A} + d\mathbf{B} = \mathbf{I}$. Find a, b, c and d.

10 Explain why for any two matrices $\mathbf{A}$ and $\mathbf{B}$ that have the same dimensions, $(\mathbf{A} + \mathbf{B})^\mathrm{T} = \mathbf{A}^\mathrm{T} + \mathbf{B}^\mathrm{T}$.

Section 2: Matrix multiplication

Matrices have a variety of uses, and most involve multiplication. You might find the rules for matrix multiplication a little strange at first sight, and an illustration may help explain them.

Matrix $\mathbf{A} = \begin{pmatrix} 1 & 3 \\ 2 & 5 \end{pmatrix}$ and matrix $\mathbf{B} = \begin{pmatrix} -1 & 4 \\ 0 & -2 \end{pmatrix}$. Find the product $\mathbf{C} = \mathbf{AB}$.

$$\underbrace{\begin{pmatrix} 1 & 3 \\ 2 & 5 \end{pmatrix}}_{\mathbf{A}} \underbrace{\begin{pmatrix} -1 & 4 \\ 0 & -2 \end{pmatrix}}_{\mathbf{B}} = \underbrace{\begin{pmatrix} c_{11} & c_{12} \\ c_{21} & c_{22} \end{pmatrix}}_{\mathbf{C}}$$

To find each element c_{ij} you take row i from the left matrix $\mathbf{A}$ and column j from the right matrix $\mathbf{B}$.

Multiply each pair of values together and calculate the total of these products to find c_{ij}.

For example, to work out c_{11} you look at the **first row** of $\mathbf{A}$ and the **first column** of $\mathbf{B}$:

$$\underbrace{\begin{pmatrix} 1 & 3 \\ 2 & 5 \end{pmatrix}}_{\mathbf{A}} \underbrace{\begin{pmatrix} -1 & 4 \\ 0 & -2 \end{pmatrix}}_{\mathbf{B}}$$

$c_{11} = 1 \times (-1) + 3 \times 0 = -1$

To work out c_{12} you look at the **first row** of $\mathbf{A}$ and the **second column** of $\mathbf{B}$:

$$\underbrace{\begin{pmatrix} 1 & 3 \\ 2 & 5 \end{pmatrix}}_{\mathbf{A}} \underbrace{\begin{pmatrix} -1 & 4 \\ 0 & -2 \end{pmatrix}}_{\mathbf{B}}$$

$c_{12} = 1 \times 4 + 3 \times (-2) = -2$

Continuing in this way, you calculate each element of $\mathbf{C}$ to find

$\mathbf{C} = \begin{pmatrix} -1 & -2 \\ -2 & -2 \end{pmatrix}$

An example in context might help you understand why matrix multiplication is defined in this way.

> **WORKED EXAMPLE 1.5**
>
> Two sweet shops, Express Tills and Youchooz, sell aniseed balls, bonbons and chocolate drops.
>
> Express Tills charges £1.00 for a kilogram of aniseed balls, £1.80 for a kilogram of bonbons and £2.50 for a kilogram of chocolate drops.
>
> Youchooz charges £1.10 for a kilogram of aniseed balls, £2.00 for a kilogram of bonbons and £2.10 for a kilogram of chocolate drops.
>
> **a** Write down a pricing matrix for this information, of the form
> $$\mathbf{P} = \begin{matrix} & A & B & C \\ X & \\ Y & \end{matrix}\begin{pmatrix} a_x & b_x & c_x \\ a_y & b_y & c_y \end{pmatrix}.$$
>
> I wish to buy 2 kg of aniseed balls, 3 kg of bonbons and 7 kg of chocolate drops. How much will this cost in each shop?
>
> **b** Represent the shopping list as a column matrix, of the form
> $$\mathbf{R} = \begin{pmatrix} r_a \\ r_b \\ r_c \end{pmatrix} \begin{matrix} A \\ B \\ C \end{matrix}$$
>
> **c** Calculate the cost matrix **PR** and determine which shop would charge less for this shopping list.
>
> **a** $\underline{P} = \begin{matrix} & A & B & C \\ X & \\ Y & \end{matrix}\begin{pmatrix} 1.0 & 1.8 & 2.5 \\ 1.1 & 2.0 & 2.1 \end{pmatrix}$ .... Enter the prices for each item and for each shop.
>
> **b** $\underline{R} = \begin{pmatrix} 2 \\ 3 \\ 7 \end{pmatrix} \begin{matrix} A \\ B \\ C \end{matrix}$ .... Enter the requirements for each item.
>
> **c** $\underline{PR} = \begin{matrix} X \\ Y \end{matrix}\begin{pmatrix} 1.0 & 1.8 & 2.5 \\ 1.1 & 2.0 & 2.1 \end{pmatrix}\begin{pmatrix} 2 \\ 3 \\ 7 \end{pmatrix}$ .... To calculate the product, you need to multiply a row of the left matrix with the column of the right matrix.
>
> $= \begin{matrix} X \\ Y \end{matrix}\begin{pmatrix} 1.0 \times 2 + 1.8 \times 3 + 2.5 \times 7 \\ 1.1 \times 2 + 2.0 \times 3 + 2.1 \times 7 \end{pmatrix}$
>
> $= \begin{matrix} X \\ Y \end{matrix}\begin{pmatrix} 24.9 \\ 22.9 \end{pmatrix}$
>
> *The shopping costs £24.90 at Express Tills but only £22.90 at Youchooz, so Youchooz would charge less.*

1 Matrices

For the matrix multiplication method to work, the left matrix must have the same number of columns as the right matrix has rows. If this is not the case, the matrices are not conformable for multiplication, and the product is not defined.

Key point 1.6

When an $m \times n$ matrix **A** and an $n \times p$ matrix **B** are multiplied together, the result is an $m \times p$ matrix $\mathbf{C} = \mathbf{AB}$.

To find the element in row i and column j of **C**:

1. Take row i of **A** and column j of **B**.
2. Multiply each pair of corresponding values and add all the products together.

Explore

The rule for multiplying matrices may be written as: $c_{ij} = \sum_{k=1}^{n} a_{ik} b_{kj}$. This may look complicated, but is in fact just another way of describing the process in Key point 1.6. Does this sort of notation help or hinder understanding? Find out about **summation convention**, which is used in many branches of mathematics and physics, such as general relativity.

Tip

Remember that you can use your calculator to multiply matrices. However, you also need to be able to do it without one.

WORKED EXAMPLE 1.6

The 2×2 matrix **A** is given by $\mathbf{A} = \begin{pmatrix} 1 & 3 \\ 2 & -5 \end{pmatrix}$.

For each of the following, determine **AB** and **BA** or explain why the product does not exist.

a $\mathbf{B}_1 = \begin{pmatrix} 3 & -4 \\ 1 & 2 \end{pmatrix}$

b $\mathbf{B}_2 = \begin{pmatrix} 4 & 5 & -3 \\ 2 & 22 & -1 \end{pmatrix}$

c $\mathbf{B}_3 = \begin{pmatrix} 2 & 1 \\ 2 & -3 \\ 2 & 3 \end{pmatrix}$

d $\mathbf{B}_4 = \mathbf{A}$

a $\mathbf{AB}_1 = \begin{pmatrix} 1 & 3 \\ 2 & -5 \end{pmatrix} \begin{pmatrix} 3 & -4 \\ 1 & 2 \end{pmatrix}$

$= \begin{pmatrix} 1 \times 3 + 3 \times 1 & 1 \times (-4) + 3 \times 2 \\ 2 \times 3 + (-5) \times 1 & 2 \times (-4) + (-5) \times 2 \end{pmatrix}$

$= \begin{pmatrix} 6 & 2 \\ 1 & -18 \end{pmatrix}$

Same number of columns in **A** (2×2) as rows in **B** (2×2) so the product exists.

For the **top left** element of the product, multiply the **top** row of **A** with the **left** column of **B**, and continue in the same way for every element.

Continues on next page ...

$B_1A = \begin{pmatrix} 3 & -4 \\ 1 & 2 \end{pmatrix} \begin{pmatrix} 1 & 3 \\ 2 & -5 \end{pmatrix}$

$= \begin{pmatrix} 3\times1-4\times2 & 3\times3-4\times(-5) \\ 1\times1+2\times2 & 1\times3+2\times(-5) \end{pmatrix}$

$= \begin{pmatrix} -5 & 29 \\ 5 & -7 \end{pmatrix}$

> Same number of columns in **B** (2×2) as rows in **A** (2×2) so the product exists.
>
> For the top left element of the product, multiply the top row of **A** with the left column of **B**, and continue in the same way for every element.

b $AB_2 = \begin{pmatrix} 1 & 3 \\ 2 & -5 \end{pmatrix} \begin{pmatrix} 4 & 5 & -3 \\ 2 & 22 & -1 \end{pmatrix}$

$= \begin{pmatrix} 1\times4+3\times2 & 1\times5+3\times22 & 1\times(-3)+3\times(-1) \\ 2\times4-5\times2 & 2\times5-5\times22 & 2\times(-3)-5\times(-1) \end{pmatrix}$

$= \begin{pmatrix} 10 & 71 & -6 \\ -2 & -100 & -1 \end{pmatrix}$

> Same number of columns in **A** (2×2) as rows in **B** (2×3) so the product exists.
>
> For the top left element of the product, multiply the top row of **A** with the left column of **B**, and continue in the same way for every element.

$B_2A = \begin{pmatrix} 4 & 5 & -3 \\ 2 & 22 & -1 \end{pmatrix} \begin{pmatrix} 1 & 3 \\ 2 & -5 \end{pmatrix}$

Not conformable: B_2 has 3 columns but A has 2 rows.

> Different number of columns in **B** (2×3) and rows in **A** (2×2) so the product does not exist.

c $AB_3 = \begin{pmatrix} 1 & 3 \\ 2 & -5 \end{pmatrix} \begin{pmatrix} 2 & 1 \\ 2 & -3 \\ 2 & 3 \end{pmatrix}$

Not conformable: A has 2 columns but B_3 has 3 rows.

> Different number of columns in **A** (2×2) and rows in **B** (3×2) so the product does not exist.

$B_3A = \begin{pmatrix} 2 & 1 \\ 2 & -3 \\ 2 & 3 \end{pmatrix} \begin{pmatrix} 1 & 3 \\ 2 & -5 \end{pmatrix}$

$= \begin{pmatrix} 2\times1+1\times2 & 2\times3+1\times(-5) \\ 2\times1-3\times2 & 2\times3-3\times(-5) \\ 2\times1+3\times2 & 2\times3+3\times(-5) \end{pmatrix}$

$= \begin{pmatrix} 4 & 1 \\ -4 & 21 \\ 8 & -9 \end{pmatrix}$

> Same number of columns in **B** (3×2) as rows in **A** (2×2) so the product exists.

d $B_4A = AB_4 = A^2 = \begin{pmatrix} 1 & 3 \\ 2 & -5 \end{pmatrix} \begin{pmatrix} 1 & 3 \\ 2 & -5 \end{pmatrix}$

$= \begin{pmatrix} 1\times1+2\times3 & 1\times3+3\times(-5) \\ 2\times1-5\times2 & 2\times3-5\times(-5) \end{pmatrix}$

$= \begin{pmatrix} 7 & -12 \\ -8 & 31 \end{pmatrix}$

> Same number of columns in **A** (2×2) as rows in **A** (2×2) so the product exists.

In part **d** of Worked example 1.6, the standard index notation A^2 represents a matrix **A** multiplied by itself. Similarly $A^3 = AAA$ and onwards, for higher integer powers.

Notice that in part **a** of Worked example 1.6, AB_1 and B_1A did not give the same result. Matrix multiplication is not generally **commutative**; that is, **AB** does not necessarily equal **BA**. However, some matrices will **commute** with each other and, as you will see, there are some matrices that commute with all other matrices of suitable dimensions.

> **Focus on ...**
>
> Powers of matrices have some interesting applications, including counting the number of paths in a network — see Focus on ... Modelling 1.

Key point 1.7

Two matrices **A** and **B** commute (are commutative) if **AB** equals **BA**.

Although matrix multiplication is not generally commutative, it is **associative**; that is, a multiple product **ABC** can be calculated as **(AB)C** or as **A(BC)**, and the result is still the same. (However, **(AC)B** may be different.)

WORKED EXAMPLE 1.7

$$A = \begin{pmatrix} 1 & 2 \\ 4 & -2 \end{pmatrix}, B = \begin{pmatrix} 3 & 1 \\ -1 & -1 \end{pmatrix}, C = \begin{pmatrix} -2 & -1 \\ 1 & 1 \end{pmatrix}$$

a Calculate $X = AB$ and $Y = BC$.
b Calculate **XC** and **AY** and explain your findings.

a $X = AB = \begin{pmatrix} 1 & 2 \\ 4 & -2 \end{pmatrix}\begin{pmatrix} 3 & 1 \\ -1 & -1 \end{pmatrix}$ 　　You can use standard matrix multiplication.

$= \begin{pmatrix} 1 & -1 \\ 14 & 6 \end{pmatrix}$

$Y = BC = \begin{pmatrix} 3 & 1 \\ -1 & -1 \end{pmatrix}\begin{pmatrix} -2 & -1 \\ 1 & 1 \end{pmatrix}$

$= \begin{pmatrix} -5 & -2 \\ 1 & 0 \end{pmatrix}$

b $XC = \begin{pmatrix} 1 & -1 \\ 14 & 6 \end{pmatrix}\begin{pmatrix} -2 & -1 \\ 1 & 1 \end{pmatrix}$

$= \begin{pmatrix} -3 & -2 \\ -22 & -8 \end{pmatrix}$

$AY = \begin{pmatrix} 1 & 2 \\ 4 & -2 \end{pmatrix}\begin{pmatrix} -5 & -2 \\ 1 & 0 \end{pmatrix}$

$= \begin{pmatrix} -3 & -2 \\ -22 & -8 \end{pmatrix}$

$XC = (AB)C$
$AY = A(BC)$ 　　The products give the same result because matrix multiplication is associative.

EXERCISE 1B

1 State whether the two matrices can be multiplied, and the dimension of their product when multiplied in the order given.

a **i** $\begin{pmatrix} 1 & 1 & 2 \\ 0 & 3 & 5 \end{pmatrix}$ and $\begin{pmatrix} 3 & 1 \\ 3 & 1 \\ 3 & 2 \end{pmatrix}$ **ii** $\begin{pmatrix} 1 & 0 \\ 0 & 1 \end{pmatrix}$ and $\begin{pmatrix} 3 & -1 & 1 \\ 2 & 1 & 3 \end{pmatrix}$

b **i** $\begin{pmatrix} 3 & -1 \\ 1 & 0 \end{pmatrix}$ and $\begin{pmatrix} 1 & 1 \\ 2 & 1 \\ 2 & 2 \end{pmatrix}$ **ii** $\begin{pmatrix} 1 & 0 & 0 \\ 0 & 1 & 0 \end{pmatrix}$ and $\begin{pmatrix} 0 & 1 \\ 1 & 0 \end{pmatrix}$

c **i** $(3 \; -2)$ and $\begin{pmatrix} 0 & 0 \\ 0 & 0 \end{pmatrix}$ **ii** $(1 \; -1 \; 2)$ and $\begin{pmatrix} 3 \\ 1 \\ 4 \end{pmatrix}$

d **i** $\begin{pmatrix} 3 & 1 \\ 2 & 1 \end{pmatrix}$ and $\begin{pmatrix} 2 & -2 \\ 2 & 1 \end{pmatrix}$ **ii** $\begin{pmatrix} 1 & a \\ 2 & 2 \end{pmatrix}$ and $\begin{pmatrix} -a & 2a \\ 1 & 2 \end{pmatrix}$

e **i** $\begin{pmatrix} 1 & a & 0 \\ 2 & 2 & a \\ 1 & 0 & 5 \end{pmatrix}$ and $\begin{pmatrix} 2 & 1 & 1 \\ -1 & a & 5 \\ 2 & 0 & a \end{pmatrix}$ **ii** $\begin{pmatrix} 2 \\ 1 \\ 3 \end{pmatrix}$ and $(-1 \; 1 \; 3)$

2 Multiply the matrices from question **1** when possible. Use a calculator to check your answers (where possible).

3 Determine whether the following matrices commute.

a **i** $\begin{pmatrix} 2 & 0 \\ 0 & 3 \end{pmatrix}$ and $\begin{pmatrix} 4 & 1 \\ 2 & 5 \end{pmatrix}$ **ii** $\begin{pmatrix} 1 & 5 \\ 0 & 1 \end{pmatrix}$ and $\begin{pmatrix} 1 & -3 \\ 0 & 1 \end{pmatrix}$

b **i** $\begin{pmatrix} 3 & -1 \\ 2 & 3 \end{pmatrix}$ and $\begin{pmatrix} 2 & 0 \\ 0 & 2 \end{pmatrix}$ **ii** $\begin{pmatrix} 2 & 3 \\ -3 & 2 \end{pmatrix}$ and $\begin{pmatrix} -1 & 5 \\ -5 & -1 \end{pmatrix}$

c **i** $\begin{pmatrix} 1 & 2 \\ 2 & 3 \end{pmatrix}$ and $\begin{pmatrix} 1 & 3 \\ 0 & 2 \end{pmatrix}$ **ii** $\begin{pmatrix} 2 & 0 \\ -3 & 3 \end{pmatrix}$ and $\begin{pmatrix} 1 & -5 \\ 0 & 1 \end{pmatrix}$

4 Find the values of the unknown scalars in each equation.

a **i** $\begin{pmatrix} 2 & -3 \\ 1 & 0 \end{pmatrix}\begin{pmatrix} 1 & x \\ y & 2 \end{pmatrix} = \begin{pmatrix} -4 & 0 \\ 1 & 3 \end{pmatrix}$ **ii** $\begin{pmatrix} a & 2 \\ -3 & b \end{pmatrix}\begin{pmatrix} 1 & 2 \\ -2 & 3 \end{pmatrix} = \begin{pmatrix} 0 & 14 \\ -5 & -3 \end{pmatrix}$

b **i** $\begin{pmatrix} x & y \\ 2 & -1 \end{pmatrix}\begin{pmatrix} 3 & 1 \\ 1 & 2 \end{pmatrix} = \begin{pmatrix} 8 & 11 \\ 5 & 0 \end{pmatrix}$ **ii** $\begin{pmatrix} 2 & 1 \\ -1 & 2 \end{pmatrix}\begin{pmatrix} 1 & p \\ -3 & q \end{pmatrix} = \begin{pmatrix} -1 & 0 \\ -7 & -5 \end{pmatrix}$

5 Given that $\mathbf{A} = \begin{pmatrix} 7 & -1 \\ 0 & 5 \end{pmatrix}$ and $\mathbf{B} = \begin{pmatrix} 3 & 3 \\ 1 & 6 \end{pmatrix}$, find:

a $\mathbf{A} + 3\mathbf{B} - 2\mathbf{I}$ **b** $\mathbf{AB}$ **c** $\mathbf{A}^3$

6 Given that $\mathbf{A} = (2 \; -3)$, $\mathbf{B} = \begin{pmatrix} 1 \\ 5 \end{pmatrix}$ and $\mathbf{C} = (-1 \; 7)$, find:

a $\mathbf{A} + \mathbf{C}$ **b** $\mathbf{AB}$ **c** $\mathbf{BC}$

7 Let $\mathbf{M} = \begin{pmatrix} 2 & -1 & 5 \\ 0 & 1 & 4 \\ -4 & 0 & 2 \end{pmatrix}$ and $\mathbf{N} = \begin{pmatrix} 3 & 0 & -1 \\ 2 & 2 & 5 \\ -1 & 3 & 0 \end{pmatrix}$. Calculate:

   a $3\mathbf{M} - 2\mathbf{I}$
   b $\mathbf{MN}$
   c $\mathbf{N}^2$

8 Let $\mathbf{P} = \begin{pmatrix} 2 & a \\ 3a & -1 \end{pmatrix}$ and $\mathbf{Q} = \begin{pmatrix} 2a & -2 \\ a & 3 \end{pmatrix}$. Find in terms of a:

   a $\mathbf{P} - 3\mathbf{Q}$
   b $\mathbf{PQ}$

9 Given that $\mathbf{A} = (2 \ 1 \ 3)$, $\mathbf{B} = \begin{pmatrix} p & 2 \\ 1 & 2p \\ -1 & 2 \end{pmatrix}$ and $\mathbf{C} = \begin{pmatrix} 3p \\ -2 \end{pmatrix}$, find in terms of p:

   a $\mathbf{AB}$

   b $\mathbf{BC}$

   c   Explain why $\mathbf{B}^2$ does not exist.

10 Find the value of b so that the matrices $\begin{pmatrix} 3 & 1 \\ 0 & 3 \end{pmatrix}$ and $\begin{pmatrix} -5 & 2 \\ 0 & b \end{pmatrix}$ commute.

11 Prove that the matrices $\begin{pmatrix} a & b \\ -b & a \end{pmatrix}$ and $\begin{pmatrix} c & d \\ -d & c \end{pmatrix}$ commute for all values of a, b, c and d.

12 Given that the matrices $\begin{pmatrix} 2 & 3 \\ 3 & -2 \end{pmatrix}$ and $\begin{pmatrix} c & d \\ d & -c \end{pmatrix}$ commute, find an expression for d in terms of c.

13 $\mathbf{A} = \begin{pmatrix} a_{11} & a_{12} \\ a_{21} & a_{22} \end{pmatrix}$, $\mathbf{B} = \begin{pmatrix} b_{11} & b_{12} \\ b_{21} & b_{22} \end{pmatrix}$ and $\mathbf{C} = \begin{pmatrix} c_{11} & c_{12} \\ c_{21} & c_{22} \end{pmatrix}$.

   a   Calculate $\mathbf{X} = \mathbf{AB}$ and $\mathbf{Y} = \mathbf{BC}$.

   b   Show that $\mathbf{XC} = \mathbf{AY}$.

14 Prove that for two 2×2 matrices $\mathbf{A}$ and $\mathbf{B}$, $(\mathbf{AB})^T = \mathbf{B}^T\mathbf{A}^T$.

   Explain whether this is the case for matrices of other dimensions for which the product exists.

Section 3: Determinants and inverses of 2 × 2 matrices

In this section you will learn to do the following:

Given two matrices, $\mathbf{A}$ and $\mathbf{B}$, find a matrix $\mathbf{X}$ such that $\mathbf{AX} = \mathbf{B}$.

Initially, you will focus on 2×2 matrices.

> **Fast forward**
>
> In Section 4 you will extend these ideas to 3×3 matrices.

The identity matrix

In arithmetic, an identity is a number which, for a given operation, produces no changes. So, for addition in the real numbers, zero is the identity because for any real value x:

$x + 0 = 0 + x = x$

For 2 × 2 matrix addition, the zero matrix has this property:

$\mathbf{Z} + \mathbf{A} = \mathbf{A} + \mathbf{Z} = \mathbf{A}$

However, the zero matrix is not an identity for multiplication, as any matrix multiplied by the zero matrix gives the zero matrix:

$\mathbf{ZA} = \mathbf{AZ} = \mathbf{Z}$

The identity for multiplication of the real numbers is 1, because for any real value x:

$1 \times x = x \times 1 = x$

In matrix multiplication, the identity matrix, which was defined in Section 1, has this property:

$\mathbf{IA} = \mathbf{AI} = \mathbf{A}$

You can prove this for 2 × 2 matrices by considering the general matrix $\mathbf{A} = \begin{pmatrix} a & b \\ c & d \end{pmatrix}$:

$\mathbf{IA} = \begin{pmatrix} 1 & 0 \\ 0 & 1 \end{pmatrix} \begin{pmatrix} a & b \\ c & d \end{pmatrix} = \begin{pmatrix} 1 \times a + 0 \times c & 1 \times b + 0 \times d \\ 0 \times a + 1 \times c & 0 \times b + 1 \times d \end{pmatrix} = \begin{pmatrix} a & b \\ c & d \end{pmatrix} = \mathbf{A}$

$\mathbf{AI} = \begin{pmatrix} a & b \\ c & d \end{pmatrix} \begin{pmatrix} 1 & 0 \\ 0 & 1 \end{pmatrix} = \begin{pmatrix} 1 \times a + 0 \times b & 0 \times a + 1 \times b \\ 1 \times c + 0 \times d & 0 \times c + 1 \times d \end{pmatrix} = \begin{pmatrix} a & b \\ c & d \end{pmatrix} = \mathbf{A}$

This result generalises for multiplication of the $n \times n$ identity matrix with any $n \times n$ matrix.

> **Explore**
>
> With real numbers, if $xa = 0$ then either $x = 0$ or $a = 0$. This is not the case for matrices. Can you find two non-zero matrices whose product is the zero matrix?

> **Key point 1.8**
>
> The $n \times n$ identity matrix $\mathbf{I}$ has the unique property that:
> - for any $n \times n$ matrix $\mathbf{A}$, $\mathbf{IA} = \mathbf{A}$
> - for any $n \times n$ matrix $\mathbf{B}$, $\mathbf{BI} = \mathbf{B}$.

> **Tip**
>
> In the definition of the identity, we need to require that both $\mathbf{IA} = \mathbf{A}$ and $\mathbf{BI} = \mathbf{B}$. This is because, generally, matrices don't commute. If $\mathbf{M}$ is a square $n \times n$ matrix, then $\mathbf{I}$ commutes with $\mathbf{M}$: $\mathbf{MI} = \mathbf{IM}$.

> **Focus on …**
>
> In Focus on … Proof 1 you will see how to prove that there can be only one identity matrix.

Determinants

When you compare real numbers you can say that one is greater or less than another. If you want to compare vectors you can use their

1 Matrices

magnitudes. Although you cannot meaningfully write that $\begin{pmatrix}3\\1\end{pmatrix} > \begin{pmatrix}2\\2\end{pmatrix}$ or that $\begin{pmatrix}3\\1\end{pmatrix} < \begin{pmatrix}2\\2\end{pmatrix}$, you know that you can compare their magnitudes, as given by the modulus of the vector.

 $\left|\begin{pmatrix}3\\1\end{pmatrix}\right| = \sqrt{10} > \left|\begin{pmatrix}2\\2\end{pmatrix}\right| = \sqrt{8}$

Is there an analogue for modulus when considering matrices? The answer is that for a square matrix, you can calculate a **determinant**, which, in many respects, can be considered the magnitude of the matrix. However, unlike a vector modulus, the determinant can take positive or negative values.

Key point 1.9

The determinant of a 2×2 matrix $\mathbf{A} = \begin{pmatrix} a & b \\ c & d \end{pmatrix}$ is written as det $\mathbf{A}$, $|\mathbf{A}|$ or $\begin{vmatrix} a & b \\ c & d \end{vmatrix}$, and equals $ad - bc$.

That is, the determinant is the product of the **lead diagonal** elements less the product of the **reverse diagonal** elements.

Fast forward

In Chapter 3 you will see that determinants can be used to deduce a scale factor of an enlargement, as well as to decide whether a system of simultaneous equations has a unique solution.

WORKED EXAMPLE 1.8

Calculate the determinant of the matrix $\mathbf{A} = \begin{pmatrix} 1 & 5 \\ 2 & -2 \end{pmatrix}$.

$|\underline{A}| = \begin{Vmatrix} 1 & 5 \\ 2 & -2 \end{Vmatrix}$

$= 1 \times (-2) - (5 \times 2)$

$= -2 - 10$

$= -12$

> The determinant of a 2×2 matrix is the product of the lead diagonal elements less the product of the reverse diagonal elements.

You can prove some useful properties for 2×2 matrix determinants algebraically. To do this, you need to use unknowns in each position in the matrices.

Key point 1.10

For two 2×2 matrices $\mathbf{A}$ and $\mathbf{B}$ and a scalar k:

- det $\mathbf{AB}$ = det $\mathbf{BA}$ = det $\mathbf{A} \times$ det $\mathbf{B}$
- $\det(k\mathbf{A}) = k^2 \det \mathbf{A}$

The proof of the first result is shown here. You are asked to prove the second result in question **3** of Exercise 1C.

PROOF 1

Let $\underline{A} = \begin{pmatrix} a & b \\ c & d \end{pmatrix}$ and $\underline{B} = \begin{pmatrix} p & q \\ r & s \end{pmatrix}$. ...... You need to introduce some variables so you can do the calculation.

Then: ...... First, find the individual determinants of **A** and **B**.

$\det \underline{A} = ad - bc$

$\det \underline{B} = ps - qr$

$\underline{AB} = \begin{pmatrix} ap+br & aq+bs \\ cp+dr & cq+ds \end{pmatrix}$ ...... Use the rule for multiplying matrices to find **AB** and **BA**. Remember that they are not the same!

$\underline{BA} = \begin{pmatrix} ap+cq & bp+dq \\ ar+cs & br+ds \end{pmatrix}$

$\det \underline{AB} = (ap+br)(cq+ds) - (aq+bs)(cp+dr)$ ...... Expand and simplify the expression for det **AB**.

$\quad = acpq + adps + bcqr + bdrs$

$\quad\quad - (acpq + adqr + bcps + bdrs)$

$\quad = adps + bcqr - adqr - bcps$

$\det \underline{A} \times \det \underline{B} = (ad-bc)(ps-qr)$ ...... It's not obvious how to simplify this, so you need to look at det **A** × det **B**.

$\quad = adps - adqr + bcqr - bcps$

Hence, ... The two expressions contain the same four terms.

$\det \underline{AB} = \det \underline{A} \times \det \underline{B}$

$\det \underline{BA} = (ap+cq)(br+ds) - (bp+dq)(ar+cs)$ ...... Since **BA** is not the same as **AB** you need to expand det **BA** as well.

$\quad = (abpr + adps + cbqr + cdqs)$

$\quad\quad - (abpr + bcps + adqr + cqds)$

$\quad = adps + cbqr - bcps - adqr$ ...... This is again the same as det **A** × det **B**.

So $\det \underline{AB} = \det \underline{BA} = \det \underline{A} \times \det \underline{B}$ ...... Write a conclusion, summarising what you have proved.

EXERCISE 1C

1 Find the determinants of each matrix.

   a   **i** $\begin{pmatrix} 3 & -1 \\ 7 & 4 \end{pmatrix}$ **ii** $\begin{pmatrix} 1 & 1 \\ -3 & 2 \end{pmatrix}$

   b   **i** $\begin{pmatrix} 2 & -3 \\ 1 & 5 \end{pmatrix}$ **ii** $\begin{pmatrix} 3 & -2 \\ 1 & 3 \end{pmatrix}$

c i $\begin{pmatrix} 2a & a \\ 3 & -1 \end{pmatrix}$ 　　ii $\begin{pmatrix} 1 & -a \\ 5 & 2a \end{pmatrix}$

d i $\begin{pmatrix} a & -3 \\ 2 & 5a \end{pmatrix}$ 　　ii $\begin{pmatrix} 1 & 2a \\ -a & 3 \end{pmatrix}$

2 Find the determinants of the matrices $\mathbf{A} = \begin{pmatrix} 2 & -3 \\ 1 & 5 \end{pmatrix}$, $\mathbf{B} = \begin{pmatrix} 3 & -2 \\ 1 & 3 \end{pmatrix}$ and **AB**. Confirm that $\det \mathbf{AB} = \det \mathbf{A} \times \det \mathbf{B}$.

3 Prove that for any 2×2 matrix **A** and a scalar k, $\det k\mathbf{A} = k^2 \det \mathbf{A}$.

Inverse matrices

Remember that you started this section with the aim of finding a matrix **X** such that **AX** = **B**. In other words, you are trying to 'undo' matrix multiplication.

For real numbers, you can reverse multiplication by division or, equivalently, use multiplication by the reciprocal: if $ax = b$ then $x = \dfrac{b}{a} = \dfrac{1}{a} \times b$. The matrix equivalent of a reciprocal is called the **inverse matrix**.

Key point 1.11

A matrix $\mathbf{A}^{-1}$ is the inverse of a square matrix **A** and has the property that:

$$\mathbf{AA}^{-1} = \mathbf{A}^{-1}\mathbf{A} = \mathbf{I}$$

You can use a calculator to find the inverse of a matrix with numerical entries, but sometimes you also need to use the following formula.

Key point 1.12

For a matrix $\mathbf{A} = \begin{pmatrix} a & b \\ c & d \end{pmatrix}$ with $ad - bc \neq 0$, the inverse is:

$$\mathbf{A}^{-1} = \frac{1}{ad - bc} \begin{pmatrix} d & -b \\ -c & a \end{pmatrix}$$

To prove that this formula gives the inverse matrix, you need to show that multiplying it by **A** gives the identity matrix.

PROOF 2

$$AA^{-1} = \begin{pmatrix} a & b \\ c & d \end{pmatrix} \times \frac{1}{ad-bc}\begin{pmatrix} d & -b \\ -c & a \end{pmatrix}$$

> The definition of the inverse is that $AA^{-1} = A^{-1}A = I$. So you can multiply the two matrices and check that you get the identity.

$$= \begin{pmatrix} a & b \\ c & d \end{pmatrix}\begin{pmatrix} \frac{d}{ad-bc} & \frac{-b}{ad-bc} \\ \frac{-c}{ad-bc} & \frac{a}{ad-bc} \end{pmatrix}$$

> Firstly multiply the second matrix by the scalar (by multiplying each element by the scalar).

$$= \begin{pmatrix} \frac{ad-bc}{ad-bc} & \frac{-ab+ba}{ad-bc} \\ \frac{cd-dc}{ad-bc} & \frac{-bc+da}{ad-bc} \end{pmatrix}$$

$$= \begin{pmatrix} 1 & 0 \\ 0 & 1 \end{pmatrix} = I, \text{ as required.}$$

> This is the result you wanted: $AA^{-1} = I$.

A similar calculation shows that $A^{-1}A = I$.

> **Focus on ...**
>
> In fact, it turns out that you don't need to check this. In Focus on ... Proof 2 you will prove that, if $AA^{-1} = I$, then $A^{-1}A = I$ as well.

In the formula in Key point 1.12, the expression at the bottom of the fraction is the determinant of **A**. It turns out that when det **A** = 0, the matrix **A** has no inverse.

🔑 Key point 1.13

A matrix **A** with det **A** = 0 is called **singular** and has no inverse.

A matrix that has an inverse is called **non-singular**.

To find the inverse of a 2 × 2 matrix with non-zero determinant you use the formula from Key Point 1.12:

- swap the elements on the lead diagonal
- change the sign of the elements on the reverse diagonal
- multiply by the reciprocal of the determinant of the original matrix.

WORKED EXAMPLE 1.9

For each of the following matrices, find the inverse matrix or establish that there is no inverse.

Verify where there is an inverse that the product with the original matrix is **I**.

a $A = \begin{pmatrix} 4 & 1 \\ 6 & 2 \end{pmatrix}$

b $B = \begin{pmatrix} 2 & 4 \\ -1 & 3 \end{pmatrix}$

c $C = \begin{pmatrix} 1 & -2 \\ -3 & 6 \end{pmatrix}$

d $D = \begin{pmatrix} 0 & 1 \\ 1 & 0 \end{pmatrix}$

Continues on next page ...

1 Matrices

a $\det \underline{A} = 4 \times 2 - 1 \times 6 = 2$

$\underline{A}^{-1} = \dfrac{1}{2}\begin{pmatrix} 2 & -1 \\ -6 & 4 \end{pmatrix} = \begin{pmatrix} 1 & -0.5 \\ -3 & 2 \end{pmatrix}$

$\underline{AA}^{-1} = \begin{pmatrix} 4 & 1 \\ 6 & 2 \end{pmatrix}\begin{pmatrix} 1 & -0.5 \\ -3 & 2 \end{pmatrix}$

$= \begin{pmatrix} 4 \times 1 + 1 \times (-3) & 4 \times (-0.5) + 1 \times 2 \\ 6 \times 1 + 2 \times (-3) & 6 \times (-0.5) + 2 \times 2 \end{pmatrix}$

$= \begin{pmatrix} 1 & 0 \\ 0 & 1 \end{pmatrix} = \underline{I}$

Find det **A**; if it is non-zero, then then $\mathbf{A}^{-1}$ exists.

Swap the elements on the lead diagonal.

Change the sign of the elements on the reverse diagonal.

Multiply by the reciprocal of the determinant of the original matrix.

Check the answer by multiplication to **I**.

b $\det \underline{B} = 2 \times 3 - 4 \times (-1) = 10$

$\underline{B}^{-1} = \dfrac{1}{10}\begin{pmatrix} 3 & -4 \\ 1 & 2 \end{pmatrix} = \begin{pmatrix} 0.3 & -0.4 \\ 0.1 & 0.2 \end{pmatrix}$

$\underline{BB}^{-1} = \begin{pmatrix} 2 & 4 \\ -1 & 3 \end{pmatrix}\begin{pmatrix} 0.3 & -0.4 \\ 0.1 & 0.2 \end{pmatrix}$

$= \begin{pmatrix} 2 \times 0.3 + 4 \times 0.1 & 2 \times (-0.4) + 4 \times 0.2 \\ (-1) \times 0.3 + 3 \times 0.1 & (-1) \times (-0.4) + 3 \times 0.2 \end{pmatrix}$

$= \begin{pmatrix} 1 & 0 \\ 0 & 1 \end{pmatrix} = \underline{I}$

Find det **B**; if it is non-zero, then then $\mathbf{B}^{-1}$ exists.

Swap the elements on the lead diagonal.

Change the sign of the elements on the reverse diagonal.

Multiply by the reciprocal of the determinant of the original matrix.

Check the answer by multiplication to **I**.

c $\det \underline{C} = 1 \times 6 - (-2) \times (-3) = 0$

$\underline{C}$ is singular and has no inverse.

Find det **C**; if it is zero, then $\mathbf{C}^{-1}$ does not exist.

d $\det \underline{D} = 0 \times 0 - 1 \times 1 = -1$

$\underline{D}^{-1} = -\begin{pmatrix} 0 & -1 \\ -1 & 0 \end{pmatrix} = \begin{pmatrix} 0 & 1 \\ 1 & 0 \end{pmatrix}$

$\underline{DD}^{-1} = \begin{pmatrix} 0 & 1 \\ 1 & 0 \end{pmatrix}\begin{pmatrix} 0 & 1 \\ 1 & 0 \end{pmatrix}$

$= \begin{pmatrix} 0 \times 0 + 1 \times 1 & 0 \times 1 + 1 \times 0 \\ 1 \times 0 + 0 \times 1 & 1 \times 1 + 0 \times 0 \end{pmatrix}$

$= \begin{pmatrix} 1 & 0 \\ 0 & 1 \end{pmatrix} = \underline{I}$

Find det **D**; if it is non-zero, then then $\mathbf{D}^{-1}$ exists.

Swap the elements on the lead diagonal.

Change the sign of the elements on the reverse diagonal.

Multiply by the reciprocal of the determinant of the original matrix.

Check the answer by multiplication to **I**.

Using the inverse

You can use the inverse matrix to 'undo' matrix multiplication. Because matrix multiplication is generally not commutative, you need to be careful to multiply the matrices in the correct order.

If **A** is a non-singular matrix and if **AX** = **B**, we can left-multiply both sides by A^{-1} on the left:

$A^{-1}(AX) = A^{-1}B$

$\Rightarrow (A^{-1}A)X = A^{-1}B$

$\Rightarrow IX = A^{-1}B$

$\Rightarrow X = A^{-1}B$

However, if you want to solve the equation **XA** = **B**, you need to multiply by A^{-1} on the right, so that **A** and A^{-1} are next to each other:

$XAA^{-1} = BA^{-1} \Rightarrow X = BA^{-1}$

WORKED EXAMPLE 1.10

$A = \begin{pmatrix} 4 & 1 \\ 7 & 2 \end{pmatrix}$ and $B = \begin{pmatrix} 3 & -4 \\ 0 & 8 \end{pmatrix}$.

a Find **X** such that **AX** = **B**.
b Find **Y** such that **YA** = **B**.

$\det A = 4 \times 2 - 1 \times 7 = 1$

$A^{-1} = \begin{pmatrix} 2 & -1 \\ -7 & 4 \end{pmatrix}$

*You need to multiply through by A^{-1} in order to find **X** and **Y**.*

*Calculate det **A** and then use this to find A^{-1}.*

a $AX = B$

$A^{-1}AX = A^{-1}B$

$X = A^{-1}B = \begin{pmatrix} 2 & -1 \\ -7 & 4 \end{pmatrix}\begin{pmatrix} 3 & -4 \\ 0 & 8 \end{pmatrix}$

$= \begin{pmatrix} 6 & -16 \\ -21 & 60 \end{pmatrix}$

*You need to cancel **A** from the left side of the product, so you must multiply by A^{-1} on both sides of the equation.*

*Then use $A^{-1}A = I$ and $IX = X$ for any **X**.*

b $YA = B$

$YAA^{-1} = BA^{-1}$

$Y = BA^{-1} = \begin{pmatrix} 3 & -4 \\ 0 & 8 \end{pmatrix}\begin{pmatrix} 2 & -1 \\ -7 & 4 \end{pmatrix}$

$= \begin{pmatrix} 34 & -19 \\ -56 & 32 \end{pmatrix}$

*You need to cancel **A** from the right side of the product, so you must multiply by A^{-1} on the right on both sides of the equation.*

*Then use $AA^{-1} = I$ and $YI = Y$ for any **Y**.*

You will see later that you often need to use the inverse of a product of two matrices. With real numbers, the reciprocal of a product is the product of the reciprocals: $\frac{1}{ab} = \frac{1}{a} \times \frac{1}{b}$. Because matrix multiplication is not commutative, you need to be a little more careful.

> **Fast forward**
>
> You will use the inverse of a matrix product when you work with transformations in Chapter 3.

WORKED EXAMPLE 1.11

For non-singular square matrices **A** and **B**:

a show that $(\mathbf{AB})^{-1}$ exists
b write down $(\mathbf{AB})^{-1}$ in terms of $\mathbf{A}^{-1}$ and $\mathbf{B}^{-1}$.

a If A and B are non-singular then
   det A and det B are both non-zero.
   Since det AB = det A × det B, it follows that det AB is also non-zero and so AB is non-singular and has an inverse.

   > The statements 'non-singular', 'has non-zero determinant', 'has an inverse' are all equivalent (they mean the same thing).
   > The determinant of a matrix product is the product of the determinants of the original matrices. So if neither is singular, the product is also non-singular.

b By definition of an inverse,

   (AB)(AB)⁻¹ = I

   AB(AB)⁻¹ = I

   Multiply by A⁻¹ on the left:

   A⁻¹AB(AB)⁻¹ = A⁻¹I

   Simplify: A⁻¹A = I and XI = IX = X

   B(AB)⁻¹ = A⁻¹

   Now multiply by B⁻¹ on the left:

   B⁻¹B(AB)⁻¹ = B⁻¹A⁻¹

   Simplify:

   B⁻¹B = I and IX = X

   (AB)⁻¹ = B⁻¹A⁻¹

   > Multiply by inverses on the left of each side to find $(\mathbf{AB})^{-1}$.

🔑 Key point 1.14

The inverse of a product consists of the product of the inverses of the individual matrices, but listed in the opposite order:

$$(\mathbf{AB})^{-1} = \mathbf{B}^{-1}\mathbf{A}^{-1}$$

$$(\mathbf{ABC})^{-1} = \mathbf{C}^{-1}\mathbf{B}^{-1}\mathbf{A}^{-1}$$

EXERCISE 1D

1. Find the inverse of each matrix, stating any values of a for which the inverse does not exist. Use a calculator to check your answers.

   a i $\begin{pmatrix} 3 & -1 \\ 7 & 4 \end{pmatrix}$ ii $\begin{pmatrix} 1 & 1 \\ -3 & 2 \end{pmatrix}$

   b i $\begin{pmatrix} 2 & -3 \\ 1 & 5 \end{pmatrix}$ ii $\begin{pmatrix} 3 & -2 \\ 1 & 3 \end{pmatrix}$

   c i $\begin{pmatrix} 2a & a \\ 3 & -1 \end{pmatrix}$ ii $\begin{pmatrix} 1 & -a \\ 5 & 2a \end{pmatrix}$

   d i $\begin{pmatrix} a & -3 \\ 2 & 5a \end{pmatrix}$ ii $\begin{pmatrix} 1 & 2a \\ -a & 3 \end{pmatrix}$

2. Find all possible values of x for which each matrix is singular.

   a i $\begin{pmatrix} x & -3 \\ 1 & 2 \end{pmatrix}$ ii $\begin{pmatrix} x & 1 \\ 1 & 5 \end{pmatrix}$

   b i $\begin{pmatrix} 2x & -x \\ 5 & 2 \end{pmatrix}$ ii $\begin{pmatrix} 3 & -1 \\ x & 3x \end{pmatrix}$

   c i $\begin{pmatrix} 4x & 1 \\ 2 & 2x \end{pmatrix}$ ii $\begin{pmatrix} 1 & x \\ 2x & 8 \end{pmatrix}$

   d i $\begin{pmatrix} 2x & -x \\ 4 & x \end{pmatrix}$ ii $\begin{pmatrix} 1 & x \\ 5x & x \end{pmatrix}$

3. Answer this question without a calculator, then use a calculator to check your answer.

   Given that $\mathbf{A} = \begin{pmatrix} 1 & 1 \\ 3 & -1 \end{pmatrix}$ and $\mathbf{B} = \begin{pmatrix} -1 & 1 \\ 2 & 3 \end{pmatrix}$, find the matrix $\mathbf{X}$ so that:

   a i $\mathbf{AX} = \mathbf{B}$ ii $\mathbf{XA} = \mathbf{B}$

   b i $\mathbf{XB} = \begin{pmatrix} 1 & -1 \\ 3 & 2 \end{pmatrix}$ ii $\mathbf{BX} = \begin{pmatrix} 3 & 1 \\ 1 & 5 \end{pmatrix}$

   c i $\mathbf{AX} = \begin{pmatrix} 1 \\ 4 \end{pmatrix}$ ii $\mathbf{XB} = (-3 \quad 1)$

4. If $\mathbf{A} = \begin{pmatrix} 3 & -1 \\ 2 & 1 \end{pmatrix}$, find the matrix $\mathbf{B}$ such that $\mathbf{BA} = \begin{pmatrix} -1 & 1 \\ 3 & 5 \end{pmatrix}$.

5. $\mathbf{A} = \begin{pmatrix} -3 & 1 \\ 1 & 8 \end{pmatrix}$ and $\mathbf{B} = \begin{pmatrix} 2 & 1 \\ 1 & 5 \end{pmatrix}$.

   a Show that $\mathbf{A}$ is non-singular.

   b Find $\mathbf{A}^{-1}\mathbf{B}$.

6. If $\mathbf{A} = \begin{pmatrix} 1 & 0 \\ 2 & 1 \end{pmatrix}$, find the matrix $\mathbf{X}$ such that $\mathbf{AX} = \begin{pmatrix} 3 \\ -2 \end{pmatrix}$.

7 Find the values of k for which the matrix $\begin{pmatrix} 3k & 1 \\ 9 & k \end{pmatrix}$ is singular.

8 Let $\mathbf{A} = \begin{pmatrix} 5 & 3c \\ -c & 1 \end{pmatrix}$.

   a Show that $\mathbf{A}$ is non-singular for all values of c.

   b Find $\mathbf{A}^{-1}$ in terms of c.

9 Given that $\mathbf{M} = \begin{pmatrix} 1 & -3 \\ 1 & 5 \end{pmatrix}$, find the matrix $\mathbf{X}$ such that $\mathbf{M}^{-1}\mathbf{X}\mathbf{M} = \begin{pmatrix} 4 & 0 \\ 0 & -2 \end{pmatrix}$.

10 Given that $\mathbf{A}$ and $\mathbf{B}$ are non-singular matrices with inverses $\mathbf{A}^{-1}$ and $\mathbf{B}^{-1}$:

   a show that $\frac{1}{3}\mathbf{A}^{-1}$ is the inverse of $3\mathbf{A}$

   b simplify $\left(\mathbf{A}^{-1}\mathbf{B}\right)^{-1}(3\mathbf{A})^{-1}$.

11 Given that $\mathbf{A}$ and $\mathbf{B}$ are non-singular matrices, simplify $\left(\mathbf{A}^{-1}\mathbf{B}^{-1}\mathbf{A}\right)^{-1}$.

12 If $\mathbf{P}$ and $\mathbf{Q}$ are non-singular matrices, simplify:

   a $\mathbf{P}(\mathbf{QP})^{-1}$

   b $(2\mathbf{PQ})(3\mathbf{PQ})^{-1}$

13 Prove that, if the non-singular matrices $\mathbf{A}$ and $\mathbf{B}$ commute, then so do $\mathbf{A}^{-1}$ and $\mathbf{B}^{-1}$.

14 For a non-singular square matrix $\mathbf{A}$, find in terms of $\det \mathbf{A}$:

   a $\det(\mathbf{A}^{-1})$

   b $\det(\mathbf{A}^T)$, where $\mathbf{A}$ is a 2×2 matrix

   c $\det(\mathbf{A}^n)$, where n is an integer.

Section 4: Determinants and inverses of 3 × 3 matrices

Determinant of a 3 × 3 matrix

You already know how to perform addition and multiplication for a 3×3 matrix. To find a determinant of a 3×3 matrix you use determinants of the smaller 2×2 matrices.

Key point 1.15

$$\det \begin{pmatrix} a & b & c \\ d & e & f \\ g & h & i \end{pmatrix} = a \begin{vmatrix} e & f \\ h & i \end{vmatrix} - b \begin{vmatrix} d & f \\ g & i \end{vmatrix} + c \begin{vmatrix} d & e \\ g & h \end{vmatrix}$$

In this formula, each number in the top row is multiplied by the determinant obtained by deleting the row and column containing that element. Notice that the middle term has a negative sign.

WORKED EXAMPLE 1.12

Find the determinant of matrix $\mathbf{A} = \begin{pmatrix} 1 & 2 & 0 \\ 2 & -1 & 3 \\ -2 & 0 & 1 \end{pmatrix}$.

$\det \underline{A} = +1 \times \begin{vmatrix} -1 & 3 \\ 0 & 1 \end{vmatrix}$

$\phantom{\det \underline{A} =} -2 \times \begin{vmatrix} 2 & 3 \\ -2 & 1 \end{vmatrix}$

$\phantom{\det \underline{A} =} +0 \times \begin{vmatrix} 2 & -1 \\ -2 & 0 \end{vmatrix}$

For each element in the top row, multiply by the corresponding determinant. Remember that the middle term has a negative sign.

$\det \underline{A} = +1 \times (-1) - 2 \times 8 + 0$

$\phantom{\det \underline{A}} = -17$

Evaluate each 2×2 determinant.

Tip

You are permitted to use a calculator to find determinants (and inverses) of numerical 3×3 matrices. Remember, you can still check your answer to a non-numerical matrix problem on a calculator by substituting one or more trial values for any unknowns and checking that your formula matches the numerical output from your calculator!

WORKED EXAMPLE 1.13

Find the value of a for which matrix $\mathbf{A} = \begin{pmatrix} 1 & 2 & 0 \\ 2 & a & 3 \\ -2 & 0 & 1 \end{pmatrix}$ is singular.

We want to find when $\det \underline{A} = 0$.

A singular matrix has zero determinant.

$\det \begin{pmatrix} 1 & 2 & 0 \\ 2 & a & 3 \\ -2 & 0 & 1 \end{pmatrix} = 1 \times \begin{vmatrix} a & 3 \\ 0 & 1 \end{vmatrix}$

$ -2 \times \begin{vmatrix} 2 & 3 \\ -2 & 1 \end{vmatrix}$

$ +0 \times \begin{vmatrix} 2 & a \\ -2 & 0 \end{vmatrix}$

For each element in the top row, multiply by the corresponding determinant, changing the middle sign to negative.

$\det \underline{A} = 1 \times a - 2 \times 8 + 0$

$\phantom{\det \underline{A}} = a - 16$

$\det \underline{A} = 0 \Rightarrow a = 16$

A singular matrix has a zero determinant.

1 Matrices

Explore

You don't need to use the first row in the calculation of the determinant; using any other row or column will give the same answer. Find out how the procedure generalises to find determinants of square matrices of any size.

Inverse of a 3 × 3 matrix

Finding the inverse of a 3×3 matrix involves several steps. First you need to find the **cofactor** of each element.

- For each element of the matrix, delete the row and column containing that element.
- Find the determinant of the remaining 2×2 matrix.
- Determine the sign according to the alternating sign matrix:

$$\begin{pmatrix} + & - & + \\ - & + & - \\ + & - & + \end{pmatrix}$$

Fast forward

An alternative method for finding the inverse matrix involves the vector product. You may wish to read Chapter 2, Section 5 and then choose which method you prefer to use.

For example, consider the matrix $\mathbf{A} = \begin{pmatrix} 1 & 2 & 3 \\ 4 & 5 & 6 \\ 7 & 8 & 9 \end{pmatrix}$.

To find the cofactor of element 2, remove the first row and the second column: $\begin{pmatrix} 1 & 2 & 3 \\ 4 & 5 & 6 \\ 7 & 8 & 9 \end{pmatrix}$. The remaining determinant is $\begin{vmatrix} 4 & 6 \\ 7 & 9 \end{vmatrix} = 36 - 42 = -6$.

The alternating sign matrix has a '−' in place of element 2, so you need to change the sign; the cofactor of element 2 is 6.

To find the cofactor of element 7, remove the third row and the first column: $\begin{pmatrix} 1 & 2 & 3 \\ 4 & 5 & 6 \\ 7 & 8 & 9 \end{pmatrix}$. The remaining determinant is $\begin{vmatrix} 2 & 3 \\ 5 & 6 \end{vmatrix} = 12 - 15 = -3$.

The alternating sign matrix has a '+' in place of element 7 so the sign doesn't change; the cofactor of element 7 is −3.

Key point 1.16

To calculate the inverse of a non-singular matrix **A**:

- calculate cofactors for each of the nine elements, and assemble these into a **cofactor matrix C**
- take the transpose of the cofactor matrix
- divide by the determinant of **A**.

In summary: $\mathbf{A}^{-1} = \dfrac{1}{\det \mathbf{A}} \mathbf{C}^{\mathrm{T}}$

WORKED EXAMPLE 1.14

Find the inverse of non-singular matrix $\mathbf{A} = \begin{pmatrix} 2 & 3 & 1 \\ 2 & 3 & -3 \\ -2 & 1 & 4 \end{pmatrix}$.

The matrix of cofactors:

$\underline{C} = \begin{pmatrix} +\begin{vmatrix} 3 & -3 \\ 1 & 4 \end{vmatrix} & -\begin{vmatrix} 2 & -3 \\ -2 & 4 \end{vmatrix} & +\begin{vmatrix} 2 & 3 \\ -2 & 1 \end{vmatrix} \\ -\begin{vmatrix} 3 & 1 \\ 1 & 4 \end{vmatrix} & +\begin{vmatrix} 2 & 1 \\ -2 & 4 \end{vmatrix} & -\begin{vmatrix} 2 & 3 \\ -2 & 1 \end{vmatrix} \\ +\begin{vmatrix} 3 & 1 \\ 3 & -3 \end{vmatrix} & -\begin{vmatrix} 2 & 1 \\ 2 & -3 \end{vmatrix} & +\begin{vmatrix} 2 & 3 \\ 2 & 3 \end{vmatrix} \end{pmatrix}$

> For each cofactor, find the relevant determinant and apply the alternating sign matrix.

$= \begin{pmatrix} 15 & -2 & 8 \\ -11 & 10 & -8 \\ -12 & 8 & 0 \end{pmatrix}$

$\underline{C}^T = \begin{pmatrix} 15 & -11 & -12 \\ -2 & 10 & 8 \\ 8 & -8 & 0 \end{pmatrix}$

> Write down $\mathbf{C}^T$.

$\det \underline{A} = 2 \times \begin{vmatrix} 3 & -3 \\ 1 & 4 \end{vmatrix} - 3 \times \begin{vmatrix} 2 & -3 \\ -2 & 4 \end{vmatrix} + 1 \times \begin{vmatrix} 2 & 3 \\ -2 & 1 \end{vmatrix}$

> Find the determinant of **A**.

$= 2 \times 15 - 3 \times 2 + 1 \times 8$

$= 32$

$\underline{A}^{-1} = \frac{1}{32} \underline{C}^T = \frac{1}{32} \begin{pmatrix} 15 & -11 & -12 \\ -2 & 10 & 8 \\ 8 & -8 & 0 \end{pmatrix}$

> The inverse is the transpose of the cofactor matrix divided by the determinant. You can leave the factor $\frac{1}{32}$ outside the matrix.

💡 Tip

You can check your answer on a calculator.

EXERCISE 1E

1 Find the determinant of each matrix. Check your answer using a calculator.

a i $\begin{pmatrix} 1 & 3 & 2 \\ 2 & 4 & 0 \\ 5 & -3 & 0 \end{pmatrix}$ **ii** $\begin{pmatrix} 2 & 4 & 1 \\ 1 & 2 & 6 \\ -3 & -6 & 8 \end{pmatrix}$

b i $\begin{pmatrix} 3 & 1 & -4 \\ -5 & 1 & 0 \\ 1 & -2 & 6 \end{pmatrix}$ **ii** $\begin{pmatrix} 3 & d & 2 \\ -4 & 2 & -3 \\ 0 & 1 & -1 \end{pmatrix}$

2 Find the inverse of each matrix. Check your answer using a calculator.

a i $\begin{pmatrix} 1 & 3 & 2 \\ 2 & 4 & 0 \\ 5 & -3 & 0 \end{pmatrix}$ **ii** $\begin{pmatrix} 2 & 3 & 1 \\ 1 & 2 & 6 \\ -3 & -6 & 8 \end{pmatrix}$

b i $\begin{pmatrix} 3 & 1 & -4 \\ -5 & 1 & 0 \\ 1 & -2 & 6 \end{pmatrix}$ **ii** $\begin{pmatrix} 3 & d & 2 \\ -4 & 2 & -3 \\ 0 & 1 & -1 \end{pmatrix}$

3 Find all possible values of x for which each matrix is singular.

a i $\begin{pmatrix} 1 & x & -4 \\ -1 & 0 & -x \\ 2 & 1 & 1+x \end{pmatrix}$ **ii** $\begin{pmatrix} 1 & 2 & 1 \\ 0 & x & 0 \\ -7 & x^2 & 1 \end{pmatrix}$

b i $\begin{pmatrix} 2x & 1 & -1 \\ 1 & x & 1-x \\ 0 & 1 & 1 \end{pmatrix}$ **ii** $\begin{pmatrix} 0 & x & 1 \\ -x & x-1 & 2 \\ 4 & 1 & -1 \end{pmatrix}$

4 Given that $\mathbf{A} = \begin{pmatrix} 1 & 1 & 2 \\ 0 & -2 & -1 \\ -2 & -1 & -3 \end{pmatrix}$ and $\mathbf{B} = \begin{pmatrix} 1 & 0 & 1 \\ 9 & 4 & -2 \\ -2 & -1 & 1 \end{pmatrix}$, find the matrix $\mathbf{X}$ such that:

a i $\mathbf{AX} = \mathbf{B}$ **ii** $\mathbf{XA} = \mathbf{B}$

b i $\mathbf{BX} = \begin{pmatrix} 1 & 3 & 2 \\ 4 & 0 & 1 \\ -1 & 2 & -3 \end{pmatrix}$ **ii** $\mathbf{XB} = \begin{pmatrix} -2 & 1 & 1 \\ -4 & -2 & 0 \\ 0 & 1 & 2 \end{pmatrix}$

c i $\mathbf{AX} = \begin{pmatrix} 1 \\ 3 \\ -1 \end{pmatrix}$ **ii** $\mathbf{XB} = \begin{pmatrix} -1 & 2 & -4 \end{pmatrix}$

5 Find all possible values of x for which $\begin{vmatrix} x & 6 & -9 \\ 2 & 4 & x \\ -1 & -2 & 3 \end{vmatrix} = 0$.

6 Find all values of x for which $\mathbf{A}$ is singular, where $\mathbf{A} = \begin{pmatrix} 2x & 1 & x^2 \\ 1 & 2 & x \\ -1 & 3 & -1 \end{pmatrix}$.

27

7 In this question you must show detailed reasoning.

Given $\mathbf{M} = \begin{pmatrix} 2 & 1 & -1 \\ 0 & 2 & 1 \\ 3 & 3 & -1 \end{pmatrix}$, find $\mathbf{X}$ such that $\mathbf{M}^{-1}\mathbf{X}\mathbf{M} = \begin{pmatrix} 4 & 0 & 0 \\ 0 & 2 & 0 \\ 0 & 0 & -3 \end{pmatrix}$.

> **Tip**
>
> Remember that 'show detailed reasoning' means that you need to show all the steps in your working, although you may use a calculator to check your answer.

8 Matrix $\mathbf{A}$ is given by $\mathbf{A} = \begin{pmatrix} 1 & 0 & a \\ 4 & 2 & 1+a \\ 3 & 4 & -1 \end{pmatrix}$.

  a Find the inverse $\mathbf{A}^{-1}$ in terms of a.

  b Given that $\mathbf{AX} = \begin{pmatrix} 2 & -1 & 1 \\ 0 & 1 & 0 \\ 1 & 2 & -1 \end{pmatrix}$, find $\mathbf{X}$ in terms of a.

  c If $\det \mathbf{X} = 2$, find the value of a.

9 Matrix $\mathbf{A}$ is given by $\mathbf{A} = \begin{pmatrix} 1 & 0 & 1 \\ -2 & x & 2 \\ 3 & 1 & -1 \end{pmatrix}$.

  a Find a condition on x for matrix $\mathbf{A}$ to be non-singular.

  b Assuming the condition found in part **a** is true, find $\mathbf{B}$ where

  $\mathbf{AB} = \begin{pmatrix} 2 \\ 0 \\ -1 \end{pmatrix}$, giving $\mathbf{B}$ in terms of x.

10 The procedure for finding the inverse matrix applies to matrices of any size. Check that following the procedure in Key point 1.16 for a 2×2 matrix gives the same answer as the procedure we used in Section 2.

11 For an $n \times n$ matrix $\mathbf{M}$, $\mathbf{M}^{-1} = \dfrac{1}{|\mathbf{M}|}\mathbf{C}^{\mathrm{T}}$, where $\mathbf{C}$ is the matrix of cofactors for $\mathbf{M}$.

Find the matrix $\mathbf{A}^{-1}$, where $\mathbf{A} = \begin{pmatrix} 1 & 0 & 0 & a \\ 2 & 1 & 3 & 0 \\ 0 & -1 & 0 & 1 \\ 1 & -2 & 1 & 0 \end{pmatrix}$.

1 Matrices

📎 Checklist of learning and understanding

- An $m \times n$ matrix **A** is a rectangular array of numerical or algebraic elements with m rows and n columns.
- Addition (or subtraction) of conformable matrices **A** and **B** involves adding (or subtracting) elements of matching position.
- Scalar multiplication of a matrix involves multiplying each element by the scalar.
- When an $m \times n$ matrix **A** and an $n \times p$ matrix **B** are multiplied together, the result is an $m \times p$ matrix **C** = **AB**. To find the element in row i and column j of **C**:
  1. Take row i of **A** and column j of **B**.
  2. Multiply each pair of corresponding values and add all the products together.
- The zero matrix **Z** has all elements equal to 0.
- The identity matrix **I** is a square ($n \times n$) matrix with elements equal to 1 on the lead diagonal and 0 elsewhere.
  - For suitably sized **I**, **AI** = **A**, **IA** = **A** for any matrix **A**.
- The inverse matrix satisfies $\mathbf{AA}^{-1} = \mathbf{A}^{-1}\mathbf{A} = \mathbf{I}$.
  - A matrix is singular if its determinant is zero. Otherwise it is non-singular. Only non-singular matrices have an inverse matrix.
  - For two non-singular matrices **A** and **B**, $(\mathbf{AB})^{-1} = \mathbf{B}^{-1}\mathbf{A}^{-1}$.
- Inverse matrices can be used to solve equations:
  - If **AX** = **B**, then **X** = $\mathbf{A}^{-1}\mathbf{B}$.
  - If **XA** = **B**, then **X** = $\mathbf{BA}^{-1}$.
- The determinant of a 2×2 matrix $\mathbf{M} = \begin{pmatrix} a & b \\ c & d \end{pmatrix}$ is $|\mathbf{M}| = ad - bc$.
- The inverse of a non-singular 2×2 matrix $\mathbf{M} = \begin{pmatrix} a & b \\ c & d \end{pmatrix}$ is $\mathbf{M}^{-1} = \dfrac{1}{|\mathbf{M}|}\begin{pmatrix} d & -b \\ -c & a \end{pmatrix}$.
- The determinant of a 3×3 matrix $\mathbf{M} = \begin{pmatrix} a & b & c \\ d & e & f \\ g & h & i \end{pmatrix}$ is $|\mathbf{M}| = a\begin{vmatrix} e & f \\ h & i \end{vmatrix} - b\begin{vmatrix} d & f \\ g & i \end{vmatrix} + c\begin{vmatrix} d & e \\ g & h \end{vmatrix}$.
- The inverse of a non-singular 3×3 matrix **M** is $\mathbf{M}^{-1} = \dfrac{1}{|\mathbf{M}|}\mathbf{C}^{\mathrm{T}}$, where **C** is the matrix of cofactors for **M**.

Mixed practice 1

1 $A = \begin{pmatrix} p & -1 \\ -4 & 2p \end{pmatrix}$ and $B = \begin{pmatrix} 3 & -1 \\ 0 & 4 \end{pmatrix}$.

Find, in terms of p, the matrix AB.

2 Matrices A, B and C are given by:

$A = \begin{pmatrix} a & -1 \\ 2 & 1 \end{pmatrix}$, $B = \begin{pmatrix} 3 & b \\ 0 & -4 \end{pmatrix}$, $C = \begin{pmatrix} 1 & 4 \\ 2 & c \end{pmatrix}$

If $AB + kC = I$, find a, b, c and k.

3 Matrices A and B are given by $A = \begin{pmatrix} k & -1 \\ 1 & k \end{pmatrix}$ and $B = \begin{pmatrix} 2 & 2 \\ -2 & 2 \end{pmatrix}$ where k is a constant.

  a Show that $AB = BA$.

  b Show, by choosing matrices C and D, that matrix multiplication is not always commutative.

4 The matrices A, B and C are given by $A = (5 \ \ 1)$, $B = (2 \ \ -5)$ and $C = \begin{pmatrix} 3 \\ 2 \end{pmatrix}$.

  a Find $3A - 4B$.

  b Find CB. Determine whether CB is singular or non-singular, giving a reason for your answer.

© OCR, AS GCE Further Mathematics, Paper 4725, June 2013
[Question part reference style adapted]

5 In this question you must show detailed reasoning.

$A = \begin{pmatrix} 2 & 3 \\ -2 & -5 \end{pmatrix}$ and $C = \begin{pmatrix} 1 & 2 \\ 0 & 3 \end{pmatrix}$.

Given $AB = C$, find B.

6 Matrix A is given by $A = \begin{pmatrix} a & -2 \\ 2 & 4 \end{pmatrix}$.

  a If A is singular, calculate a.

  b Given A is non-singular, express A^{-1} in terms of a.

7 The matrix A is given by $A = \begin{pmatrix} 2 & a \\ 0 & 1 \end{pmatrix}$, where a is a constant.

  a Find A^{-1}.

The matrix B is given by $B = \begin{pmatrix} 2 & a \\ 4 & 1 \end{pmatrix}$.

  b Given that $PA = B$, find the matrix P.

© OCR, AS GCE Further Mathematics, Paper 4725, June 2015
[Question part reference style adapted]

8 Find the determinant of the matrix $\begin{pmatrix} a & 4 & -1 \\ 3 & a & 2 \\ a & 1 & 1 \end{pmatrix}$.

© OCR, AS GCE Further Mathematics, Paper 4725, June 2014

9 Find all values of x for which the matrix $\begin{pmatrix} x & -1 & -1 \\ 3 & 4 & 1 \\ 0 & 2x & 1 \end{pmatrix}$ is singular.

10 **In this question you must show detailed reasoning.**

Given matrices $\mathbf{A} = \begin{pmatrix} 2 & 0 & 1 \\ 1 & -1 & 0 \\ 0 & 3 & -2 \end{pmatrix}$ and $\mathbf{AX} = \begin{pmatrix} 3 & -1 \\ 2 & 5 \\ 0 & 4 \end{pmatrix}$, find $\mathbf{X}$.

11 Matrix $\mathbf{A} = \begin{pmatrix} 1 & 2 \\ x & y \end{pmatrix}$. Given $\mathbf{A}$ is non-singular and $\mathbf{A} + \mathbf{A}^{-1} = \mathbf{I}$, find x and y.

12 a Show that for two 2×2 matrices $\mathbf{A}$ and $\mathbf{B}$, where neither $\mathbf{A}$ nor $\mathbf{B}$ is the zero matrix $\mathbf{Z}$, that if $\mathbf{AB} = \mathbf{Z}$ then both $\mathbf{A}$ and $\mathbf{B}$ must be singular.

   b Find two matrices $\mathbf{C}$ and $\mathbf{D}$, where no element of either matrix is zero, for which $\mathbf{CD} = \mathbf{Z}$.

13 a For two 2×2 matrices $\mathbf{A}$ and $\mathbf{B}$, show that if

   $\det(\mathbf{A} + \mathbf{B}) = 0 = \det(\mathbf{A} - \mathbf{B})$

   then

   $\det \mathbf{A} + \det \mathbf{B} = 0$.

   b Give an example of two matrices $\mathbf{A}$ and $\mathbf{B}$ for which

   $\det \mathbf{A} + \det \mathbf{B} = 0$ but $\det(\mathbf{A} + \mathbf{B}) \neq 0$.

2 Further vectors

In this chapter you will learn how to:

- write an equation of a straight line in three dimensions, using both vectors and coordinates
- find the intersection point of two lines
- calculate an angle between two vectors or two straight lines (using a scalar product)
- decide whether two lines are parallel or perpendicular
- find a line that is perpendicular to two given lines (using a vector product)
- solve problems involving distances between points and lines.

Before you start…

A Level Mathematics Student Book 1, Chapter 12; A Level Mathematics Student Book 2, Chapter 19	You should be able to describe vectors using components in two and three dimensions.	1	a Write $\begin{pmatrix} 3 \\ -5 \end{pmatrix}$ using $\mathbf{i}$ and $\mathbf{j}$ base vectors. b Write $3\mathbf{i} - 2\mathbf{k}$ as a three-dimensional column vector.
	You should be able to recognise when two vectors are equal.	2	Find the values of a and b such that $\begin{pmatrix} 3a-2 \\ b+1 \end{pmatrix} = \begin{pmatrix} b-3 \\ 2a+1 \end{pmatrix}$.
	You should be able to recognise when two vectors are parallel.	3	Find the values of p and q such that the vectors $2\mathbf{i} + p\mathbf{j} - \mathbf{k}$ and $q\mathbf{i} + 3\mathbf{j} + 5\mathbf{k}$ are parallel.
A Level Mathematics Student Book 1, Chapter 10; A Level Mathematics Student Book 2, Chapter 7	You should be able to solve trigonometric equations to find an unknown angle, working in both degrees and radians.	4	a Find two possible values of angle $\theta \in [0°, 360°]$ such that $12 - 5\cos\theta = 14$. b Find the size of angle A in radians.

2 Further vectors

Describing lines in three dimensions

Many situations involve lines in three-dimensional space; for example, representing flight paths of aeroplanes or describing motion of a character in a computer game. In order to solve problems involving lines in space, we need a way of deciding whether a point lies on a given straight line.

Suppose you are given two points, A and B. These two points determine a unique straight line (by a 'straight line' we mean a line extending indefinitely in both directions). How can you check whether a third point lies on the same line, or describe all points on this line? You can use vectors to answer this question.

Section 1: Vector equation of a line

Consider, as an example, the straight line passing through points $A(-1, 1, 4)$ and $B(1, 4, 2)$, and another point $C(5, 10, -2)$. Then:

$$\overrightarrow{AB} = \begin{pmatrix} 2 \\ 3 \\ -2 \end{pmatrix} \text{ and } \overrightarrow{AC} = \begin{pmatrix} 6 \\ 9 \\ -6 \end{pmatrix} = 3\overrightarrow{AB}$$

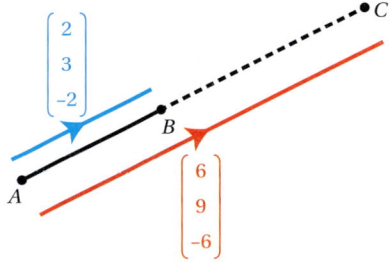

This means that the line AC is parallel to AB. But since they both contain the point A, they must be the same straight line; in other words, C lies on the line AB.

> **Tip**
>
> 'Line AB' refers to the infinite line passing through A and B.

You can now characterise all the points on the line AB. Using the idea above, a point R lies on AB if AR and AB are parallel. But you know that this can be expressed using vectors by saying that $\overrightarrow{AR} = \lambda \overrightarrow{AB}$ for some value of the scalar λ.

So $\overrightarrow{AR} = \begin{pmatrix} 2\lambda \\ 3\lambda \\ -2\lambda \end{pmatrix}$. However, you also know that $\overrightarrow{AR} = \mathbf{r} - \mathbf{a}$, where $\mathbf{r}$ and $\mathbf{a}$ are the position vectors of R and A, respectively.

> **Tip**
>
> Remember that a scalar means a number.

> **Rewind**
>
> See A Level Mathematics Student Book 1, Chapter 12, Section 2, for a reminder of vector algebra.

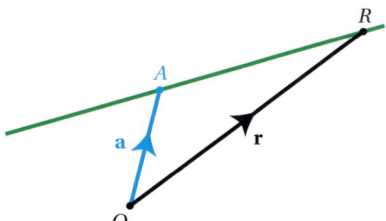

This means that $\mathbf{r} = \begin{pmatrix} -1 \\ 1 \\ 4 \end{pmatrix} + \begin{pmatrix} 2\lambda \\ 3\lambda \\ -2\lambda \end{pmatrix}$ is the position vector of a general point on the line AB. In other words, R has coordinates $(-1 + 2\lambda, 1 + 3\lambda, 4 - 2\lambda)$ for some value of λ. Different values of λ correspond to different points on the line; for example, $\lambda = 0$ corresponds to point A, $\lambda = 1$ to point B and $\lambda = 3$ to point C.

> **Tip**
>
> It doesn't matter what letter you choose for the scalar. The letters most commonly used are λ (lambda), μ (mu), t and s.

The line is parallel to the vector $\begin{pmatrix} 2 \\ 3 \\ -2 \end{pmatrix}$, so this vector determines the direction of the line. The expression for the position vector of **r** is usually written as $\mathbf{r} = \begin{pmatrix} -1 \\ 1 \\ 4 \end{pmatrix} + \lambda \begin{pmatrix} 2 \\ 3 \\ -2 \end{pmatrix}$, so it is easy to identify the **direction vector**.

> ▶▶ **Fast forward**
>
> You will see below and in Worked example 2.3 that there is more than one possible vector equation of a line.

🔑 Key point 2.1

The expression $\mathbf{r} = \mathbf{a} + \lambda \mathbf{d}$ is a **vector equation** of the line.

The vector **d** is the direction vector of the line and **a** is the position vector of one point on the line.

The vector **r** is the position vector of a general point on the line; different values of parameter λ give positions of different points on the line.

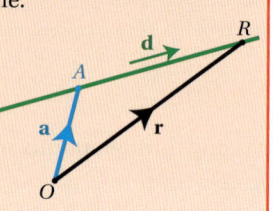

WORKED EXAMPLE 2.1

Write down a vector equation of the line passing through the point $(-1, 1, 2)$ in the direction of the vector $\begin{pmatrix} 2 \\ 2 \\ 1 \end{pmatrix}$.

$\underline{\mathbf{r}} = \begin{pmatrix} -1 \\ 1 \\ 2 \end{pmatrix} + \lambda \begin{pmatrix} 2 \\ 2 \\ 1 \end{pmatrix}$ .... The equation of the line is $\mathbf{r} = \mathbf{a} + \lambda \mathbf{d}$, where **a** is the position vector of a point on the line and **d** is the direction vector.

The vector equation also can be used for lines in two dimensions. For example, a line with direction vector $\begin{pmatrix} 1 \\ 3 \end{pmatrix}$ has gradient 3, because an increase of 1 unit in x produces an increase of 3 units in y.

In three dimensions you cannot use a single number to represent the direction vector. For example, for a line with direction vector $\begin{pmatrix} 2 \\ 2 \\ 1 \end{pmatrix}$, an increase of 2 units in x produces an increase of 2 units in y and an increase of 1 unit in z.

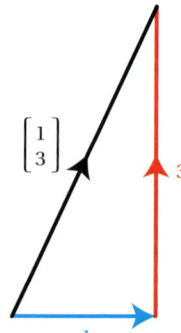

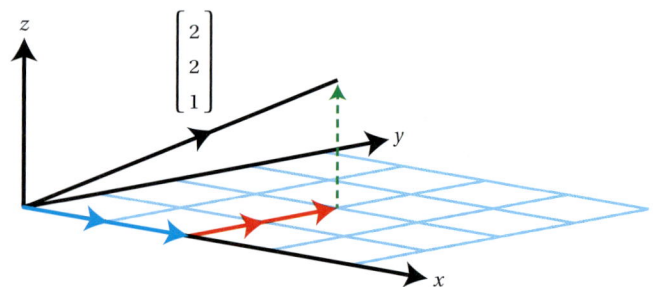

The next example shows how to find a vector equation of the line when two points on the line are given.

WORKED EXAMPLE 2.2

Find a vector equation of the line through points $A(-1, 1, 2)$ and $B(3, 5, 4)$.

$\underline{r} = \underline{a} + \lambda \underline{d}$ — To write down an equation of the line, you need to know one point and the direction vector.

$\underline{a} = \begin{pmatrix} -1 \\ 1 \\ 2 \end{pmatrix}$ — The line passes through $A(-1, 1, 2)$.

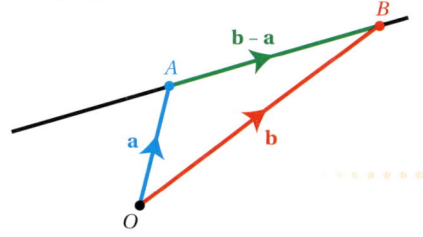

— The line is in the direction of $\overrightarrow{AB}$, as you can see by drawing a diagram.

$\underline{d} = \overrightarrow{AB} = \underline{b} - \underline{a} = \begin{pmatrix} 4 \\ 4 \\ 2 \end{pmatrix}$

$\underline{r} = \begin{pmatrix} -1 \\ 1 \\ 2 \end{pmatrix} + \lambda \begin{pmatrix} 4 \\ 4 \\ 2 \end{pmatrix}$ — A vector equation of the line is $\mathbf{r} = \mathbf{a} + \lambda \mathbf{d}$.

What if, for '**a**' in the formula, you used the position vector of point B instead? Then you would get the equation $\mathbf{r} = \begin{pmatrix} 3 \\ 5 \\ 4 \end{pmatrix} + \lambda \begin{pmatrix} 4 \\ 4 \\ 2 \end{pmatrix}$. This equation represents the same line, but the values of the parameter λ corresponding to particular points will be different.

For example, with the first equation point A has $\lambda = 0$ and point B has $\lambda = 1$, whereas with the second equation point A has $\lambda = -1$ and point B has $\lambda = 0$.

The direction vector is not unique either, since you are interested only in its direction and not its magnitude. Hence, you could use any multiple of the direction vector instead, for example $\begin{pmatrix} 2 \\ 2 \\ 1 \end{pmatrix}$ or $\begin{pmatrix} -6 \\ -6 \\ -3 \end{pmatrix}$.

So yet another form of the equation of the same line would be

$\mathbf{r} = \begin{pmatrix} -1 \\ 1 \\ 2 \end{pmatrix} + \lambda \begin{pmatrix} -6 \\ -6 \\ -3 \end{pmatrix}$. With this equation, point A has $\lambda = 0$ and point B has $\lambda = -\frac{2}{3}$.

> **Tip**
>
> When there is more than one line in a question, you should use different letters for the parameters.

WORKED EXAMPLE 2.3

a Show that the equations $\mathbf{r} = \begin{pmatrix} -1 \\ 1 \\ 2 \end{pmatrix} + \lambda \begin{pmatrix} 2 \\ 2 \\ 1 \end{pmatrix}$ and $\mathbf{r} = \begin{pmatrix} 5 \\ 7 \\ 5 \end{pmatrix} + \mu \begin{pmatrix} 6 \\ 6 \\ 3 \end{pmatrix}$ represent the same straight line.

b Show that the equation $\mathbf{r} = \begin{pmatrix} -5 \\ -3 \\ 1 \end{pmatrix} + t \begin{pmatrix} -4 \\ -4 \\ -2 \end{pmatrix}$ represents a different straight line.

> You need to show that the two lines have parallel direction vectors (they will then be parallel) and one common point (then they will be the same line).

a Direction vectors are parallel, as

$\begin{pmatrix} 6 \\ 6 \\ 3 \end{pmatrix} = 3 \begin{pmatrix} 2 \\ 2 \\ 1 \end{pmatrix}$

> Two vectors are parallel if one is a scalar multiple of the other.

> You now need to check that the point $(5, 7, 5)$ lies on the first line. This will be the case if you can find the value of the parameter λ for the first line that gives the position vector of $(5, 7, 5)$.

$-1 + 2\lambda = 5$
$\lambda = 3$

> Find the value of λ that gives the first coordinate.

$\begin{cases} 1 + 3 \times 2 = 7 \\ 2 + 3 \times 1 = 5 \end{cases}$

> This value of λ must give the other two coordinates.

$(5, 7, 5)$ lies on the line.

Hence, the two lines are the same.

b $\begin{pmatrix} -4 \\ -4 \\ -2 \end{pmatrix} = -2 \begin{pmatrix} 2 \\ 2 \\ 1 \end{pmatrix}$

> Check whether the direction vectors are parallel.

So the line is parallel to the other two.

$-1 + 2\lambda = -5$
$\lambda = -2$

> Check whether $(-5, -3, 1)$ lies on the first line. Find the value of λ that gives the first coordinate.

$\begin{cases} 1 + (-2) \times 2 = -3 \\ 2 + (-2) \times 1 = 0 \neq 1 \end{cases}$

> This value of λ must give the other two coordinates.

$(-5, -3, 1)$ does not lie on the line.

Hence, the line is not the same as the first line.

WORK IT OUT 2.1

Find a vector equation of the line containing points $A(-3, 4, 2)$ and $B(5, 1, 1)$.

Which is the correct solution? Can you identify the errors made in the incorrect solutions?

Solution 1	Solution 2	Solution 3
$\mathbf{b} - \mathbf{a} = 8\mathbf{i} - 3\mathbf{j} - \mathbf{k}$ $\mathbf{r} = 8\mathbf{i} - 3\mathbf{j} - \mathbf{k} + t(-3\mathbf{i} + 4\mathbf{j} + 2\mathbf{k})$	$\mathbf{r} = \begin{pmatrix} -3 \\ 4 \\ 2 \end{pmatrix} + \lambda \begin{pmatrix} 5 \\ 1 \\ 1 \end{pmatrix}$	$\mathbf{a} - \mathbf{b} = -8\mathbf{i} + 3\mathbf{j} + \mathbf{k}$ $\mathbf{r} = 5\mathbf{i} + \mathbf{j} + \mathbf{k} + t(-8\mathbf{i} + 3\mathbf{j} + \mathbf{k})$

Sometimes you only know that a point lies on a given line, but not its precise coordinates. The next example shows you how to work with a general point on the line (with an unknown value of λ).

WORKED EXAMPLE 2.4

Point $B(3, 5, 4)$ lies on the line with equation $\mathbf{r} = \begin{pmatrix} -1 \\ 1 \\ 2 \end{pmatrix} + \lambda \begin{pmatrix} 2 \\ 2 \\ 1 \end{pmatrix}$. Find the possible positions of a point Q on the line such that $BQ = 15$.

$\mathbf{q} = \begin{pmatrix} -1 \\ 1 \\ 2 \end{pmatrix} + \lambda \begin{pmatrix} 2 \\ 2 \\ 1 \end{pmatrix}$

$= \begin{pmatrix} -1 + 2\lambda \\ 1 + 2\lambda \\ 2 + \lambda \end{pmatrix}$

You know that Q lies on the line, so it has the position vector $\begin{pmatrix} -1 \\ 1 \\ 2 \end{pmatrix} + \lambda \begin{pmatrix} 2 \\ 2 \\ 1 \end{pmatrix}$ for some value of λ. You need to find the possible values of λ and substitute them to find the position vector of Q.

$\overrightarrow{BQ} = \mathbf{q} - \mathbf{b}$

$= \begin{pmatrix} -1 + 2\lambda \\ 1 + 2\lambda \\ 2 + \lambda \end{pmatrix} - \begin{pmatrix} 3 \\ 5 \\ 4 \end{pmatrix}$

$= \begin{pmatrix} 2\lambda - 4 \\ 2\lambda - 4 \\ \lambda - 2 \end{pmatrix}$

You can express vector $\overrightarrow{BQ}$ in terms of λ and then set its magnitude equal to 15.

$|\overrightarrow{BQ}| = 15$:

$(2\lambda - 4)^2 + (2\lambda - 4)^2 + (\lambda - 2)^2 = 15^2$
$9\lambda^2 - 36\lambda - 189 = 0$
$\lambda = -3 \text{ or } 7$

It is easier to work without the square root, so square the magnitude equation $|\mathbf{a}| = \sqrt{a_1^2 + a_2^2 + a_3^2}$.

$\mathbf{q} = \begin{pmatrix} -7 \\ -5 \\ -1 \end{pmatrix} \text{ or } \begin{pmatrix} 13 \\ 15 \\ 9 \end{pmatrix}$

You can now find the position vector of Q, using $\mathbf{q} = \begin{pmatrix} -1 + 2\lambda \\ 1 + 2\lambda \\ 2 + \lambda \end{pmatrix}$.

EXERCISE 2A

1 Find the vector equation of the line in the given direction through the given point.

   a **i** direction $\begin{pmatrix} 1 \\ 4 \end{pmatrix}$, point $(4, -1)$ **ii** direction $\begin{pmatrix} 2 \\ -3 \end{pmatrix}$, point $(4, 1)$

   b **i** point $(1, 0, 5)$, direction $\begin{pmatrix} 1 \\ 3 \\ -3 \end{pmatrix}$ **ii** point $(-1, 1, 5)$, direction $\begin{pmatrix} 3 \\ -2 \\ 2 \end{pmatrix}$

   c **i** point $(4, 0)$, direction $2\mathbf{i} + 3\mathbf{j}$ **ii** point $(0, 2)$, direction $\mathbf{i} - 3\mathbf{j}$

   d **i** direction $\mathbf{i} - 3\mathbf{k}$, point $(0, 2, 3)$ **ii** direction $2\mathbf{i} + 3\mathbf{j} - \mathbf{k}$, point $(4, -3, 0)$

2 Find the vector equation of the line through two given points.

   a **i** $(4, 1)$ and $(1, 2)$ **ii** $(2, 7)$ and $(4, -2)$

   b **i** $(-5, -2, 3)$ and $(4, -2, 3)$ **ii** $(1, 1, 3)$ and $(10, -5, 0)$

3 Decide whether or not the given point lies on the given line.

   a **i** line $\mathbf{r} = \begin{pmatrix} 2 \\ 1 \\ 5 \end{pmatrix} + t\begin{pmatrix} -1 \\ 2 \\ 2 \end{pmatrix}$, point $(0, 5, 9)$ **ii** line $\mathbf{r} = \begin{pmatrix} -1 \\ 0 \\ 3 \end{pmatrix} + t\begin{pmatrix} 4 \\ 1 \\ 5 \end{pmatrix}$, point $(-1, 0, 3)$

   b **i** line $\mathbf{r} = \begin{pmatrix} 4 \\ 0 \\ 3 \end{pmatrix} + t\begin{pmatrix} 4 \\ 0 \\ 3 \end{pmatrix}$, point $(0, 0, 0)$ **ii** line $\mathbf{r} = \begin{pmatrix} -1 \\ 5 \\ 1 \end{pmatrix} + t\begin{pmatrix} 0 \\ 0 \\ 7 \end{pmatrix}$, point $(-1, 3, 8)$

4 Determine whether the two equations describe the same straight line.

   a **i** $\mathbf{r} = \begin{pmatrix} 3 \\ -1 \\ 2 \end{pmatrix} + \lambda\begin{pmatrix} 1 \\ 1 \\ 3 \end{pmatrix}$ and $\mathbf{r} = \begin{pmatrix} 4 \\ 0 \\ 5 \end{pmatrix} + \mu\begin{pmatrix} 2 \\ 1 \\ 1 \end{pmatrix}$ **ii** $\mathbf{r} = \begin{pmatrix} 4 \\ 1 \\ 2 \end{pmatrix} + \lambda\begin{pmatrix} 3 \\ 4 \\ 1 \end{pmatrix}$ and $\mathbf{r} = \begin{pmatrix} 7 \\ 5 \\ 1 \end{pmatrix} + \mu\begin{pmatrix} 3 \\ 4 \\ 1 \end{pmatrix}$

   b **i** $\mathbf{r} = 3\mathbf{i} + 2\mathbf{j} - 2\mathbf{k} + t(2\mathbf{i} - 5\mathbf{j} + 3\mathbf{k})$ and $\mathbf{r} = 3\mathbf{i} + 2\mathbf{j} - 2\mathbf{k} + s(-4\mathbf{i} + 10\mathbf{j} - 6\mathbf{k})$

   ii $\mathbf{r} = 3\mathbf{i} + 2\mathbf{j} - 2\mathbf{k} + t(2\mathbf{i} - 5\mathbf{j} + 3\mathbf{k})$ and $\mathbf{r} = -\mathbf{i} + 12\mathbf{j} - 8\mathbf{k} + s(-4\mathbf{i} + 10\mathbf{j} - 6\mathbf{k})$

5 A line passes through the point $A(3, -1, 4)$ and has the direction vector $5\mathbf{i} - \mathbf{j} + 2\mathbf{k}$.

   a Write down the vector equation of the line.

   b Point B has coordinates $(-7, 1, 0)$. Show that B lies on the line.

   c Find the exact distance AB.

6 **a** Find the vector equation of the line through the points with coordinates $(4, -1, 5)$ and $(7, 7, 2)$.

   b Determine whether the point with coordinates $(10, 15, 1)$ lies on this line.

7 Line l_1 has vector equation $\mathbf{r} = \begin{pmatrix} 3 \\ -1 \\ 1 \end{pmatrix} + \lambda\begin{pmatrix} 1 \\ -6 \\ 2 \end{pmatrix}$. Find the vector equation of the line parallel to l_1 that passes through the point $P(4, 1, 7)$.

8 Find the vector equation of the line containing the point $(4, -1, 2)$ that is parallel to the line with equation $\mathbf{r} = (3 + 2\lambda)\mathbf{i} + (5 - \lambda)\mathbf{j} + (3\lambda)\mathbf{k}$.

9 a Show that the points $A(4, -1, -8)$ and $B(2, 1, -4)$ lie on the line l with equation $\mathbf{r} = \begin{pmatrix} 2 \\ 1 \\ -4 \end{pmatrix} + t \begin{pmatrix} -1 \\ 1 \\ 2 \end{pmatrix}$.

   b Find the coordinates of the point C on the line l such that $AB = BC$.

10 a Find the vector equation of line l through points $P(7, 1, 2)$ and $Q(3, -1, 5)$.

   b Point R lies on l and $PR = 3PQ$. Find the possible coordinates of R.

11 a Write down the vector equation of the line l through the point $A(2, 1, 4)$ parallel to the vector $2\mathbf{i} - 3\mathbf{j} + 6\mathbf{k}$.

   b Calculate the magnitude of the vector $2\mathbf{i} - 3\mathbf{j} + 6\mathbf{k}$.

   c Find the possible coordinates of point P on l such that $AP = 35$.

Section 2: Cartesian equation of a line

In the previous section you worked with vector equations of lines in both two and three dimensions. You already know that, in two dimensions, the equation of a straight line also can be written in the form $y = mx + c$ or $ax + by = c$. In this section we look at how the two forms are related.

WORKED EXAMPLE 2.5

A straight line passes through the point $(3, -5)$ and has gradient $-\dfrac{2}{7}$. Find the vector equation of the line.

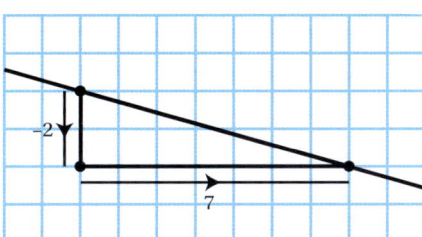

Draw a gradient triangle to identify the direction vector: 2 units down and 7 to the right.

The direction vector is $\underline{d} = \begin{pmatrix} 7 \\ -2 \end{pmatrix}$

and the line passes through point $\underline{a} = \begin{pmatrix} 3 \\ -5 \end{pmatrix}$, so the equation is:

The vector equation of the line is $\mathbf{r} = \mathbf{a} + \lambda \mathbf{b}$.

$\underline{r} = \begin{pmatrix} 3 \\ -5 \end{pmatrix} + \lambda \begin{pmatrix} 7 \\ -2 \end{pmatrix}$

A Level Further Mathematics for OCR A Pure Core Student Book 1

Key point 2.2

In two dimensions, a line with gradient $\frac{p}{q}$ has the direction vector $\begin{pmatrix} q \\ p \end{pmatrix}$.

WORKED EXAMPLE 2.6

A straight line has the equation $\mathbf{r} = \begin{pmatrix} 1 \\ 2 \end{pmatrix} + \lambda \begin{pmatrix} 5 \\ 3 \end{pmatrix}$. Write the equation of the line in the form $ax + by + c = 0$.

The line has gradient $\frac{3}{5}$ and passes through the point $(1, 2)$.

You can find the gradient from the direction vector. The vector equation also shows the coordinates of one point on the line.

$y - 2 = \frac{3}{5}(x - 1)$

Use $y - y_1 = m(x - x_1)$.

$\Leftrightarrow 5y - 10 = 3x - 3$
$\Leftrightarrow 3x - 5y + 7 = 0$

The equation of a line in the form $ax + by + c = 0$ is called a **Cartesian equation**. This means that the equation is in terms of x- and y-coordinates, rather than in terms of position vectors.

There is another way to change from a vector to a Cartesian equation. The key is to realise that the position vector $\mathbf{r}$ gives the coordinates of a point on the line: $\mathbf{r} = \begin{pmatrix} x \\ y \end{pmatrix}$.

> **Tip**
>
> The Cartesian equation of the line in two dimensions can be written as $ax + by + c = 0$, $ax + by = c$ or $y = mx + c$.

WORKED EXAMPLE 2.7

A line has vector equation $\mathbf{r} = \begin{pmatrix} 1 \\ 2 \end{pmatrix} + \lambda \begin{pmatrix} 5 \\ 3 \end{pmatrix}$. By expressing x and y in terms of λ, write the equation of the line in the form $ax + by = c$.

$\begin{pmatrix} x \\ y \end{pmatrix} = \begin{pmatrix} 1 \\ 2 \end{pmatrix} + \lambda \begin{pmatrix} 5 \\ 3 \end{pmatrix}$

The position vector is related to coordinates $\mathbf{r} = \begin{pmatrix} x \\ y \end{pmatrix}$.

$\Rightarrow \begin{cases} x = 1 + 5\lambda \\ y = 2 + 3\lambda \end{cases}$

$\lambda = \dfrac{x - 1}{5} = \dfrac{y - 2}{3}$

Make λ the subject of both equations.

$\Rightarrow 3x - 3 = 5y - 10$
$\Rightarrow 3x - 5y = -7$

Rearrange into the required form.

In three dimensions, there is no equivalent of the gradient – you cannot use a single number to represent the direction vector. However, you can still use the method from Worked example 2.7 to find a Cartesian equation of the line.

WORKED EXAMPLE 2.8

A line has vector equation $\mathbf{r} = \begin{pmatrix} 1 \\ 4 \\ -1 \end{pmatrix} + \lambda \begin{pmatrix} 3 \\ 2 \\ 5 \end{pmatrix}$. Express y and z in terms of x.

$\begin{pmatrix} x \\ y \\ z \end{pmatrix} = \begin{pmatrix} 1 \\ 4 \\ -1 \end{pmatrix} + \lambda \begin{pmatrix} 3 \\ 2 \\ 5 \end{pmatrix}$ .... Write $\mathbf{r} = \begin{pmatrix} x \\ y \\ z \end{pmatrix}$.

$\Rightarrow \begin{cases} x = 1 + 3\lambda \\ y = 4 + 2\lambda \\ z = -1 + 5\lambda \end{cases}$

$\lambda = \dfrac{x-1}{3}$ .... Express λ from the first equation and substitute into the second and third.

$\Rightarrow y = \dfrac{2}{3}x + \dfrac{10}{3}, \; z = \dfrac{5}{3}x - \dfrac{8}{3}$

It is possible to combine these two equations. You make λ the subject of all three equations and equate them to each other:

$\begin{cases} \lambda = \dfrac{x-1}{3} \\ \lambda = \dfrac{y-4}{2} \\ \lambda = \dfrac{z+1}{5} \end{cases} \Rightarrow \dfrac{x-1}{3} = \dfrac{y-4}{2} = \dfrac{z+1}{5}$

> ⏪ **Rewind**
>
> Writing x, y and z in terms of λ gives the parametric equation of the line. This is covered in A Level Mathematics Student Book 2, Chapter 12.

🔑 Key point 2.3

To find the Cartesian equation of a line given its vector equation:

- write $\begin{pmatrix} x \\ y \\ z \end{pmatrix}$ in terms of λ, giving three equations
- make λ the subject of each equation
- equate the three expressions for λ to get an equation of the form $\dfrac{x-a}{k} = \dfrac{y-b}{m} = \dfrac{z-c}{n}$.

Sometimes a Cartesian equation cannot be written in the previous form described, and you need to make a slight adjustment to the procedure.

WORKED EXAMPLE 2.9

Find the Cartesian equation of the line with vector equation $\mathbf{r} = \begin{pmatrix} 1 \\ 1/2 \\ -3 \end{pmatrix} + \lambda \begin{pmatrix} 1/3 \\ 5 \\ 0 \end{pmatrix}$.

$\begin{cases} x = 1 + \dfrac{1}{3}\lambda \implies \lambda = \dfrac{x-1}{1/3} \\ y = \dfrac{1}{2} + 5\lambda \implies \lambda = \dfrac{y - 1/2}{5} \\ z = -3 \end{cases}$

You need an equation involving x, y and z. Remembering that $\mathbf{r} = \begin{pmatrix} x \\ y \\ z \end{pmatrix}$, you can express λ in terms of x, y and z.

$\dfrac{x-1}{1/3} = \dfrac{y - 1/2}{5}, \; z = -3$

You can equate the expressions for λ from the first two equations. However, the third equation does not contain λ, so you have to leave it as a separate equation.

$\dfrac{3x-3}{1} = \dfrac{2y-1}{10}, \; z = -3$

It will look neater if you rewrite the equation without 'fractions within fractions'.

You can reverse the procedure presented in Worked example 2.9 and go from a Cartesian to a vector equation. A vector equation is convenient if you need to identify the direction vector of the line, or to solve problems involving the intersections of lines.

> **Tip**
>
> The Cartesian equation can sometimes be 'read off' the vector equation: if the vector equation is $\mathbf{r} = \begin{pmatrix} a \\ b \\ c \end{pmatrix} + \lambda \begin{pmatrix} k \\ m \\ n \end{pmatrix}$, then the Cartesian equation is $\dfrac{x-a}{k} = \dfrac{y-b}{m} = \dfrac{z-c}{n}$. However, if any of the components of the direction vector is 0, you have to go through the whole procedure described in Key point 2.3.

🔑 Key point 2.4

To find a vector equation of a line from a Cartesian equation in the form $\dfrac{x-a}{k} = \dfrac{y-b}{m} = \dfrac{z-c}{n}$:

- set each of the three expressions equal to λ
- express x, y and z in terms of λ
- write $\mathbf{r} = \begin{pmatrix} x \\ y \\ z \end{pmatrix}$ to obtain $\mathbf{r}$ in terms of λ.

You can adapt this procedure even when the Cartesian equation is not of the previous form, as in the next example.

WORKED EXAMPLE 2.10

Find a vector equation of the line with Cartesian equation $x = -2, \dfrac{3y+1}{4} = \dfrac{2-z}{5}$ and, hence, write down the direction vector of the line.

$\begin{cases} \dfrac{3y+1}{4} = \lambda \\ \dfrac{2-z}{5} = \lambda \end{cases}$ .... You need to introduce a parameter λ. As the two expressions involving y and z are equal, you can set them both equal to λ.

$\begin{cases} x = -2 \\ y = \dfrac{4\lambda - 1}{3} \\ z = 2 - 5\lambda \end{cases}$ .... You can now express x, y and z in terms of λ.

$\underline{r} = \begin{pmatrix} -2 \\ -1/3 \\ 2 \end{pmatrix} + \lambda \begin{pmatrix} 0 \\ 4/3 \\ -5 \end{pmatrix}$ .... The vector equation is an equation for $\mathbf{r} = \begin{pmatrix} x \\ y \\ z \end{pmatrix}$ in terms of λ.

We usually separate the expression into a part without λ and a part involving λ.

The direction vector is $\begin{pmatrix} 0 \\ 4/3 \\ -5 \end{pmatrix}$ .... You can now identify the direction vector.

or $\begin{pmatrix} 0 \\ 4 \\ -15 \end{pmatrix}$. .... You can change the magnitude of the direction vector so that it does not contain fractions.

If you want to check whether a given point lies on a given line, you can do this by substituting in the numbers for the x-, y- and z-coordinates.

WORKED EXAMPLE 2.11

Does the point $A(3, -2, 2)$ lie on the line with equation $\dfrac{x+1}{2} = \dfrac{4-y}{3} = \dfrac{2z}{3}$?

Substituting in the coordinates of A:

$\begin{cases} \dfrac{x+1}{2} = \dfrac{3+1}{2} = 2 \\ \dfrac{4-y}{3} = \dfrac{4+2}{3} = 2 \\ \dfrac{2z}{3} = \dfrac{2 \times 2}{3} = \dfrac{4}{3} \end{cases}$ .... If the point lies on the line, the coordinates should satisfy the Cartesian equation. This means that all three expressions should be equal.

$2 \neq \dfrac{4}{3}$, so the point does not lie on the line. .... The equality is not satisfied.

EXERCISE 2B

1 Write down the Cartesian equation of each line.

a i $\mathbf{r} = \begin{pmatrix} 3 \\ -1 \end{pmatrix} + \lambda \begin{pmatrix} -7 \\ 4 \end{pmatrix}$ ii $\mathbf{r} = \begin{pmatrix} -1 \\ 5 \end{pmatrix} + \lambda \begin{pmatrix} 2 \\ 3 \end{pmatrix}$

b i $\mathbf{r} = \begin{pmatrix} 4 \\ -1 \\ 5 \end{pmatrix} + \lambda \begin{pmatrix} 2 \\ -1 \\ 7 \end{pmatrix}$ ii $\mathbf{r} = \begin{pmatrix} 1 \\ 7 \\ 2 \end{pmatrix} + \lambda \begin{pmatrix} -1 \\ 1 \\ 2 \end{pmatrix}$

c i $\mathbf{r} = \begin{pmatrix} -1 \\ 5 \\ 0 \end{pmatrix} + \lambda \begin{pmatrix} 0 \\ -2 \\ 2 \end{pmatrix}$ ii $\mathbf{r} = \begin{pmatrix} 3 \\ 0 \\ 6 \end{pmatrix} + \lambda \begin{pmatrix} 7 \\ 1 \\ 0 \end{pmatrix}$

2 Find a vector equation of each line.

a i $y = \dfrac{3}{5}x + 2$ ii $y = -\dfrac{4}{3}x - 1$

b i $3x - 5y = 17$ ii $2x + 3y + 4 = 0$

3 Write down a vector equation of each line.

a i $\dfrac{x-2}{5} = \dfrac{y-2}{3} = \dfrac{z+1}{7}$ ii $\dfrac{x+1}{4} = \dfrac{y-6}{-1} = \dfrac{z-5}{3}$

b i $\dfrac{x+1}{3} = \dfrac{y}{-7} = \dfrac{z-1}{-5}$ ii $\dfrac{x-3}{2} = \dfrac{y+1}{-4} = \dfrac{z}{5}$

c i $\dfrac{x-11}{3} = \dfrac{y+1}{6}, z = -2$ ii $\dfrac{x+1}{5} = \dfrac{3-z}{2}, y = 1$

4 Determine whether the following pairs of lines are parallel, the same line or neither.

a $\mathbf{r} = \begin{pmatrix} 1 \\ 1 \\ 2 \end{pmatrix} + \lambda \begin{pmatrix} -1 \\ 1 \\ 3 \end{pmatrix}$ and $\mathbf{r} = 4\mathbf{i} - \mathbf{j} - 2\mathbf{k} + t(5\mathbf{i} + 2\mathbf{j} + \mathbf{k})$

b $\mathbf{r} = \begin{pmatrix} 13/2 \\ -7 \\ 1 \end{pmatrix} + t \begin{pmatrix} 2 \\ -3 \\ -2/3 \end{pmatrix}$ and $\dfrac{2x-1}{4} = \dfrac{y-2}{-3} = \dfrac{6-3z}{2}$

c $\dfrac{x-5}{7} = \dfrac{y-2}{-1} = 4 - z$ and $\mathbf{r} = \begin{pmatrix} 2\lambda + 1 \\ 4 \\ 5 - \lambda \end{pmatrix}$

d $x = 2t + 1, y = 1 - 4t, z = 3$ and $\mathbf{r} = \begin{pmatrix} 8 \\ -13 \\ 3 \end{pmatrix} + s \begin{pmatrix} -1 \\ 2 \\ 0 \end{pmatrix}$

5 Find a vector equation of the line $5x + 3y = 30$.

6 Determine whether the point with coordinates $(2, 4, 5)$ lies on the line with equation $\dfrac{2x-1}{3} = \dfrac{y+1}{5} = \dfrac{3-z}{2}$.

7 a Find the Cartesian equation of the line with vector equation $\mathbf{r} = (3\lambda + 1)\mathbf{i} + (4 - 2\lambda)\mathbf{j} + (3\lambda - 1)\mathbf{k}$.

 b Find a unit vector in the direction of the line.

8 Line l has Cartesian equation $\dfrac{x-4}{3} = \dfrac{2y+1}{4}$, $z = -2$. Point $M(-2, p, q)$ lies on the line.

  a Find the values of p and q.

  b Point N also lies on the line and the distance $MN = \sqrt{52}$. Find the possible coordinates of N.

Section 3: Intersections of lines

Suppose two lines have vector equations $\mathbf{r}_1 = \mathbf{a} + \lambda \mathbf{d}_1$ and $\mathbf{r}_2 = \mathbf{b} + \mu \mathbf{d}_2$. If they intersect, then there is a point that lies on both lines. The position vector of this point will satisfy both equations, so you need to find the values of λ and μ that make $\mathbf{r}_1 = \mathbf{r}_2$.

WORKED EXAMPLE 2.12

Find the coordinates of the point of intersection of the lines $\mathbf{r}_1 = \begin{pmatrix} 0 \\ -4 \\ 1 \end{pmatrix} + \lambda \begin{pmatrix} 1 \\ 2 \\ 1 \end{pmatrix}$ and $\mathbf{r}_2 = \begin{pmatrix} 1 \\ 3 \\ 5 \end{pmatrix} + \mu \begin{pmatrix} 4 \\ -2 \\ -2 \end{pmatrix}$.

$\begin{pmatrix} 0 \\ -4 \\ 1 \end{pmatrix} + \lambda \begin{pmatrix} 1 \\ 2 \\ 1 \end{pmatrix} = \begin{pmatrix} 1 \\ 3 \\ 5 \end{pmatrix} + \mu \begin{pmatrix} 4 \\ -2 \\ -2 \end{pmatrix}$ You need to make $\mathbf{r}_1 = \mathbf{r}_2$.

$\Leftrightarrow \begin{pmatrix} 0+\lambda \\ -4+2\lambda \\ 1+\lambda \end{pmatrix} = \begin{pmatrix} 1+4\mu \\ 3-2\mu \\ 5-2\mu \end{pmatrix}$

$\Leftrightarrow \begin{cases} 0+\lambda = 1+4\mu \\ -4+2\lambda = 3-2\mu \\ 1+\lambda = 5-2\mu \end{cases}$ If two vectors are equal, then all their components are equal.

$\Leftrightarrow \begin{cases} \lambda - 4\mu = 1 \quad (1) \\ 2\lambda + 2\mu = 7 \quad (2) \\ \lambda + 2\mu = 4 \quad (3) \end{cases}$

$(3)-(1): 6\mu = 3$ You know how to solve two simultaneous equations in two variables. You can pick any two of the three equations. Here it is helpful to use the first and third equations because subtracting them eliminates λ.

$\mu = \dfrac{1}{2},\ \lambda = 3$

$(2): 2 \times 3 + 2 \times \dfrac{1}{2} = 7$ The values of λ and μ you have found must also satisfy the second equation.

The lines intersect.

$\mathbf{r}_1 = \begin{pmatrix} 0 \\ -4 \\ 1 \end{pmatrix} + 3 \begin{pmatrix} 1 \\ 2 \\ 1 \end{pmatrix} = \begin{pmatrix} 3 \\ 2 \\ 4 \end{pmatrix}$ The position of the intersection point is given by the vector $\mathbf{r}_1$ (or $\mathbf{r}_2$; they should be the same).

The lines intersect at the point $(3, 2, 4)$.

In a plane, two different straight lines either intersect or are parallel. However, in three dimensions it is possible to have lines that are not parallel but do not intersect, like the red and the blue lines in the diagram.

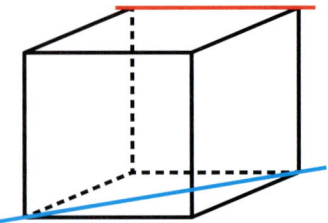

Such lines are called **skew lines**.

When two lines are skew, it is not possible to find values of λ and μ such that $\mathbf{r}_1 = \mathbf{r}_2$.

> **Tip**
>
> You may be able to use your calculator to solve simultaneous equations.

WORKED EXAMPLE 2.13

Show that the lines $\mathbf{r} = \begin{pmatrix} -4 \\ 3 \\ 3 \end{pmatrix} + \mu \begin{pmatrix} 1 \\ 1 \\ 4 \end{pmatrix}$ and $\mathbf{r} = \begin{pmatrix} 2 \\ 1 \\ 1 \end{pmatrix} + \lambda \begin{pmatrix} 2 \\ -3 \\ 2 \end{pmatrix}$ do not intersect.

$\begin{pmatrix} -4 \\ 3 \\ 3 \end{pmatrix} + \mu \begin{pmatrix} 1 \\ 1 \\ 4 \end{pmatrix} = \begin{pmatrix} 2 \\ 1 \\ 1 \end{pmatrix} + \lambda \begin{pmatrix} 2 \\ -3 \\ 2 \end{pmatrix}$

Make the two position vectors equal and try to solve the three equations to find λ and μ.

$\begin{cases} \mu - 2\lambda = 6 & (1) \\ \mu + 3\lambda = -2 & (2) \\ 4\mu - 2\lambda = -2 & (3) \end{cases}$

(1) and (2): $\lambda = -\dfrac{8}{5}, \mu = \dfrac{14}{5}$

You can find μ and λ from the first two equations.

$4 \times \dfrac{14}{5} - 2 \times \left(-\dfrac{8}{5}\right) = \dfrac{72}{5} \neq -2$

The values found must also satisfy the third equation.

The two lines do not intersect.

As the lines do not intersect, it is impossible to find μ and λ to make $\mathbf{r}_1 = \mathbf{r}_2$.

It is also possible to check whether a given line crosses one of the coordinate axes. In the next example you will use the Cartesian equation of a line.

WORKED EXAMPLE 2.14

a Find the coordinates of the point where the line with equation $\frac{x-6}{2} = \frac{y+1}{7} = \frac{z+9}{-3}$ intersects the y-axis.

b Show that the line does not intersect the z-axis.

a $\frac{0-6}{2} = \frac{k+1}{7} = \frac{0+9}{-3}$ *A point on the y-axis has coordinates $(0, k, 0)$. You can substitute these into the Cartesian equation.*

$-3 = \frac{k+1}{7} = -3$

$k + 1 = -21$ *You can now find k.*
$k = -22$

The point of intersection is $(0, -22, 0)$.

b $\frac{0-6}{2} \neq \frac{0+1}{7}$ *A point on the z-axis has coordinates $(0, 0, m)$.*

The line does not intersect the z-axis. *The first equality is not satisfied.*

EXERCISE 2C

1 Determine whether the following pairs of lines intersect and, if they do, find the coordinates of the intersection point.

a i $\mathbf{r} = \begin{pmatrix} 6 \\ 1 \\ 2 \end{pmatrix} + \lambda \begin{pmatrix} -1 \\ 2 \\ 1 \end{pmatrix}$ and $\mathbf{r} = \begin{pmatrix} 2 \\ 1 \\ -14 \end{pmatrix} + \mu \begin{pmatrix} 2 \\ -2 \\ 3 \end{pmatrix}$

  ii $\mathbf{r} = \begin{pmatrix} 4 \\ -1 \\ 2 \end{pmatrix} + \lambda \begin{pmatrix} 1 \\ 2 \\ -4 \end{pmatrix}$ and $\mathbf{r} = \begin{pmatrix} 6 \\ -2 \\ 0 \end{pmatrix} + \mu \begin{pmatrix} 3 \\ -4 \\ 0 \end{pmatrix}$

b i $\mathbf{r} = \begin{pmatrix} 1 \\ 2 \\ 3 \end{pmatrix} + t \begin{pmatrix} -1 \\ 1 \\ 2 \end{pmatrix}$ and $\mathbf{r} = \begin{pmatrix} -4 \\ -4 \\ -11 \end{pmatrix} + s \begin{pmatrix} 5 \\ 1 \\ 2 \end{pmatrix}$

  ii $\mathbf{r} = \begin{pmatrix} 4 \\ 0 \\ 2 \end{pmatrix} + t \begin{pmatrix} 2 \\ 0 \\ 1 \end{pmatrix}$ and $\mathbf{r} = \begin{pmatrix} -1 \\ 2 \\ 3 \end{pmatrix} + s \begin{pmatrix} 1 \\ -2 \\ -2 \end{pmatrix}$

c i $\frac{x+1}{2} = \frac{y-6}{-2} = \frac{z+7}{1}$ and $\frac{x-2}{-1} = \frac{y-5}{3} = \frac{z}{5}$

  ii $\frac{x-2}{-3} = \frac{y+1}{2} = \frac{z-1}{2}$ and $\frac{x+1}{1} = \frac{y}{6} = \frac{z-1}{3}$

2. Show that the lines with equations $\mathbf{r} = (3+2t)\mathbf{i} + (3-t)\mathbf{j} + (6+3t)\mathbf{k}$ and $\mathbf{r} = (2-3s)\mathbf{i} + (2s)\mathbf{j} + 6\mathbf{k}$ are skew.

3. Show that the lines $\mathbf{r} = \begin{pmatrix} 7 \\ 1 \\ 5 \end{pmatrix} + t\begin{pmatrix} 2 \\ 2 \\ 1 \end{pmatrix}$ and $\mathbf{r} = \begin{pmatrix} 4 \\ -6 \\ -3 \end{pmatrix} + s\begin{pmatrix} -3 \\ 1 \\ 5 \end{pmatrix}$ intersect, and find the coordinates of the intersection point.

4. Determine whether the line with equation $\mathbf{r} = \begin{pmatrix} 3 \\ -7 \\ 2 \end{pmatrix} + \lambda\begin{pmatrix} -1 \\ 1 \\ 5 \end{pmatrix}$ crosses the x-axis.

5. The line with equation $\dfrac{x-p}{3} = \dfrac{y+2}{4} = \dfrac{z-12}{8}$ crosses the y-axis. Find the value of p.

6. Show that the lines with equations $\mathbf{r} = \begin{pmatrix} 1 \\ 1 \\ 2 \end{pmatrix} + \lambda\begin{pmatrix} 1 \\ 0 \\ 3 \end{pmatrix}$, $\mathbf{r} = \begin{pmatrix} -2 \\ 3 \\ -1 \end{pmatrix} + \mu\begin{pmatrix} 1 \\ -1 \\ 0 \end{pmatrix}$ and $\mathbf{r} = \begin{pmatrix} 2 \\ -1 \\ -1 \end{pmatrix} + t\begin{pmatrix} -1 \\ 2 \\ 3 \end{pmatrix}$ form a triangle, and find its area.

Section 4: Angles and the scalar product

The diagram shows two lines with angle θ between them. **a** and **b** are vectors in the directions of the two lines, arranged so that both arrows are pointing away from the intersection point. Hence, $\cos\theta$ can be expressed in terms of the components of the two vectors.

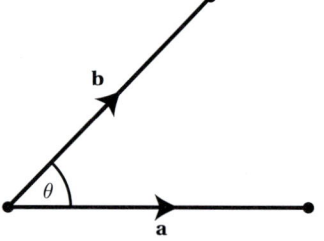

Key point 2.5

If θ is the angle between vectors $\mathbf{a} = \begin{pmatrix} a_1 \\ a_2 \\ a_3 \end{pmatrix}$ and $\mathbf{b} = \begin{pmatrix} b_1 \\ b_2 \\ b_3 \end{pmatrix}$, then

$$\cos\theta = \dfrac{a_1 b_1 + a_2 b_2 + a_3 b_3}{|\mathbf{a}||\mathbf{b}|}.$$

The expression in the numerator of the previous fraction has some important uses, so it has been given a special name.

Key point 2.6

The quantity $a_1 b_1 + a_2 b_2 + a_3 b_3$ is called the **scalar product** (or **dot product**) of **a** and **b** and is denoted by $\mathbf{a} \cdot \mathbf{b}$.

If θ is the angle between vectors **a** and **b** then $\mathbf{a} \cdot \mathbf{b} = |\mathbf{a}||\mathbf{b}|\cos\theta$.

2 Further vectors

WORKED EXAMPLE 2.15

Given points $A(3, -5, 2)$, $B(4, 1, 1)$ and $C(-1, 1, 2)$, find the size of the angle BAC, in degrees.

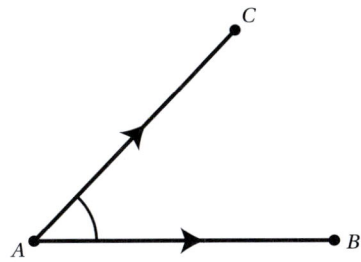

It is always a good idea to draw a diagram to see which vectors you need to use.

Let $\theta = \angle BAC$

$\cos \theta = \dfrac{\overrightarrow{AB} \cdot \overrightarrow{AC}}{|\overrightarrow{AB}||\overrightarrow{AC}|}$

You can see that the required angle is between vectors $\overrightarrow{AB}$ and $\overrightarrow{AC}$.

Note that you need both vectors to be directed away from the angle you want to find.

$\overrightarrow{AB} = \begin{pmatrix} 4 \\ 1 \\ 1 \end{pmatrix} - \begin{pmatrix} 3 \\ -5 \\ 2 \end{pmatrix} = \begin{pmatrix} 1 \\ 6 \\ -1 \end{pmatrix}$

$\overrightarrow{AC} = \begin{pmatrix} -1 \\ 1 \\ 2 \end{pmatrix} - \begin{pmatrix} 3 \\ -5 \\ 2 \end{pmatrix} = \begin{pmatrix} -4 \\ 6 \\ 0 \end{pmatrix}$

You need to find the components of vectors $\overrightarrow{AB}$ and $\overrightarrow{AC}$.
$\overrightarrow{AB} = \mathbf{b} - \mathbf{a}$ and $\overrightarrow{AC} = \mathbf{c} - \mathbf{a}$.

$\overrightarrow{AB} \cdot \overrightarrow{AC} = \begin{pmatrix} 1 \\ 6 \\ -1 \end{pmatrix} \cdot \begin{pmatrix} -4 \\ 6 \\ 0 \end{pmatrix}$

$= 1 \times (-4) + 6 \times 6 + (-1) \times 0$

$= 32$

Find the dot product.

$\cos \theta = \dfrac{32}{\sqrt{1^2 + 6^2 + 1^2} \sqrt{4^2 + 6^2 + 0^2}}$

$= \dfrac{32}{\sqrt{38} \sqrt{52}}$

$= 0.7199$

$\theta = \cos^{-1}(0.7199) = 44.0°$

Use $\cos \theta = \dfrac{\overrightarrow{AB} \cdot \overrightarrow{AC}}{|\overrightarrow{AB}||\overrightarrow{AC}|}$

When you have two lines given by their equations, you can use direction vectors to find the angle between them.

WORKED EXAMPLE 2.16

Find the acute angle between lines with equations $\mathbf{r} = \begin{pmatrix} 4 \\ 1 \\ -2 \end{pmatrix} + t \begin{pmatrix} 1 \\ -1 \\ 3 \end{pmatrix}$ and $\mathbf{r} = \begin{pmatrix} 4 \\ 1 \\ -2 \end{pmatrix} + \lambda \begin{pmatrix} -1 \\ 4 \\ 1 \end{pmatrix}$.

$\cos \theta = \dfrac{\mathbf{a} \cdot \mathbf{b}}{|\mathbf{a}||\mathbf{b}|}$

> You know the formula for the angle between two vectors.
> But which vectors **a** and **b** should you use?

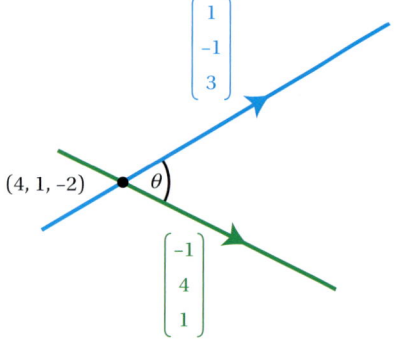

> Drawing a diagram is a good way of identifying which two vectors make the required angle.
> The diagram indicates that you should take **a** and **b** to be the direction vectors of the two lines.

$\mathbf{a} = \begin{pmatrix} 1 \\ -1 \\ 3 \end{pmatrix}, \mathbf{b} = \begin{pmatrix} -1 \\ 4 \\ 1 \end{pmatrix}$

$\cos \theta = \dfrac{-1 - 4 + 3}{\sqrt{(1+1+9)}\sqrt{1+16+1}}$

$= -\dfrac{2}{\sqrt{11}\sqrt{18}}$

$\theta = 98.2°$

> Now use the formula to calculate the angle.

Acute angle $= 180° - 98.2° = 81.8°$

> The angle found is obtuse. The question asked for the acute angle.

🔑 **Key point 2.7**

The angle between two lines is equal to the angle between their direction vectors.

💡 **Tip**

The angle between two lines can be found even if the lines don't intersect.

WORK IT OUT 2.2

Find the angle between the lines $\mathbf{r} = \begin{pmatrix} 1 \\ 3 \\ 3 \end{pmatrix} + \lambda \begin{pmatrix} -1 \\ 1 \\ 2 \end{pmatrix}$ and $\mathbf{r} = \begin{pmatrix} 1 \\ -1 \\ 0 \end{pmatrix} + \mu \begin{pmatrix} 1 \\ 0 \\ 3 \end{pmatrix}$.

Which is the correct solution? Can you identify the errors made in the incorrect solutions?

Solution 1	Solution 2	Solution 3
$\mathbf{a} = \begin{pmatrix} 1 \\ 3 \\ 3 \end{pmatrix}$, $\mathbf{b} = \begin{pmatrix} 1 \\ -1 \\ 0 \end{pmatrix}$ $\cos\theta = \dfrac{1-3+0}{\sqrt{19}\sqrt{2}} = -0.324$ $\Rightarrow \theta = 109°$	$\mathbf{a} = \begin{pmatrix} 1 \\ 3 \\ 3 \end{pmatrix} + \begin{pmatrix} -1 \\ 1 \\ 2 \end{pmatrix} = \begin{pmatrix} 0 \\ 4 \\ 5 \end{pmatrix}$ $\mathbf{b} = \begin{pmatrix} 1 \\ -1 \\ 0 \end{pmatrix} + \begin{pmatrix} 1 \\ 0 \\ 3 \end{pmatrix} = \begin{pmatrix} 2 \\ -1 \\ 3 \end{pmatrix}$ $\cos\theta = \dfrac{(0-4+15)}{\sqrt{41}\sqrt{14}} = 0.459$ $\Rightarrow \theta = 62.7°$	$\mathbf{a} = \begin{pmatrix} -1 \\ 1 \\ 2 \end{pmatrix}$, $\mathbf{b} = \begin{pmatrix} 1 \\ 0 \\ 3 \end{pmatrix}$ $\cos\theta = \dfrac{-1+0+6}{\sqrt{6}\sqrt{10}} = 0.645$ $\Rightarrow \theta = 49.8°$

The formula in Key point 2.5 is very convenient for checking whether two vectors are perpendicular. If $\theta = 90°$ then $\cos\theta = 0$, so the numerator of the fraction in the formula must be zero. This means that you don't even need to calculate the magnitudes of the two vectors.

🔑 Key point 2.8

Two vectors $\mathbf{a}$ and $\mathbf{b}$ are perpendicular if $\mathbf{a} \cdot \mathbf{b} = 0$.

Two lines are perpendicular if their direction vectors satisfy $\mathbf{d}_1 \cdot \mathbf{d}_1 = 0$.

WORKED EXAMPLE 2.17

Given that $\mathbf{p} = \begin{pmatrix} 4 \\ -1 \\ 2 \end{pmatrix}$ and $\mathbf{q} = \begin{pmatrix} 2 \\ 1 \\ 1 \end{pmatrix}$, find the value of the scalar t such that $\mathbf{p} + t\mathbf{q}$ is perpendicular to $\begin{pmatrix} 3 \\ 5 \\ 1 \end{pmatrix}$.

$(\underline{p} + t\underline{q}) \cdot \begin{pmatrix} 3 \\ 5 \\ 1 \end{pmatrix} = 0$ — Two vectors are perpendicular if their scalar product equals 0.

Continues on next page ...

$$\underline{p}+t\underline{q}=\begin{pmatrix}4+2t\\-1+t\\2+t\end{pmatrix}$$

So

$$\begin{pmatrix}4+2t\\-1+t\\2+t\end{pmatrix}\cdot\begin{pmatrix}3\\5\\1\end{pmatrix}=0$$

> You need to find the components of $\mathbf{p}+t\mathbf{q}$ in terms of t and then form an equation.

$\Leftrightarrow 3(4+2t)+5(-1+t)+1(2+t)=0$

$\Leftrightarrow 9+12t=0$

> Use the definition of a scalar product.

$\Leftrightarrow t=-\dfrac{3}{4}$

WORKED EXAMPLE 2.18

Prove that the lines $2x+1=\dfrac{y+1}{2}=\dfrac{5-z}{4}$ and $\dfrac{x-2}{4}=\dfrac{y}{6}=\dfrac{2z-6}{7}$ are perpendicular.

$2x+1=\dfrac{y+1}{2}=\dfrac{5-z}{4}$

$\Leftrightarrow \dfrac{x+1/2}{1/2}=\dfrac{y+1}{2}=\dfrac{z-5}{-4}\Rightarrow \underline{d}_1=\begin{pmatrix}1/2\\2\\-4\end{pmatrix}$

> You need to identify the two direction vectors. To do this, you need to rearrange the equations slightly.

$\dfrac{x-2}{4}=\dfrac{y}{6}=\dfrac{2z-6}{7}$

$\Leftrightarrow \dfrac{x-2}{4}=\dfrac{y}{6}=\dfrac{z-3}{7/2}\Rightarrow \underline{d}_2=\begin{pmatrix}4\\6\\7/2\end{pmatrix}$

$\underline{d}_1\cdot \underline{d}_2=\left(\dfrac{1}{2}\right)(4)+(2)(6)+(-4)\left(\dfrac{7}{2}\right)$

> $\mathbf{d}_1$ and $\mathbf{d}_2$ are perpendicular if their scalar product equals zero.

$=2+12-14=0$

Hence, the two lines are perpendicular.

Perpendicular lines can be used to find the shortest distance from a point to a line, as shown in the next example.

WORKED EXAMPLE 2.19

Line l has the equation $\mathbf{r} = \begin{pmatrix} 3 \\ -1 \\ 0 \end{pmatrix} + \lambda \begin{pmatrix} 1 \\ -1 \\ 1 \end{pmatrix}$ and point A has coordinates $(3, 9, -2)$.

a Find the coordinates of point B on l so that AB is perpendicular to l.

b Hence, find the shortest distance from A to l.

c Find the coordinates of the reflection of the point A in l.

a

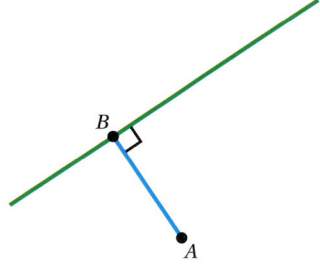

$\overrightarrow{AB} \cdot \begin{pmatrix} 1 \\ -1 \\ 1 \end{pmatrix} = 0$

> Draw a diagram. The line AB should be perpendicular to the direction vector of l.

$\overrightarrow{OB} = \underline{r} = \begin{pmatrix} 3+\lambda \\ -1-\lambda \\ \lambda \end{pmatrix}$

> You know that B lies on l, so its position vector is given by the equation for $\mathbf{r}$.

$\overrightarrow{AB} = \begin{pmatrix} 3+\lambda \\ -1-\lambda \\ \lambda \end{pmatrix} - \begin{pmatrix} 3 \\ 9 \\ -2 \end{pmatrix} = \begin{pmatrix} \lambda \\ -10-\lambda \\ \lambda+2 \end{pmatrix}$

$\begin{pmatrix} \lambda \\ -10-\lambda \\ \lambda+2 \end{pmatrix} \cdot \begin{pmatrix} 1 \\ -1 \\ 1 \end{pmatrix} = 0$

> You can now find the value of λ for which the two lines are perpendicular.

$(\lambda) + (10+\lambda) + (\lambda+2) = 0$

$\lambda = -4$

$\underline{r} = \begin{pmatrix} -1 \\ 3 \\ -4 \end{pmatrix}$

> Using this value of λ in the equation of the line gives the position vector of B.

B has coordinates $(-1, 3, -4)$.

b $\overrightarrow{AB} = \begin{pmatrix} -1 \\ 3 \\ -4 \end{pmatrix} - \begin{pmatrix} 3 \\ 9 \\ -2 \end{pmatrix} = \begin{pmatrix} -4 \\ -6 \\ -2 \end{pmatrix}$

> The shortest distance from a point to a line is the perpendicular distance; in other words, the distance AB.

$|\overrightarrow{AB}| = \sqrt{16+36+4} = 2\sqrt{14}$

Continues on next page ...

c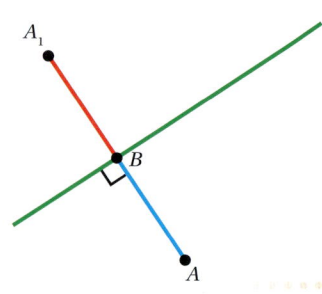

$\overrightarrow{BA_1} = \overrightarrow{AB}$

$\underline{a}_1 - \underline{b} = \overrightarrow{AB}$

$\underline{a}_1 = \begin{pmatrix} -4 \\ -6 \\ -2 \end{pmatrix} + \begin{pmatrix} -1 \\ 3 \\ -4 \end{pmatrix}$

So A_1 has the coordinates $(-5, -3, -6)$.

The reflection A_1 lies on the line AB, and $BA_1 = AB$. As they are also in the same direction, $\overrightarrow{BA_1} = \overrightarrow{AB}$.

Part **c** of Worked example 2.19 illustrates the power of vectors: as they contain both distance and direction information, just one equation $(\overrightarrow{BA_1} = \overrightarrow{AB})$ is needed to express both the fact that A_1 lies on the line AB and that $BA_1 = AB$.

 Focus on …

Worked example 2.19 illustrates one possible way to find the shortest distance from a point to a line. You can explore other methods in Focus on … Problem-solving 1.

EXERCISE 2D

1 Calculate the scalar product for each pair of vectors.

  a **i** $\begin{pmatrix} 5 \\ 1 \\ 2 \end{pmatrix}$ and $\begin{pmatrix} 1 \\ -2 \\ 3 \end{pmatrix}$ **ii** $\begin{pmatrix} 3 \\ 0 \\ 2 \end{pmatrix}$ and $\begin{pmatrix} 0 \\ -1 \\ 1 \end{pmatrix}$

  b **i** $2\mathbf{i} + 2\mathbf{j} - \mathbf{k}$ and $\mathbf{i} - \mathbf{j} + 3\mathbf{k}$ **ii** $3\mathbf{i} + \mathbf{j}$ and $\mathbf{i} - 2\mathbf{k}$

  c **i** $\begin{pmatrix} 3 \\ 2 \end{pmatrix}$ and $\begin{pmatrix} -1 \\ 4 \end{pmatrix}$ **ii** $\mathbf{i} - \mathbf{j}$ and $2\mathbf{i} + 3\mathbf{j}$

2 Calculate the angle between the pairs of vectors from question **1**. Give your answers in degrees.

3 The angle between vectors **a** and **b** is θ. Find the exact value of $\cos\theta$ in the following cases.

  a **i** $\mathbf{a} = 2\mathbf{i} + 3\mathbf{j} - \mathbf{k}$ and $\mathbf{b} = \mathbf{i} + 2\mathbf{j} - \mathbf{k}$ **ii** $\mathbf{a} = \mathbf{i} - 3\mathbf{j} + 3\mathbf{k}$ and $\mathbf{b} = \mathbf{i} + 5\mathbf{j} - 2\mathbf{k}$

  b **i** $\mathbf{a} = \begin{pmatrix} 2 \\ 2 \\ 3 \end{pmatrix}$ and $\mathbf{b} = \begin{pmatrix} 1 \\ 1 \\ -2 \end{pmatrix}$ **ii** $\mathbf{a} = \begin{pmatrix} 5 \\ 1 \\ -3 \end{pmatrix}$ and $\mathbf{b} = \begin{pmatrix} 2 \\ -1 \\ 2 \end{pmatrix}$

  c **i** $\mathbf{a} = -2\mathbf{k}$ and $\mathbf{b} = 4\mathbf{i}$ **ii** $\mathbf{a} = 5\mathbf{i}$ and $\mathbf{b} = 3\mathbf{j}$

2 Further vectors

4 a The vertices of a triangle have position vectors $\mathbf{a} = \begin{pmatrix} 1 \\ 1 \\ 3 \end{pmatrix}$, $\mathbf{b} = \begin{pmatrix} 2 \\ -1 \\ 1 \end{pmatrix}$ and $\mathbf{c} = \begin{pmatrix} 5 \\ 1 \\ 2 \end{pmatrix}$. Find, in degrees, the angles of the triangle.

  b Find, in degrees, the angles of the triangle with vertices (2, 1, 2), (4, −1, 5) and (7, 1, −2).

5 Determine whether the following pairs of vectors are perpendicular.

  a i $\begin{pmatrix} 2 \\ 1 \\ -3 \end{pmatrix}$ and $\begin{pmatrix} 1 \\ -2 \\ 2 \end{pmatrix}$ **ii** $\begin{pmatrix} 3 \\ -1 \\ 2 \end{pmatrix}$ and $\begin{pmatrix} 2 \\ 6 \\ 0 \end{pmatrix}$

  b i $5\mathbf{i} - 2\mathbf{j} + \mathbf{k}$ and $3\mathbf{i} + 4\mathbf{j} - 7\mathbf{k}$ **ii** $\mathbf{i} - 3\mathbf{k}$ and $2\mathbf{i} + \mathbf{j} + \mathbf{k}$

6 Find the acute angle between the following pairs of lines, giving your answer in degrees.

  a i $\mathbf{r} = \begin{pmatrix} 5 \\ -1 \\ 2 \end{pmatrix} + \lambda \begin{pmatrix} 2 \\ 2 \\ 3 \end{pmatrix}$ and $\mathbf{r} = \begin{pmatrix} 1 \\ 1 \\ 0 \end{pmatrix} + \mu \begin{pmatrix} 4 \\ -1 \\ 3 \end{pmatrix}$

  ii $\mathbf{r} = \begin{pmatrix} 4 \\ 0 \\ 2 \end{pmatrix} + \lambda \begin{pmatrix} 2 \\ -1 \\ 1 \end{pmatrix}$ and $\mathbf{r} = \begin{pmatrix} 1 \\ 0 \\ 2 \end{pmatrix} + \mu \begin{pmatrix} -5 \\ 1 \\ 3 \end{pmatrix}$

  b i $\mathbf{r} = \begin{pmatrix} 2 \\ 0 \\ 1 \end{pmatrix} + t \begin{pmatrix} -1 \\ 0 \\ 0 \end{pmatrix}$ and $\mathbf{r} = \begin{pmatrix} 1 \\ 3 \\ 3 \end{pmatrix} + s \begin{pmatrix} 4 \\ 0 \\ 2 \end{pmatrix}$

  ii $\mathbf{r} = \begin{pmatrix} 6 \\ 6 \\ 2 \end{pmatrix} + t \begin{pmatrix} -1 \\ 0 \\ 3 \end{pmatrix}$ and $\mathbf{r} = \begin{pmatrix} 1 \\ 0 \\ 0 \end{pmatrix} + s \begin{pmatrix} 4 \\ -1 \\ 2 \end{pmatrix}$

7 Points A and B have position vectors $\overrightarrow{OA} = \begin{pmatrix} 2 \\ 2 \\ 3 \end{pmatrix}$ and $\overrightarrow{OB} = \begin{pmatrix} -1 \\ 7 \\ 2 \end{pmatrix}$. Find the angle between $\overrightarrow{AB}$ and $\overrightarrow{OA}$.

8 Four points are given with coordinates $A(2, -1, 3)$, $B(1, 1, 2)$, $C(6, -1, 2)$ and $D(7, -3, 3)$. Find the angle between $\overrightarrow{AC}$ and $\overrightarrow{BD}$.

9 Four points have coordinates $A(2, 4, 1)$, $B(k, 4, 2k)$, $C(k+4, 2k+4, 2k+2)$ and $D(6, 2k+4, 3)$.

  a Show that $ABCD$ is a parallelogram for all values of k.

  b When $k = 1$ find the angles of the parallelogram.

  c Find the value of k for which $ABCD$ is a rectangle.

10 Vertices of a triangle have position vectors $\mathbf{a} = \mathbf{i} - 2\mathbf{j} + 2\mathbf{k}$, $\mathbf{b} = 3\mathbf{i} - \mathbf{j} + 7\mathbf{k}$ and $\mathbf{c} = 5\mathbf{i}$.

  a Show that the triangle is right-angled.

  b Calculate the other two angles of the triangle.

  c Find the area of the triangle.

11 Line l has the equation $\mathbf{r} = \begin{pmatrix} 4 \\ 2 \\ -1 \end{pmatrix} + \lambda \begin{pmatrix} 2 \\ -1 \\ 2 \end{pmatrix}$ and point P has coordinates $(7, 2, 3)$. Point C lies on l and PC is perpendicular to l. Find the coordinates of C.

12 Find the shortest distance from the point (−1, 1, 2) to the line with equation $\mathbf{r} = \begin{pmatrix} 1 \\ 0 \\ 2 \end{pmatrix} + t \begin{pmatrix} -3 \\ 1 \\ 1 \end{pmatrix}$.

13 Find the distance of the line with equation $\mathbf{r} = \begin{pmatrix} 1 \\ -2 \\ 2 \end{pmatrix} + \lambda \begin{pmatrix} 2 \\ 2 \\ 1 \end{pmatrix}$ from the origin.

14 The lines l_1 and l_2 have equations $\mathbf{r} = \begin{pmatrix} 0 \\ -1 \\ 2 \end{pmatrix} + \lambda \begin{pmatrix} 1 \\ 5 \\ 3 \end{pmatrix}$ and $\mathbf{r} = \begin{pmatrix} 2 \\ 2 \\ 1 \end{pmatrix} + t \begin{pmatrix} -1 \\ 1 \\ 3 \end{pmatrix}$, respectively. The two lines intersect at point P.

  a Find the coordinates of P.
  b Find, in degrees, the acute angle between the two lines.
  c Point Q has coordinates (−1, 5, 10). Show that Q lies on l_2.
  d Find the distance PQ.
  e Hence, find the shortest distance from Q to the line l_1.

15 Line l has equation $\mathbf{r} = \begin{pmatrix} 5 \\ 1 \\ 2 \end{pmatrix} + \lambda \begin{pmatrix} 2 \\ -3 \\ 3 \end{pmatrix}$ and point P has coordinates (21, 5, 10).

  a Find the coordinates of point M on l such that PM is perpendicular to l.
  b Show that the point $Q(15, -14, 17)$ lies on l.
  c Find the coordinates of point R on l such that $|PR| = |PQ|$.

Section 5: The vector product

You know that you can use the scalar product to check whether two lines are perpendicular. But can you answer the reverse question: find a line that is perpendicular to a given line?

In two dimensions, if a line has gradient m then a perpendicular line has gradient $\dfrac{-1}{m}$. Furthermore, there is only one perpendicular line passing through any given point.

In three dimensions, if you try to find a line through a given point and perpendicular to a given line, you will find that there is more than one possible answer. In fact, there are infinitely many such lines.

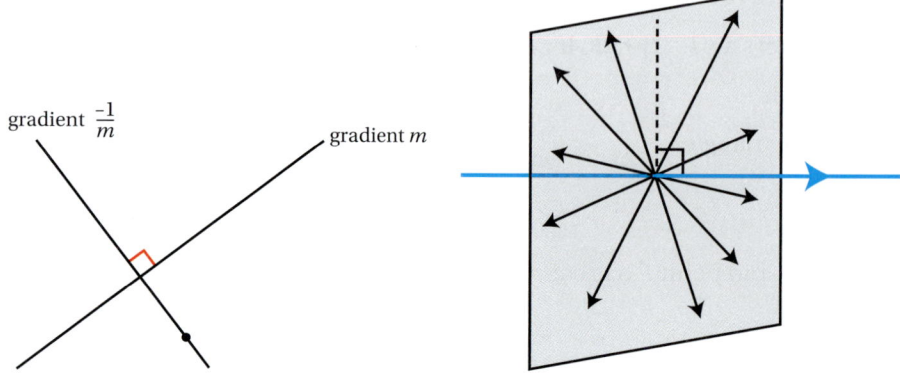

2 Further vectors

However, if you are given two non-parallel lines, then there is only one direction that is perpendicular to both of them. This direction is given by the **vector product** (or **cross product**).

Key point 2.9

Given vectors $\mathbf{a} = \begin{pmatrix} a_1 \\ a_2 \\ a_3 \end{pmatrix}$ and $\mathbf{b} = \begin{pmatrix} b_1 \\ b_2 \\ b_3 \end{pmatrix}$, their vector product is

$$\mathbf{a} \times \mathbf{b} = \begin{pmatrix} a_2 b_3 - a_3 b_2 \\ a_3 b_1 - a_1 b_3 \\ a_1 b_2 - a_2 b_1 \end{pmatrix}.$$

This vector is perpendicular to both $\mathbf{a}$ and $\mathbf{b}$.

Tip

The formula for the vector product also can be written using determinant notation:

$$\mathbf{a} \times \mathbf{b} = \begin{vmatrix} \mathbf{i} & a_1 & b_1 \\ \mathbf{j} & a_2 & b_2 \\ \mathbf{k} & a_3 & b_3 \end{vmatrix}$$

It is important to use the '×' symbol to denote the vector product, so that it is distinct from the scalar product.

This will appear in your formula book, but you can also use a calculator.

One important example of this is the base vectors; for example, you can check that $\mathbf{i} \times \mathbf{j} = \mathbf{k}$ and $\mathbf{i} \times \mathbf{k} = -\mathbf{j}$.

Tip

You need to be careful to get the vectors $\mathbf{a}$ and $\mathbf{b}$ the right way around. The vector product is not commutative, and $\mathbf{a} \times \mathbf{b} = -\mathbf{b} \times \mathbf{a}$.

WORKED EXAMPLE 2.20

The lines l_1 and l_2 have equations $\mathbf{r} = \begin{pmatrix} 1 \\ 5 \\ -2 \end{pmatrix} + \lambda \begin{pmatrix} 3 \\ -4 \\ 1 \end{pmatrix}$ and $\mathbf{r} = \begin{pmatrix} 1 \\ 5 \\ -2 \end{pmatrix} + \mu \begin{pmatrix} 3 \\ 5 \\ 2 \end{pmatrix}$, respectively.

a Calculate $\begin{pmatrix} 3 \\ -4 \\ 1 \end{pmatrix} \times \begin{pmatrix} 3 \\ 5 \\ 2 \end{pmatrix}$.

b Hence, find the equation of the line through the point $(1, 5, -2)$ that is perpendicular to both l_1 and l_2.

a $\begin{pmatrix} 3 \\ -4 \\ 1 \end{pmatrix} \times \begin{pmatrix} 3 \\ 5 \\ 2 \end{pmatrix} = \begin{pmatrix} (-4)(2) & -(1)(5) \\ (1)(3) & -(3)(2) \\ (3)(5) & -(-4)(3) \end{pmatrix}$

$= \begin{pmatrix} -13 \\ -3 \\ 27 \end{pmatrix}$

Use a calculator, or the formula from Key point 2.9:

$\begin{pmatrix} a_1 \\ a_2 \\ a_3 \end{pmatrix} \times \begin{pmatrix} b_1 \\ b_2 \\ b_3 \end{pmatrix} = \begin{pmatrix} a_2 b_3 - a_3 b_2 \\ a_3 b_1 - a_1 b_3 \\ a_1 b_2 - a_2 b_1 \end{pmatrix}$

Continues on next page ...

b $\quad \mathbf{r} = \begin{pmatrix} 1 \\ 5 \\ -2 \end{pmatrix} + \lambda \begin{pmatrix} -13 \\ -3 \\ 27 \end{pmatrix}$ ········· Vector equation of a line is $\mathbf{r} = \mathbf{a} + \lambda \mathbf{d}$.

The direction is the perpendicular vector you have just found.

The line passes through $(1, 5, -2)$.

🔍 Explore

Find out about some uses of the vector product, both in pure mathematics and in applications. For example, the area of a triangle can be calculated using the magnitude of the vector product. In Pure Core Student Book 2 you will use the vector product to find the equation of a plane. In mechanics, the moment of a force is actually a vector, given by $\mathbf{M} = \mathbf{F} \times \mathbf{r}$. You may also know the 'right-hand rule' for determining the direction of the magnetic force.

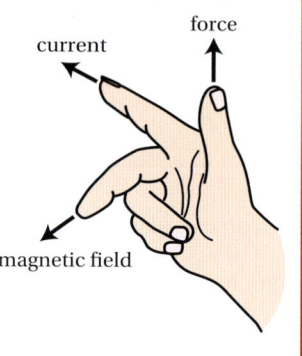

Application to inverse matrices

Vector product also can be used to find an inverse of a 3×3 matrix.

The procedure is best illustrated by an example: find the inverse of the matrix $\mathbf{A} = \begin{pmatrix} 2 & 3 & 1 \\ 2 & 3 & -3 \\ -2 & 1 & 4 \end{pmatrix}$. This is the same matrix as that used in Worked example 1.14, so you can compare the two methods.

> ⏮ **Rewind**
>
> You learnt about the cofactor method for finding inverse matrix in Chapter 1, Section 4.

Let $\mathbf{c}_1$ and $\mathbf{c}_2$ be the first two columns of $\mathbf{A}$, so $\mathbf{c}_1 = \begin{pmatrix} 2 \\ 2 \\ -2 \end{pmatrix}$ and $\mathbf{c}_2 = \begin{pmatrix} 3 \\ 3 \\ 1 \end{pmatrix}$.

Find the vector product of these two vectors: $\mathbf{c}_1 \times \mathbf{c}_2 = \begin{pmatrix} 2+6 \\ -6-2 \\ 6-6 \end{pmatrix} = \begin{pmatrix} 8 \\ -8 \\ 0 \end{pmatrix}$. Then use $(8\ -8\ 0)$ in the third row of $\mathbf{A}^{-1}$.

For the first row of $\mathbf{A}^{-1}$ use the vector product of the second and third columns of $\mathbf{A}$: $\mathbf{c}_2 \times \mathbf{c}_3 = \begin{pmatrix} 3 \\ 3 \\ 1 \end{pmatrix} \times \begin{pmatrix} 1 \\ -3 \\ 4 \end{pmatrix} = \begin{pmatrix} 15 \\ -11 \\ -12 \end{pmatrix}$, and for the second row use $\mathbf{c}_3 \times \mathbf{c}_1 = \begin{pmatrix} -2 \\ 10 \\ 8 \end{pmatrix}$.

Finally, divide the matrix by $\det \mathbf{A}$ (which you can calculate to be 32). So:

$$\mathbf{A}^{-1} = \frac{1}{32} \begin{pmatrix} 8 & -8 & 0 \\ 15 & -11 & -12 \\ -2 & 10 & 8 \end{pmatrix}$$

Key point 2.10

To find the inverse matrix $\mathbf{A}^{-1}$:

- The rows are found from vector products of columns of $\mathbf{A}$:
  - For the first row, use $\mathbf{c}_2 \times \mathbf{c}_3$.
  - For the second row, use $\mathbf{c}_3 \times \mathbf{c}_1$.
  - For the third row, use $\mathbf{c}_1 \times \mathbf{c}_2$.
- Then divide by det $\mathbf{A}$.

Explore

Can you see why this procedure gives the inverse matrix? Imagine multiplying $\mathbf{A}^{-1}\mathbf{A}$. For example, to find the entry in the first row and second column, you need to multiply the entries from the first row of $\mathbf{A}^{-1}$ and the second column of $\mathbf{A}$; this is $(\mathbf{c}_2 \times \mathbf{c}_3) \cdot \mathbf{c}_2$. But $\mathbf{c}_2 \times \mathbf{c}_3$ is perpendicular to $\mathbf{c}_2$ so this scalar product equals zero. You can show similarly that all the other off-diagonal entries in $\mathbf{A}^{-1}\mathbf{A}$ are zero. To understand why the diagonal elements equal 1, you need to investigate the link between the determinant and something called the triple scalar product.

EXERCISE 2E

1 In each case, calculate $\mathbf{a} \times \mathbf{b}$ and $\mathbf{b} \times \mathbf{a}$.

  a   **i** $\mathbf{a} = \begin{pmatrix} 3 \\ 4 \\ 1 \end{pmatrix}, \mathbf{b} = \begin{pmatrix} 2 \\ 1 \\ 5 \end{pmatrix}$ **ii** $\mathbf{a} = \begin{pmatrix} 1 \\ -4 \\ 1 \end{pmatrix}, \mathbf{b} = \begin{pmatrix} -2 \\ 2 \\ 3 \end{pmatrix}$

  b   **i** $\mathbf{a} = 4\mathbf{i} + 3\mathbf{j}, \mathbf{b} = 5\mathbf{i} - \mathbf{j} + 2\mathbf{k}$ **ii** $\mathbf{a} = \mathbf{i} + 2\mathbf{j} - \mathbf{k}, \mathbf{b} = 3\mathbf{i} - \mathbf{k}$

2 In each case, calculate $\mathbf{a} \times \mathbf{b}$ and verify that it is perpendicular to both $\mathbf{a}$ and $\mathbf{b}$.

  a   **i** $\mathbf{a} = \begin{pmatrix} 1 \\ 1 \\ 2 \end{pmatrix}, \mathbf{b} = \begin{pmatrix} -1 \\ 2 \\ 5 \end{pmatrix}$ **ii** $\mathbf{a} = \begin{pmatrix} 2 \\ 3 \\ -7 \end{pmatrix}, \mathbf{b} = \begin{pmatrix} -1 \\ 1 \\ 3 \end{pmatrix}$

  b   **i** $\mathbf{a} = 4\mathbf{i} + \mathbf{j} - 3\mathbf{k}, \mathbf{b} = \mathbf{i} - \mathbf{j} + 3\mathbf{k}$ **ii** $\mathbf{a} = \mathbf{i} - \mathbf{j} + 5\mathbf{k}, \mathbf{b} = 2\mathbf{i} + \mathbf{j} - \mathbf{k}$

3 Find the inverse of each matrix. Check your answer using a calculator.

  a   **i** $\begin{pmatrix} 1 & 3 & 2 \\ 2 & 4 & 0 \\ 5 & -3 & 0 \end{pmatrix}$ **ii** $\begin{pmatrix} 2 & 3 & 1 \\ 1 & 2 & 6 \\ -3 & -6 & 8 \end{pmatrix}$

  b   **i** $\begin{pmatrix} 3 & 1 & -4 \\ -5 & 1 & 0 \\ 1 & -2 & 6 \end{pmatrix}$ **ii** $\begin{pmatrix} 3 & d & 2 \\ -4 & 2 & -3 \\ 0 & 1 & -1 \end{pmatrix}$

4. Find a vector that is perpendicular to both $\mathbf{a} = 3\mathbf{i} - \mathbf{j} + 5\mathbf{k}$ and $\mathbf{b} = \mathbf{j} - 3\mathbf{k}$.

5. A line is perpendicular to the vectors $\begin{pmatrix} -1 \\ 0 \\ 2 \end{pmatrix}$ and $\begin{pmatrix} 1 \\ 0 \\ 1 \end{pmatrix}$, and passes through the point $(-1, 1, 7)$. Find the vector equation of the line.

6. A line passes through the point $(3, 1, 6)$ and is perpendicular to the lines with equations $\mathbf{r} = \begin{pmatrix} 2 \\ 0 \\ 1 \end{pmatrix} + t \begin{pmatrix} -1 \\ 0 \\ 2 \end{pmatrix}$ and $\mathbf{r} = \begin{pmatrix} 2 \\ 0 \\ 0 \end{pmatrix} + s \begin{pmatrix} -3 \\ 3 \\ 2 \end{pmatrix}$. Find the equation of the line in vector form.

7. Find the Cartesian equation of the line that passes through the point $(3, 1, 2)$ and is perpendicular to the lines with equations $\frac{x+1}{3} = -\frac{y-2}{5} = \frac{z-1}{2}$ and $\frac{x-3}{4} = \frac{y-1}{5} = \frac{z+1}{1}$.

8. Find the Cartesian equation of the line through the point $(-3, 1, 1)$ that is perpendicular to the lines $\frac{x}{3} = \frac{y}{3} = \frac{z-1}{1}$ and $\frac{x+1}{3} = \frac{y}{1} = \frac{z-1}{5}$.

Checklist of learning and understanding

- A vector equation of a straight line has the form $\mathbf{r} = \mathbf{a} + \lambda \mathbf{d}$, where $\mathbf{a}$ is the position vector of one point on the line and $\mathbf{b}$ is the direction vector.
  - In two dimensions, a line with gradient $\frac{p}{q}$ has the direction vector $\begin{pmatrix} q \\ p \end{pmatrix}$.
  - To find the equation of the line through two points with position vectors $\mathbf{a}$ and $\mathbf{b}$, use the direction vector $\mathbf{d} = \mathbf{b} - \mathbf{a}$.
- The Cartesian equation of a line has the form $\frac{x-a}{k} = \frac{y-b}{m} = \frac{z-c}{n} (=\lambda)$, where (a, b, c) is one point on the line and $\begin{pmatrix} k \\ m \\ n \end{pmatrix}$ is the direction vector.
  - If, for example, $k = 0$, the term $\frac{(x-a)}{k}$ in the previous equation is replaced by $x = a$. The line is parallel to the y–z plane.
  - To convert from vector to Cartesian equation, set $\mathbf{r} = \begin{pmatrix} x \\ y \\ z \end{pmatrix}$ and set three expressions for λ equal to each other.
  - To convert from a Cartesian to a vector equation, express x, y and z in terms of λ.
- To find the intersection of two non-parallel lines, solve simultaneous equations. If there is no solution, the lines are skew.
  - To find the intersection of a line with one of the coordinate axes, set the other two coordinates equal to zero.
- The **scalar product** (or dot product) of two vectors can be calculated in two ways:
$$\mathbf{a} \cdot \mathbf{b} = a_1 b_1 + a_2 b_2 + a_3 b_3 \quad \text{or} \quad \mathbf{a} \cdot \mathbf{b} = |\mathbf{a}||\mathbf{b}|\cos\theta$$
  - Two vectors are perpendicular if $\mathbf{a} \cdot \mathbf{b} = 0$.

Continues on next page ...

- The angle between two vectors can be found using $\cos\theta = \dfrac{\mathbf{a}\cdot\mathbf{b}}{|\mathbf{a}||\mathbf{b}|}$.
  - The angle between two lines is the angle between their direction vectors.
  - The vector product of two vectors is given by:
  $$\mathbf{a}\times\mathbf{b} = \begin{pmatrix} a_2b_3 - a_3b_2 \\ a_3b_1 - a_1b_3 \\ a_1b_2 - a_2b_1 \end{pmatrix} = \begin{vmatrix} \mathbf{i} & a_1 & b_1 \\ \mathbf{j} & a_2 & b_2 \\ \mathbf{k} & a_3 & b_3 \end{vmatrix}$$
- If $\mathbf{a}$ and $\mathbf{b}$ are not parallel, the vector product is perpendicular to both $\mathbf{a}$ and $\mathbf{b}$.
- If two vectors are parallel, their vector product is zero.
- You can use the vector product to find the inverse of a 3×3 matrix.

For a 3×3 matrix $\mathbf{A}$ with columns $\mathbf{c}_1$, $\mathbf{c}_2$ and $\mathbf{c}_3$, to find the inverse matrix $\mathbf{A}^{-1}$:
- The rows are found from vector products of columns of $\mathbf{A}$:
  - For the first row, use $\mathbf{c}_2 \times \mathbf{c}_3$.
  - For the second row, use $\mathbf{c}_3 \times \mathbf{c}_1$.
  - For the third row, use $\mathbf{c}_1 \times \mathbf{c}_2$.
- Then divide by $\det \mathbf{A}$.

Mixed practice 2

1. Find the vector equation of the line passing through points $(-1, 2, 5)$ and $(7, 0, 3)$.

2. **In this question you must show detailed reasoning.**

   Two lines have equations $\mathbf{r} = (3\mathbf{i} - \mathbf{j} + 3\mathbf{k}) + t(2\mathbf{i} + \mathbf{j} + \mathbf{k})$ and $\mathbf{r} = (-2\mathbf{i} - 2\mathbf{j} - 2\mathbf{k}) + s(\mathbf{i} - \mathbf{j} + 3\mathbf{k})$ and the lines intersect.

   a Find the coordinates of the intersection point.

   b Find the angle between the lines.

3. Show that the lines with equations $\mathbf{r} = (5\mathbf{i} - 2\mathbf{j} + \mathbf{k}) + t(2\mathbf{i} - \mathbf{j} - \mathbf{k})$ and $\mathbf{r} = (\mathbf{i} + \mathbf{j} - \mathbf{k}) + s(-2\mathbf{i} + \mathbf{j} + 5\mathbf{k})$ are skew.

4. Find a vector perpendicular to $\mathbf{a} = 3\mathbf{i} - 5\mathbf{j} - \mathbf{k}$ and $\mathbf{b} = 3\mathbf{i} - \mathbf{k}$.

5. Find the acute angle between the skew lines
   $$\frac{x+3}{1} = \frac{y-2}{1} = \frac{z-4}{-1} \text{ and } \frac{x-5}{2} = \frac{y-1}{-3} = \frac{z+3}{1}.$$

   © OCR, GCE Further Mathematics, Paper 4727, January 2006

6. a Find a vector equation of the line with Cartesian equation
   $$\frac{2x-1}{4} = \frac{y+2}{3} = \frac{4-3z}{6}.$$

   b Determine whether the line intersects the x-axis.

   c Find the angle the line makes with the x-axis.

   > **Tip**
   >
   > The direction vectors of the three coordinate axes are
   > $\begin{pmatrix} 1 \\ 0 \\ 0 \end{pmatrix}, \begin{pmatrix} 0 \\ 1 \\ 0 \end{pmatrix}$ and $\begin{pmatrix} 0 \\ 0 \\ 1 \end{pmatrix}$.

7. a Find the coordinates of the point of intersection of the lines with Cartesian equations
   $$\frac{x-2}{3} = \frac{y+1}{4} = \frac{z+1}{1} \text{ and } 5-x = \frac{y+2}{-3} = \frac{z-7}{2}.$$

   b Show that the line with equation $\mathbf{r} = \begin{pmatrix} 7 \\ 8 \\ -1 \end{pmatrix} + \lambda \begin{pmatrix} 1 \\ -1 \\ 2 \end{pmatrix}$ passes through the intersection point above.

8. Four points have coordinates $A(-1, 5, 4)$, $B(0, 1, 7)$, $C(-1, 1, 2)$ and $D(0, 0, 5)$. Determine whether the (infinite) lines AB and CD intersect.

9. Find the vector equation of the line through the point $(-1, 0, 3)$ that is perpendicular to the lines
   $$\mathbf{r} = \begin{pmatrix} -2 \\ 3 \\ 3 \end{pmatrix} + \lambda \begin{pmatrix} -1 \\ 1 \\ 1 \end{pmatrix} \text{ and } \mathbf{r} = \begin{pmatrix} 1 \\ 0 \\ 2 \end{pmatrix} + \mu \begin{pmatrix} 2 \\ 2 \\ 5 \end{pmatrix}.$$

10 The two lines l_1 and l_2 have equations $\mathbf{r} = \begin{pmatrix} 2 \\ -1 \\ 0 \end{pmatrix} + \lambda \begin{pmatrix} 1 \\ -2 \\ 2 \end{pmatrix}$ and

$\mathbf{r} = \begin{pmatrix} 2 \\ -1 \\ 0 \end{pmatrix} + \mu \begin{pmatrix} 1 \\ 1 \\ 2 \end{pmatrix}$, respectively, and intersect at point P.

a Show that $Q(5, 2, 6)$ lies on l_2.

b R is a point on l_1 such that $|PR| = |PQ|$. Find the possible coordinates of R.

11 The position vectors of the points P and Q with respect to an origin O are $5\mathbf{i} + 2\mathbf{j} - 9\mathbf{k}$ and $4\mathbf{i} + 4\mathbf{j} - 6\mathbf{k}$ respectively.

a Find a vector equation for the line PQ.

The position vector of the point T is $\mathbf{i} + 2\mathbf{j} - \mathbf{k}$.

b Write down a vector equation for the line OT and show that OT is perpendicular to PQ.

It is given that OT intersects PQ.

c Find the position vector of the point of intersection of OT and PQ.

d Hence find the perpendicular distance from O to PQ, giving your answer in an exact form.

© OCR, GCE Further Mathematics, Paper 4724,
January 2007
[Question part reference style adapted]

12 The two lines l_1 and l_2 are given by $\mathbf{r} = \begin{pmatrix} -5 \\ 1 \\ 10 \end{pmatrix} + \lambda \begin{pmatrix} -3 \\ 0 \\ 4 \end{pmatrix}$ and

$\mathbf{r} = \begin{pmatrix} 3 \\ 0 \\ -9 \end{pmatrix} + \mu \begin{pmatrix} 1 \\ 1 \\ 7 \end{pmatrix}$, respectively.

a l_1 and l_2 intersect at P. Find the coordinates of P.

b Show that the point $Q(5, 2, 5)$ lies on l_2.

c Find the coordinates of point M on l_1 such that QM is perpendicular to l_1.

d Find the area of the triangle PQM.

3 Applications of matrices

In this chapter you will learn how to:

- use matrices to solve sets of simultaneous equations
- interpret matrices as linear transformations in two and three dimensions
- find a matrix representing a combined transformation
- find invariant points and invariant lines of a linear transformation.

Before you start…

GCSE	You should know how to solve linear simultaneous equations in two variables.	1	Solve the simultaneous equations: $\begin{cases} 2x-3y=5 \\ x+2y=-1 \end{cases}$
Chapter 2	You should be able to use position vectors to represent points in two and three dimensions.	2	Write down the position vectors of points $A(5, 3, -2)$ and $B(0, -1, 1)$.
GCSE	You should understand simple transformations: rotation, reflection, enlargement.	3	Triangle PQR is given by $P(1, 2)$, $Q(1, 4)$, $R(2, 2)$. Find the image of PQR under each transformation: a rotation 90° anticlockwise about the origin b reflection in the line $y=-x$ c enlargement centred at the origin, scale factor 2.
A Level Mathematics Student Book 1, Chapter 10	You should be able to solve trigonometric equations.	4	Find θ in $[0°, 360°]$ for which $\sin\theta = \dfrac{1}{2}$, $\cos\theta = -\dfrac{\sqrt{3}}{2}$.
Chapter 1	You should know how to find determinants and inverses of 2×2 and 3×3 matrices.	5	For the matrix $A = \begin{pmatrix} 3 & 1 & -1 \\ 2 & 4 & 1 \\ 0 & -4 & 1 \end{pmatrix}$, find: a $\det A$ b A^{-1}.
Chapter 1	You should be able to identify a singular matrix.	5	Find the value of k such that the matrix $\begin{pmatrix} 1 & 2 \\ 5 & k \end{pmatrix}$ is singular.

Why are matrices useful?

In Chapter 1 you learnt about the structure and arithmetic of matrices, how to calculate inverses and determinants, and how to solve equations involving matrices. In this chapter you will explore two of the most common applications of matrices. The first is to solve systems of linear equations, which is an essential tool in both pure and applied mathematics. The second is to describe geometric transformations. This allows visual information to be recorded mathematically, which is needed in applications such as computer game design.

3 Applications of matrices

Section 1: Linear simultaneous equations

You already know several methods for solving two simultaneous equations with two unknowns (probably elimination and substitution). These methods become increasingly difficult when you have more than two equations. In this section, you will learn how to represent a system of equations as a matrix equation, which you can then solve using inverse matrices.

When you multiply a column vector by a square matrix you get another column vector. For example:

$$\begin{pmatrix} 3 & 2 \\ 2 & -7 \end{pmatrix} \begin{pmatrix} x \\ y \end{pmatrix} = \begin{pmatrix} 3x+2y \\ 2x-7y \end{pmatrix}$$

The two components of this new vector look like expressions that appear in simultaneous equations. So, for example, the system of equations

$$\begin{cases} 3x+2y=5 \\ 2x-7y=20 \end{cases}$$

can be written as $\begin{pmatrix} 3 & 2 \\ 2 & -7 \end{pmatrix} \begin{pmatrix} x \\ y \end{pmatrix} = \begin{pmatrix} 5 \\ 20 \end{pmatrix}$.

WORKED EXAMPLE 3.1

Solve the simultaneous equations:

$$\begin{cases} 3x+2y=5 \\ 2x-7y=20 \end{cases}$$

$\begin{pmatrix} 3 & 2 \\ 2 & -7 \end{pmatrix} \begin{pmatrix} x \\ y \end{pmatrix} = \begin{pmatrix} 5 \\ 20 \end{pmatrix}$ Re-write the problem as a matrix multiplication.

This is an equation of the form $\mathbf{A}\begin{pmatrix} x \\ y \end{pmatrix} = \mathbf{B}$, so the solution is $\begin{pmatrix} x \\ y \end{pmatrix} = \mathbf{A}^{-1}\mathbf{B}$.

$\begin{pmatrix} 3 & 2 \\ 2 & -7 \end{pmatrix}^{-1} = \dfrac{1}{25}\begin{pmatrix} 7 & 2 \\ 2 & -3 \end{pmatrix}$ Find the inverse of the square matrix.

$\begin{pmatrix} x \\ y \end{pmatrix} = \begin{pmatrix} 3 & 2 \\ 2 & -7 \end{pmatrix}^{-1} \begin{pmatrix} 5 \\ 20 \end{pmatrix}$

$= \dfrac{1}{25}\begin{pmatrix} 7 & 2 \\ 2 & -3 \end{pmatrix}\begin{pmatrix} 5 \\ 20 \end{pmatrix}$

$= \dfrac{1}{25}\begin{pmatrix} 75 \\ -50 \end{pmatrix}$

$= \begin{pmatrix} 3 \\ -2 \end{pmatrix}$

$x=3, y=-2$

You can use the same idea with systems of three equations. Now you need a column vector with three components and a 3×3 matrix.

> **Tip**
>
> Remember, you are allowed to perform all numerical matrix multiplication on your calculator.

WORKED EXAMPLE 3.2

Solve the simultaneous equations:
$$\begin{cases} 3x + y - z = 3 \\ 2x + 4y + z = -8 \\ -4y + z = 6 \end{cases}$$

$\begin{pmatrix} 3 & 1 & -1 \\ 2 & 4 & 1 \\ 0 & -4 & 1 \end{pmatrix} \begin{pmatrix} x \\ y \\ z \end{pmatrix} = \begin{pmatrix} 3 \\ -8 \\ 6 \end{pmatrix}$ ⋯ Rewrite the problem as a matrix multiplication. The coefficients from the first equation (3, 1, −1) give the top row of the matrix, and so on.

$\begin{pmatrix} 3 & 1 & -1 \\ 2 & 4 & 1 \\ 0 & -4 & 1 \end{pmatrix}^{-1} = \dfrac{1}{30}\begin{pmatrix} 8 & 3 & 5 \\ -2 & 3 & -5 \\ -8 & 12 & 10 \end{pmatrix}$ ⋯ Find the inverse of the square matrix.

$\begin{pmatrix} x \\ y \\ z \end{pmatrix} = \begin{pmatrix} 3 & 1 & -1 \\ 2 & 4 & 1 \\ 0 & -4 & 1 \end{pmatrix}^{-1} \begin{pmatrix} 3 \\ -8 \\ 6 \end{pmatrix}$ ⋯ Multiply by the inverse on both sides of the equation to find the values x, y and z.

$= \dfrac{1}{30} \begin{pmatrix} 8 & 3 & 5 \\ -2 & 3 & -5 \\ -8 & 12 & 10 \end{pmatrix} \begin{pmatrix} 3 \\ -8 \\ 6 \end{pmatrix}$

$= \dfrac{1}{30} \begin{pmatrix} 30 \\ -60 \\ -60 \end{pmatrix}$

$= \begin{pmatrix} 1 \\ -2 \\ -2 \end{pmatrix}$

$x = 1, y = -2, z = -2$

Sometimes simultaneous equations don't have a unique solution. For example, the system $\begin{cases} x + y = 1 \\ x + y = 2 \end{cases}$ doesn't have any solutions, whereas the system $\begin{cases} x + y = 1 \\ 2x + 2y = 2 \end{cases}$ has infinitely many.

> **Tip**
>
> Remember that you can use a calculator to find the inverse with no extra working.

With elimination and substitution methods, you have to go through the whole process of solving the equations before establishing that there is

3 Applications of matrices

no unique solution. With the matrix method, there is no unique solution whenever the determinant is zero (which means it is not possible to find the inverse matrix).

> **Key point 3.1**
>
> A system of simultaneous equations can be written as a matrix multiplication problem:
>
> $$MX = B$$
>
> where **M** contains the coefficients and **X** is a column vector of the variables.
>
> If **M** is non-singular then there is a unique solution for the variables:
>
> $$X = M^{-1}B$$
>
> If **M** is singular, there is no unique solution.

> **Tip**
>
> Remember that 'singular' means that the matrix has a zero determinant.

> **Fast forward**
>
> In Pure Core Student Book 2 you will learn to interpret the various possible solutions where **M** is singular.

WORKED EXAMPLE 3.3

Consider the system of equations:
$$\begin{cases} x + z = 2 \\ -2x + ay + 2z = 0 \\ 3x + y - z = -1 \end{cases}$$

a Find the value of a for which the system does not have a unique solution.

b Now assume that a is such that the system does have a unique solution. Find the solution in terms of a.

a $\underline{A} = \begin{pmatrix} 1 & 0 & 1 \\ -2 & a & 2 \\ 3 & 1 & -1 \end{pmatrix}$

$\det \underline{A} = 1 \begin{vmatrix} a & 2 \\ 1 & -1 \end{vmatrix} - 0 \begin{vmatrix} -2 & 2 \\ 3 & -1 \end{vmatrix} + 1 \begin{vmatrix} -2 & a \\ 3 & 1 \end{vmatrix}$ .... The solution is not unique when $\det \underline{A} = 0$.

$= 1(-a - 2) - 0 + 1(-2 - 3a)$

$= -4 - 4a$

$\det \underline{A} = 0$ when $a = -1$.

b When $a \neq -1$, find $\underline{A}^{-1}$: .... When **A** is non-singular, you can use the inverse matrix to solve the system.

Matrix of cofactors: $\underline{C} = \begin{pmatrix} -a-2 & 4 & -2-3a \\ 1 & -4 & -1 \\ -a & -4 & a \end{pmatrix}$ .... First find the matrix of cofactors (remember to apply the alternating signs matrix).

Continues on next page ...

67

A Level Further Mathematics for OCR A Pure Core Student Book 1

$$\underline{A}^{-1} = \frac{1}{\det \underline{A}} \underline{C}^T$$

The inverse matrix is $\mathbf{C}^T$ divided by the determinant.

$$= -\frac{1}{4a+4} \begin{pmatrix} -a-2 & 1 & -a \\ 4 & -4 & -4 \\ -2-3a & -1 & a \end{pmatrix}$$

$$= \frac{1}{4a+4} \begin{pmatrix} a+2 & -1 & a \\ -4 & 4 & 4 \\ 2+3a & 1 & -a \end{pmatrix}$$

Solving the equations:

Now use the inverse matrix to solve the system.

$$\underline{A} \begin{pmatrix} x \\ y \\ z \end{pmatrix} = \begin{pmatrix} 2 \\ 0 \\ -1 \end{pmatrix} \text{ so}$$

$$\begin{pmatrix} x \\ y \\ z \end{pmatrix} = \underline{A}^{-1} \begin{pmatrix} 2 \\ 0 \\ -1 \end{pmatrix}$$

$$= \frac{1}{4a+4} \begin{pmatrix} a+2 & -1 & a \\ -4 & 4 & 4 \\ 2+3a & 1 & -a \end{pmatrix} \begin{pmatrix} 2 \\ 0 \\ -1 \end{pmatrix}$$

$$= \frac{1}{4a+4} \begin{pmatrix} a+4 \\ -12 \\ 4+7a \end{pmatrix}$$

So the solution is:

You need to give x, y and z in terms of a.

$$x = \frac{a+4}{4a+4}, \quad y = -\frac{3}{a+1}, \quad z = \frac{4+7a}{4a+4}$$

EXERCISE 3A

1 By rewriting each of the following sets of simultaneous equations as a matrix problem, solve for x and y.

a i $\begin{cases} x+2y=3 \\ 4x-2y=-8 \end{cases}$ ii $\begin{cases} 7x-3y=13 \\ 2x+4y=11 \end{cases}$

b i $\begin{cases} 4y-x=2 \\ 3x-2y=-1 \end{cases}$ ii $\begin{cases} 4x+19y=12 \\ -8x-2y=36 \end{cases}$

c i $\begin{cases} x-7y=17 \\ 2x+3y=-17 \end{cases}$ ii $\begin{cases} 3x-4y+2=0 \\ x-2y-8=0 \end{cases}$

2 By rewriting each of the following sets of simultaneous equations as a matrix problem, solve for x and y.

a i $\begin{cases} x+y-z=3 \\ x+z=-8 \\ -2y+z=6 \end{cases}$ ii $\begin{cases} x+y-z=1 \\ x-y+z=-3 \\ 2x-3y+5z=-2 \end{cases}$

b i $\begin{cases} 2x+3y-z=4 \\ x-7y+2z=0 \\ -3x-y+z=2 \end{cases}$ **ii** $\begin{cases} 3x+y-2z=1 \\ -5x+y+3z=-2 \\ x-2y+z=5 \end{cases}$

3 Find the value of a for which the simultaneous equations
$\begin{cases} ax+y-z=1 \\ x+z=0 \\ -2y+z=2 \end{cases}$
do not have a unique solution.

4 Consider the system of equations
$\begin{cases} 2x+ay+z=1 \\ y+z=0 \\ x+(a+1)y+z=-1 \end{cases}$
Given that the system has a unique solution, find the set of possible values of a.

5 a Find the value of k for which the simultaneous equations
$\begin{cases} kx+2y=1 \\ (k-2)x+3y=-1 \end{cases}$
do not have a unique solution.

b Assuming that the equations have a unique solution, find the solution in terms of k.

6 The system of equations
$\begin{cases} ax+3y=2 \\ 5x+(a-2)y=1 \end{cases}$
has a unique solution.

a Find the set of possible values of a.

b Find the solution in terms of a.

7 Alessia has a set of coloured blocks. Two green, one purple and one yellow block together have mass 115 g. One green, two purple and three yellow blocks have mass 210 g. One green, one purple and two yellow blocks have mass 135 g.

a Write this information as a matrix equation.

b Hence, find the mass of a yellow block.

> **Tip**
> You can use your calculator to find inverses and multiply matrices.

8 A teacher orders books from three different shops. He orders 50 books and spends £157 in total. He orders twice as many books from shop Y as from shop Z. The books in shop X cost £3.50 each, the books in shop Y cost £2.80 each and the books in shop Z cost £3.10 each.

a Formulate this problem as a matrix equation.

b Hence, find out how many books the teacher ordered from each shop.

9 f(x) is a quadratic function. It is given that f(1)=4, f(2)=7 and f(3)=14. Find f(4).

10 Consider the system of linear equations
$$\begin{cases} x + cy - 2z = 3 \\ 2x - cy + z = 1 \\ x - 3y + 3z = 5 \end{cases}$$

a Find the set of values of c for which the system has a unique solution.

b Given that c is one of the values from part **a**, find the solution in terms of c.

11 a Show that the system
$$\begin{cases} (k-1)x + 2z = 1 \\ (k+1)y + z = 0 \\ -3x + 3y + z = -1 \end{cases}$$
has a unique solution for all values of k.

b Express the solution in terms of k.

Section 2: Matrices as linear transformations

You are familiar with transformations in two dimensions, such as reflections, rotations or enlargements, where points (making up the **object**) are moved under a consistent rule to new (**image**) points. If we represent the points by their position vectors, then this rule can be written as a matrix equation.

For example, consider the rotation 90° anticlockwise about the origin, applied to the triangle with vertices $P(1, 3)$, $Q(2, 3)$ and $R(1, 1)$, as shown in the diagram.

The image points have coordinates $P'(-3, 1)$, $Q'(-3, 2)$ and $R'(-1, 1)$. Look at how the transformation affects the position vectors:

$$\begin{pmatrix} 1 \\ 3 \end{pmatrix} \to \begin{pmatrix} -3 \\ 1 \end{pmatrix}, \begin{pmatrix} 2 \\ 3 \end{pmatrix} \to \begin{pmatrix} -3 \\ 2 \end{pmatrix}, \begin{pmatrix} 1 \\ 1 \end{pmatrix} \to \begin{pmatrix} -1 \\ 1 \end{pmatrix}$$

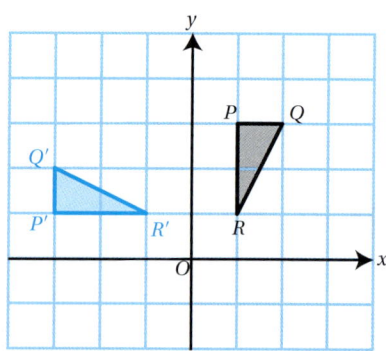

It looks as though the rule can be written as:
$$\begin{pmatrix} x \\ y \end{pmatrix} \to \begin{pmatrix} -y \\ x \end{pmatrix}$$

We can express this as a matrix equation:
$$\begin{pmatrix} x' \\ y' \end{pmatrix} = \begin{pmatrix} 0 & -1 \\ 1 & 0 \end{pmatrix} \begin{pmatrix} x \\ y \end{pmatrix}$$

Here the matrix $\mathbf{M}_1 = \begin{pmatrix} 0 & -1 \\ 1 & 0 \end{pmatrix}$ represents the 90° anticlockwise rotation about the origin. You can now use this matrix to find the image of any other point after the rotation; for example, the point with position vector $\begin{pmatrix} 5 \\ -8 \end{pmatrix}$ would be rotated to the point with position vector $\begin{pmatrix} 0 & -1 \\ 1 & 0 \end{pmatrix} \begin{pmatrix} 5 \\ -8 \end{pmatrix} = \begin{pmatrix} 8 \\ 5 \end{pmatrix}$.

> **Tip**
>
> The direction of a rotation, if not specified, is conventionally interpreted as being anticlockwise. Nevertheless, it is wise to specify clockwise or anticlockwise in any working or answers.

The easiest way to identify what transformation a matrix represents is to look at the image of the **unit square**, the square with coordinates $O(0, 0)$, $A(1, 0)$, $B(1, 1)$ and $C(0, 1)$.

WORKED EXAMPLE 3.4

A transformation $\mathbf{M}_2$ is given by $\mathbf{M}_2 = \begin{pmatrix} 0 & -1 \\ -1 & 0 \end{pmatrix}$. Find the image of the unit square under transformation $\mathbf{M}_2$, and show this on a coordinate grid. Hence, describe the transformation.

$O: \begin{pmatrix} 0 & -1 \\ -1 & 0 \end{pmatrix} \begin{pmatrix} 0 \\ 0 \end{pmatrix} = \begin{pmatrix} 0 \\ 0 \end{pmatrix}$

$A: \begin{pmatrix} 0 & -1 \\ -1 & 0 \end{pmatrix} \begin{pmatrix} 1 \\ 0 \end{pmatrix} = \begin{pmatrix} 0 \\ -1 \end{pmatrix}$

$B: \begin{pmatrix} 0 & -1 \\ -1 & 0 \end{pmatrix} \begin{pmatrix} 1 \\ 1 \end{pmatrix} = \begin{pmatrix} -1 \\ -1 \end{pmatrix}$

$C: \begin{pmatrix} 0 & -1 \\ -1 & 0 \end{pmatrix} \begin{pmatrix} 0 \\ 1 \end{pmatrix} = \begin{pmatrix} -1 \\ 0 \end{pmatrix}$

Label the vertices of the unit square $O(0, 0)$, $A(1, 0)$, $B(1, 1)$ and $C(0, 1)$. Multiply the position vector of each vertex by the transformation matrix.

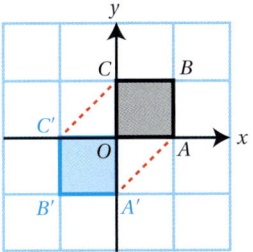

The transformation represents a reflection in the line $y = -x$.

Looking at the images of A and C helps identify the line of reflection.

Looking at the diagram in Worked example 3.4, it is not immediately clear whether it shows a 180° rotation about the origin or a reflection in the line $y = -x$. In this case A' is $(0, -1)$ and C' is $(-1, 0)$. A rotation would produce the image the other way around, as shown to the right.

The matrix representing the 180° rotation is $\mathbf{M}_3 = \begin{pmatrix} -1 & 0 \\ 0 & -1 \end{pmatrix}$.

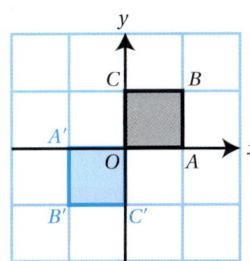

You can use the unit square to find the matrix to represent a given transformation. For a transformation $\mathbf{M} = \begin{pmatrix} a & b \\ c & d \end{pmatrix}$:

$\mathbf{M} \begin{pmatrix} 1 \\ 0 \end{pmatrix} = \begin{pmatrix} a \\ c \end{pmatrix}$ and $\mathbf{M} \begin{pmatrix} 0 \\ 1 \end{pmatrix} = \begin{pmatrix} b \\ d \end{pmatrix}$

The image of the fourth corner of the unit square is $\begin{pmatrix} a+c \\ b+d \end{pmatrix}$. Notice that a matrix transformation never changes the position of the origin, as

$\mathbf{M} \begin{pmatrix} 0 \\ 0 \end{pmatrix} = \begin{pmatrix} 0 \\ 0 \end{pmatrix}$.

This means that, to find the transformation matrix, you need only the images of the points $(1, 0)$ and $(0, 1)$.

> **Tip**
>
> Since a matrix transformation never moves the origin, translations can not be represented by matrices.

Key point 3.2

The first column of the transformation matrix is the image of $\begin{pmatrix} 1 \\ 0 \end{pmatrix}$ and the second column is the image of $\begin{pmatrix} 0 \\ 1 \end{pmatrix}$.

WORKED EXAMPLE 3.5

By considering the image of the unit square, find the matrix representing the enlargement with scale factor 3 and centre at the origin.

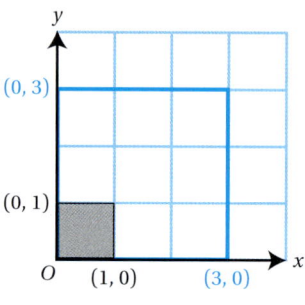

$\begin{pmatrix} 1 \\ 0 \end{pmatrix} \rightarrow \begin{pmatrix} 3 \\ 0 \end{pmatrix}$ and $\begin{pmatrix} 0 \\ 1 \end{pmatrix} \rightarrow \begin{pmatrix} 0 \\ 3 \end{pmatrix}$ — The images of the points (1, 0) and (0, 1) give the columns of the transformation matrix.

So the matrix is $\begin{pmatrix} 3 & 0 \\ 0 & 3 \end{pmatrix}$.

Using this method you can find a matrix for any linear transformation in two dimensions. You need to know the transformation matrices for the rotations, reflections and enlargement given in Key point 3.3.

> **Tip**
>
> The transformations that can be represented by matrices are called 'linear' because the image of a straight line is always another straight line.

 Key point 3.3

Rotation anticlockwise about the origin with the given angle:

90°	180°	270°
$\begin{pmatrix} 0 & -1 \\ 1 & 0 \end{pmatrix}$	$\begin{pmatrix} -1 & 0 \\ 0 & -1 \end{pmatrix}$	$\begin{pmatrix} 0 & 1 \\ -1 & 0 \end{pmatrix}$

Reflection in the given mirror line:

x-axis	y-axis	y = x	y = −x
$\begin{pmatrix} 1 & 0 \\ 0 & -1 \end{pmatrix}$	$\begin{pmatrix} -1 & 0 \\ 0 & 1 \end{pmatrix}$	$\begin{pmatrix} 0 & 1 \\ 1 & 0 \end{pmatrix}$	$\begin{pmatrix} 0 & -1 \\ -1 & 0 \end{pmatrix}$

> **Fast forward**
>
> You will meet rotations with other angles in Section 3.

3 Applications of matrices

Enlargement with centre at the origin:

Scale factor k
$\begin{pmatrix} k & 0 \\ 0 & k \end{pmatrix}$

The determinant

In some cases it can be difficult to distinguish between a rotation and a reflection. You saw this when you compared the reflection in the line $y = -x$ from Worked example 3.4 and the rotation through $180°$.

The image of the unit square is the same in both cases, but the points are arranged in a different order. Reading anticlockwise around the shape, the square $OABC$ is mapped to $OA'B'C'$ by the rotation, and to $OC'B'A'$ by the reflection. We say that the rotation **preserves the orientation** and the reflection **reverses the orientation** of the shape.

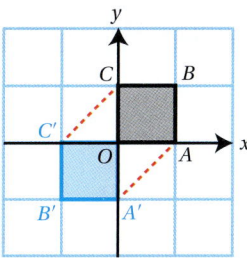

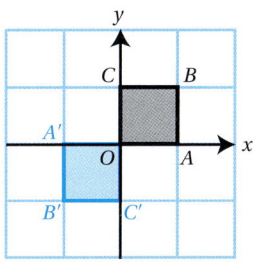

It turns out that a good way to distinguish between the two is to use the determinant of the transformation matrix. For the transformations in two dimensions you have met so far:

Rotation	Reflection	Enlargement
$\det \mathbf{M} = 1$	$\det \mathbf{M} = -1$	$\det \mathbf{M} = k^2$

So the transformations that reverse the orientation have a negative determinant. Also, rotations and reflections don't change the size of the shape, whereas enlargements do; the determinant is related to the scale factor.

🔑 Key point 3.4

For a matrix transformation in two dimensions:

- The determinant of the transformation matrix gives the area scale factor for the transformation.
- If the determinant is negative the orientation of the shape is reversed.

Successive transformations

When two transformations are applied in succession, the overall result is another transformation. You can find its matrix as follows.

Suppose the original point (the object) has the position vector $\mathbf{X} = \begin{pmatrix} x \\ y \end{pmatrix}$. If the matrix representing the first transformation is $\mathbf{A}$, then the first image is $\mathbf{AX}$. After applying the second transformation with matrix $\mathbf{B}$, the final image is $\mathbf{B}(\mathbf{AX})$.

Since matrix multiplication is associative, this is the same as $(\mathbf{BA})\mathbf{X}$. Hence, the matrix representing the combined transformation is $\mathbf{BA}$.

73

> **Key point 3.5**
>
> For two transformations **A** and **B**, if **C** represents **A** followed by **B**, transformation **C** is given by **C**=**BA**.

Notice that the matrix for the transformation that is applied first is written on the right.

WORKED EXAMPLE 3.6

$\mathbf{R} = \begin{pmatrix} 0 & 1 \\ 1 & 0 \end{pmatrix}$ represents a reflection in the line $y=x$ and $\mathbf{S} = \begin{pmatrix} 0 & 1 \\ -1 & 0 \end{pmatrix}$ represents a rotation 270° anticlockwise about the origin.

Transformation $\mathbf{T}_1$ is defined as **R** followed by **S**, and $\mathbf{T}_2$ is defined by **S** followed by **R**.

B is the image of the point $A(2, 3)$ under $\mathbf{T}_1$ and C is the image of A under $\mathbf{T}_2$.

a Find the coordinates of B and C. Do the transformations **R** and **S** commute?
b Describe the transformations $\mathbf{T}_1$ and $\mathbf{T}_2$.

a $\mathbf{T}_1 = \mathbf{SR} = \begin{pmatrix} 0 & 1 \\ -1 & 0 \end{pmatrix}\begin{pmatrix} 0 & 1 \\ 1 & 0 \end{pmatrix} = \begin{pmatrix} 1 & 0 \\ 0 & -1 \end{pmatrix}$ .... R followed by S is represented by **SR**.

$\mathbf{T}_1 \begin{pmatrix} 2 \\ 3 \end{pmatrix} = \begin{pmatrix} 1 & 0 \\ 0 & -1 \end{pmatrix}\begin{pmatrix} 2 \\ 3 \end{pmatrix} = \begin{pmatrix} 2 \\ -3 \end{pmatrix}$

B has coordinates $(2, -3)$.

$\mathbf{T}_2 = \mathbf{RS} = \begin{pmatrix} 0 & 1 \\ 1 & 0 \end{pmatrix}\begin{pmatrix} 0 & 1 \\ -1 & 0 \end{pmatrix} = \begin{pmatrix} -1 & 0 \\ 0 & 1 \end{pmatrix}$ .... S followed by R is represented by **RS**.

$\mathbf{T}_2 \begin{pmatrix} 2 \\ 3 \end{pmatrix} = \begin{pmatrix} -1 & 0 \\ 0 & 1 \end{pmatrix}\begin{pmatrix} 2 \\ 3 \end{pmatrix} = \begin{pmatrix} -2 \\ 3 \end{pmatrix}$

C has coordinates $(-2, 3)$.

b $\mathbf{T}_1$ is a reflection in the x-axis. .... Looking at the columns of $\mathbf{T}_1$, the unit vector **i** is unchanged and the vector **j** is reversed.

$\mathbf{T}_2$ is a reflection in the y-axis. .... $\mathbf{T}_2$ leaves the **j** vector unchanged and reverses the direction of **i**.

Inverse transformations

You can also use a matrix to reverse the effect of a transformation. If a transformation has matrix **M**, and if the image of the object **X** under this transformation is **X**′=**MX**, then you can recover the original object by using the inverse matrix: $\mathbf{M}^{-1}\mathbf{X}' = \mathbf{X}$.

3 Applications of matrices

🔑 Key point 3.6

If a linear transformation is represented by a matrix **M**, then its inverse transformation is represented by the matrix **M**⁻¹.

Notice that all the transformations we have met so far have non-zero determinants, so their inverse matrices exist.

When you have two successive transformations, the inverse transformations are applied in reverse order. This corresponds to the inverse of a product of two matrices:
$$(\mathbf{AB})^{-1} = \mathbf{B}^{-1}\mathbf{A}^{-1}$$

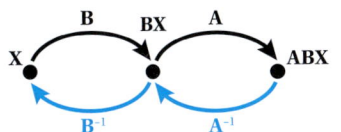

WORKED EXAMPLE 3.7

Point P is rotated $180°$ about the origin, and then reflected in the y-axis. The final image has coordinates $(-3, 7)$. Find the coordinates of P.

The matrix for the $180°$ rotation is $\underline{A} = \begin{pmatrix} -1 & 0 \\ 0 & -1 \end{pmatrix}$ and for the reflection $\underline{B} = \begin{pmatrix} -1 & 0 \\ 0 & 1 \end{pmatrix}$.	You are looking for the inverse of the combined transformation. Start by writing down the individual transformation matrices first.
Combined transformation: $\underline{C} = \underline{BA} = \begin{pmatrix} -1 & 0 \\ 0 & 1 \end{pmatrix}\begin{pmatrix} -1 & 0 \\ 0 & -1 \end{pmatrix} = \begin{pmatrix} 1 & 0 \\ 0 & -1 \end{pmatrix}$	Find the combined transformation. Remember that the second transformation is written on the left.
We know that $\underline{C}\begin{pmatrix} x \\ y \end{pmatrix} = \begin{pmatrix} -3 \\ 7 \end{pmatrix}$, where (x, y) are the coordinates of P.	
Hence, $\begin{pmatrix} x \\ y \end{pmatrix} = \underline{C}^{-1}\begin{pmatrix} -3 \\ 7 \end{pmatrix}$	You can multiply on the left by the inverse matrix.
$\underline{C}^{-1} = \dfrac{1}{-1}\begin{pmatrix} -1 & 0 \\ 0 & 1 \end{pmatrix} = \begin{pmatrix} 1 & 0 \\ 0 & -1 \end{pmatrix}$	The inverse of $\begin{pmatrix} a & b \\ c & d \end{pmatrix}$ is $\dfrac{1}{ad-bc}\begin{pmatrix} d & -b \\ -c & a \end{pmatrix}$
And so: $\begin{pmatrix} x \\ y \end{pmatrix} = \begin{pmatrix} 1 & 0 \\ 0 & -1 \end{pmatrix}\begin{pmatrix} -3 \\ 7 \end{pmatrix} = \begin{pmatrix} -3 \\ -7 \end{pmatrix}$ The coordinates of P are $(-3, -7)$.	

EXERCISE 3B

In this exercise, all rotations are anticlockwise (in the positive direction) unless stated otherwise.

1. Draw the image of the unit square under the transformations represented by the following matrices:

   a i $\begin{pmatrix} 1 & 2 \\ 1 & 0 \end{pmatrix}$ ii $\begin{pmatrix} -1 & 0 \\ 0 & 1 \end{pmatrix}$ b i $\begin{pmatrix} 3 & 0 \\ 0 & 3 \end{pmatrix}$ ii $\begin{pmatrix} 0 & 2 \\ -3 & 0 \end{pmatrix}$

2. Each diagram shows the image of the unit square under a linear transformation. Write down the matrix representing each transformation.

   a i 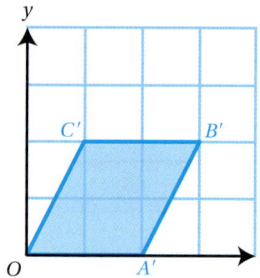   ii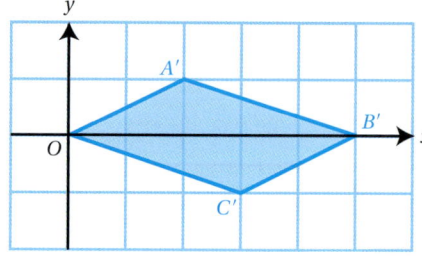

   b i 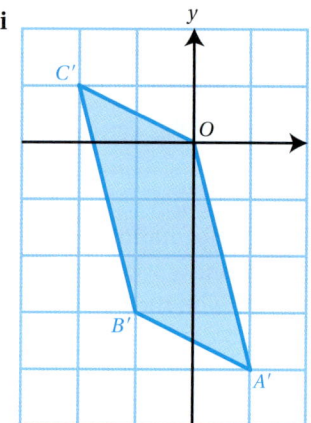   ii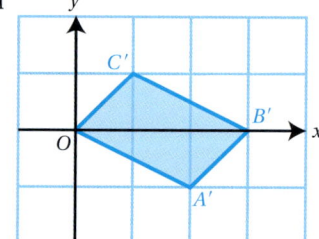

3. By considering the image of the unit square and the determinant, classify the following transformations as rotation, reflection or neither. Where appropriate, state the angle of rotation or the equation of the line of symmetry.

   a $\begin{pmatrix} 0 & -1 \\ -1 & 0 \end{pmatrix}$ b $\begin{pmatrix} 0 & 1 \\ 1 & 0 \end{pmatrix}$ c $\begin{pmatrix} 1 & -1 \\ -1 & 2 \end{pmatrix}$

   d $\begin{pmatrix} -1 & 0 \\ 0 & 1 \end{pmatrix}$ e $\begin{pmatrix} -1 & 0 \\ 0 & -1 \end{pmatrix}$ f $\begin{pmatrix} 1 & 1 \\ -1 & 1 \end{pmatrix}$

4. Find the image of the given point after the given transformation (or sequence of transformations).

   a i point (3, 5), reflection in the line $y=x$

      ii point (3, 5), reflection in the y-axis

   b i point (−1, 3), rotation 270° about the origin

      ii point (−1, 3), rotation 180° about the origin

3 Applications of matrices

    c   **i**   point (4, −7), enlargement with scale factor 3 followed by rotation 90° about the origin

        ii   point (4, −7), reflection in the line $y=x$ followed by enlargement with scale factor 4

    d   **i**   point (4, 1), rotation 180° about the origin followed by enlargement with scale factor $\frac{1}{2}$

        ii   point (4, 1), enlargement with scale factor $\frac{1}{3}$ followed by reflection in the x-axis

5 You are given a transformation (or a sequence of transformations) and the coordinates of the image. Find the coordinates of the original object.

    a   **i**   rotation 90° about the origin, image (3, 6)

        ii   rotation 270° about the origin, image (3, 6)

    b   **i**   reflection in the x-axis, image (7, 2)

        ii   reflection in the line $y=-x$, image (7, 2)

    c   **i**   enlargement with scale factor 3 followed by a reflection in the line $y=x$, image (−5, 2)

        ii   reflection in the y-axis followed by enlargement with scale factor 5, image (−5, 2)

    d   **i**   rotation 90° about the origin followed by a reflection in the x-axis, image (6, 2)

        ii   reflection in the line $y=x$ followed by a rotation 180° about the origin, image (6, 2)

6 Write down a matrix that represents:

    a   a rotation 540° anticlockwise about the origin

    b   a rotation 90° clockwise about the origin.

7   **a**   Find the matrix for the resulting transformation when a rotation 90° about the origin is followed by a rotation 180° about the origin. Describe the transformation.

    b   Repeat part **a** for some other pairs of rotations, including combining a rotation with itself. What do you notice?

    c   Find the matrix for the resulting transformation when reflection in the line $y=x$ is followed by reflection in the y-axis. Describe the transformation.

    d   Repeat part **c** for other pairs of reflections. What do you notice?

8 What is the inverse of these transformations?

    a   reflection in the line $y=x$

    b   rotation 90° clockwise about the origin

9 The triangle with vertices $P(1, 1)$, $Q(6, 1)$ and $R(4, -2)$ is rotated 90° anticlockwise about the origin. Find the coordinates of the vertices of the image.

10 The triangle with vertices $A(-1, 3)$, $B(2, 4)$ and $C(2, 3)$ is reflected in the line $y=-x$.

    a   Find the coordinates of the vertices of the image. Show the original and the image triangle on a grid.

    b   Find the determinant of the transformation. Explain briefly how this relates to your diagram in part **a**.

11 Transformation **T** is defined as a reflection in the line $y=x$ followed by an enlargement with scale factor 3.

    a   Find the matrix representing **T**.

    b   The image of the point P, under the transformation **T**, has coordinates (3, −9). Find the coordinates of P.

    c   The rectangle with vertices (0, 0), (2, 0), (2, 5) and (0, 5) is transformed using the transformation **T**. Find the area of the image.

Section 3: Further transformations in 2-D

There are five types of basic transformation that can be produced by 2×2 matrices. In the previous section, you worked with enlargements, and special cases of rotations and reflections. In this section, you will extend to general rotations, and also meet stretches and shears.

One important point to note is that every matrix transformation maps the origin to itself. This is because $\mathbf{M}\begin{pmatrix}0\\0\end{pmatrix}=\begin{pmatrix}0\\0\end{pmatrix}$ for every matrix $\mathbf{M}$.

Remember that the columns of the transformation matrices correspond to the images of $\begin{pmatrix}1\\0\end{pmatrix}$ and $\begin{pmatrix}0\\1\end{pmatrix}$; this allows you to write down the matrix for each of these transformations.

Rotations

The origin can never move under a matrix transformation, so it has to be the centre of rotation.

A rotation of angle θ (anticlockwise) about the origin moves the point $(1, 0)$ to the point $(\cos\theta, \sin\theta)$ and $(0, 1)$ to $(-\sin\theta, \cos\theta)$, so the matrix for this transformation is:

$$\mathbf{M}=\begin{pmatrix}\cos\theta & -\sin\theta\\ \sin\theta & \cos\theta\end{pmatrix}$$

> **Rewind**
>
> Check that using $\theta=90°$, $180°$ and $270°$ gives the three rotation matrices from Section 2.

WORKED EXAMPLE 3.8

Find the image of the point $(-4, 2)$ after a rotation $75°$ anticlockwise about the origin.

The matrix is: Find the rotation matrix using the general
                                   expression above.
$\underline{M}=\begin{pmatrix}\cos 75° & -\sin 75°\\ \sin 75° & \cos 75°\end{pmatrix}$

$=\begin{pmatrix}0.259 & -0.966\\ 0.966 & 0.259\end{pmatrix}$

The image of $(-4, 2)$ is:

$\begin{pmatrix}0.259 & -0.966\\ 0.966 & 0.259\end{pmatrix}\begin{pmatrix}-4\\ 2\end{pmatrix}=\begin{pmatrix}-2.97\\ -3.35\end{pmatrix}$

Reflections

You need to work with only four special reflections: those in the two coordinate axes and in the lines $y = x$ and $y = -x$, as given in Key point 3.3.

3 Applications of matrices

Explore

You can use a diagram similar to that used previously in the rotations section, to work out a matrix for a general reflection. Investigate what transformations you can get by combining two reflections, or a reflection and a rotation.

Stretches

A stretch with scale factor c parallel to the x-axis leaves the y-axis unchanged (this is called the invariant axis). Hence, its matrix is $\begin{pmatrix} c & 0 \\ 0 & 1 \end{pmatrix}$.

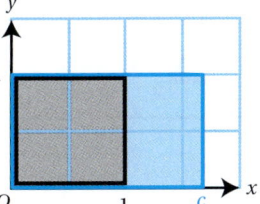

Tip

A stretch with a negative scale factor is in fact a stretch followed by a reflection.

Similarly, a stretch with scale factor d parallel to the y-axis leaves the x-axis invariant and has matrix $\begin{pmatrix} 1 & 0 \\ 0 & d \end{pmatrix}$.

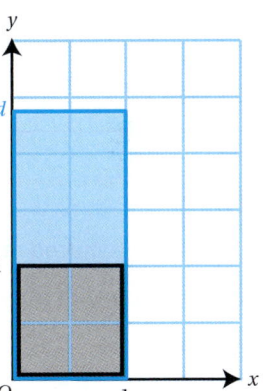

Explore

Investigate how to produce stretches in other directions, by combining the basic stretches with other transformations.

WORKED EXAMPLE 3.9

Transformation **S** is a stretch with scale factor 3 with the x-axis invariant. Transformation **T** is a stretch with scale factor 5 with the y-axis invariant. Transformation **V** is the result of **S** followed by **T**.

a Find the matrix representing **V**.

b The triangle with vertices $A(1, 1)$, $B(2, 1)$ and $C(1, 3)$ is transformed using **V**. Draw triangle ABC and its image on a grid, and find the area of the image.

a $\underline{TS} = \begin{pmatrix} 5 & 0 \\ 0 & 1 \end{pmatrix}\begin{pmatrix} 1 & 0 \\ 0 & 3 \end{pmatrix} = \begin{pmatrix} 5 & 0 \\ 0 & 3 \end{pmatrix}$ The combined matrix is **TS** (be careful about the order!).

b $A': \begin{pmatrix} 5 & 0 \\ 0 & 3 \end{pmatrix}\begin{pmatrix} 1 \\ 1 \end{pmatrix} = \begin{pmatrix} 5 \\ 3 \end{pmatrix}$ Multiply each position vector by the transformation matrix.

$B': \begin{pmatrix} 5 & 0 \\ 0 & 3 \end{pmatrix}\begin{pmatrix} 2 \\ 1 \end{pmatrix} = \begin{pmatrix} 10 \\ 3 \end{pmatrix}$

$C': \begin{pmatrix} 5 & 0 \\ 0 & 3 \end{pmatrix}\begin{pmatrix} 1 \\ 3 \end{pmatrix} = \begin{pmatrix} 5 \\ 9 \end{pmatrix}$

Continues on next page ...

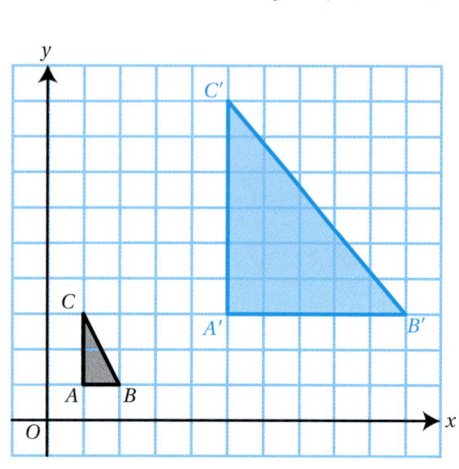

The area of ABC is $\frac{1}{2}(1)(2) = 1$.

$\det \underline{V} = 15$

The determinant of **V** is the scale factor for the area.

Hence, the area of $A'B'C'$ is 15.

Enlargements

An enlargement (centred at the origin) is a combination of a vertical and horizontal stretch with the same scale factors. Its matrix is $\begin{pmatrix} k & 0 \\ 0 & k \end{pmatrix}$, where k is the scale factor.

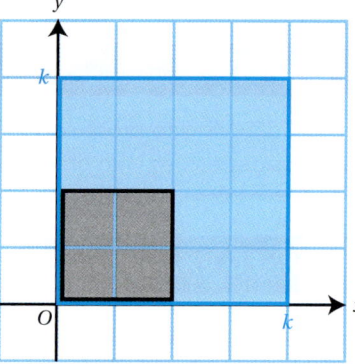

> **Tip**
>
> An enlargement with a negative scale factor is in fact an enlargement followed by a 180° rotation.

Shears

A stretch moves points away from an axis, with points that are further away moving more. It is also possible to have a transformation that moves points parallel to an axis, but still with those points further away from the axis moving more. This sort of transformation is called a **shear**.

You will only need to consider shears parallel to one of the coordinate axes. A shear always leaves one line invariant. For example, a shear parallel to the y-axis leaves all the points on the y-axis invariant and all other points are moved vertically by the amount proportional to their distance from the y-axis. To define the shear fully, you need to give the image of one point. (In this case you could give the image of $(1, 0)$.)

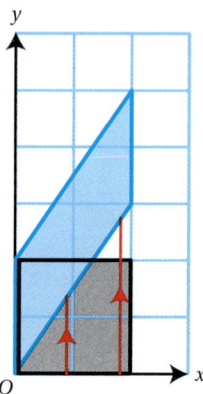

3 Applications of matrices

WORKED EXAMPLE 3.10

Describe the transformation represented by matrix $\mathbf{M}_4 = \begin{pmatrix} 1 & 2 \\ 0 & 1 \end{pmatrix}$.

Image of the unit square:

$\begin{pmatrix} 1 \\ 0 \end{pmatrix} \mapsto \begin{pmatrix} 1 \\ 0 \end{pmatrix}, \begin{pmatrix} 0 \\ 1 \end{pmatrix} \mapsto \begin{pmatrix} 2 \\ 1 \end{pmatrix}, \begin{pmatrix} 1 \\ 1 \end{pmatrix} \mapsto \begin{pmatrix} 3 \\ 1 \end{pmatrix}$

Use the two columns of the matrix to find the images of (1, 0) and (0, 1).

Sketch the unit square and its image.

The transformation is a shear with the x-axis invariant, mapping (0, 1) to (2, 1).

The table in Key point 3.7 summarises all the 2-D linear transformations.

Key point 3.7

Transformation	Matrix	Determinant
Rotation about O, angle θ (anticlockwise)	$\begin{pmatrix} \cos\theta & -\sin\theta \\ \sin\theta & \cos\theta \end{pmatrix}$ **This will appear in your formula book.**	1
Reflection in the coordinate axes	x-axis $\quad$ y-axis $\begin{pmatrix} 1 & 0 \\ 0 & -1 \end{pmatrix} \begin{pmatrix} -1 & 0 \\ 0 & 1 \end{pmatrix}$	-1
Reflection in the lines $y = \pm x$	$\begin{pmatrix} 0 & \pm 1 \\ \pm 1 & 0 \end{pmatrix}$ **This will appear in your formula book.**	-1
Stretch, scale factor c, with the y-axis invariant	$\begin{pmatrix} c & 0 \\ 0 & 1 \end{pmatrix}$	c

Tip

You should remember that positive angles represent anticlockwise, and negative angles represent clockwise rotation.

Stretch, scale factor d, with the x-axis invariant	$\begin{pmatrix} 1 & 0 \\ 0 & d \end{pmatrix}$	d
Enlargement, centre O, scale factor k	$\begin{pmatrix} k & 0 \\ 0 & k \end{pmatrix}$	k^2
Shear, x-axis invariant, $(0, 1) \mapsto (k, 1)$	$\begin{pmatrix} 1 & k \\ 0 & 1 \end{pmatrix}$	1
Shear, y-axis invariant, $(1, 0) \mapsto (1, k)$	$\begin{pmatrix} 1 & 0 \\ k & 1 \end{pmatrix}$	1

EXERCISE 3C

1 Find the angle of (anticlockwise) rotation represented by each matrix.

   a $\begin{pmatrix} 1/2 & -\sqrt{3}/2 \\ \sqrt{3}/2 & 1/2 \end{pmatrix}$ **b** $\begin{pmatrix} 0.6 & -0.8 \\ 0.8 & 0.6 \end{pmatrix}$ **c** $\begin{pmatrix} -\sqrt{2}/2 & -\sqrt{2}/2 \\ \sqrt{2}/2 & -\sqrt{2}/2 \end{pmatrix}$ **d** $\begin{pmatrix} -3/5 & 4/5 \\ -4/5 & -3/5 \end{pmatrix}$

2 Describe these shears:

   a $\begin{pmatrix} 1 & 6 \\ 0 & 1 \end{pmatrix}$ **b** $\begin{pmatrix} 1 & 0 \\ 2 & 1 \end{pmatrix}$ **c** $\begin{pmatrix} 1 & -3 \\ 0 & 1 \end{pmatrix}$ **d** $\begin{pmatrix} 1 & -3/2 \\ 0 & 1 \end{pmatrix}$

3 Write down a matrix to represent each of these transformations in two dimensions:

   a rotation anticlockwise $60°$ about the origin

   b shear with the x-axis invariant, mapping $(0, 1)$ to $(3, 1)$

   c reflection in the y-axis

   d shear with the y-axis invariant, mapping $(1, 0)$ to $(1, \frac{1}{2})$

   e rotation $150°$ clockwise about the origin

   f enlargement with scale factor 5 centred at the origin.

4 Find the image of the point $(3, -1)$ under each of these transformations:

   a reflection in the line $y = -x$

   b rotation $45°$ clockwise about the origin

   c shear with the y-axis invariant, mapping $(1, 0)$ to $(1, 4)$

   d rotation $120°$ about the origin

   e enlargement with scale factor $\frac{1}{3}$ centred at the origin

   f shear with the x-axis invariant, mapping $(0, 1)$ to $(\frac{1}{3}, 1)$.

3 Applications of matrices

5 For each transformation, find the point whose image is (−1, 2).

   a reflection in the line $y=x$

   b rotation 90° about the origin

   c enlargement with scale factor 2 with the centre at the origin

   d shear with the y-axis invariant, mapping (1, 0) to (1, 2)

   e rotation 60° about the origin

   f shear with the x-axis invariant, mapping (0, 1) to ($\frac{1}{2}$, 1).

6 Find the image of the point (2, −3) under a rotation 135° anticlockwise about the origin.

7 The vertices of a rectangle are $A(-2, 1)$, $B(3, 1)$, $C(3, -2)$ and $D(-2, -2)$. $PQRS$ is the image of $ABCD$ under the shear with the x-axis invariant, mapping (0, 1) to (3, 1).

   a Find the coordinates of P, Q, R and S.

   b Find the ratio (area of $PQRS$):(area of $ABCD$).

8 a Write down the 2×2 matrix representing a shear with the y-axis invariant, mapping (1, 0) to (1, 1.5).

   b A shear with the y-axis invariant, mapping (1, 0) to (1, 1.5) is applied to a triangle. The image has vertices with coordinates (0, 0), (1, 3) and (−3, 1). Find the coordinates of the vertices of the original triangle.

Section 4: Invariant points and invariant lines

You already know that every linear transformation maps the origin to itself; we say that O is an **invariant point**. Some transformations, such as rotations, have no other invariant points – all other points are moved by the transformation. In this section you will learn how to determine whether a transformation has any invariant points.

Consider the transformation represented by matrix $\mathbf{R} = \begin{pmatrix} -0.6 & 0.8 \\ 0.8 & 0.6 \end{pmatrix}$.

If a point with position vector $\begin{pmatrix} u \\ v \end{pmatrix}$ is invariant, then its image will have the same position vector:

$$\mathbf{R}\begin{pmatrix} u \\ v \end{pmatrix} = \begin{pmatrix} 0.8v - 0.6u \\ 0.6v + 0.8u \end{pmatrix} = \begin{pmatrix} u \\ v \end{pmatrix}$$

This is a system of linear equations:

$$\begin{cases} 0.8v - 0.6u = u \\ 0.6v + 0.8u = v \end{cases} \Leftrightarrow \begin{cases} 0.8v - 1.6u = 0 \\ -0.4v + 0.8u = 0 \end{cases}$$

You can see that the two equations are the same, and equivalent to $v = 2u$. This means that every invariant point must lie on the line $y = 2x$. We say that $y = 2x$ is a **line of invariant points**.

> **Explore**
>
> Matrix $\mathbf{R}$ in fact represents a reflection in the line $y = 2x$. Find a matrix to represent a reflection in the line $y = kx$ and use this method to prove that this is a line of invariant points.

A Level Further Mathematics for OCR A Pure Core Student Book 1

> ### 🔑 Key point 3.8
>
> An invariant point is any point that is unaffected by the transformation; that is, the image of the point is the point itself: $\mathbf{M}\begin{pmatrix} u \\ v \end{pmatrix} = \begin{pmatrix} u \\ v \end{pmatrix}$.
>
> There may be infinitely many invariant points, forming a line of invariant points. In that case, the previous equation will have infinitely many solutions of the form $v = ku$.

> ### 🔎 Explore
>
> Can you prove that, if a transformation has two invariant points, then it must have infinitely many? Is it possible to have two lines of invariant points?

WORKED EXAMPLE 3.11

Determine whether the transformation represented by the matrix $\mathbf{B} = \begin{pmatrix} 3 & -2 \\ 2 & -1 \end{pmatrix}$ has any lines of invariant points.

We are looking for points (u, v) such that $\begin{pmatrix} 3 & -2 \\ 2 & -1 \end{pmatrix}\begin{pmatrix} u \\ v \end{pmatrix} = \begin{pmatrix} u \\ v \end{pmatrix}$	Invariant points satisfy $\mathbf{B}\begin{pmatrix} u \\ v \end{pmatrix} = \begin{pmatrix} u \\ v \end{pmatrix}$.
$\Rightarrow \begin{cases} 3u - 2v = u \\ 2u - v = v \end{cases}$	Re-write this as a system of equations.
Both equations are equivalent to $u - v = 0$; i.e. $v = u$.	Check whether both equations are in fact the same.
Hence, $y = x$ is a line of invariant points.	If so, they give a line of invariant points.

WORKED EXAMPLE 3.12

Show that the transformation represented by the matrix $\mathbf{M} = \begin{pmatrix} -4 & 1 \\ 3 & -2 \end{pmatrix}$ has no invariant points other than the origin.

Invariant points satisfy: $\begin{pmatrix} -4 & 1 \\ 3 & -2 \end{pmatrix}\begin{pmatrix} u \\ v \end{pmatrix} = \begin{pmatrix} u \\ v \end{pmatrix}$	Write the condition for invariant points and turn it into simultaneous equations.
$\Rightarrow \begin{cases} -4u + v = u \\ 3u - 2v = v \end{cases}$	
$\Rightarrow \begin{cases} -5u + v = 0 \\ 3u - 3v = 0 \end{cases}$	
The only solution is $u = 0, v = 0$.	Solve the equations.
Hence, the only invariant point is $(0, 0)$.	

3 Applications of matrices

Consider again the reflection in the line $y=2x$. All the points on the reflection line are invariant. Every other point moves under the reflection. However, it stays on the same line perpendicular to the reflection line. This means that each of these perpendicular lines, considered as a whole, is invariant.

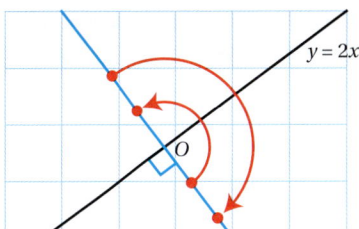

 Key point 3.9

An **invariant line** l is a line for which the image of any point on l is also on l (although is not necessarily the same point).

 Tip

Strictly speaking, it also needs to be checked that the image of the line covers the whole line. For example, the transformation represented by the zero matrix maps each point on the line $y = x$ to (0, 0). Thus, the image of every point on the line also lies on the line, but we would not call $y = x$ an invariant line for this transformation. However, in this course you will not encounter such examples.

Any line of invariant points is an invariant line. However, the opposite is not true; there can be an invariant line that contains non-invariant points (e.g., any line perpendicular to a line of reflection).

WORKED EXAMPLE 3.13

Show that $y = -\frac{1}{2}x + 3$ is an invariant line for the reflection in $y=2x$, represented by the matrix $\mathbf{R} = \begin{pmatrix} -0.6 & 0.8 \\ 0.8 & 0.6 \end{pmatrix}$.

Any point on the line $y = -\frac{1}{2}x + 3$ has coordinates of the form $(u, -0.5u + 3)$.

⇢ You are going to find the image of a general point on the line $y = -\frac{1}{2}x + 3$.

Its image is
$$\begin{pmatrix} u' \\ v' \end{pmatrix} = \begin{pmatrix} -0.6 & 0.8 \\ 0.8 & 0.6 \end{pmatrix} \begin{pmatrix} u \\ -0.5u + 3 \end{pmatrix}$$
$$= \begin{pmatrix} -0.6u - 0.4u + 2.4 \\ 0.8u - 0.3u + 1.8 \end{pmatrix}$$
$$= \begin{pmatrix} -u + 2.4 \\ 0.5u + 1.8 \end{pmatrix}$$

Then
$$-\frac{1}{2}u' + 3 = -\frac{1}{2}(-u + 2.4) + 3$$
$$= 0.5u + 1.8$$
$$= v'$$

⇢ To check whether this image lies on the same line, you need to check that $v' = -\frac{1}{2}u' + 3$.

Hence, (u', v') also lies on the line $y = -\frac{1}{2}x + 3$, and so this line is invariant.

WORKED EXAMPLE 3.14

Show that an enlargement has infinitely many invariant lines through the origin.

The matrix for an enlargement is $\begin{pmatrix} k & 0 \\ 0 & k \end{pmatrix}$.

For a line through the origin, $v = mu$. ········· Lines through the origin have the form $y = mx$.

$\begin{pmatrix} u' \\ v' \end{pmatrix} = \begin{pmatrix} k & 0 \\ 0 & k \end{pmatrix} \begin{pmatrix} u \\ mu \end{pmatrix}$ ········· Write an equation for the image of any point on the line.

$\Rightarrow \begin{cases} u' = ku \\ v' = kmu \end{cases}$

Hence, $v' = mu'$ for all m, so every line through the origin is invariant. ········· If a line is invariant, then the coordinates of the image also satisfy $y = mx$.

WORKED EXAMPLE 3.15

A transformation is represented by the matrix $\mathbf{A} = \begin{pmatrix} -4 & 1 \\ 3 & -2 \end{pmatrix}$. Find the equations of invariant lines through the origin.

The image of (u, mu): ········· Any line through the origin has the form $y = mx$.

$\begin{pmatrix} u' \\ v' \end{pmatrix} = \begin{pmatrix} -4 & 1 \\ 3 & -2 \end{pmatrix} \begin{pmatrix} u \\ mu \end{pmatrix}$

$= \begin{pmatrix} -4u + mu \\ 3u - 2mu \end{pmatrix}$

For an invariant line: ········· If the line is invariant, the image also lies on the line.

$3u - 2mu = m(-4u + mu)$

$\Rightarrow u(m^2 - 2m - 3) = 0$ ········· If the whole line is invariant, then this is true for all u.

$\Rightarrow m^2 - 2m - 3 = 0$

$\Rightarrow m = -1$ or 3

The invariant lines are $y = -x$ and $y = 3x$.

3 Applications of matrices

Notice that, as you found in Worked example 3.12, this transformation has no invariant points (other than the origin). Hence, none of the invariant lines can be lines of invariant points.

EXERCISE 3D

1 For each matrix, find any lines of invariant points and any other invariant lines through the origin.

a $\begin{pmatrix} 1 & 1 \\ 0 & 4 \end{pmatrix}$ 	b $\begin{pmatrix} 2 & 5 \\ 0 & 4 \end{pmatrix}$ 	c $\begin{pmatrix} 1 & 4 \\ 2 & -1 \end{pmatrix}$ 	d $\begin{pmatrix} 3 & -2 \\ 4 & -3 \end{pmatrix}$

2 **R** is a reflection in the line $y = 2x$ with matrix $\begin{pmatrix} -0.6 & 0.8 \\ 0.8 & 0.6 \end{pmatrix}$.

S is a 90° rotation anticlockwise about the origin.

T is a stretch, scale factor 3, parallel to the y-axis.

Find the invariant lines, if any, of:

a **R** followed by **S** 	b **S**$^{-1}$**RS** 	c **TR** 	d **RT**

e **TS** 	f **S**$^{-1}$**TS**

3 Transformation **A** is given by $\mathbf{A} = \begin{pmatrix} 3 & -1 \\ 6 & a \end{pmatrix}$.

a If $y = 2x$ is an invariant line under transformation **A**, find the value of a.

b For this value a, determine whether there is a second invariant line.

4 Transformations **A** and **B** are given by $\mathbf{A} = \begin{pmatrix} 3 & 1 \\ 2 & 4 \end{pmatrix}$, $\mathbf{B} = \begin{pmatrix} 5 & -3 \\ -1 & 7 \end{pmatrix}$.

a Show that they have a common invariant line.

b Find any invariant lines of the product **AB**.

5 Transformation **A** is given by $\mathbf{A} = \begin{pmatrix} -3 & -2 \\ 9 & 8 \end{pmatrix}$.

a Find any invariant lines of **A** and determine whether there is a line of invariant points.

b Transformation $\mathbf{B} = \mathbf{A}^2$. Write down the equations of any invariant lines of **B**.

6 **R** is a reflection in the line $y = 2x$ with matrix $\begin{pmatrix} -0.6 & 0.8 \\ 0.8 & 0.6 \end{pmatrix}$.

S is a clockwise rotation about the origin by angle θ.

Find a condition of θ for which $y = x$ is an invariant line of **S**$^{-1}$**RS**.

7 Transformation **A** is given by $\mathbf{A} = \begin{pmatrix} 3 & 1 \\ 0 & 1 \end{pmatrix}$.

a Find any invariant lines of **A** and determine for each such line whether it is a line of invariant points.

Transformation **B** is given by $\mathbf{B} = \begin{pmatrix} -1 & b \\ 7 & -4 \end{pmatrix}$.

b Given that $y = 7x$ is an invariant line of the product **AB**, find the value b.

8 For this question, two distinct lines are said to be **twinned** under a transformation if each line is the image of the other.

a Under transformation $\mathbf{T} = \begin{pmatrix} 4 & 1 \\ a & b \end{pmatrix}$, line $y = -2x$ is twinned with $y = 3x$.

Calculate the values a and b.

b For transformation $\mathbf{S} = \begin{pmatrix} 1 & 2 \\ -4 & -1 \end{pmatrix}$, find the line that is twinned with $y = 3x$.

Section 5: Transformations in 3-D

When you move from the plane to three-dimensional space, some of the basic transformations need to be described in a different way. For example, while in two dimensions a rotation is about a point, in three dimensions it is about an **axis of rotation**. Similarly, you can't reflect a three-dimensional object in a line, but you can use a **plane of reflection**.

In two dimensions, it is useful to consider the image of the unit square. In three dimensions, you can look at the unit cube. This is the cube with edge length 1, with a vertex at the origin and edges parallel to the coordinate axes. Three of the edges are given by the unit vectors, $\mathbf{i} = \begin{pmatrix} 1 \\ 0 \\ 0 \end{pmatrix}$, $\mathbf{j} = \begin{pmatrix} 0 \\ 1 \\ 0 \end{pmatrix}$ and $\mathbf{k} = \begin{pmatrix} 0 \\ 0 \\ 1 \end{pmatrix}$.

The three columns of a transformation matrix give the image positions for these three unit vectors, and so outline the three edges of the image of the unit cube.

In each of the two types of transformation you will consider in this section, at least one of the unit direction vectors will be unaffected. By fixing the row and column of that direction vector in the matrix, you can use your understanding of 2-D transformations to define the 3-D matrix.

Reflections

In this course you need to consider only three possible planes of reflection: the x–y plane, the y–z plane and the x–z plane. The x–y plane contains the x- and y-axes. Every point in this plane has the z-coordinate equal to zero, so this plane also can be described as the $z = 0$ plane. The other two planes are the $x = 0$ and the $y = 0$ planes.

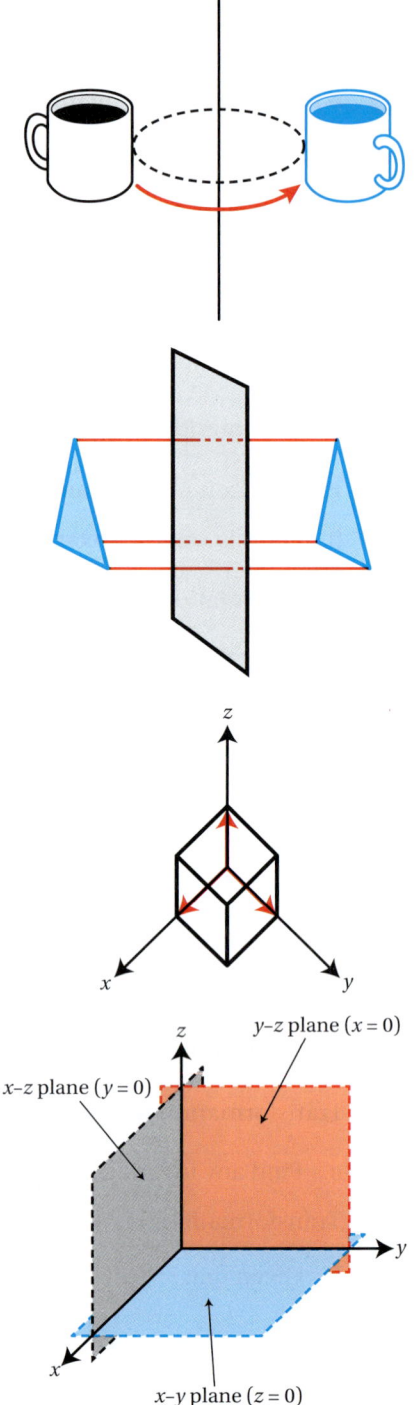

3 Applications of matrices

WORKED EXAMPLE 3.16

Transformation **R** represents a reflection in the plane $x=0$. Write down the 3×3 matrix for **R**.

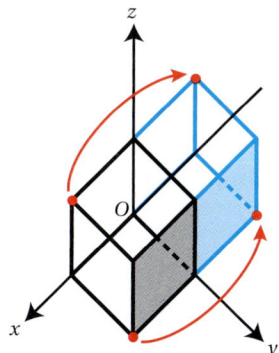

Sketch or imagine the unit cube being reflected in the plane ($x=0$ is the y–z plane).

Images of unit vectors:

$$\begin{pmatrix}1\\0\\0\end{pmatrix} \mapsto \begin{pmatrix}-1\\0\\0\end{pmatrix}, \begin{pmatrix}0\\1\\0\end{pmatrix} \mapsto \begin{pmatrix}0\\1\\0\end{pmatrix}, \begin{pmatrix}0\\0\\1\end{pmatrix} \mapsto \begin{pmatrix}0\\0\\1\end{pmatrix}$$

The unit vectors **j** and **k** lie in the plane of reflection, so are unaffected by the reflection. The **i** vector has its direction reversed.

Hence,

$$\underline{R} = \begin{pmatrix} -1 & 0 & 0 \\ 0 & 1 & 0 \\ 0 & 0 & 1 \end{pmatrix}$$

The images of the unit vectors give the columns of the transformation matrix.

Rotations

You need to work with rotations only about one of the coordinate axes. The axis of rotation is unaffected by the transformation, so one of the columns in the transformation matrix will be just the unit vector. To find the rest of the matrix you need to think about the other two unit vectors being rotated in two dimensions.

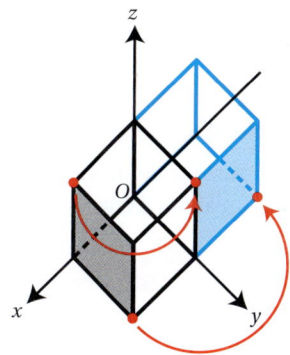

WORKED EXAMPLE 3.17

Transformation **S** represents the rotation 60° anticlockwise about the y-axis. Find the 3×3 matrix for **S**.

The axis of rotation is along direction **j**, so

$$\begin{pmatrix}0\\1\\0\end{pmatrix} \mapsto \begin{pmatrix}0\\1\\0\end{pmatrix} \qquad \underline{S} = \begin{pmatrix} ? & 0 & ? \\ 0 & 1 & 0 \\ ? & 0 & ? \end{pmatrix}$$

The unit vector **j** lies along the axis of rotation so is unaffected by the rotation. This means that the second row and column are as shown in red.

Continues on next page ...

A 60° rotation about the origin has 2-D matrix:

$$\begin{pmatrix} 1/2 & -\sqrt{3}/2 \\ \sqrt{3}/2 & 1/2 \end{pmatrix}$$

Filling in the gaps with this rotation matrix gives

$$\underline{S} = \begin{pmatrix} 1/2 & 0 & \sqrt{3}/2 \\ 0 & 1 & 0 \\ -\sqrt{3}/2 & 0 & 1/2 \end{pmatrix}$$

The **i** and **k** vectors are rotated in the x–z plane. Thus the remaining four elements form the 2×2 matrix of a 60° rotation.

You need to be a little careful: the anticlockwise rotation goes from z towards x, so the image of the unit vectors **k** has both components positive, and the image of **i** has one negative component. This means that the negative entry (from $-\sin 60°$) is in the first column rather than the third.

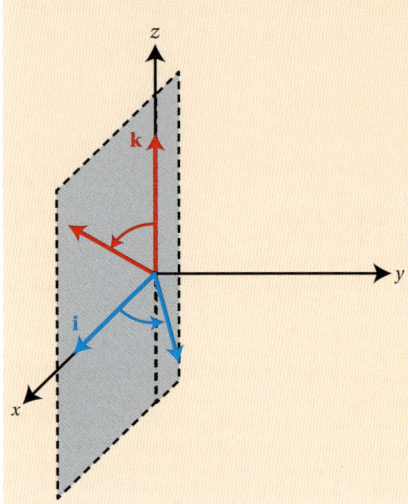

The six 3-D transformation matrices you need to know are summarised in Key point 3.10.

Key point 3.10

3-D transformations can be represented by 3×3 matrices.

Rotation about a given axis:

x-axis	y-axis	z-axis
$\begin{pmatrix} 1 & 0 & 0 \\ 0 & \cos\theta & -\sin\theta \\ 0 & \sin\theta & \cos\theta \end{pmatrix}$	$\begin{pmatrix} \cos\theta & 0 & \sin\theta \\ 0 & 1 & 0 \\ -\sin\theta & 0 & \cos\theta \end{pmatrix}$	$\begin{pmatrix} \cos\theta & -\sin\theta & 0 \\ \sin\theta & \cos\theta & 0 \\ 0 & 0 & 1 \end{pmatrix}$

This will appear in your formula book.

Reflection in a given plane:

$x=0$	$y=0$	$z=0$
$\begin{pmatrix} -1 & 0 & 0 \\ 0 & 1 & 0 \\ 0 & 0 & 1 \end{pmatrix}$	$\begin{pmatrix} 1 & 0 & 0 \\ 0 & -1 & 0 \\ 0 & 0 & 1 \end{pmatrix}$	$\begin{pmatrix} 1 & 0 & 0 \\ 0 & 1 & 0 \\ 0 & 0 & -1 \end{pmatrix}$

3 Applications of matrices

Other transformations

As in two dimensions, combining transformations corresponds to multiplying their matrices.

WORKED EXAMPLE 3.18

Find the matrix of the resulting transformation when a rotation 90° about the x-axis is followed by a rotation 90° about the y-axis.

Let $\underline{A}$ represent the rotation about the x-axis and $\underline{B}$ the rotation about the y-axis. Then:

$$\underline{A} = \begin{pmatrix} 1 & 0 & 0 \\ 0 & 0 & -1 \\ 0 & 1 & 0 \end{pmatrix} \text{ and } \underline{B} = \begin{pmatrix} 0 & 0 & 1 \\ 0 & 1 & 0 \\ -1 & 0 & 0 \end{pmatrix}.$$

Start by writing down the two standard rotation matrices.

The combined transformation is:

$\underline{C} = \underline{BA}$

$= \begin{pmatrix} 0 & 0 & 1 \\ 0 & 1 & 0 \\ -1 & 0 & 0 \end{pmatrix} \begin{pmatrix} 1 & 0 & 0 \\ 0 & 0 & -1 \\ 0 & 1 & 0 \end{pmatrix}$

$= \begin{pmatrix} 0 & 1 & 0 \\ 0 & 0 & -1 \\ -1 & 0 & 0 \end{pmatrix}$

The combined transformation corresponds to the matrix product.

This doesn't seem to be any of the three standard rotations, and you don't need to be able to interpret such a compound transformation.

The determinant of the transformation matrix still tells you about the scale factor, but when in three dimensions it is the scale factor for volume rather than for area. You can see from the table in Key point 3.10 that all rotations have determinant 1 and all reflections have determinant −1.

🔑 Key point 3.11

For a transformation matrix in 3-D:

- The determinant gives the scale factor for the volume.
- If the determinant is negative, the transformation changes the orientation of the object.

WORKED EXAMPLE 3.19

A linear transformation is described by matrix $\mathbf{T} = \begin{pmatrix} 2 & 1 & -1 \\ 0 & 3 & 3 \\ -2 & 5 & 0 \end{pmatrix}$.

A cuboid C with its vertex at the origin and edge vectors $3\mathbf{i}$, $2\mathbf{j}$ and $4\mathbf{k}$ is transformed under $\mathbf{T}$. Find the volume of the image.

C has volume $2 \times 3 \times 4 = 24$.

$|\mathbf{T}| = 2\begin{vmatrix} 3 & 3 \\ 5 & 0 \end{vmatrix} - 1\begin{vmatrix} 0 & 3 \\ -2 & 0 \end{vmatrix} - 1\begin{vmatrix} 0 & 3 \\ -2 & 5 \end{vmatrix}$ .... The scale factor for the volume is given by the determinant.

$= 2(-15) - 1(6) - 1(6)$

$= -42$

The volume of the image equals $24 \times 42 = 1008$. .... The image is also in reversed orientation, as shown by the negative determinant.

EXERCISE 3E

1 Write down a matrix to represent each transformation in three dimensions:

  a rotation 90° about the x-axis

  b rotation 30° about the z-axis

  c reflection in the plane $x = 0$

  d reflection in the plane $y = 0$.

2 Find the image of the point $(2, -1, 1)$ under each transformation in three dimensions:

  a rotation 60° about the y-axis

  b rotation 180° about the z-axis

  c reflection in the plane $z = 0$

  d reflection in the plane $y = 0$.

3 Point A is reflected in the plane $x = 0$. The coordinates of the image are $(2, -5, 1)$. Find the coordinates of A.

4 Transformation $\mathbf{T}$ is a reflection in the plane $y = 0$. Transformation $\mathbf{S}$ is a rotation 180° about the x-axis. Transformation $\mathbf{M}$ is $\mathbf{T}$ followed by $\mathbf{S}$.

  a Write down the matrices representing $\mathbf{T}$ and $\mathbf{S}$.

  b Find the matrix representing $\mathbf{M}$. Hence, describe the transformation $\mathbf{M}$.

  c Find the determinant of $\mathbf{M}$ and explain briefly how this relates to the transformation.

3 Applications of matrices

5 **R** represents a rotation 90° clockwise about the *x*-axis.

Triangle *ABC* is given by $A(1, 1, 1)$, $B(1, 3, 1)$, $C(1, 1, 4)$.

Find the image of triangle *ABC* under transformation **R**.

6 $(4, 2, -1)$ are the coordinates of the image of point *A* after a rotation 135° about the *z*-axis. Find the coordinates of the object point *A*.

7 Find the coordinates of the image when the point $(-3, 1, 1)$ is rotated 30° clockwise about the *y*-axis.

8 A rotation 90° anticlockwise about the *z*-axis is followed by the reflection in the plane $x=0$. Find the matrix representing the resulting transformation.

9 The 90° anticlockwise rotation about the *x*-axis is followed by the 90° clockwise rotation about the *y*-axis. Find the matrix representing the resulting transformation.

10 Point *P* is rotated 90° about the *z*-axis and then reflected in the plane $y=0$. The coordinates of the image are $(3, -1, 4)$. Find the coordinates of *P*.

11 Transformation **T** represents a 90° anticlockwise rotation about the *x*-axis followed by a 90° anticlockwise rotation about the *y*-axis.

    a Find matrix **T**.   **b** Show that $\mathbf{T}^3 = \mathbf{I}$.

12 A transformation is represented by a 3×3 matrix **T**.

The image under **T** of triangle *XYZ*, with $X(1, 3, -1)$, $Y(0, 1, 2)$ and $Z(4, -2, -3)$ is *X'Y'Z'*, with coordinates $X'(8, 2, -1)$, $Y'(7, 3, 4)$ and $Z'(-8, -5, -2)$.

    a By forming a matrix equation of the form $\mathbf{TA} = \mathbf{B}$ or otherwise, find **T**.

    b The image of each of three distinct points (other than the origin) will uniquely define a three-dimensional transformation, as long as a condition is fulfilled. In terms of the geometry of the three points, state this condition.

13 A transformation in three dimensions is represented by the matrix $\mathbf{M} = \begin{pmatrix} 5 & 2 & 3 \\ 1 & 1 & 2 \\ 0 & 3 & 2 \end{pmatrix}$.

    a Find the volume of the image of the unit cube under this transformation.

    b Explain the significance of the sign of the determinant of **M**.

14 By considering the image of the unit cube, identify the transformations represented by the following 3×3 matrices:

    a $\mathbf{A} = \begin{pmatrix} 1 & 0 & 0 \\ 0 & 4 & 0 \\ 0 & 0 & 1 \end{pmatrix}$ **b** $\mathbf{B} = \begin{pmatrix} 3 & 0 & 0 \\ 0 & 3 & 0 \\ 0 & 0 & 3 \end{pmatrix}$ **c** $\mathbf{C} = \begin{pmatrix} -0.5 & 0 & 0 \\ 0 & -0.5 & 0 \\ 0 & 0 & -0.5 \end{pmatrix}$

15 A transformation in three dimensions has matrix $\begin{pmatrix} 2 & 2 & 3 \\ 4 & -1 & 2 \\ 2 & 2 & 0 \end{pmatrix}$. The image of a cube *C* under this transformation is a three-dimensional object with volume 240 units^3. Find the edge length of cube *C*.

Checklist of learning and understanding

- A set of simultaneous equations can be solved by rewriting as a matrix multiplication, where the coefficients form a matrix **M**, with $\mathbf{M}\begin{pmatrix} x \\ y \\ z \end{pmatrix} = \mathbf{C}$ for some column matrix **C**.
- A matrix can represent a linear transformation: the image of a point with position vector $\begin{pmatrix} u \\ v \end{pmatrix}$ is $\mathbf{M}\begin{pmatrix} u \\ v \end{pmatrix}$.
- Two-dimensional linear transformations include:
  - rotation about the origin
  - reflection in line $y = mx$
  - stretch parallel to the x-axis or y-axis
  - enlargement centred at the origin
  - shear parallel to the x-axis or y-axis.
- Three-dimensional linear transformations include:
  - rotation about the x-axis, y-axis or z-axis
  - reflection in the plane $x=0$, $y=0$ or $z=0$.
- The determinant of a 2×2 transformation matrix is an area scale factor; the determinant of a 3×3 transformation matrix is a volume scale factor.
- A negative determinant means that the transformation changes the orientation of the image.
- An invariant line is one whose image is the original line.
- An invariant point is one whose image is the same point.
  - The origin is always an invariant point.
  - Invariant points may form a line of invariant points.

Mixed practice 3

1 A reflection is represented by the matrix $\begin{pmatrix} -1 & 0 \\ 0 & 1 \end{pmatrix}$.

State the equation of the line of invariant points.

2 **R** is a clockwise rotation by 120° about the z-axis.

S is the matrix $\dfrac{1}{2}\begin{pmatrix} -1 & -\sqrt{3} & 0 \\ \sqrt{3} & -1 & 0 \\ 0 & 0 & -2 \end{pmatrix}$.

  a **T = RS**. Calculate matrix **T**.

  b Describe the transformation represented by **T**.

3 $\mathbf{M} = \begin{pmatrix} 3 & 5 \\ 7 & k \end{pmatrix}$

  a **i** Find the value of k for which **M** is singular.

    ii Given that **M** is non-singular, find $\mathbf{M}^{-1}$, the inverse of **M**, in terms of k.

  b When $k = 12$, use $\mathbf{M}^{-1}$ to solve the simultaneous equations:
$$\begin{cases} 3x + 5y = 9 \\ 7x + 12y = 11 \end{cases}$$

4 **a** Describe the single transformation given by each matrix.

    i $\mathbf{A} = \begin{pmatrix} 1 & 5 \\ 0 & 1 \end{pmatrix}$ **ii** $\mathbf{B} = \dfrac{1}{5}\begin{pmatrix} -3 & 4 \\ 4 & 3 \end{pmatrix}$

  b Write down the 3×3 matrix describing a rotation 60° about the x-axis.

5 For matrices **A** and **B**, find any invariant lines of the form $y = mx$ and determine whether any are lines of invariant points.

  a $\mathbf{A} = \begin{pmatrix} 4 & 1 \\ -27 & -8 \end{pmatrix}$ **b** $\mathbf{B} = \begin{pmatrix} 4 & 1 \\ -1 & 2 \end{pmatrix}$

6 Transformation **A** is a 90° rotation clockwise about the origin and transformation **B** is a stretch, scale factor 3, parallel to the y-axis.

  a Write down the 2×2 matrices for **A** and **B**.

  b Matrix **C** is such that **BC = AC**. Find det **C**.

7 **a** Find the matrix that represents a shear with the y-axis invariant, the image of the point $(1, 0)$ being the point $(1, 4)$.

  b The matrix **X** is given by $\mathbf{X} = \begin{pmatrix} \frac{1}{2}\sqrt{2} & \frac{1}{2}\sqrt{2} \\ -\frac{1}{2}\sqrt{2} & \frac{1}{2}\sqrt{2} \end{pmatrix}$.

    i Describe fully the geometrical transformation represented by **X**.

    ii Find the value of the determinant of **X** and describe how this value relates to the transformation represented by **X**.

© OCR, AS GCE Further Mathematics, Paper 4725, June 2014

8. The matrix $\mathbf{A}$ is given by $\mathbf{A} = \begin{pmatrix} a & 2 & 1 \\ 1 & 3 & 2 \\ 4 & 1 & 1 \end{pmatrix}$.

   a Find the value of a for which $\mathbf{A}$ is singular.

   b Given that $\mathbf{A}$ is non-singular, find $\mathbf{A}^{-1}$ and, hence, solve the equations $\begin{cases} ax + 2y + z = 1 \\ x + 3y + 2z = 2 \\ 4x + y + z = 3 \end{cases}$

   © OCR, AS GCE Further Mathematics, Paper 4725, June 2013

   [Question and question part reference style adapted]

9. The transformation represented by matrix $\mathbf{A} = \begin{pmatrix} -a & a^2 \\ -2 & 2 \end{pmatrix}$ has a line of invariant points $y = bx$.

   Find a and b.

10. Under transformation $\mathbf{T}$, the images of points $P(1, 3)$ and $Q(-2, 5)$ are $P'(11, 6)$ and $Q'(11, 10)$.

    a By considering $\mathbf{T}\begin{pmatrix} 1 & -2 \\ 3 & 5 \end{pmatrix}$ or otherwise, calculate the matrix representing $\mathbf{T}$.

    b $\mathbf{T}$ is the result of an enlargement, scale factor $k > 0$ and a transformation with matrix $\mathbf{S}$, where $\det \mathbf{S} = 1$.

       i Find k.

       ii Describe the transformation $\mathbf{S}$.

11. Transformation $\mathbf{A}$ is given by matrix $\mathbf{A} = \begin{pmatrix} -2 & 6 \\ 3 & -5 \end{pmatrix}$.

    a A rectangle $OPQR$ with coordinates $P(2, 1)$ and $R(-2, 4)$ is transformed by $\mathbf{A}$.

       i Write down the coordinates of Q.

       ii Find the image $OP'Q'R'$ of $OPQR$ under transformation $\mathbf{A}$.

    b i Write down the equation of the line of invariant points for $\mathbf{A}$.

       ii Determine whether there is a second invariant line for transformation $\mathbf{A}$ and, if so, find its equation.

12. Matrices $\mathbf{A}$ and $\mathbf{B}$ are given by

    $\mathbf{A} = \begin{pmatrix} 8 - 3k & -1 \\ 12 - 9k & 1 \end{pmatrix}$ and $\mathbf{B} = \begin{pmatrix} 9 - 2k & -2 \\ 0 & 3 - 2k \end{pmatrix}$.

    a Find, in terms of k, the invariant lines of $\mathbf{A}$.

    Given that $\det \mathbf{A} = \det \mathbf{B} + 1$:

    b Find the possible values of k.

    c Show that $\mathbf{A}$ and $\mathbf{B}$ have a common invariant line.

    d For each value of k, find the equation of any other invariant lines of $\mathbf{A}$.

3 Applications of matrices

13 Matrices **A** and **B** are given by $\mathbf{A} = \begin{pmatrix} -1 & 2 \\ 0 & a \end{pmatrix}$ and $\mathbf{B} = \begin{pmatrix} -2 & 2 \\ b & -2 \end{pmatrix}$.

    a Given **A** and **B** commute under multiplication, find a and b.

    b The matrix **AB** can be written as $k\mathbf{T}$, where det $\mathbf{T} = 1$.

       i Write down the matrix **T** and the value of k.

      ii Describe **AB** as a combination of two linear transformations.

14 a Matrix **A** is defined by $\mathbf{A} = \begin{pmatrix} -1 & s \\ t & 2 \end{pmatrix}$.

    Given that the image of the point (2, 1) under the transformation represented by **A** is (1, 10), find the value of s and the value of t.

  b Matrix **B** is defined by $\mathbf{B} = \begin{pmatrix} \sqrt{2} & -\sqrt{2} \\ \sqrt{2} & \sqrt{2} \end{pmatrix}$.

    i Show that $\mathbf{B}^4 = k\mathbf{I}$, where k is an integer and **I** is the 2×2 identity matrix.

   ii Describe the transformation represented by matrix **B** as a combination of two geometrical transformations.

  iii Find the matrix $\mathbf{B}^{15}$.

FOCUS ON ... PROOF 1

Proving properties of identity and inverse matrices

Throughout Chapters 1 and 3 you used various properties of identity and inverse matrices without really checking that they must be true. But in mathematics, all properties you use must be proved. This is particularly important when working with structures such as matrices, which have many properties similar to numbers but also some that are different. (For example, matrix multiplication is not commutative, and not all non-zero matrices have an inverse.) This means that our intuition about what 'works' may be wrong.

In Section 3 of Chapter 1 we stated that the identity matrix **I** has the unique property that **IA** = **AI** = **A** for every square matrix **A**. It is reasonable to ask: How can we be sure that there is only one matrix with this property? Would it be possible to have two different identity matrices?

You are going to prove that the identity matrix is indeed unique.

PROOF 3

If **J** is a matrix such that **JA** = **AJ** = **A** for every matrix **A**, then **J** = **I**.

Consider the product **IJ**.	You can use any matrix for **A**. It makes sense to choose the identity matrix, as we know a lot of its properties.
By the definition of **I**, **IJ** = **J**.	**I** is the identity matrix so **IA** = **A** for any conformable matrix **A**.
But by the proposed property of **J**, **IJ** = **I**.	You are proposing that **AJ** = **A** for any conformable matrix **A**.
Then **J** = **IJ** = **I** so **J** = **I**.	State your conclusion.

ⓘ Did you know?

You can adapt this proof to a wide variety of contexts to show that an identity element for a binary operation must be unique; for example, in standard arithmetic, 0 is the only identity for addition and 1 is the only identity for multiplication.

The statement in Key point 1.8 requires that both **IA** = **A** and **AI** = **A**. You know that matrix multiplication is generally not commutative (**AB** ≠ **BA** for some matrices). So it is sensible to ask: is there some other matrix **J**, such that **JA** = **A** but **AJ** ≠ **A**? (In advanced mathematics, we would say that **J** is a 'left identity' but not a 'right identity'.)

We are going to prove that this is not the case.

Focus on ... Proof 1

PROOF 4

If **J** is a matrix such that **JA** = **A** for all **A**, then also **AJ** = **A**.

If JA = A for all A then
AJ = (AJ)I   by the definition of the identity matrix **I**

> One way to prove the required result is to introduce the identity matrix on the right, since multiplication by **I** by definition does not change a matrix.

    = A(JI)

> Remember that you can group the matrices any way you like, as long as you don't change the order!

    = AI   by the proposed property of J

    = A

> Use the given property of **J** in its product with **I**.

Hence, if JA = A for all A then also AJ = A.

> State your conclusion.

Questions

1 Use arguments similar to those presented above to prove these properties of inverse matrices.

  a Every non-singular matrix has a unique inverse:

    If **A** is a non-singular matrix with inverse A^{-1}, and if **B** is another matrix such that **AB** = **I**, then **B** = A^{-1}.

  b If **A** is a non-singular matrix, then its 'right inverse' and its 'left inverse' are the same:

    If AA^{-1} = **I** then also $A^{-1}A$ = **I**.

2 In matrix algebra, you cannot simply 'cancel' a matrix from both sides of an equation. In other words, **AB** = **AC** does not necessarily imply that **B** = **C**.

  a Find a counter example to prove that **AB** = **AC** $\Rightarrow$ **B** = **C** is not true.

  b Can you find an example of two non-zero matrices whose product is zero? (This would show that it is not true that **AB** = **Z** $\Rightarrow$ **A** = **Z** or **B** = **Z**.)

FOCUS ON ... PROBLEM-SOLVING 1

Alternative approaches to calculating distances

In Worked example 2.19, you looked at the following problem:

Line l has equation $\mathbf{r} = \begin{pmatrix} 3 \\ -1 \\ 0 \end{pmatrix} + \lambda \begin{pmatrix} 1 \\ -1 \\ 1 \end{pmatrix}$ and point A has coordinates $(3, 9, -2)$.

Find the shortest distance from A to l.

You used this strategy to solve the problem.

Strategy 1

- Write down the position vector of a general point B on the line (in terms of λ):

$$\mathbf{b} = \begin{pmatrix} 3+\lambda \\ -1-\lambda \\ \lambda \end{pmatrix}$$

- To get the shortest distance, AB must be perpendicular to the line.

This means that $\overrightarrow{AB} \cdot \begin{pmatrix} 1 \\ -1 \\ 1 \end{pmatrix} = 0$, which gives an equation for λ:

$$\begin{pmatrix} (3+\lambda)-3 \\ (-1-\lambda)-9 \\ \lambda+2 \end{pmatrix} \cdot \begin{pmatrix} 1 \\ -1 \\ 1 \end{pmatrix} = 0$$

$$\Rightarrow 1(\lambda) - 1(-10-\lambda) + 1(\lambda+2) = 0$$

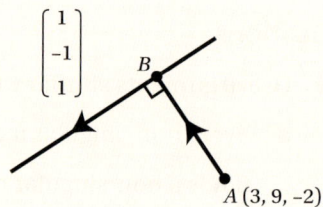

- Find λ and, hence, find the coordinates of B.
- Calculate the distance AB.

This problem can be solved in several different ways. Work through the two alternative solutions that follow. Which of the three strategies do you find the simplest?

Strategy 2

This also starts by expressing the vector $\overrightarrow{AB}$ in terms of λ, but you then use algebra or calculus to minimise this expression.

- Show that $AB^2 = 3\lambda^2 + 24\lambda + 104$.
- Either by completing the square, or by using differentiation, find the minimum value of AB^2.
- Hence, show that the required minimum distance is $2\sqrt{14}$.

> **Tip**
>
> AB^2 is the square of the length of AB.

Focus on ... Problem-solving 1

Strategy 3

This strategy uses a geometrical approach. You find the minimum distance directly, without finding the coordinates of B (or the value of λ).

The point $P(3, -1, 0)$ lies on the line. The shortest distance, marked h, equals $|\overrightarrow{PA}|\sin\theta$.

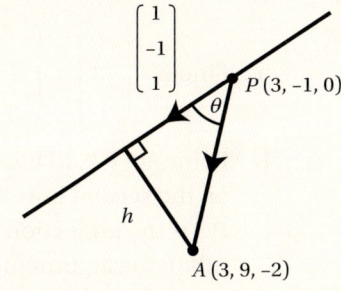

- Find the exact value of $|\overrightarrow{PA}|$.
- Use the scalar product to show that $\cos\theta = -\dfrac{6}{\sqrt{78}}$ and find the exact value of $\sin\theta$.
- Hence, show that $h = 2\sqrt{14}$.

Questions

1 Strategy 3 can be simplified slightly by introducing the concept of **projection**. Consider a line with direction vector **d** through the point with position vector **b**, and another point with position vector **a**.

Let M be the foot of the perpendicular from A to the line. The length of BM is the projection of BA onto the line.

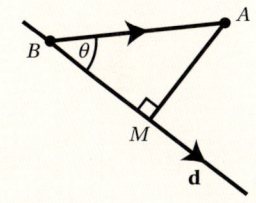

a Use the right-angled triangle ABM to express the length BM in terms of BA and θ.

b Use the scalar product to write $\cos\theta$ in terms of $(\mathbf{a} - \mathbf{b})$ and $\mathbf{d}$.

c Hence, show that $BM = \dfrac{|(\mathbf{a}-\mathbf{b})\cdot\mathbf{d}|}{|\mathbf{d}|}$.

d Use this formula for the previous example. Hence, use $AM^2 = BA^2 - BM^2$ to find the shortest distance from A to the line.

2 The lines with equations $\mathbf{r} = \begin{pmatrix} -1 \\ 2 \\ 0 \end{pmatrix} + \lambda \begin{pmatrix} 3 \\ -1 \\ 1 \end{pmatrix}$ and $\mathbf{r} = \begin{pmatrix} -1 \\ 3 \\ 8 \end{pmatrix} + \mu \begin{pmatrix} -1 \\ 2 \\ 3 \end{pmatrix}$ are skew. Find the shortest distance between them.

Try solving the problem in three different ways.

i This uses the scalar product, as in Strategy 1. Let P be a point on the first line and Q a point on the second line. The shortest distance is achieved when PQ is perpendicular to both lines.

    a Write $\overrightarrow{PQ}$ in terms of λ and μ.

    b Use the scalar product to obtain two equations for λ and μ.

    c Hence, find the minimum distance PQ.

ii Starting from part **a** above, show that $\left|\overrightarrow{PQ}\right|^2 = 14\mu^2 + 11\lambda^2 + 4\mu\lambda + 52\mu - 14\lambda + 65$. How could you find the minimum value of this expression?

101

iii Since PQ is perpendicular to both lines, the direction of $\overrightarrow{PQ}$ is parallel to the vector product of the two direction vectors.

a Find $\mathbf{n} = \begin{pmatrix} 3 \\ -1 \\ 1 \end{pmatrix} \times \begin{pmatrix} -1 \\ 2 \\ 3 \end{pmatrix}$.

b Point $A(-1, 2, 0)$ lies on the first line and point $B(-1, 3, 8)$ lies on the second line. Since $\mathbf{n}$ is perpendicular to both lines, PQ is the projection of AB onto the line with direction $\mathbf{n}$. Adapt the argument from question **1** to show that the length of PQ is $\dfrac{(\mathbf{a}-\mathbf{b})\cdot\mathbf{n}}{|\mathbf{n}|}$. Hence, show that the shortest distance between the two lines is $\sqrt{6}$.

> ▶▶ **Fast forward**
>
> You will learn a general version of this formula in Pure Core Student Book 2.

Focus on ... Modelling 1

Counting paths in networks: choosing the right representation

Describing the situation

There are many situations where we are interested in connections between places or people. Examples include road systems and social networks. For many purposes we can model such a situation as a **network** (or **graph**). This is a system of points (**nodes**) connected by lines (**edges**).

> **Fast forward**
>
> You will learn about graph theory if you study the Discrete option of Further Mathematics.

This kind of model shows only which nodes are connected by an edge; it ignores things like the shape of the road, the exact position of towns, or the nature of friendship in a social network (close friend, family, etc.) The model can be refined in several ways: the edges can have numbers associated with them (representing, for example, time or cost); sometimes edges can be directed (for example, in a network of one-way streets). There can also be more than one edge connecting two nodes; for example, there may be both a motorway and an A-road connecting two cities, or two people may be friends on several social networking sites.

One of the most famous network models is the map of the London Underground (the Tube).

The network in the diagram has three nodes (labelled A, B, C) and four edges (labelled p, q, r, s).

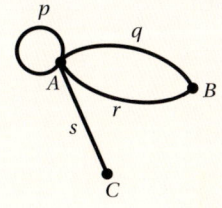

Selecting a mathematical representation

Although there are some problems that can be solved efficiently using pictures (e.g. in geometry and some probability), using equations is a far more common way in which to represent mathematical models. Furthermore, most network problems deal with very large networks and need to be solved using a computer; this means that we need to represent the information in a way that can be used in a computer program.

A useful way of representing a network is as a matrix. Each row and column corresponds to a node, and each entry is the number of edges connecting two nodes. This is called the **adjacency matrix** for the network. For example, the network shown can be represented by the matrix on the right.

$$\begin{array}{c} \\ A\\ B\\ C \end{array} \begin{array}{ccc} A & B & C \end{array} \\ \begin{pmatrix} 1 & 2 & 1 \\ 2 & 0 & 0 \\ 1 & 0 & 0 \end{pmatrix}$$

The circled number 2 shows that there are two edges between A and B. (Notice that, since the edges are not directed, the matrix is symmetrical.)

103

Here we will consider networks in which:

- there can be more than one edge connecting two nodes
- a node can be connected to itself
- the edges are not directed; this means that if A is connected to B then B is also connected to A
- we are interested only in the number of edges between two nodes, not their length or shape as drawn.

Using the model

A **path** between two nodes is a sequence of edges starting at the first node and ending at the second. For example, one path between C and B is $B \xrightarrow{r} A \xrightarrow{p} A \xrightarrow{s} C$; this path has 'length' 3 (it consists of three edges). A path can use the same edge more than once; for example, $A \xrightarrow{s} C \xrightarrow{s} A \xrightarrow{q} B \xrightarrow{r} A \xrightarrow{q} B$ is a path of length 5 between A and B.

You are going to solve this problem:

How can you count the number of paths of a given length between two given nodes?

For example, in the previous network, there are 6 paths of length 3 between A and C:

$A \xrightarrow{p} A \xrightarrow{p} A \xrightarrow{s} C$
$A \xrightarrow{s} C \xrightarrow{s} A \xrightarrow{s} C$
$A \xrightarrow{q} B \xrightarrow{q} A \xrightarrow{s} C$
$A \xrightarrow{q} B \xrightarrow{r} A \xrightarrow{s} C$
$A \xrightarrow{r} B \xrightarrow{q} A \xrightarrow{s} C$
$A \xrightarrow{r} B \xrightarrow{r} A \xrightarrow{s} C$

To get a feel for the problem, answer the following questions.

Questions

1 List all the paths of length 2 between:

    a A and B **b** A and A.

2 List all the paths of length 3 between:

    a B and C **b** B and B.

Even listing all the paths of length 3 seems reasonably complicated. How would you count all the paths of length 10? What would you do if your network had 1000 nodes?

It turns out that, with the matrix representation, it is possible to prove the following result:

The number of paths of length n between two nodes is given by the corresponding entry in the matrix M^n.

For example, $\mathbf{M}^3 = \begin{pmatrix} 11 & 12 & 6 \\ 12 & 4 & 2 \\ 6 & 2 & 1 \end{pmatrix}$, which shows that there are 6 paths of length 3 between A and C (as we saw earlier).

> **Fast forward**
>
> You can actually prove this result by induction (which you will meet in Chapter 6). To count the number of paths of length $k + 1$ between A and B, think about using paths of length k to get from A to another node, and then taking the final step from that node to B. The way you add up the number of different paths is the same as the way you multiply matrices.

3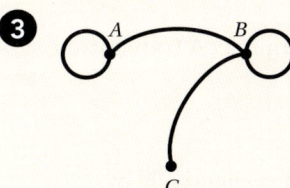

By representing this network as an adjacency matrix, find the number of paths:

a of length 2 between A and B
b of length 5 between A and C.

4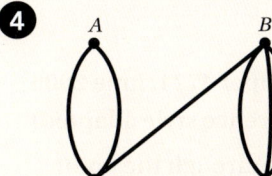

Find the number of paths:

a of length 10 between A and C
b of length 4 between A and A.

5 Can you adapt the model to answer the question about the number of paths in a directed network, such as this one?

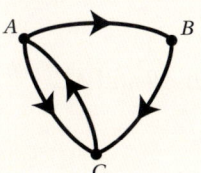

Find the number of paths of length 6:

a from B to A **b** from A to B **c** from C to C.

CROSS-TOPIC REVIEW EXERCISE 1

1. Find the value of c for which the matrix $\begin{pmatrix} 3 & -c \\ 1 & c+5 \end{pmatrix}$ is singular.

2. Find a vector equation of the line passing through the points $P(3, 12, -5)$ and $Q(-1, 1, 6)$.

3. Consider the matrix $\mathbf{A} = \begin{pmatrix} -3 & 1 \\ 1 & 2 \end{pmatrix}$.

   a Find det $\mathbf{A}$.

   S is a square with vertices $(1, 0)$, $(3, 0)$, $(1, 2)$ and $(3, 2)$. The transformation with matrix $\mathbf{A}$ transforms S into T.

   b Find the area of T.

4. The position vectors of three points, A, B and C relative to an origin O are given respectively by

   $\overrightarrow{OA} = 7\mathbf{i} + 3\mathbf{j} - 3\mathbf{k}$,

   $\overrightarrow{OB} = 4\mathbf{i} + 2\mathbf{j} - 4\mathbf{k}$,

   and $\overrightarrow{OC} = 5\mathbf{i} + 4\mathbf{j} - 5\mathbf{k}$.

   a Find the angle between AB and AC.

   b Find the area of triangle ABC.

   © OCR, GCE Further Mathematics, Paper 4724, June 2006
   [Question part reference style adapted]

5. The line L_1 passes through the points $(2, -3, 1)$ and $(-1, -2, -4)$. The line L_2 passes through the point $(3, 2, -9)$ and is parallel to the vector $4\mathbf{i} - 4\mathbf{j} + 5\mathbf{k}$.

   a Find an equation for L_1 in the form $\mathbf{r} = \mathbf{a} + t\mathbf{b}$.

   b Prove that L_1 and L_2 are skew.

   © OCR, GCE Further Mathematics, Paper 4724, June 2005
   [Question part reference style adapted]

6. Points A, B and C have coordinates $(-3, 1, 1)$, $(0, 5, 2)$ and $(1, -3, 6)$.

   a Find $\overrightarrow{AB} \times \overrightarrow{AC}$.

   b Hence, find a vector equation of the line through A that is perpendicular to both AB and AC.

7. The 3×3 matrix $\mathbf{R}$ represents the reflection in the plane $y = 0$.

   a By considering the images of the unit vectors $\mathbf{i}$, $\mathbf{j}$ and $\mathbf{k}$, find $\mathbf{R}$.

   b Find the determinant of $\mathbf{R}$ and explain what its value tells you about the reflection in the plane $y = 0$.

8. Two friends buy some fruit and vegetables. Arianne buys 2 bags of apples, 3 bags of bananas and 3 bags of carrots. She spends a total of £15. Filip buys 4 bags of apples, 1 bag of bananas and 5 bags of carrots. He spends a total of £15.20. A bag of bananas costs £1.20 more than a bag of apples.

   a Represent this information as a matrix equation.

   b Hence, find the cost of:

      i a bag of apples

      ii a bag of bananas

      iii a bag of carrots.

Cross-topic review exercise 1

9 Line l_1 passes through points $M(3, -7, 1)$ and $N(5, -5, 5)$.

   a Find a vector equation of l_1.

   b Given that l_1 intersects the line with equation $\mathbf{r} = (\mathbf{i} + 6\mathbf{k}) + \mu(-2\mathbf{i} + \mathbf{j} + p\mathbf{k})$, find the value of p.

10 Points A, B and C have coordinates $(-1, 4)$, $(1, 7)$ and $(3, 3)$.

   a Find, in degrees, the size of angle BAC.

   b Find the area of triangle ABC.

   A linear transformation $\mathbf{M}$ is represented by the matrix $\begin{pmatrix} 3 & -2 \\ -1 & 5 \end{pmatrix}$. The image of triangle ABC under $\mathbf{M}$ is PQR.

   c Find the area of the triangle PQR.

11 Given that $\mathbf{A}$ and $\mathbf{B}$ are 2×2 non-singular matrices and $\mathbf{I}$ is the 2×2 identity matrix, simplify $\mathbf{B(AB)}^{-1}\mathbf{A} - \mathbf{I}$.

© OCR, AS GCE Further Mathematics, Paper 4725, January 2009

12 Determine whether the lines $\dfrac{x-1}{1} = \dfrac{y+2}{-1} = \dfrac{z+4}{2}$ and $\dfrac{x+3}{2} = \dfrac{y-1}{3} = \dfrac{z-5}{4}$ intersect or are skew.

© OCR, GCE Further Mathematics, Paper 4727, January 2010

13 The matrix $\mathbf{D}$ is given by $\mathbf{D} = \begin{pmatrix} a & 2 & 0 \\ 3 & 1 & 2 \\ 0 & -1 & 1 \end{pmatrix}$, where $a \neq 2$.

   a Find $\mathbf{D}^{-1}$.

   b Hence, or otherwise, solve the equations

   $ax + 2y = 3$,

   $3x + y + 2z = 4$,

   $-y + z = 1$.

© OCR, AS GCE Further Mathematics, Paper 4725, January 2007
[Question part reference style adapted]

14 The transformation represented by the matrix $\mathbf{M} = \begin{pmatrix} -3 & 4 \\ 4 & 3 \end{pmatrix}$ has an invariant line $y = cx$ with $c > 0$.

   a Find the value of c.

   b Show that this is not a line of invariant points.

15 Let $\mathbf{R}$ be a rotation $90°$ anticlockwise about the x-axis.

   a Write down the 3×3 matrix for $\mathbf{R}$.

   Points A and B have coordinates $(2, 0, 5)$ and $(-1, 3, 7)$. Their images under the transformation $\mathbf{R}$ are points M and N.

   b Show that the line MN is not perpendicular to the line AB.

16 The equation of a straight line l is $\mathbf{r} = \begin{pmatrix} 3 \\ 1 \\ 1 \end{pmatrix} + t \begin{pmatrix} 1 \\ -1 \\ 2 \end{pmatrix}$. O is the origin.

   a The point P on l is given by $t = 1$. Calculate the acute angle between OP and l.
   b Find the position vector of the point Q on l such that OQ is perpendicular to l.
   c Find the length of OQ.

   © OCR, GCE Further Mathematics, Paper 4724, January 2010
   [Question part reference style adapted]

17 A linear transformation is represented by the matrix $\mathbf{M} = \begin{pmatrix} 3 & -1 \\ 0 & a \end{pmatrix}$. Line l_1 has equation $\mathbf{r} = \begin{pmatrix} 1 \\ 0 \end{pmatrix} + t \begin{pmatrix} -3 \\ 1 \end{pmatrix}$. Line l_2 is the image of l_1 under the transformation $\mathbf{M}$. Find the value of a such that l_2 is perpendicular to l_1.

4 Complex numbers

In this chapter you will learn:

- about a new set of numbers called the complex numbers
- how to do arithmetic with complex numbers
- why complex roots of real polynomials occur in conjugate pairs
- about a geometric representation of complex numbers
- how arithmetic with complex numbers can be interpreted as geometric transformations
- how to represent equations and inequalities with complex numbers graphically.

Before you start …

GCSE	You should be able to use the quadratic formula.	1	Solve the equation $3x^2 - 6x + 2 = 0$, giving your answers in simplified surd form.
A Level Mathematics Student Book 1, Chapter 5	You should be able to solve simultaneous equations.	2	Solve the simultaneous equations: $$\begin{cases} x + 2y = 5 \\ x^2 + y^2 = 10 \end{cases}$$
A Level Mathematics Student Book 2, Chapter 7	You should be able to use radians.	3	Write each angle in radians. a 60°　b 150°　c 240°
		4	Find the exact value of: a $\sin\left(\dfrac{3\pi}{4}\right)$ b $\cos\left(-\dfrac{\pi}{6}\right)$ c $\tan\left(\dfrac{4\pi}{3}\right)$.
GCSE	You should be able to represent a locus of points on a diagram.	5	Draw two points, P and Q, 5 cm apart. Shade the locus of all the points that are less than 3 cm from P and closer to Q than to P.

Extending the number system

Until now, every number you have met has probably been a real number. You may have also been told that it is not possible to find the square root of a negative number. However, in this chapter, you are introduced to the idea that there is a number that can be squared to give -1. We do not claim that this number is real; in fact, we call it an **imaginary number**. This idea leads to a whole new branch of numbers: complex numbers. Remarkably, these numbers end up having many useful applications in the real world, from electrical impedance in electronics to the Schrödinger equation in quantum mechanics!

A Level Further Mathematics for OCR A Pure Core Student Book 1

Section 1: Definition and basic arithmetic of i

There is no real number that is a solution to the equation $x^2 = -1$, but mathematicians have defined there to be an imaginary number that solves this equation. This imaginary number is given the symbol i.

> **Key point 4.1**
>
> $$i^2 = -1$$
>
> In all other ways, i acts just like a normal constant.

> **Tip**
>
> $(-i)^2$ also equals -1.

WORKED EXAMPLE 4.1

Simplify the following:

a i^3 **b** i^4 **c** i^5

a $i^3 = i^2 \times i$ *Use normal laws of indices.*

$ = (-1)i$

$ = -i$ $i^2 = -1$

b $i^4 = i^2 \times i^2$

$ = (-1)^2$

$ = 1$

c $i^5 = i^4 \times i$

$ = 1 \times i$

$ = i$

You need to be familiar with some common terminology.

- A **complex number** is one that can be written in the form $x + iy$, where x and y are real. Commonly, z is used to denote an unknown complex number and $\mathbb{C}$ is used for the set of all complex numbers.
- In the previous definition, x is the **real part** of z and is given the symbol $\text{Re}(z)$; y is the **imaginary part** of z and is given the symbol $\text{Im}(z)$. So, for example, $\text{Re}(3 - i)$ is 3 and $\text{Im}(3 - i)$ is -1.

> **Tip**
>
> Remember that the symbol for the set of real numbers is $\mathbb{R}$.

> **Tip**
>
> Note that the imaginary part is itself real, that is, 'y' not 'iy'.

You can now do some arithmetic with complex numbers.

> **Tip**
>
> Your calculator may have a 'complex' mode, which you can use to check your calculations.

WORKED EXAMPLE 4.2

If $z = 3 + \text{i}$ and $w = 5 - 2\text{i}$, find:

a $z + w$ **b** $z - w$ **c** zw **d** $w \div 2$

a $(3+\text{i})+(5-2\text{i}) = (3+5)+(\text{i}-2\text{i})$
$= 8 - \text{i}$

Group the real and imaginary parts.

b $(3+\text{i})-(5-2\text{i}) = (3+5)+(\text{i}+(-2\text{i}))$
$= -2 + 3\text{i}$

Group real and imaginary parts.

c $(3+\text{i})\times(5-2\text{i}) = (3\times5)+(3\times(-2\text{i}))$
$+(\text{i}\times5)+(\text{i}\times(-2\text{i}))$

Multiply out the brackets.

$= 15 - 6\text{i} + 5\text{i} - 2\text{i}^2$
$= 15 - \text{i} - (2\times -1)$
$= 17 - \text{i}$

Remember, $\text{i}^2 = -1$.

d $\frac{5-2\text{i}}{2} = \frac{5}{2} - \frac{2\text{i}}{2}$
$= 2.5 - \text{i}$

Use normal rules of fractions.

The original purpose of introducing complex numbers is to solve quadratic equations with negative discriminants.

Tip

You will see later that the square root of a complex number cannot be uniquely defined. However, it is common to use the square root symbol in the quadratic formula.

WORKED EXAMPLE 4.3

a Find $\sqrt{-4}$.

b Hence, solve the equation $x^2 - 4x + 5 = 0$.

a $\sqrt{-4} = \sqrt{4}\sqrt{-1}$

Use standard rules of square roots, $\sqrt{ab} = \sqrt{a}\sqrt{b}$.

$= 2\text{i}$

Use $\text{i} = \sqrt{-1}$.

b $x = \frac{4 \pm \sqrt{16 - 4\times1\times5}}{2}$

Use the quadratic formula.

$= \frac{4 \pm \sqrt{-4}}{2}$

$= \frac{4 \pm 2\text{i}}{2}$

Use the expression for $\sqrt{-4}$ from part **a**.

$= 2 \pm \text{i}$

Did you know?

You may be sceptical about the idea of 'imagining' numbers. However, when negative numbers were introduced by the Indian mathematician Brahmagupta in the 7th century there was just as much scepticism. 'How can you have −2 carrots?' people would ask. In Europe, it took until the 17th century for negative numbers to be accepted. Mathematicians had worked successfully for thousands of years without using negative numbers, treating equations like $x + 3 = 0$ as having no solution. However, once negative numbers were 'invented' it took only a hundred years or so to accept that equations such as $x^2 + 3 = 0$ also have a solution.

Focus on …

Focus on … Problem-solving 2 shows how you can use complex numbers to solve some cubic equations.

When you look at a new number system, one of the most important questions to ask is: When are two numbers equal?

Key point 4.2

If two complex numbers are equal, then their real parts are the same and their imaginary parts are the same.

Tip

A complex number is zero if and only if both real and imaginary parts are both zero.

Although this may seem obvious, in mathematics it pays to be careful. For example, if two rational numbers $\frac{a}{b}$ and $\frac{c}{d}$ are equal, it does not mean that $a = c$ and $b = d$.

Despite its apparent simplicity, Key point 4.2 has some remarkably powerful uses. One is to find square roots of complex numbers.

WORKED EXAMPLE 4.4

Solve the equation $z^2 = 8 - 6i$.

Let $z = x + iy$ — z is a complex number, so write $z = x + iy$, where x and y are real.

$$z^2 = 8 - 6i$$

$$(x + iy)^2 = 8 - 6i$$

$$x^2 + 2xyi + (iy)^2 = 8 - 6i$$ — Expand the brackets.

$$x^2 + 2xyi - y^2 = 8 - 6i$$ — Remember that $i^2 = -1$.

Real: $x^2 - y^2 = 8$ \quad (1)

Imaginary: $2xy = -6$ \quad (2)

Now equate the real and imaginary parts.

From (2): $y = -\dfrac{3}{x}$ — Use substitution to solve these simultaneous equations.

Continues on next page …

Substituting into (1):
$$x^2 - \frac{9}{x^2} = 8$$
$$x^4 - 9 = 8x^2$$
$$x^4 - 8x^2 - 9 = 0$$
$$(x^2 - 9)(x^2 + 1) = 0$$
$$x^2 - 9 = 0 \text{ or } x^2 + 1 = 0$$
$$x = \pm 3$$

Multiplying through by x^2 leads to a disguised quadratic.

There are two possible values for x^2. However, x is real so $x^2 + 1 = 0$ is impossible.

$$y = -\frac{3}{x}$$
$$= \mp 1$$

Find y for each x (using equation (2)).

$$z = 3 - i \text{ or } -3 + i$$

Write the answer in the form $z = x + iy$.

Notice that there are two numbers that have the same square; this is consistent with what you have already seen with real numbers.

EXERCISE 4A

In questions **2–7**, you may be able to use a calculator to check your answer. However, you need to be able to show full non–calculator working.

1 State the imaginary part of each complex number.

   a   **i** $-3 + 5i$ **ii** $8 - 2i$

   b   **i** $6 + i$ **ii** $19 - i$

   c   **i** $2i - 8$ **ii** $7i - 2$

   d   **i** 15 **ii** $-3i$

   e   **i** i^2 **ii** $(1 + i) - i$

   f   **i** $1 + ai + b - i \quad a, b \in \mathbb{R}$ **ii** $2 - 4i - (bi - a) \quad a, b \in \mathbb{R}$

2 Evaluate, giving your answer in the form $x + iy$.

   a   **i** $2i + 3i$ **ii** $i - 9i$

   b   **i** $5i^2$ **ii** $-i^2$

   c   **i** $(-3i)^2$ **ii** $(4i)^2$

   d   **i** $(4i + 3) - (6i - 2)$ **ii** $2(2i - 1) - 3(4 - 2i)$

3 Evaluate, giving your answer in the form $x + iy$.

   a   **i** $i(1 + i)$ **ii** $3i(2 - 5i)$

   b   **i** $(2 + i)(1 + 2i)$ **ii** $(5 + 2i)(4 + 3i)$

   c   **i** $(2 + 3i)(1 - 2i)$ **ii** $(3 + i)(5 - i)$

   d   **i** $(3 + i)^2$ **ii** $(4 - 3i)^2$

   e   **i** $\left(\frac{\sqrt{3}}{2} + \frac{1}{2}i\right)\left(\frac{\sqrt{3}}{2} - \frac{1}{2}i\right)$ **ii** $(3 + 2i)(3 - 2i)$

> **Tip**
>
> 'giving your answer in the form $x + iy$' requires x and y to be real values. If either is zero, there is no need to write "0 +" or "+ 0i"; for example, an answer of $0 + 2i$ can be given simply as $2i$.

A Level Further Mathematics for OCR A Pure Core Student Book 1

4 Evaluate, giving your answer in the form $x + iy$.

  a **i** $\dfrac{6+8i}{2}$ **ii** $\dfrac{9-3i}{3}$

  b **i** $\dfrac{5+2i}{10}$ **ii** $\dfrac{i-4}{8}$

  c **i** $\dfrac{3+i}{2} + i$ **ii** $9i - \dfrac{6-4i}{2}$

5 Evaluate, giving your answer in the form $x + iy$.

  a **i** $\sqrt{-4}$ **ii** $\sqrt{-49}$

  b **i** $\sqrt{-8}$ **ii** $\sqrt{-50}$

  c **i** $\dfrac{4-\sqrt{-36}}{3}$ **ii** $\dfrac{-1+\sqrt{-25}}{3}$

  d **i** $\dfrac{2+\sqrt{16-25}}{6}$ **ii** $\dfrac{5-2\sqrt{4-9}}{4}$

6 Solve the equations, simplifying your answers.

  a **i** $x^2 + 9 = 0$ **ii** $x^2 + 36 = 0$

  b **i** $x^2 = -10$ **ii** $x^2 = -13$

  c **i** $x^2 - 2x + 5 = 0$ **ii** $x^2 - x + 10 = 0$

  d **i** $3x^2 + 20 = 6x$ **ii** $6x + 5 = -5x^2$

7 Evaluate, simplifying your answers.

  a **i** i^3 **ii** i^4

  b **i** $(-2i)^4$ **ii** $(-5i)^3$

  c **i** $(1 - \sqrt{3}i)^3$ **ii** $(\sqrt{3} + i)^3$

  d **i** $\left(\dfrac{\sqrt{3}}{2} + \dfrac{1}{2}i\right)^3$ **ii** $\left(-\dfrac{\sqrt{3}}{2} + \dfrac{1}{2}i\right)^3$

8 Find real numbers a and b such that:

  a **i** $(a+bi)(3-2i) = 5i + 1$ **ii** $(6+i)(a+bi) = 2$

  b **i** $(a+2i)(1+2i) = 4 - bi$ **ii** $(1+ai)(1+i) = b + 2i$

  c **i** $(a+bi)(2+i) = 2a - (b-1)i$ **ii** $i(a+bi) = a - 6i$

9 By writing $z = x + iy$, solve these equations.

  a **i** $z^2 = -4i$ **ii** $z^2 = 9i$

  b **i** $z^2 = 2 + 2\sqrt{3}i$ **ii** $z^2 = 5 + i$

10 Find the exact values of $a, b \in \mathbb{R}$ such that $(3 + ai)(b - i) = -4i$. Give your answers in the form $k\sqrt{3}$.

11 Let $\mathbf{A} = \begin{pmatrix} 0 & i \\ i & 0 \end{pmatrix}$.

  a Find $\mathbf{A}^2$ and $\mathbf{A}^3$, and show that $\mathbf{A}^4 = \mathbf{I}$.

  b Hence, find $\mathbf{A}^{26}$.

⏮ **Rewind**

Operations with matrices were covered in Chapter 1.

12 Find the determinant of the matrix $\begin{pmatrix} 4-i & 2i \\ 1+i & 1+3i \end{pmatrix}$.

13 Find the exact values of $a, b \in \mathbb{R}$ such that $(1+ai)(1+bi) = b + 9i - a$.

14 By writing $z = x + iy$, solve the equation $iz + 2 = i - 3z$.

15 **In this question you must show detailed reasoning.**
   a Find values x and y such that $(x + iy)(2 + i) = -i$.
   b Hence, express $\dfrac{-3i}{2+i}$ in the form $x + iy$.

16 By writing $z = x + iy$, solve the equation $z^2 = -3 - 4i$.

17 Solve the equation $z^2 = i$.

18 Use an algebraic method to solve the equation $z^2 = 12 - 5i$.

Section 2: Division and complex conjugates

In Section 1, you saw that quadratic equations may have two complex roots. In Worked example 4.3, the roots were $2 + i$ and $2 - i$; the imaginary part arises from the term after the $\pm$ sign in the quadratic formula. These two numbers form what is called a **conjugate pair**. They differ only in the sign of the imaginary part.

> **Key point 4.3**
>
> If $z = x + iy$, then the **complex conjugate** of z is $z^* = x - iy$.

So, for example, the complex conjugate of $z = 2 + i$ is $z^* = 2 - i$.

At first, the concept of conjugates may not appear to be particularly useful, but they are needed when it comes to dividing complex numbers. This is best illustrated with an example.

WORKED EXAMPLE 4.5

Write $\dfrac{3+2i}{5-i}$ in the form $x + iy$.

$\dfrac{3+2i}{5-i} = \dfrac{3+2i}{5-i} \times \dfrac{5+i}{5+i}$ — Multiply numerator and denominator by the complex conjugate of the denominator.

$= \dfrac{15 + 10i + 3i + 2i^2}{5^2 - i^2}$ — Use the difference of two squares in the denominator: $(a-b)(a+b) = a^2 - b^2$.

$= \dfrac{13 + 13i}{25 - (-1)}$ — Remember that $i^2 = -1$.

$= 0.5 + 0.5i$

Worked example 4.5 illustrates the general procedure for dividing by a complex number.

Key point 4.4

To divide by a complex number, multiply the numerator and denominator by its conjugate.

 Tip

This procedure should remind you of rationalising the denominator, which is also based on the difference of two squares.

You can prove that this procedure always results in a real number in the denominator.

PROOF 5

Prove that zz^* is always real.

Let $z = x + iy$, where x and y are real

Then $z^* = x - iy$

Writing z and z^* in terms of their real and imaginary parts is often the best way to prove results about complex conjugates.

So
$zz^* = (x + iy)(x - iy)$
$= x^2 - ixy + iyx - i^2y^2$
$= x^2 - (-y^2)$
$= x^2 + y^2$

Use the fact that $i^2 = -1$.

… which is real.

Remember that x and y are real numbers, so their squares are also real.

The next example shows how the idea of equating real and imaginary parts can be used to solve equations involving complex conjugates.

WORKED EXAMPLE 4.6

Find the complex number z such that $3z + 2z^* = 5 + 2i$.

Let $z = x + iy$

Then

As you saw in Proof 5, the best way to approach a problem involving complex conjugates is often to write z and z^* in terms of their real and imaginary parts.

$3z + 2z^* = 5 + 2i$

$3(x + iy) + 2(x - iy) = 5 + 2i$

$5x + iy = 5 + 2i$

Real: $5x = 5$

You can now equate real and imaginary parts.

Imaginary: $y = 2$

$x = 1, y = 2$

So $z = 1 + 2i$

Being able to divide complex numbers means that you can solve more complicated equations.

WORKED EXAMPLE 4.7

Solve these simultaneous equations:

$$\begin{cases}(1+i)z+(2-i)w=3+4i \\ iz+(3+i)w=-1+5i\end{cases}$$

$\begin{cases}(1+i)z+(2-i)w=3+4i \\ iz+(3+i)w=-1+5i\end{cases}$ The best method to use here is elimination: multiply the first equation by i and the second by $(1+i)$ …

$\begin{cases}i(1+i)z+i(2-i)w=i(3+4i) \\ (1+i)iz+(1+i)(3+i)w=(1+i)(-1+5i)\end{cases}$

$\begin{cases}(1+i)iz+(1+2i)w=-4+3i \\ (1+i)iz+(2+4i)w=-6+4i\end{cases}$

Subtracting: … and then subtract them to eliminate z.

$(-1-2i)w=2-i$

$w=\dfrac{2-i}{-1-2i}\times\dfrac{-1+2i}{-1+2i}$ Divide by $(-1-2i)$: multiply the top and bottom by the complex conjugate.

$=\dfrac{5i}{1+4}$

$=i$

$iz+(3+i)w=-1+5i$ Substitute back to find z: use the second equation as it looks simpler.

$iz+(3+i)(i)=-1+5i$

$iz+(-1+3i)=-1+5i$

$iz=2i$

$z=2$

So $z=2$, $w=i$

Tip

You can also use matrix methods from Chapter 3, Section 1 to solve simultaneous equations.

EXERCISE 4B

1   State the complex conjugate of each number.

   a   **i** $2-3i$ **ii** $4+4i$

   b   **i** $i-3$ **ii** $3i+2$

   c   **i** $3i$ **ii** $-i$

   d   **i** -45 **ii** 9

2 Write the following in the form $x+iy$. Use a calculator to check your answers.

  a i $\dfrac{3-2i}{1+2i}$ **ii** $\dfrac{4i}{3-5i}$

  b i $\dfrac{4}{i}$ **ii** $-\dfrac{1}{i}$

  c i $\dfrac{4+i}{4-i}$ **ii** $\dfrac{2i+1}{2i-1}$

  d i $\dfrac{(1+i)^2}{1-i}$ **ii** $\dfrac{(i-2)^2}{i+2}$

3 Solve these equations.

  a $2z-3=4-3(i+z)$ **b** $2iz+1=4i(z-3)$

4 Solve these simultaneous equations.

  a $\begin{cases} 2z-3iw=5 \\ (1+i)z+3w=-4i \end{cases}$ **b** $\begin{cases} (1+i)z+(1-i)w=1 \\ (1-i)z+2iw=i \end{cases}$

> **Tip**
>
> In question **4** you can use either inverse matrices, or the method shown in Worked example 4.7.

5 Find the complex number z if:

  a $2z^*-1=4i$ **b** $3z^*+2=9i$

6 By writing $z=x+iy$, solve these equations.

  a $z+2z^*=2-7i$ **b** $2z+iz^*=-3-i$

7 If x and y are real numbers, find the complex conjugate z^* when:

  a i $z=3+(x+iy)$ **ii** $z=x-(2-iy)$

  b i $z=(x+3iy)+(2-i)$ **ii** $z=(3+3i)-(x-iy)$

  c i $z=x+iy+\dfrac{1}{x+iy}$ **ii** $z=x+iy-\dfrac{1}{x+iy}$

  d i $z=\dfrac{x}{x+iy}-\dfrac{x}{x-iy}$ **ii** $z=\dfrac{x}{x+iy}+\dfrac{x}{x-iy}$

8 Write $\dfrac{3-5i}{2i-1}$ in the form $a+bi$. Show all your working.

9 Let $z=x+iy$.

  a Find in terms of x and y the real and imaginary parts of $3iz+2z^*$.

  b Find the complex number z such that $3iz+2z^*=4-4i$.

10 Find real numbers x and y such that $x+3iy=z+4iz^*$, where $z=2+i$.

11 By writing $z=x+iy$ prove that $(z^*)^2=(z^2)^*$.

12 Solve $z+3z^*=i$.

13 Solve $z+i=1-z^*$.

14 The matrix $\mathbf{A}$ is given by $\mathbf{A}=\begin{pmatrix} 1+i & 2-i \\ i & 3+i \end{pmatrix}$.

  a Show that $\mathbf{A}^{-1}=\dfrac{1}{1+2i}\begin{pmatrix} 3+i & -2+i \\ -i & 1+i \end{pmatrix}$.

> **Rewind**
>
> Compare this to the method used in Worked example 4.7. Which do you prefer?

b Hence, solve the system of equations:
$$\begin{cases}(1+i)z+(2-i)w=3+4i\\iz+(3+i)w=-1+5i\end{cases}$$

15 If $z = x + iy$, find the real and the imaginary parts of $\dfrac{z}{z+1}$ in terms of x and y, simplifying your answers as far as possible.

Section 3: Geometric representation

Real numbers can be represented on a number line:

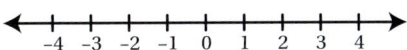

To represent complex numbers you can add another axis, perpendicular to the real number line, to show the imaginary part. The result is called an **Argand diagram**. The two axes are called the **real axis** and the **imaginary axis**.

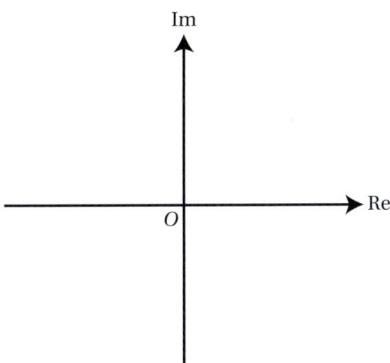

> **i) Did you know?**
>
> Using real and imaginary axes was first suggested by the land surveyor Caspar Wessel. However, this type of diagram is named after Jean–Robert Argand, who popularised the idea.

WORKED EXAMPLE 4.8

Represent $3 - 2i$ on an Argand diagram.

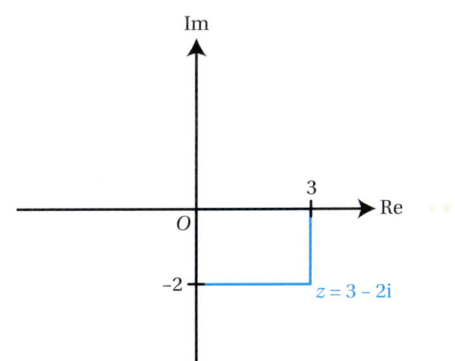

The real part is 3; this is represented by 3 units on the horizontal axis.

The imaginary part is −2; this is represented as 2 units on the negative vertical axis.

Operations with complex numbers have useful representations on an Argand diagram.

Consider two numbers, $z_1 = x_1 + iy_1$ and $z_2 = x_2 + iy_2$. On the diagram they are represented by points with coordinates (x_1, y_1) and (x_2, y_2). Their sum, $z_1 + z_2 = (x_1 + x_2) + i(y_1 + y_2)$, has coordinates $(x_1 + x_2, y_1 + y_2)$.

But you can also think of coordinates as position vectors:

$$\begin{pmatrix} x_1 \\ y_1 \end{pmatrix} + \begin{pmatrix} x_2 \\ y_2 \end{pmatrix} = \begin{pmatrix} x_1 + x_2 \\ y_1 + y_2 \end{pmatrix}$$

So you can add complex numbers geometrically by adding vectors:

You can represent subtraction similarly, by adding the negative of the second number.

Taking a complex conjugate results in a reflection in the real axis.

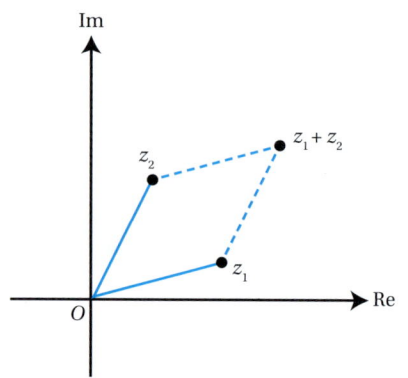
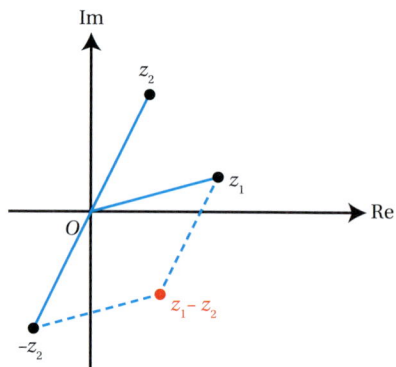
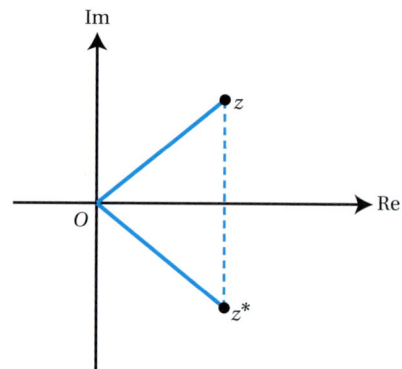

WORKED EXAMPLE 4.9

Two complex numbers, z and w, are shown on the Argand diagram.

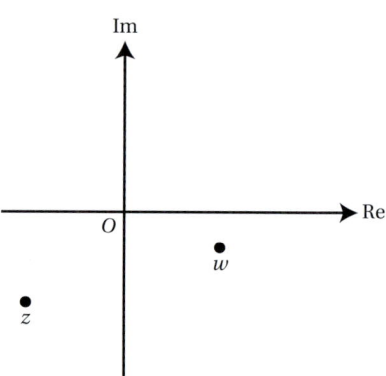

On the same diagram represent the numbers:

a $w - z$ **b** z^*

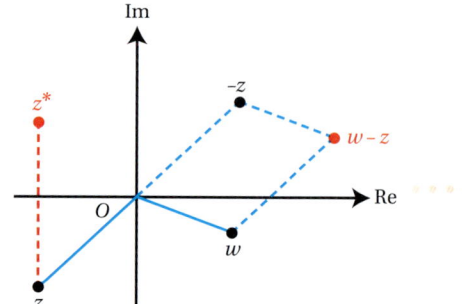

a To find $w - z$, first label $-z$ and then draw a parallelogram.

b z^* is the reflection of z in the real axis.

4 Complex numbers

EXERCISE 4C

1 Represent the following numbers on an Argand diagram. Use a separate diagram for each part.

   a   **i** $z = 4 + i$ and $w = 2i$ **ii** $z = -3 + i$ and $w = -3i$

   b   **i** $z, -z$ and iz when $z = 4 + 3i$ **ii** $z, -z$ and iz when $z = -2 + 5i$

   c   **i** $z, 3z, -2z$ and $-iz$ when $z = 2 + i$ **ii** $z, 2z$ and $2iz$ when $z = 1 - 3i$

2 Solve these quadratic equations and represent the solutions on an Argand diagram.

   a   **i** $z^2 - 4z + 13 = 0$ **ii** $z^2 - 10z + 26 = 0$

   b   **i** $z^2 + 2z + 17 = 0$ **ii** $z^2 + 6z + 13 = 0$

3 Each diagram shows two complex numbers, z and w. Copy each diagram and add the points corresponding to z^*, $-w$ and $z + w$.

   a   **i**

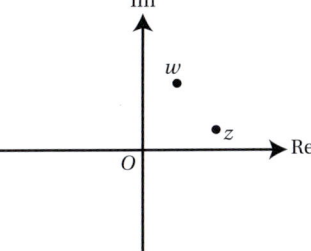

         ii

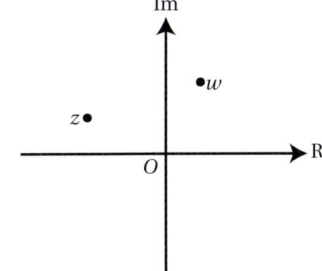

   b   **i**

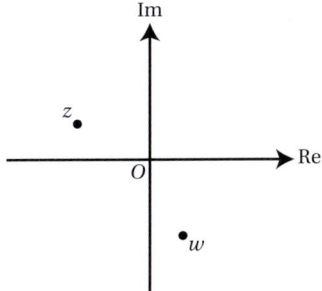

         ii

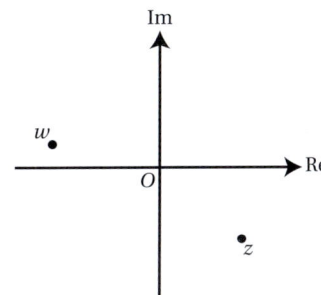

Section 4: Modulus and argument

When a complex number is represented on an Argand diagram, its distance from the origin is called the **modulus**. There are lots of complex numbers with the same modulus; they form a circle centred at the origin. You can uniquely describe a particular complex number by also giving its angle relative to the real axis; this is called the **argument**. The argument is conventionally measured in radians, anticlockwise from the positive real axis.

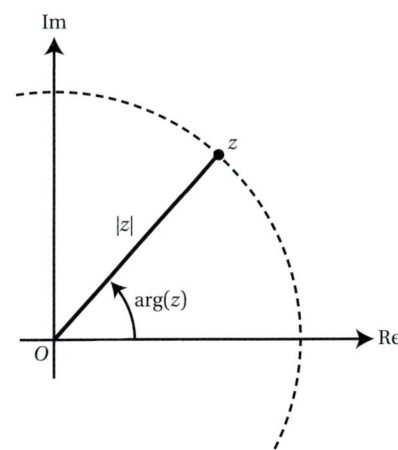

The symbols used for these are:

- $|z|$ or r for the modulus
- $\arg(z)$ or θ for the argument.

The notation $z = [r, \theta]$ is used for a complex number z with modulus r and argument θ.

The description of a complex number like this is called the **modulus-argument form**.

The description in terms of the real and imaginary parts, $z = x + iy$ is called the **Cartesian form**.

Review of radians

Radian is an alternative measure of angle, and is the most commonly used unit for angles in advanced mathematics. A full turn measures 2π radians. From this, you can deduce the sizes of other common angles; for example, a right angle is one-quarter of a full turn, so it measures $2\pi \div 4 = \frac{\pi}{2}$ radians. Although the sizes of common angles measured in radians are often expressed as fractions of π, you can also use decimal approximations. Thus, a right angle measures approximately 1.57 radians.

> **Explore**
>
> Is this definition of $|z|$ the same as or different from $|x|$, where x is real? In what other situations is the modulus sign used?

> **Rewind**
>
> Radians are covered in more detail in A Level Mathematics Student Book 2, Chapter 7.

WORKED EXAMPLE 4.10

a Convert 75° to radians.

b Convert 2.5 radians to degrees.

a $\dfrac{75}{360} = \dfrac{5}{24}$ What fraction of a full turn is 75°?

$\dfrac{5}{24} \times 2\pi = \dfrac{5\pi}{12}$ Calculate the same fraction of 2π.

$\therefore 75° = \dfrac{5\pi}{12}$ radians   This is the exact answer.

$75° = 1.31$ radians (3 s.f.)   You can also find the decimal equivalent, to 3 significant figures.

b $\dfrac{2.5}{2\pi} (\approx 0.3979)$ What fraction of a full turn is 2.5 radians?

$\dfrac{2.5}{2\pi} \times 360 = 143.24\ldots$ Calculate the same fraction of 360°.

2.5 radians = 143° (3 s.f.)

> **Key point 4.5**
>
> one full turn = 360° = 2π radians
>
> - To convert from degrees to radians, divide by 180 and multiply by π.
> - To convert from radians to degrees, divide by π and multiply by 180.

> **Tip**
>
> When you need to evaluate trigonometric functions of angles in radians, make sure your calculator is in the radian mode.

Here are some common angles in radians:

Degrees	0°	30°	45°	60°	90°	180°
Radians	0	$\frac{\pi}{6}$	$\frac{\pi}{4}$	$\frac{\pi}{3}$	$\frac{\pi}{2}$	π

EXERCISE 4D

1 Express each angle in radians, giving your answer in terms of π.

   a **i** 135°   **ii** 45°   **b** **i** 90°   **ii** 270°

   c **i** 120°   **ii** 150°   **d** **i** 50°   **ii** 80°

2 Express each angle in radians, correct to 3 decimal places.

   a **i** 320°   **ii** 20°   **b** **i** 270°   **ii** 90°

   c **i** 65°   **ii** 145°   **d** **i** 100°   **ii** 83°

3 Express each angle in degrees.

   a **i** $\frac{\pi}{3}$ **ii** $\frac{\pi}{4}$ **b** **i** $\frac{5\pi}{6}$ **ii** $\frac{2\pi}{3}$

   c **i** $\frac{3\pi}{2}$ **ii** $\frac{5\pi}{3}$ **d** **i** 1.22   **ii** 4.63

Converting between the modulus–argument and Cartesian forms

To convert between the modulus–argument and Cartesian forms you can use the Argand diagram and some trigonometry.

Key point 4.6

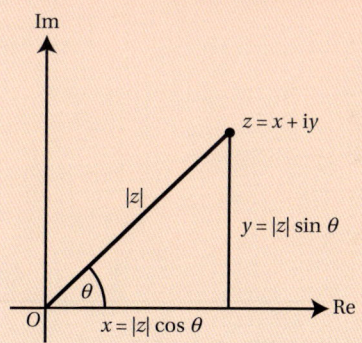

To convert from modulus-argument form to Cartesian form:

$x = |z| \cos\theta$

$y = |z| \sin\theta$

To convert from Cartesian to modulus-argument form:

$|z| = \sqrt{x^2 + y^2}$

$\tan\theta = \frac{y}{x}$

Tip

Some calculators can convert between modulus–argument and Cartesian forms.

Tip

If Re(z) > 0 then
arg(z) = arctan$\left(\frac{y}{x}\right)$

If Re(z) < 0 then
arg(z) = arctan$\left(\frac{y}{x}\right) \pm \pi$

You can draw a diagram to check.

WORKED EXAMPLE 4.11

A complex number z has modulus 3 and argument $\dfrac{\pi}{6}$. Write the number in Cartesian form.

$x = 3\cos\dfrac{\pi}{6} = \dfrac{3\sqrt{3}}{2}$ ………… Use $x = |z|\cos\theta$ and $y = |z|\sin\theta$.

$y = 3\sin\dfrac{\pi}{6} = \dfrac{3}{2}$

$\therefore z = \dfrac{3\sqrt{3}}{2} + \dfrac{3}{2}i$ ………… The Cartesian form is $z = x + iy$.

Although the argument can take any value, the **principal argument** is defined as lying between 0 and 2π or between $-\pi$ and π. In the latter case, the numbers in the bottom half of the Argand diagram will have negative principal arguments. Unless a question specifies, either of the standard intervals is acceptable.

Any arguments outside the standard interval can be converted to the equivalent principal argument by adding or subtracting the appropriate multiple of 2π, since full rotations about the origin make no difference to the position of a point in the Argand diagram.

> **Tip**
>
> Always draw the complex number in an Argand diagram before finding the argument. It is important you know which angle you need to find.

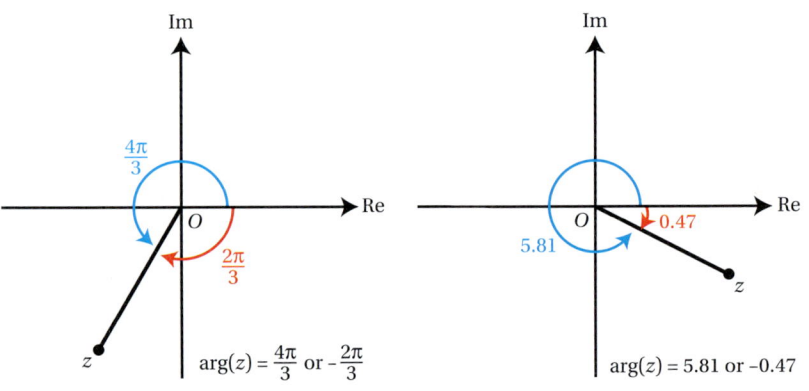

WORKED EXAMPLE 4.12

Write $2 - 3i$ in modulus-argument form, with the argument between 0 and 2π. Give your answer to 3 s.f.

$|z| = \sqrt{2^2 + (-3)^2}$ ………… Use $|z| = \sqrt{x^2 + y^2}$.

$= \sqrt{13}$

$= 3.61$ (3 s.f.)

Continues on next page ...

4 Complex numbers

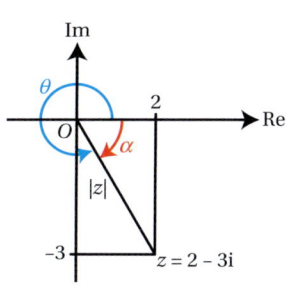

$\tan \alpha = \dfrac{3}{2}$

$\therefore \alpha = 0.983$ .... Find the angle α.

$\theta = 2\pi - 0.983$ .... From the diagram, $\theta = 2\pi - \alpha$.

$\quad = 5.30 \text{ (3 s.f.)}$

So $z = [3.61, 5.30]$ .... Remember that a complex number with modulus r and argument θ can be written as $[r, \theta]$.

.... Draw a diagram to see where the complex number actually is.

WORK IT OUT 4.1

Find the argument of $z = -5 - 3i$, where $-\pi < \arg(z) \leqslant \pi$.

Which is the correct solution? Can you identify the errors made in the incorrect solutions?

Solution 1	Solution 2	Solution 3
$\arctan\left(\dfrac{3}{5}\right) = 0.540$	$\arg(z) = -\arctan\left(\dfrac{3}{5}\right)$	$\arctan\left(\dfrac{-3}{-5}\right) = 0.540$
$\pi - 0.540 = 2.60$	$\quad = -0.540$	
$\arg(z) = -2.60$		

There is another useful way to express complex numbers:

$z = x + iy$
$\quad = |z|\cos\theta + i|z|\sin\theta$
$\quad = |z|(\cos\theta + i\sin\theta)$

Although, strictly speaking, this is a Cartesian form, it explicitly shows the modulus and the argument.

The same value of θ appears in both the cosine and the sine terms, so we can introduce a shorthand: cis θ stands for $\cos\theta + i\sin\theta$.

Focus on ...

Because modulus and argument are related to trigonometric functions, complex numbers can be used to model many periodic phenomena. Focus on … Modelling 2 shows you how they are used in electronics, to model alternating current.

Key point 4.7

A complex number z with modulus r and argument θ can be written as:

$$z = [r, \theta] = r \operatorname{cis} \theta = r(\cos\theta + i\sin\theta)$$

These three equivalent formats are all 'modulus–argument forms' of a complex number.

When you write a number in this form, there needs to be a plus sign between the two terms and the modulus must be a positive number. If this isn't the case you need to draw a diagram to find the argument.

WORKED EXAMPLE 4.13

Write $z = -2\left(\cos\left(\dfrac{\pi}{3}\right) - i\sin\left(\dfrac{\pi}{3}\right)\right)$ in the form $r\operatorname{cis}\theta$, with the argument between $-\pi$ and π.

$z = -2\cos\left(\dfrac{\pi}{3}\right) + 2i\sin\left(\dfrac{\pi}{3}\right)$

In order to draw the diagram, you need to identify the sign of the real and imaginary parts.

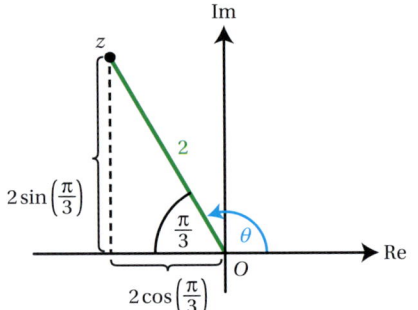

Since the sine and cosine of $\dfrac{\pi}{3}$ are both positive,

$\operatorname{Re}(z) = -2\cos\left(\dfrac{\pi}{3}\right) < 0$

and $\operatorname{Im}(z) = 2\sin\left(\dfrac{\pi}{3}\right) > 0$.

The right-angled triangle has hypotenuse 2.

The angle opposite the side marked $2\sin\left(\dfrac{\pi}{3}\right)$ is $\dfrac{\pi}{3}$.

You can therefore draw the diagram on the left.

From the diagram:

$|z| = 2,\ \arg(z) = \theta = \dfrac{2\pi}{3}$

$\theta = \pi - \dfrac{\pi}{3} = \dfrac{2\pi}{3}$

$\therefore z = 2\operatorname{cis}\left(\dfrac{2\pi}{3}\right)$

An Argand diagram can help you to identify the modulus and argument of the negative $(-z)$ and complex conjugate (z^*) of a number z.

WORKED EXAMPLE 4.14

A complex number $z = r\operatorname{cis}\theta$ is shown in the diagram. The argument is measured between $-\pi$ and π.

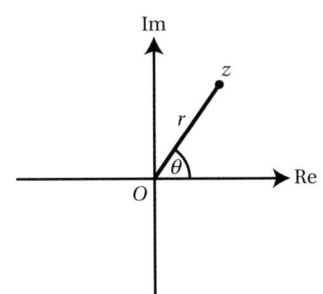

Continues on next page ...

On the same diagram, mark the numbers $-z$ and z^*. Hence, write $-z$ and z^* in the modulus–argument form.

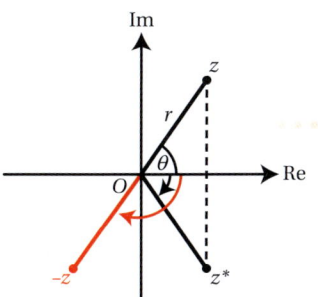

To get $-z$, make both real and imaginary parts negative.

z^* is the reflection in the real axis.

$|-z| = |z^*| = r$

All three points are the same distance from the origin, so all have the same modulus.

$\arg(-z) = -(\pi - \theta)$
$\quad\quad\quad = \theta - \pi$
$\arg(z^*) = -\theta$

As the argument is measured between $-\pi$ and π, both numbers $-z$ and z^* in the diagram have a negative argument.

$-z = r\,\text{cis}\,(\theta - \pi)$
$z^* = r\,\text{cis}\,(-\theta)$

Make sure you answer the question: write both numbers in modulus–argument form.

EXERCISE 4E

In this exercise you must show detailed reasoning.
You may be able to use your calculator to check your answers.

1 Find the modulus and the argument (measured between $-\pi$ and π) for each number.

    a   i   6   ii   13

    b   i -3 ii -1.6

    c   i $4i$ ii $0.5i$

    d   i $-2i$ ii $-5i$

    e   i $1+i$ ii $2+\sqrt{3}i$

    f   i $-1-\sqrt{3}i$ ii $4-4i$

2 Find the modulus and the argument (measured between 0 and 2π) for each number.

    a   i $4+2i$ ii $4-3i$

    b   i $i-\sqrt{3}$ ii $6i+\sqrt{2}$

    c   i $-3-i$ ii $-3+2i$

3. Write these complex numbers in Cartesian form without using trigonometric functions. Display each one on an Argand diagram.

   a i $\cos\left(\dfrac{\pi}{3}\right) + i\sin\left(\dfrac{\pi}{3}\right)$ ii $\cos\left(\dfrac{3\pi}{4}\right) + i\sin\left(\dfrac{3\pi}{4}\right)$

   b i $3\operatorname{cis}\left(\dfrac{\pi}{2}\right)$ ii $5\operatorname{cis}\left(-\dfrac{\pi}{2}\right)$

   c i $[4, 0]$ ii $[1, \pi]$

4. Given the modulus and the argument of z, write z in Cartesian form. Give real and imaginary parts either as integers or in surd form.

   a i $|z| = 4, \arg(z) = \dfrac{\pi}{3}$ ii $|z| = \sqrt{2}, \arg(z) = \dfrac{\pi}{4}$

   b i $|z| = 2, \arg(z) = \dfrac{3\pi}{4}$ ii $|z| = 2, \arg(z) = \dfrac{2\pi}{3}$

   c i $|z| = 3, \arg(z) = -\dfrac{\pi}{2}$ ii $|z| = 4, \arg(z) = -\pi$

5. Write each complex number in the form $|z|\operatorname{cis}\theta$.

   a i $z = 4i$ ii $z = -5$

   b i $z = 2 - 2\sqrt{3}i$ ii $z = \dfrac{\sqrt{3} + i}{3}$

6. Find the modulus and the argument of the following:

   a i $4\left(\cos\left(\dfrac{\pi}{3}\right) + i\sin\left(\dfrac{\pi}{3}\right)\right)$ ii $\sqrt{7}\left(\cos\left(\dfrac{3\pi}{7}\right) + i\sin\left(\dfrac{3\pi}{7}\right)\right)$

   b i $\cos\left(\dfrac{\pi}{5}\right) + i\sin\left(\dfrac{\pi}{5}\right)$ ii $\cos\left(-\dfrac{\pi}{4}\right) + i\sin\left(-\dfrac{\pi}{4}\right)$

   c i $3\left(\cos\left(\dfrac{\pi}{8}\right) - i\sin\left(\dfrac{\pi}{8}\right)\right)$ ii $7\left(\cos\left(\dfrac{4\pi}{5}\right) - i\sin\left(\dfrac{4\pi}{5}\right)\right)$

   d i $-10\left(\cos\left(\dfrac{\pi}{3}\right) + i\sin\left(\dfrac{\pi}{3}\right)\right)$ ii $-2\left(\cos\left(\dfrac{\pi}{6}\right) + i\sin\left(\dfrac{\pi}{6}\right)\right)$

   e i $6\left(\cos\left(-\dfrac{\pi}{10}\right) + i\sin\left(\dfrac{\pi}{10}\right)\right)$ ii $\dfrac{1}{2}\left(\cos\left(-\dfrac{\pi}{3}\right) - i\sin\left(-\dfrac{\pi}{3}\right)\right)$

7. a Write $3\operatorname{cis}\left(\dfrac{7\pi}{4}\right)$ in Cartesian form in terms of surds only.

   b Write $4i - 4$ in the form $|z|\operatorname{cis}\theta$.

8. Let $z = 1 + \sqrt{3}i$ and $w = 3\sqrt{3} - 3i$.

   a Find the modulus and the argument of z and w.

   b Represent z and w on the same Argand diagram.

   c Find the modulus and the argument of zw. Comment on your answer.

9 $w = 4 \operatorname{cis}\left(-\dfrac{\pi}{6}\right)$

$z = 2\sqrt{3} \operatorname{cis} \dfrac{\pi}{3}$ and $w = 4 \operatorname{cis}\left(-\dfrac{\pi}{6}\right)$

Find $z + w$ in:

a Cartesian form

b modulus–argument form

 10 If $z = r \operatorname{cis} \theta$, write in terms of r and θ, simplifying your answers as far as possible:

a $z + z^*$

b zz^*

c $\dfrac{z}{z^*}$

 11 If $z = \operatorname{cis} \theta$, express the real and imaginary parts of $\dfrac{z-1}{z+1}$ in terms of θ, simplifying your answer as far as possible.

> **Rewind**
>
> Part **c** of question **10** requires double angle formulae from A Level Mathematics Student Book 2, Chapter 8.

Section 5: Loci in the complex plane

You have met various examples of representing equations and inequalities graphically. You can represent as a graph an equation involving two variables, such as $x - 2y = 5$, show an inequality such as $2 < x \leqslant 5$ on the number line, and shade a region corresponding to an inequality in two variables, such as $y \geqslant 3x^2$.

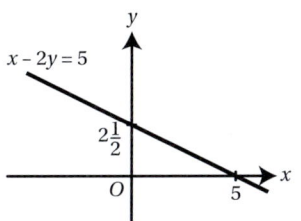
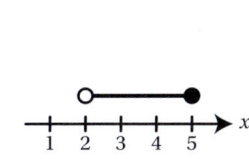
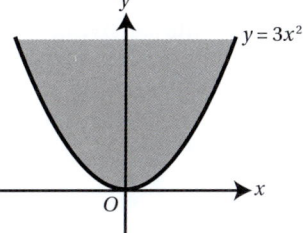

Now that you can represent complex numbers as points in the Argand diagram, there is a way to graphically show equations and inequalities involving complex numbers.

Loci involving the modulus

In Section 4, we defined the modulus of a complex number as its distance from the origin in the Argand diagram. This means that all complex numbers with the same modulus form a circle around the origin.

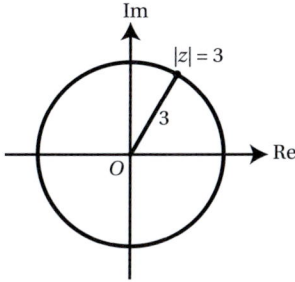

We can extend this idea to measure the distance between any two complex numbers in the Argand diagram.

If you write two numbers in Cartesian form, $z_1 = x_1 + iy_1$ and $z_2 = x_2 + iy_2$, then

$$z_1 - z_2 = (x_1 - x_2) + i(y_1 - y_2)$$

so

$$|z_1 - z_2| = \sqrt{(x_1 - x_2)^2 + (y_1 - y_2)^2}$$

Notice that the last expression is the distance between the points with coordinates (x_1, y_1) and (x_2, y_2).

Key point 4.8

The distance between points representing complex numbers z_1 and z_2 in the Argand diagram is given by $|z_1 - z_2|$.

You can now find complex numbers that satisfy equations or inequalities involving the modulus by thinking about the geometric interpretation, rather than by doing calculations.

WORKED EXAMPLE 4.15

Show on an Argand diagram a set of points satisfying the equation $|z - 2| = 3$.

Circle, centre 2, radius 3 .... The equation says 'the distance between z and 2 is 3'.

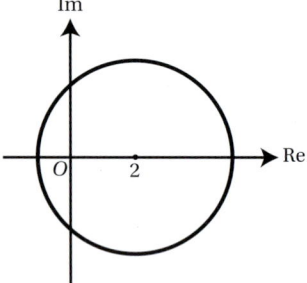

Key point 4.9

The equation $|z - a| = r$ represents a circle with radius r and centre at the point a.

4 Complex numbers

WORKED EXAMPLE 4.16

Shade on an Argand diagram the set of points satisfying the inequality $|z-2+3i|<2$.

$|z-(2-3i)|<2$ — You need to write the inequality in the form $|z-a|<2$.

Circle, centre $2-3i$, radius 2 — The inequality can be interpreted as saying 'the distance between z and $2-3i$ is less than 2'.

Remember, the dashed line means that the perimeter is not included.

You can also describe the inequality above by using (x, y) coordinates and set theory notation. The circle with centre $(2, -3)$ and radius 2 has equation $(x-2)^2 + (y+3)^2 = 4$, so the set of all points satisfying the inequality is $\{x + iy: (x-2)^2 + (y+3)^2 < 4\}$ $x, y \in \mathbb{R}$.

> **Tip**
> A **locus** is a set of all the points that satisfy a given condition.

WORKED EXAMPLE 4.17

Sketch the locus of points in the Argand diagram that satisfy:

a $|z-4| = |z-2i|$ **b** $|z-4| \geqslant |z-2i|$

a
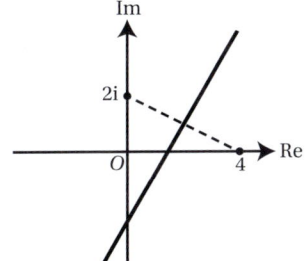

The equation says 'the distance from z to 4 is the same as the distance from z to 2i'.

This is the perpendicular bisector of the line segment joining the points 4 and 2i.

b
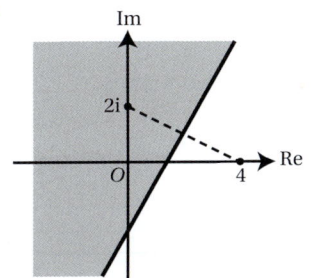

The inequality represents all the points that are closer to 2i than to 4.

Key point 4.10

The equation $|z - a| = |z - b|$ represents a straight line, which is the perpendicular bisector of the line segment joining points a and b.

Locus involving the argument

The argument measures the angle that the line connecting z to the origin makes with the positive real axis. So the three points shown on the diagram all have the same argument, θ.

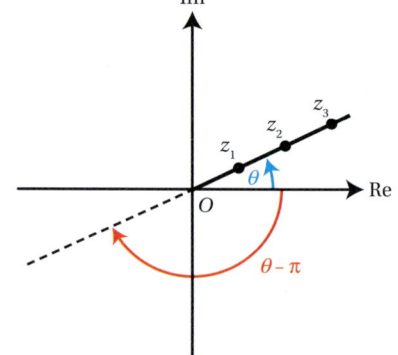

Since the argument is measured from the **positive** x-axis, any number on the dashed part of the line would have argument $\theta + \pi$ (or $\theta - \pi$ if you use negative arguments). Therefore, the locus of points with $\arg(z) = \theta$ is the half–line (shown as the solid part of the line in the diagram).

If you replace z by $z - a$, the line shifts from the origin to the point a.

 Key point 4.11

The locus of points satisfying $\arg(z - a) = \theta$ is the half–line starting from the point a and making an angle θ with the positive real axis.

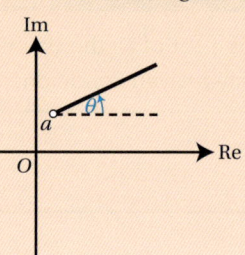

💡 **Tip**

The point a is not included in the locus (since the number zero does not have a defined argument).

WORKED EXAMPLE 4.18

Sketch the locus of points in the Argand diagram that satisfy $\arg(z - 3 + 2\mathrm{i}) = \dfrac{\pi}{4}$.

$\arg(z - (3 - 2\mathrm{i})) = \dfrac{\pi}{4}$ .... The expression in brackets needs to be written in the form $\arg(z - a) = \theta$.

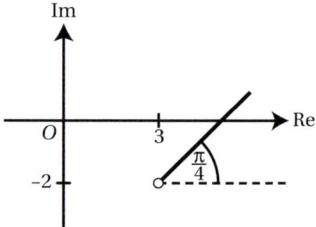

The half–line starts from the point $3 - 2\mathrm{i}$ and makes a 45° angle with the horizontal.

4 Complex numbers

WORKED EXAMPLE 4.19

On a single diagram, illustrate the locus of points that satisfy the inequalities $0 < \arg(z+1-i) < \frac{2\pi}{3}$ and $|z| \leqslant 3$.

$0 < \arg(z-(-1+i)) < \frac{2\pi}{3}$ .... The first inequality represents the region between two half-lines, starting from the point $-1+i$ and making angles 0 and $\frac{2\pi}{3}$ with the horizontal axis.

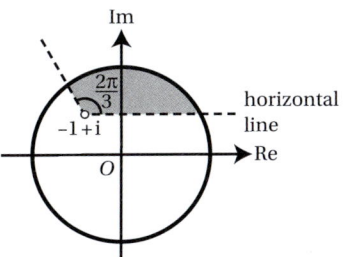

The second inequality represents the inside of the circle with radius 3 and centre at the origin.

The half-lines should be dotted and the circle perimeter solid.

You can indicate the required region by shading.

Horizontal and vertical lines

A horizontal line in an Argand diagram consists of points with a fixed imaginary part. Similarly, a vertical line consists of points with a fixed real part.

WORKED EXAMPLE 4.20

On an Argand diagram, represent the region defined by the inequalities $\text{Re}(z) < 3$ and $\text{Im}(z) \geqslant 2$.

The required region is shaded.

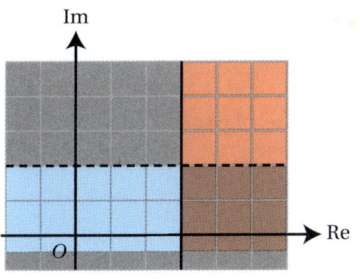

$\text{Re}(z) = 3$ represents a vertical line passing through 3 on the real axis.

$\text{Im}(z) = 2$ represents a horizontal line passing through $2i$ on the imaginary axis.

EXERCISE 4F

1 Illustrate each locus on an Argand diagram (shade the areas the inequalities cover).

    a   **i** $|z - 2i| = 5$ **ii** $|z - 3| = 5$

    b   **i** $|z + 4| = 1$ **ii** $|z + 3i| = 2$

    c   **i** $|z - i| \leqslant 2$ **ii** $|z + i| > 3$

    d   **i** $|z - 3 + i| > 2$ **ii** $|z + 1 - 2i| \leqslant 1$

2 The set of points from question **1 a i** can be described as $\{x + iy : x^2 + (y-2)^2 = 25\}$. Write the sets of points for the rest of question **1** using similar notation.

  a **ii** $|z - 3| = 5$

  b **i** $|z + 4| = 1$ **ii** $|z + 3i| = 2$

  c **i** $|z - i| \leqslant 2$ **ii** $|z + i| > 3$

  d **i** $|z - 3 + i| > 2$ **ii** $|z + 1 - 2i| \leqslant 1$

3 Sketch each locus on an Argand diagram.

  a **i** $|z - 2| = |z + 2i|$ **ii** $|z + 1| = |z - i|$

  b **i** $|z - 3i| < |z + i|$ **ii** $|z + 2| > |z - 3|$

  c **i** $\operatorname{Re}(z) = 5$ **ii** $\operatorname{Im}(z) > -2$

4 Sketch each locus on an Argand diagram.

  a **i** $\arg(z) = \dfrac{\pi}{3}$ **ii** $\arg(z) = \dfrac{\pi}{4}$

  b **i** $\arg(z) = -\dfrac{\pi}{6}$ **ii** $\arg(z) = -\dfrac{3\pi}{4}$

  c **i** $\arg(z) = \dfrac{\pi}{2}$ **ii** $\arg(z) = \pi$

5 Shade the region on an Argand diagram where $1 < |z - 3i| \leqslant 3$.

6 On an Argand diagram, sketch the locus of points where $|z - 3i| = |z + 6|$.

7 Shade the region on an Argand diagram where $\dfrac{\pi}{6} < \arg(z) < \dfrac{2\pi}{3}$.

8 **a** On the same diagram, sketch the locus of $|z + 1| = |z - 3|$ and $\arg(z) = \dfrac{\pi}{4}$.

  b Hence, find the complex number z that satisfies both equations.

9 On an Argand diagram, shade the region where $|z - 3 - i| < 3$ and $\arg(z) < \dfrac{\pi}{3}$.

10 On an Argand diagram, shade the locus of points that satisfy $\operatorname{Re}(z) \leqslant 1$, $\operatorname{Im}(z) < 3$ and $0 \leqslant \arg(z) < \dfrac{3\pi}{4}$.

11 Find the complex number z that satisfies $|z - 3i| = |z + i|$ and $|z - 1| = |z - i|$.

12 z is a complex number satisfying $|z - 2 - 2i| = 2$. Find the maximum possible value of $\arg(z)$.

Section 6: Operations in modulus–argument form

Addition and subtraction are quite straightforward in Cartesian form, but multiplication and division are more difficult. Raising to a large power is even harder. These operations are much easier in modulus–argument form, thanks to the following result.

> **Tip**
>
> The argument needs to be either between 0 and 2π, or between $-\pi$ and π. Convert any argument you calculate into the equivalent principal argument by adding or subtracting multiples of 2π.

Key point 4.12

When you multiply two complex numbers you **multiply** their moduli and **add** their arguments:

- $|zw| = |z||w|$
- $\arg(zw) = \arg(z) + \arg(w)$.

4 Complex numbers

The proof requires the use of compound angle formulae from the A Level Mathematics course:

$\sin(A + B) = \sin A \cos B + \cos A \sin B$

$\cos(A + B) = \cos A \cos B - \sin A \sin B$

> **Rewind**
>
> You learnt about more uses of these formulae in A Level Mathematics Student Book 2, Chapter 8.

PROOF 6

For two complex numbers z_1 and z_2,

$|z_1 z_2| = |z_1||z_2|$ and $\arg(z_1 z_2) = \arg(z_1) + \arg(z_2)$.

Let

$z_1 = r_1(\cos\theta_1 + i\sin\theta_1)$ and
$z_2 = r_2(\cos\theta_2 + i\sin\theta_2)$

Start by introducing variables.

$z_1 z_2 = r_1 r_2 (\cos\theta_1 + i\sin\theta_1)(\cos\theta_2 + i\sin\theta_2)$
$= r_1 r_2 (\cos\theta_1 \cos\theta_2 - \sin\theta_1 \sin\theta_2) + i(\sin\theta_1 \cos\theta_2 + \sin\theta_2 \cos\theta_1)$
$= r_1 r_2 (\cos(\theta_1 + \theta_2) + i\sin(\theta_1 + \theta_2))$

Multiply them together and group real and imaginary parts.

Use the compound angle formulae given above.

So,

$|z_1 z_2| = r_1 r_2$

$\arg(z_1 z_2) = (\theta_1 + \theta_2)$

i.e. $|z_1 z_2| = |z_1||z_2|$ and
$\arg(z_1 z_2) = \arg(z_1) + \arg(z_2)$

This is in the form $|z|\text{cis}\,\theta$ so, by comparison, you can state the modulus and argument of $z_1 z_2$.

Finish the proof with a conclusion.

A similar proof gives the result for dividing complex numbers:

Key point 4.13

When you divide two complex numbers you **divide** their moduli and **subtract** their arguments:

- $\left|\dfrac{z}{w}\right| = \dfrac{|z|}{|w|}$
- $\arg\left(\dfrac{z}{w}\right) = \arg z - \arg w$.

> **Tip**
>
> Remember that another notation for $r\,\text{cis}\,\theta$ is $[r, \theta]$. Hence, the results in Key points 4.12 and 4.13 can also be written as
> $[r_1, \theta_1][r_2, \theta_2] = [r_1 r_2, \theta_1 + \theta_2]$
> and $\dfrac{[r_1, \theta_1]}{[r_2, \theta_2]} = \left[\dfrac{r_1}{r_2}, \theta_1 - \theta_2\right]$.

WORKED EXAMPLE 4.21

a If $z = 3\,\text{cis}\left(\dfrac{\pi}{3}\right)$ and $w = 5\,\text{cis}\left(\dfrac{\pi}{4}\right)$, write zw in the form $r\,\text{cis}\,\theta$.

b Write $\dfrac{6\left(\cos\left(\dfrac{2\pi}{3}\right) + i\sin\left(\dfrac{2\pi}{3}\right)\right)}{3\left(\cos\left(\dfrac{\pi}{6}\right) + i\sin\left(\dfrac{\pi}{6}\right)\right)}$ in the form $x + iy$.

Continues on next page …

a $|zw| = 3 \times 5 = 15$

$\arg(zw) = \dfrac{\pi}{3} + \dfrac{\pi}{4} = \dfrac{7\pi}{12}$

$\therefore zw = 15 \operatorname{cis}\left(\dfrac{7\pi}{12}\right)$

Multiply the moduli and add the arguments.

b $\dfrac{6\left(\cos\left(\dfrac{2\pi}{3}\right) + i\sin\left(\dfrac{2\pi}{3}\right)\right)}{3\left(\cos\left(\dfrac{\pi}{6}\right) + i\sin\left(\dfrac{\pi}{6}\right)\right)} = \dfrac{6\operatorname{cis}\left(\dfrac{2\pi}{3}\right)}{3\operatorname{cis}\left(\dfrac{\pi}{6}\right)}$

First do the division in the modulus–argument form: divide the moduli, and subtract the arguments.

$r = \dfrac{6}{3} = 2$

$\theta = \dfrac{2\pi}{3} - \dfrac{\pi}{6} = \dfrac{\pi}{2}$

$x = 2\cos\left(\dfrac{\pi}{2}\right) = 0$

$y = 2\sin\left(\dfrac{\pi}{2}\right) = 2$

Then convert to the Cartesian form: $x = r\cos\theta$, $y = r\sin\theta$.

$\therefore \dfrac{6\left(\cos\left(\dfrac{2\pi}{3}\right) + i\sin\left(\dfrac{2\pi}{3}\right)\right)}{3\left(\cos\left(\dfrac{\pi}{6}\right) + i\sin\left(\dfrac{\pi}{6}\right)\right)} = 2i$

Remember that the argument needs to be either between 0 and 2π, or between $-\pi$ and π. Convert any argument you calculate into the equivalent principal argument by adding or subtracting multiples of 2π.

WORK IT OUT 4.2

Find the argument of $z = 3\operatorname{cis}\left(\dfrac{9\pi}{5}\right) \times 5\operatorname{cis}\left(\dfrac{4\pi}{3}\right)$.

Which is the correct solution? Can you identify the errors made in the incorrect solutions?

Solution 1	Solution 2	Solution 3
$\arg(z) = \dfrac{9\pi}{5} \times \dfrac{4\pi}{3}$ $= \dfrac{12\pi^2}{5}$	$\dfrac{9\pi}{5} + \dfrac{4\pi}{3} = \dfrac{47\pi}{15}$, so $\arg(z) = \dfrac{47\pi}{15} - 2\pi = \dfrac{17\pi}{15}$	$\arg(z) = \dfrac{9\pi}{5} + \dfrac{4\pi}{3}$ $= \dfrac{47\pi}{15}$

💡 Tip

You can also add and subtract complex numbers in modulus-argument form. So here, $z + w = 3\left(\cos\dfrac{\pi}{3} + i\sin\dfrac{\pi}{3}\right) + 5\left(\cos\dfrac{\pi}{4} + i\sin\dfrac{\pi}{4}\right) = \left(3\cos\dfrac{\pi}{3} + 5\cos\dfrac{\pi}{4}\right) + i\left(3\sin\dfrac{\pi}{3} + 5\sin\dfrac{\pi}{4}\right) = \dfrac{(3 + 5\sqrt{2})}{2} + i\dfrac{(3\sqrt{3} + 5\sqrt{2})}{2}$

EXERCISE 4G

In this exercise you must show detailed reasoning.

You may be able to use a calculator to check your answer.

1 Evaluate the following expressions, giving your answers in the form $r \operatorname{cis} \theta$.

   a **i** $3 \operatorname{cis}\left(\dfrac{\pi}{6}\right) \times 7 \operatorname{cis}\left(\dfrac{\pi}{5}\right)$ **ii** $\operatorname{cis}\left(-\dfrac{\pi}{9}\right) \times 4 \operatorname{cis}\left(\dfrac{\pi}{3}\right)$

   b **i** $\dfrac{[8, 6]}{[2, 2]}$ **ii** $\dfrac{\left[15, \dfrac{\pi}{7}\right]}{\left[5, \dfrac{\pi}{2}\right]}$

> **Tip**
>
> If you are using your calculator, make sure it is in radian mode.

2 Write in the form $\cos \theta + i \sin \theta$, where $-\pi < \arg(z) < \pi$.

   a **i** $\left(\cos\left(\dfrac{\pi}{3}\right) + i \sin\left(\dfrac{\pi}{3}\right)\right)\left(\cos\left(\dfrac{3\pi}{4}\right) + i \sin\left(\dfrac{3\pi}{4}\right)\right)$

      ii $\left(\cos\left(\dfrac{2\pi}{5}\right) + i \sin\left(\dfrac{2\pi}{5}\right)\right)\left(\cos\left(\dfrac{\pi}{4}\right) + i \sin\left(\dfrac{\pi}{4}\right)\right)$

   b **i** $\left(\cos\left(\dfrac{\pi}{3}\right) + i \sin\left(\dfrac{\pi}{3}\right)\right)\left(\cos\left(\dfrac{\pi}{4}\right) - i \sin\left(\dfrac{\pi}{4}\right)\right)$

      ii $\left(\cos\left(\dfrac{2\pi}{3}\right) + i \sin\left(\dfrac{2\pi}{3}\right)\right)\left(\cos\left(\dfrac{2\pi}{5}\right) - i \sin\left(\dfrac{2\pi}{5}\right)\right)$

   c **i** $\dfrac{\cos\left(\dfrac{3\pi}{5}\right) + i \sin\left(\dfrac{3\pi}{5}\right)}{\cos\left(\dfrac{\pi}{4}\right) + i \sin\left(\dfrac{\pi}{4}\right)}$ **ii** $\dfrac{\cos\left(\dfrac{\pi}{3}\right) + i \sin\left(\dfrac{\pi}{3}\right)}{\cos\left(\dfrac{3\pi}{4}\right) + i \sin\left(\dfrac{3\pi}{4}\right)}$

   d **i** $\dfrac{\cos\left(\dfrac{\pi}{5}\right) + i \sin\left(\dfrac{\pi}{5}\right)}{\cos\left(\dfrac{\pi}{4}\right) - i \sin\left(\dfrac{\pi}{4}\right)}$ **ii** $\dfrac{\cos\left(\dfrac{\pi}{4}\right) + i \sin\left(\dfrac{\pi}{4}\right)}{\cos\left(\dfrac{2\pi}{5}\right) - i \sin\left(\dfrac{2\pi}{5}\right)}$

3 Write $\dfrac{6\left(\cos\left(\dfrac{2\pi}{3}\right) + i \sin\left(\dfrac{2\pi}{3}\right)\right)}{2\left(\cos\left(\dfrac{\pi}{4}\right) + i \sin\left(\dfrac{\pi}{4}\right)\right)}$ in the form $r \operatorname{cis} \theta$.

4 Write $\dfrac{8 \operatorname{cis}\left(\dfrac{5\pi}{6}\right)}{4 \operatorname{cis}\left(\dfrac{2\pi}{3}\right)}$ in the form $x + iy$.

5 Let $z = \operatorname{cis}\left(\dfrac{\pi}{4}\right)$, and $w = \operatorname{cis}\left(\dfrac{\pi}{3}\right)$.

   a Write zw in the form $x + iy$, without using trigonometric functions.

   b Hence, find the exact value of $\tan\left(\dfrac{7\pi}{12}\right)$.

6 Use trigonometric identities to show that:

a $\left(\dfrac{1}{\operatorname{cis}\theta}\right) = \operatorname{cis}(-\theta) = \operatorname{cis}(2\pi - \theta)$

b $\left(\dfrac{\operatorname{cis}\theta_1}{\operatorname{cis}\theta_2}\right) = \operatorname{cis}(\theta_1 - \theta_2)$

Checklist of learning and understanding

- A complex number can be written in the form $z = x + iy$, where x and y are real and $i^2 = -1$.
  - Apart from the fact that $i^2 = -1$, the arithmetic of complex numbers is the same as for real numbers.
  - To divide by a complex number, multiply the top and bottom by its complex conjugate ($z^* = x - iy$).
- It is useful to represent complex numbers geometrically using an Argand diagram. Addition can be represented on a diagram as adding vectors, and the complex conjugate as a reflection in the real axis.
- There are two ways of describing numbers in the Argand diagram: Cartesian form ($x + iy$) and modulus–argument form ($r \operatorname{cis} \theta$, or $[r, \theta]$). The two forms are linked by:
  - $r = \sqrt{x^2 + y^2}$
  - $\tan \theta = \dfrac{y}{x}$
  - $x = r \cos \theta$
  - $y = r \sin \theta$.
- Multiplication and division can be done in modulus–argument form:
  - $\arg(zw) = \arg(z) + \arg(w)$
  - $\arg\left(\dfrac{z}{w}\right) = \arg(z) - \arg(w)$
  - $|zw| = |z||w|$
  - $\left|\dfrac{z}{w}\right| = \dfrac{|z|}{|w|}$.
- Equations and inequalities can be represented in an Argand diagram:
  - $|z - a| = r$ represents a circle with centre a and radius r.
  - $|z - a| = |z - b|$ represents the perpendicular bisector of the line segment connecting points a and b.
  - $\arg(z - a) = \theta$ represents a half–line starting from (but not including) a and making angle θ with the positive horizontal direction.
  - Vertical and horizontal lines are represented by equations of the form $\operatorname{Re}(z) = k$ or $\operatorname{Im}(z) = k$, respectively.

4 Complex numbers

Mixed practice 4

1 Let $z_1 = 1 - i$ and $z_2 = 3 + 5i$. Find in the form $x + iy$:

   a $z_1 z_2$

   b $\dfrac{z_1}{z_2}$

   Show all your working clearly.

2 **In this question you must show detailed reasoning.**

   Express $z = 3i - \dfrac{2}{i + \sqrt{3}}$ in the form $x + iy$.

3 **a** For the complex number $z = -2 + 5i$, find:

   i $|z|$

   ii $\arg(z)$, where $-\pi < \arg(z) \leqslant \pi$.

   b State the modulus and argument of z^*.

4 A complex number z is given by $z = -2 + 3i$. The argument of z can be written in the form $\pi - \arctan\left(\dfrac{a}{b}\right)$, where a and b are integers. Find the values of a and b.

5 **a** Solve the equation $z^2 + 14z + 53 = 0$.

   b Represent the solutions on an Argand diagram.

6 On an Argand diagram, illustrate the locus of points z that satisfy the equation $\text{Re}(z) + \text{Im}(z) < 2$.

7 **In this question you must show detailed reasoning.**

   Find the inverse of the matrix $\begin{pmatrix} 4 & 3i \\ -6i & 5 \end{pmatrix}$.

8 Find the complex number z such that $3z - 5z^* = 4 - 3i$.

9 By writing $z = x + iy$, where x and y are real numbers, prove that $(zz^*)^* = |z|^2$.

10 On an Argand diagram, illustrate the locus of points z that satisfy the inequality $3 < |z - 3 + 4i| \leqslant 5$.

11 The complex numbers a and b are given by $a = 7 + 6i$ and $b = 1 - 3i$. Showing clearly how you obtain your answers, find

   a $|a - 2b|$ and $\arg(a - 2b)$,

   b $\dfrac{b}{a}$, giving your answer in the form $x + iy$.

   © OCR, AS GCE Further Mathematics, Paper 4725, June 2010
   [Question part reference style adapted]

12 Given that $w = 1 + \sqrt{3}i$ and $z = 1 + i$, show that $\text{Re}\left(\dfrac{w + \sqrt{2}z}{w - \sqrt{2}z}\right) = 0$.

13 Let z and w be complex numbers satisfying $\dfrac{w + i}{w - i} = \dfrac{z + 1}{z - 1}$.

   a Express w in terms of z.

   b Show that, if $\text{Im}(z) = 0$, then $\text{Re}(w) = 0$.

14 On an Argand diagram, represent the region defined by the inequalities $0 < \arg(z - 2i) \leqslant \dfrac{3\pi}{4}$ and $|z - 2i| \geqslant 2$.

15 Two complex numbers, a and b, are shown on the Argand diagram.

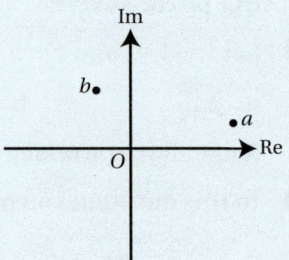

  a Copy the diagram and sketch the points representing the numbers $a + b$ and a^* on to the diagram.

  b Sketch the locus of points z that satisfy $|z - a| = |z - b|$.

16 The complex number $3 - 3i$ is denoted by a.

  a Find $|a|$ and $\arg a$.

  b Sketch on a single Argand diagram the loci given by

    i $|z - a| = 3\sqrt{2}$ **ii** $\arg(z - a) = \dfrac{1}{4}\pi$

  c Indicate, by shading, the region of the Argand diagram for which $|z - a| \geqslant 3\sqrt{2}$ and $0 \leqslant \arg(z - a) \leqslant \dfrac{1}{4}\pi$.

  © OCR, AS GCE Further Mathematics, Paper 4725, June 2009
  [Question part reference style adapted]

17 Find, in terms of w, the complex number that satisfies both $|z - w| = 2\sqrt{2}$ and $\arg(z - w) = \dfrac{\pi}{4}$.

18 Let z and w be complex numbers such that $w = \dfrac{1}{1 - z}$ and $|z|^2 = 1$. Find the real part of w.

19 If $z = \operatorname{cis} \theta$, prove that $\dfrac{z^2 - 1}{z^2 + 1} = i \tan \theta$.

20 **In this question you must show detailed reasoning.**

  If z and w are complex numbers, solve the simultaneous equations:
  $$\begin{cases} 3z + w = 9 + 11i \\ iw - z = -8 - 2i \end{cases}$$

21 **a** For a complex number z, prove that $zz^* = |z|^2$.

  b Let z be a complex number of modulus 1, and define the matrix $\mathbf{A} = \begin{pmatrix} 1 & z \\ -z^* & 1 \end{pmatrix}$.

  Show that $\mathbf{A}^3 - 2\mathbf{A} + 4\mathbf{I} = \mathbf{Z}$, where $\mathbf{Z}$ is the zero matrix.

22 **In this question you must show detailed reasoning.**

  Let $z_1 = \dfrac{\sqrt{6} + i\sqrt{2}}{2}$, and $z_2 = 1 - i$.

  a Find the value of $\dfrac{z_1}{z_2}$ in the form $a + bi$, where a and b are to be determined exactly in surd form.

  b Show that $\dfrac{z_1}{z_2} = \cos\left(\dfrac{5\pi}{12}\right) + i \sin\left(\dfrac{5\pi}{12}\right)$.

  c Hence, find the exact values of $\cos\left(\dfrac{5\pi}{12}\right)$ and $\sin\left(\dfrac{5\pi}{12}\right)$.

23 By considering the product $(2 + i)(3 + i)$, show that $\arctan \dfrac{1}{2} + \arctan \dfrac{1}{3} = \dfrac{\pi}{4}$.

24 If $0 < \theta < \dfrac{\pi}{2}$ and $z = (\sin \theta + i(1 - \cos \theta))^2$, find $\arg(z)$ in its simplest form.

5 Roots of polynomials

In this chapter you will learn:

- how to factorise polynomials and solve equations that may have complex roots
- a useful link between the roots of a polynomial and its coefficients
- how to use substitutions to solve more complicated equations.

Before you start…

A Level Mathematics Student Book 1, Chapter 4	You should be able to use the factor theorem to factorise cubic polynomials.	1 a b	Show that $x = 2$ is a root of $f(x) = 2x^3 - 9x^2 + 7x + 6$. Hence, factorise $f(x)$ completely.
Chapter 4	You should be able to perform arithmetic with complex numbers and solve quadratic equations with complex roots.	2 a b	Expand and simplify $(3 - 2i)(5 + i)$. Solve the equation $x^2 - 2x + 5 = 0$.
Chapter 4	You should be able to work with complex conjugates.	3 a b	Given that $z = 3 - 5i$, find: $z + z^*$ zz^*.

Using complex numbers in factorising

This chapter draws together ideas from the AS Mathematics course on factorising cubics and quartics, with complex numbers from Chapter 4 of this book, to enable you to find complex roots of these polynomials. It also looks at the relationship between the coefficients of a polynomial and its roots.

Section 1: Factorising polynomials

You are already familiar with the link between factorising and real roots of a polynomial; for example, the quadratic equation $x^2 - x - 6 = 0$ has solutions $x = -2$ and $x = 3$, so you can factorise it as:

$x^2 - x - 6 = (x + 2)(x - 3)$

This is the factor theorem (which you met in A Level Mathematics Book 1, Chapter 4), and it also applies to polynomials with complex roots.

WORKED EXAMPLE 5.1

a Solve the equation $x^2 - 4x + 40 = 0$.

b Hence, factorise $x^2 - 4x + 40$.

a $x = \dfrac{4 \pm \sqrt{(-4)^2 - 4 \times 40}}{2}$ Use the quadratic formula.

$= \dfrac{4 \pm \sqrt{-144}}{2}$

$= \dfrac{4 \pm 12i}{2}$

$= 2 \pm 6i$

b Hence,   Make the link between roots and factors.

$x^2 - 4x + 40 = (x - (2 + 6i))(x - (2 - 6i))$

$= (x - 2 + 6i)(x - (2 - 6i))$

You can use the same reasoning to factorise polynomials of higher degree.

WORKED EXAMPLE 5.2

Let $f(x) = x^3 - x^2 - x - 15$.

a Show that $f(3) = 0$.

b Hence, write $f(x)$ as a product of a linear factor and a real quadratic factor.

c Solve the equation $f(x) = 0$ and write $f(x)$ as a product of three linear factors.

a $f(3) = 3^3 - 3^2 - 3 - 15$ Substitute $x = 3$ into $f(x)$.

$= 27 - 9 - 3 - 15$

$= 0$

b $x^3 - x^2 - x - 15 = (x - 3)(x^2 + Bx + C)$ As 3 is a root, $(x - 3)$ is one factor. You can find the quadratic factor by long division or by comparing coefficients.

$\Rightarrow B = 2, C = 5$

$\therefore f(x) = (x - 3)(x^2 + 2x + 5)$

c $f(x) = 0$

$(x - 3)(x^2 + 2x + 5) = 0$

$x = 3$ or $x^2 + 2x + 5 = 0$

Continues on next page...

If $x^2 + 2x + 5 = 0$

$x = \dfrac{-2 \pm \sqrt{2^2 - 4 \times 5}}{2}$ •••• Solve the quadratic using the formula.

$= \dfrac{-2 \pm \sqrt{-16}}{2}$

$= \dfrac{-2 \pm 4i}{2}$

$= -1 \pm 2i$

$x = 3, -1 \pm 2i$ •••• State all three roots of $f(x) = 0$.

$\therefore f(x) = (x-3)(x-(-1+2i))(x-(-1-2i))$
$= (x-3)(x+1-2i)(x+1+2i)$ •••• Each root z has a corresponding factor $(x - z)$.

The last example shows that you can now factorise some expressions that were impossible to factorise fully using just real numbers. A particularly useful case is extending the difference of two squares identity to the sum of two squares.

Key point 5.1

$$a^2 + b^2 \equiv (a + ib)(a - ib)$$

WORKED EXAMPLE 5.3

Factorise $81z^4 - 16$.

$81z^4 - 16 = (9z^2 - 4)(9z^2 + 4)$ •••• This is a difference of two squares.

$= (3z - 2)(3z + 2)(3z - 2i)(3z + 2i)$ •••• The first factor is a difference of two squares again, but the second factor is a sum of two squares.

EXERCISE 5A

 Solve the equation $f(x) = 0$ and, hence, factorise $f(x)$.

    a   **i** $f(x) = x^2 - 2x + 2$ **ii** $f(x) = x^2 - 6x + 25$

    b   **i** $f(x) = x^2 + 3x + 4$ **ii** $f(x) = x^2 + 2x + 5$

    c   **i** $f(x) = 3x^2 - 2x + 10$ **ii** $f(x) = 5x^2 + 4x + 2$

2 Factorise each expression into linear factors.

  a **i** z^2+4 **ii** z^2+25

  b **i** $4z^2+49$ **ii** $9z^2+64$

  c **i** z^4-1 **ii** $16z^4-81$

3 Given one root of each cubic polynomial, write it as a product of a linear factor and a real quadratic factor and, hence, find all three roots.

  a **i** x^3+2x^2-x-14, root $x=2$ **ii** x^3+3x^2+7x+5, root $x=-1$

  b **i** $2x^3-5x+6$, root $x=-2$ **ii** $3x^3-x^2-2$, root $x=1$

4 Let $f(x)=x^3-13x^2+56x-78$.

  Show that $(x-3)$ is a factor of f(x) and, hence, find all the solutions of the equation f(x) = 0.

5 **a** Given that $(2x+1)$ is a factor of $2x^3+ax^2+16x+6$, show that $a=9$.

  b Factorise $2x^3+9x^2+16x+6$ completely.

6 Given that f(x) = $4x^4 - 4x^3 - 21x^2 - 9x$:

  a show that $(x-3)$ is a factor of f(x)

  b factorise f(x) and, hence, solve the equation f(x) = 0.

7 Given that f(x) = $x^4 + 3x^3 - x^2 - 13x - 10$:

  a show that $(x+1)$ and $(x-2)$ are factors of f(x)

  b write f(x) as a product of two linear factors and a quadratic factor. Hence, find all the solutions of the equation f(x) = 0.

8 **In this question you must show detailed reasoning.**

  Find all the solutions of the equation $x^4 + 21x^2 - 100 = 0$.

Section 2: Complex solutions to polynomial equations

If a quadratic equation with real coefficients has two complex solutions, then they are always a conjugate pair; for example, the equation $x^2 - 6x + 25 = 0$ has solutions $x = 3 + 4i$ and $x = 3 - 4i$. This happens because of the ± in the quadratic formula.

If you look at the cubic and quartic polynomials you factorised in Exercise 5A, you will see that the roots were either real or in a complex conjugate pair. It can be proved that this result generalises to any **real polynomial** (a polynomial for which all coefficients are real numbers).

> **Did you know?**
>
> This result is not true if the polynomial has complex coefficients. For example, the equation $z^2 - iz + 2 = 0$ has solutions $-i$ and $2i$.

5 Roots of polynomials

Key point 5.2

Complex solutions of real polynomials come in conjugate pairs:

if $f(z) = 0$ then $f(z^*) = 0$.

Focus on ...

This result is proved in Focus on ... Proof 2.

This result can be very useful when factorising real polynomials and solving real equations. If you know one complex root, then you can immediately write down another one.

WORKED EXAMPLE 5.4

Given that $1 - i\sqrt{6}$ is a root of the polynomial $f(x) = x^3 + x^2 + x + 21$, find the other two roots.

$1 - i\sqrt{6}$ is a root so $1 + i\sqrt{6}$ is also a root.	Complex roots come in conjugate pairs.
So $(x-(1-i\sqrt{6}))$ and $(x-(1-i\sqrt{6}))$ are factors of $f(x)$.	Link roots to factors (using the factor theorem).
Therefore $(x-(1-i\sqrt{6}))(x-(1+i\sqrt{6}))$ is a factor.	
$(x-(1-i\sqrt{6}))(x-(1+i\sqrt{6})) = x^2 - 2x + 7$	Multiply this out.
$x^3 + x^2 + x + 21 = (x+3)(x^2 - 2x + 7)$ So the other two roots are -3 and $1 + i\sqrt{6}$.	Use polynomial division or comparing coefficients to find the third factor. Alternatively, you can look at the constant term to see that this factor is $(x+3)$.

In Worked example 5.4, in order to find the quadratic factor of $f(x)$ you needed to expand $(x-(1-i\sqrt{6}))(x-(1+i\sqrt{6}))$. This product is of the form $(x - z)(x - z^*)$. You will get this type of expression whenever you expand two brackets corresponding to a pair of complex conjugate roots.

Tip

It is useful to know the following shortcut:

$(x-z)(x-z^*) = x^2 - 2x\,\text{Re}(z) + |z|^2$

WORKED EXAMPLE 5.5

Given that one of the roots of the polynomial $f(x) = x^4 - 5x^3 + 26x^2 + 46x - 68$ is $3 - 5i$, find the remaining roots.

$3 - 5i$ is a root so $3 + 5i$ is also a root.	Complex roots come in conjugate pairs.
So $(x-(3-5i))$ and $(x-(3+5i))$ are factors of $f(x)$.	Link roots to factors (using the factor theorem).

Continues on next page...

145

Therefore

$(x-(3-5i))(x-(3+5i)) = x^2 - 6x + 34$

is a factor.

> Multiply out the brackets (using the shortcut described in the Tip):
> Let $z = 3 + 5i$; then $\text{Re}(z) = 3$ and $|z|^2 = 3^2 + 5^2 = 34$.

Factorising:

$x^4 - 5x^3 + 26x^2 + 46x - 68$
$= (x^2 - 6x + 34)(x^2 + x - 2)$

> Divide $f(x)$ by $x^2 - 6x + 34$ (using polynomial division or comparing coefficients).

Roots of the second factor:

$x^2 + x - 2 = 0$
$(x+2)(x-1) = 0$
$x = -2$ or 1

> You already know the roots of the first factor. Find the roots of the second factor by factorising.

So the roots of $f(x)$ are: $1, -2$ and $3 \pm 5i$.

You can also reverse this method to find a polynomial with given roots.

WORKED EXAMPLE 5.6

Find the real cubic polynomial with roots 3 and $4 + i$. Give your answer in the form $f(x) = x^3 + bx^2 + cx + d$.

3 is root of $f(x)$, so $(x-3)$ is a factor.

> From the factor theorem, if z is a root then $(x - z)$ is a factor.

$4 + i$ is a root, so $4 - i$ is another root.

So $f(x)$ also has factors $(x-(4+i))$ and $(x-(4-i))$.

> Complex roots occur in conjugate pairs.

Hence,

$f(x) = (x-3)(x-(4+i))(x-(4-i))$
$= (x-3)(x^2 - 8x + 17)$
$= x^3 - 11x^2 + 41x - 51$

> Expand the brackets; you can use the shortcut for $(x - z)(x - z^*)$:
> If $z = 4 + i$, then $\text{Re}(z) = 4$ and $|z|^2 = 4^2 + 1^2 = 17$.
> Expand and simplify.

5 Roots of polynomials

WORKED EXAMPLE 5.7

The polynomial $f(x) = x^4 + bx^3 + cx^2 + dx + e$ has roots $3i$ and $5 - i$. Find the values of the real numbers b, c, d and e.

The other two roots are $-3i$ and $5 + i$.
Write down the remaining roots and use them to find factors.

Hence, the two quadratic factors are:
$(x + 3i)(x - 3i) = x^2 + 9$
and
$(x - (5 - i))(x - (5 + i)) = x^2 - 10x + 26$
The complex conjugate pairs will give quadratic factors.

Hence,
$f(x) = (x^2 + 9)(x^2 - 10x + 26)$
$= x^4 - 10x^3 + 35x^2 - 90x + 234$
So $b = -10, c = 35, d = -90, e = 234$
Multiply the two factors to get the polynomial.

WORK IT OUT 5.1

Find a cubic polynomial with real coefficients given that two of its roots are 2 and $2i - 1$.

Which is the correct solution? Can you identify the errors made in the incorrect solutions?

Solution 1	Solution 2	Solution 3
The other complex root is $2i + 1$, so the polynomial is $(x - 2)(x - (2i - 1))(x - (2i + 1))$ $= (x - 2)(x^2 - 4ix - 5)$ $= x^3 - (2 + 4i)x^2 + (8i - 5)x + 10$	The other complex root is $-2i - 1$, so the polynomial is $(x + 2)(x - (2i - 1))(x - (-2i - 1))$ $= (x + 2)(x^2 + 2x + 5)$ $= x^3 + 4x^2 + 9x + 10$	The other complex root is $-1 - 2i$, so the polynomial is $(x - 2)(x - (-1 + 2i))(x - (-1 - 2i))$ $= (x - 2)(x^2 + 2x + 5)$ $= x^3 + x - 10$

EXERCISE 5B

1. Find the real values of a and b such that the quadratic equation $x^2 + ax + b = 0$ has the given roots.

   a i $5i$ and $-5i$
   ii $-3i$ and $3i$

   b i $3 - 4i$ and $3 + 4i$
   ii $1 + 2i$ and $1 - 2i$

2. Given one complex root of the cubic polynomial, factorise the polynomial and write down all its roots.

   a i $x^3 - 11x^2 + 43x - 65$, root $x = 3 + 2i$
   ii $x^3 - x^2 - 7x + 15$, root $x = 2 + i$

   b i $x^3 - 3x^2 + 7x - 5$, root $x = 1 - 2i$
   ii $x^3 - 2x^2 - 14x + 40$, root $x = 3 - i$

3 Given one complex root of the quartic polynomial, find one real quadratic factor and, hence, find all four roots.

  a i $x^4 - 2x^3 + 14x^2 - 8x + 40$, root $x = 1 + 3i$ **ii** $x^4 - 6x^3 + 11x^2 - 6x + 10$, root $x = 3 - i$

  b i $x^4 - 2x^3 + 8x^2 + 14x + 39$, root $x = 2 - 3i$ **ii** $x^4 - 3x^3 + 27x^2 + 21x + 58$, root $x = 2 + 5i$

  c i $x^4 + 2x^3 + 10x^2 + 8x + 24$, root $-2i$ **ii** $x^4 - 4x^3 + 21x^2 - 64x + 80$, root $4i$

4 In this question you must show detailed reasoning.

  Given that $5 - i$ is one root of the equation $x^3 - 8x^2 + 6x + 52 = 0$, find the remaining two roots.

5 Let $p(x) = x^3 + 3x^2 + 16x + 48$.

  a Show that $p(4i) = 0$. **b** Hence, solve the equation $p(x) = 0$.

6 In this question you must show detailed reasoning.

  Given that $2 + 5i$ is a root of the equation $x^4 - 4x^3 + 30x^2 - 4x + 29 = 0$:

  a write down another complex root of the equation **b** find the remaining two roots.

7 Two roots of the equation $x^4 - 8x^3 + 21x^2 - 32x + 68 = 0$ are $2i$ and $4 - i$. Write down the other two roots and, hence, write $x^4 - 8x^3 + 21x^2 - 32x + 68$ as a product of two real quadratic factors.

8 Let $f(z) = z^4 + z^3 + 5z^2 + 4z + 4$.

  a Show that $f(2i) = 0$.

  b Write $f(z)$ as a product of two real quadratic factors.

  c Hence, find the remaining solutions of the equation $f(z) = 0$.

9 Find a quartic equation with real coefficients and roots $4i$ and $3 - 2i$.

Section 3: Roots and coefficients

When you first learnt to solve quadratic equations, you were probably told to look for two numbers that add up to the middle coefficient and multiply to give the constant term. For example, $x^2 - 10x + 21$ factorises as $(x - 3)(x - 7)$ because $3 + 7 = 10$ and $3 \times 7 = 21$. Hence, the roots of the equation $x^2 - 10x + 21 = 0$ are 3 and 7.

But there are infinitely many other quadratic equations with the same roots, because you can multiply the whole equation by a constant. Another example of an equation with roots 3 and 7 is $3x^2 - 30x + 63 = 0$. The two roots still add up to 10, which is $\frac{30}{3}$, and multiply to give 21, which is $\frac{63}{3}$. This is a particular example of a very useful general result.

> **Key point 5.3**
>
> If p and q are the roots of the quadratic $ax^2 + bx + c = 0$, then
>
> - $p + q = -\frac{b}{a}$
> - $pq = \frac{c}{a}$

5 Roots of polynomials

PROOF 7

If a quadratic equation has roots p and q, then

$$(x-p)(x-q)=0$$
$$x^2-(p+q)x+pq=0$$
$$ax^2-a(p+q)x+apq=0$$

Hence, $b=-a(p+q)$ and $c=apq$.

So

$$p+q=-\frac{b}{a} \text{ and } pq=\frac{c}{a}.$$

- Write the equation in factorised form.
- You can multiply the whole equation by a number, and it will still have the same roots.
- Compare coefficients with ax^2+bx+c.

You can also find other functions of roots. This requires a little bit of algebraic manipulation.

WORKED EXAMPLE 5.8

The equation $5x^2+3x+1=0$ has roots p and q. Find the values of:

a $\dfrac{1}{p}+\dfrac{1}{q}$ **b** p^2+q^2

$$p+q=-\frac{b}{a}=-\frac{3}{5}$$

$$pq=\frac{c}{a}=\frac{1}{5}$$

- You could actually find the roots (by using the quadratic formula), but Key point 5.3 gives you a much quicker way to answer the question.

a $\dfrac{1}{p}+\dfrac{1}{q}=\dfrac{p+q}{pq}$

$$=\frac{-\frac{3}{5}}{\frac{1}{5}}$$

$$=-3$$

- It is often helpful to combine fractions into a single fraction.

b $(p+q)^2=p^2+2pq+q^2$

$\Rightarrow p^2+q^2=(p+q)^2-2pq$

$$=\left(-\frac{3}{5}\right)^2-2\left(\frac{1}{5}\right)$$

$$=-\frac{1}{25}$$

- You can get p^2+q^2 by squaring $p+q$.

- p^2+q^2 is a sum of two squares, so you may think that you made a mistake because the answer is negative. However, p and q can be complex numbers, so this is in fact possible!

Tip

We sometimes use Greek letters α (alpha), β (beta) and γ (gamma) instead of p, q, r for the roots.

WORKED EXAMPLE 5.9

The equation $3x^2 + kx - (k+1) = 0$ has roots α and β.

a Write down the expressions for $\alpha + \beta$ and $\alpha\beta$ in terms of k.

b Find $\alpha^3 + \beta^3$ in terms of k.

a $\alpha + \beta = -\dfrac{k}{3}$

$\alpha\beta = -\dfrac{k+1}{3}$

Use Key point 5.3:

$\alpha + \beta = -\dfrac{b}{a}$

$\alpha\beta = \dfrac{c}{a}$

b $(\alpha + \beta)^3 = \alpha^3 + 3\alpha^2\beta + 3\alpha\beta^2 + \beta^3$

$= \alpha^3 + \beta^3 + 3\alpha\beta(\alpha + \beta)$

$\Rightarrow \alpha^3 + \beta^3 = (\alpha + \beta)^3 - 3\alpha\beta(\alpha + \beta)$

$= -\dfrac{k^3}{27} - 3\left(-\dfrac{k+1}{3}\right)\left(-\dfrac{k}{3}\right)$

$= -\dfrac{k^3}{27} - \dfrac{k(k+1)}{3}$

$= -\dfrac{k^3 + 9k^2 + 9k}{27}$

$\alpha^3 + \beta^3$ can be found from the binomial expansion of $(\alpha + \beta)^3$. You need to try and express everything in terms of $\alpha + \beta$ and $\alpha\beta$.

EXERCISE 5C

1 The equation $x^2 - kx + 2k = 0$ has roots α and β. Find the following in terms of k:

a $\alpha + \beta$ **b** $2\alpha\beta$ **c** $\alpha^2 + \beta^2$

d $\dfrac{1}{\alpha} + \dfrac{1}{\beta}$ **e** $\alpha^3 + \beta^3$ **f** $\dfrac{1}{\alpha^2} + \dfrac{1}{\beta^2}$

2 The equation $ax^2 + 3x - a^2 = 0$ has roots p and q. Find the following in terms of a:

a $3p + 3q$ **b** p^2q^2 **c** $p^2 + q^2$ **d** $(p-q)^2$

Tip

Notice that every function you calculate relating to the the roots is 'symmetrical'; that is, you can exchange the values of the roots without effecting the value of the function. You could not use the method of this chapter to calculate, for example, $2\alpha + 3\beta$, or $\alpha - \beta$.

5 Roots of polynomials

Cubic and quartic equations

For cubic equations there are three relationships between roots and coefficients. Just as in the proof of the relationships between coefficients and roots of a quadratic, if the roots of the equation $ax^3 + bx^2 + cx + d = 0$ are p, q and r, then we can write:

$$ax^3 + bx^2 + cx + d = a(x-p)(x-q)(x-r)$$

Expanding and comparing coefficients gives the following results.

Key point 5.4

If p, q and r are the roots of the cubic $ax^3 + bx^2 + cx + d = 0$, then

- $p + q + r = -\dfrac{b}{a}$
- $pq + qr + rp = \dfrac{c}{a}$
- $pqr = -\dfrac{d}{a}$

Tip

Notice that the expressions are symmetrical in the three roots.

We can again combine these relationships with algebraic identities to find other combinations of roots.

WORKED EXAMPLE 5.10

The equation $x^3 - 3x^2 + 4x + 7 = 0$ has roots α, β and γ.

Find the value of $\alpha^2 + \beta^2 + \gamma^2$.

$(\alpha + \beta + \gamma)^2 = (\alpha + (\beta + \gamma))^2$
$= \alpha^2 + 2\alpha(\beta + \gamma) + (\beta + \gamma)^2$
$= \alpha^2 + 2\alpha\beta + 2\alpha\gamma + \beta^2 + \gamma^2 + 2\beta\gamma$
$= \alpha^2 + \beta^2 + \gamma^2 + 2(\alpha\beta + \beta\gamma + \gamma\alpha)$

$\alpha^2 + \beta^2 + \gamma^2$ can be found from the expansion of $(\alpha + \beta + \gamma)^2$.

$\alpha + \beta + \gamma = 3$
$\alpha\beta + \beta\gamma + \gamma\alpha = 4$

Now use the result in Key point 5.4 to find $\alpha + \beta + \gamma$ and $\alpha\beta + \beta\gamma + \gamma\alpha$.

$\therefore \alpha^2 + \beta^2 + \gamma^2 = 3^2 - 2(4) = 1$

Similar relationships between roots and coefficients can be found for polynomial equations of any degree. The expressions get increasingly complicated. For a quartic equation they are as follows.

A Level Further Mathematics for OCR A Pure Core Student Book 1

Key point 5.5

If p, q, r and s are the roots of the quartic $ax^4 + bx^3 + cx^2 + dx + e = 0$, then

- $p + q + r + s = -\dfrac{b}{a}$
- $pq + pr + ps + qr + qs + rs = \dfrac{c}{a}$
- $pqr + pqs + prs + qrs = -\dfrac{d}{a}$
- $pqrs = \dfrac{e}{a}$

Tip

It may help you remember these equations if you notice that the pattern is always the same:

- The sum of all the roots is related to $\dfrac{b}{a}$.
- The sum of all possible products of two roots is related to $\dfrac{c}{a}$.
- The sum of all possible products of three roots is related to $\dfrac{d}{a}$.

The signs alternate between − and +.

WORKED EXAMPLE 5.11

The equation $2x^4 - 3x^3 + x - 5 = 0$ has roots p, q, r and s. Find the value of $\dfrac{1}{p} + \dfrac{1}{q} + \dfrac{1}{r} + \dfrac{1}{s}$.

$\dfrac{1}{p} + \dfrac{1}{q} + \dfrac{1}{r} + \dfrac{1}{s} = \dfrac{qrs + prs + pqs + pqr}{pqrs}$ Combine into a single fraction.

$= \dfrac{-\frac{1}{2}}{-\frac{5}{2}}$ Use Key point 5.5:

$= \dfrac{1}{5}$ $pqr + pqs + prs + qrs = -\dfrac{d}{a}$

       $pqrs = \dfrac{e}{a}$

You can use information about the roots to prove facts about the coefficients of an equation.

Tip

Remember that an arithmetic sequence is one in which the term goes up by a constant number.

WORKED EXAMPLE 5.12

The roots p, q, r of the equation $x^3 - 3x^2 + cx + d = 0$ form an arithmetic sequence.

Show that $c + d = 2$.

$q - p = r - q$ If p, q, r form an arithmetic sequence then $q - p = r - q$.
$\Rightarrow p + r = 2q$

Continues on next page...

$p+q+r = -\dfrac{-3}{1} = 3$

You know three equations relating the roots to the coefficients. The most useful one seems to be $p+q+r = -\dfrac{b}{a}$. (Note that $a=1$.)

$\therefore q + 2q = 3$
$q = 1$

Substitute from $p+r = 2q$.

$pq + qr + rp = c$

$p + r + rp = c$

$2 + rp = c$

$\Rightarrow rp = c - 2$

To involve c and d you need to use the other two relationships as well. Start with $pq+qr+rp = \dfrac{c}{a}$ with $q=1$.

You know that $p+r = 2q = 2$.

$pqr = -d$

$pr = -d$

Finally, use $pqr = -\dfrac{d}{a}$ with $q=1$.

$\therefore c - 2 = -d$
$\Rightarrow c + d = 2$, as required

Substitute from $rp = c - 2$.

EXERCISE 5D

In this exercise you must show detailed reasoning.

1 The equation $3x^3 + 6x^2 + 12x - 4 = 0$ has roots p, q and r. Find the value of:

    a $p+q+r$ **b** $\dfrac{1}{p} + \dfrac{1}{q} + \dfrac{1}{r}$

    c $p^2qr + pq^2r + pqr^2$ **d** $p^2 + q^2 + r^2$

2 α, β, γ and δ are the roots of the given quartic equation. In each case, find the value of the given expressions.

    a $2x^4 - 4x^3 + 5x^2 + 3x - 1 = 0$; $\alpha\beta\gamma\delta$ and $\alpha\beta\gamma + \alpha\beta\delta + \alpha\gamma\delta + \beta\gamma\delta$

    b $3x^4 - 2x^2 + 1 = 0$; $\alpha + \beta + \gamma + \delta$ and $\alpha\beta + \alpha\gamma + \alpha\delta + \beta\gamma + \beta\delta + \gamma\delta$

    c $5x^4 - 3x - 8 = 0$; $\alpha + \beta + \gamma + \delta$ and $\alpha\beta\gamma\delta$

3 The equation $4x^3 - 2x^2 + 4x + 1 = 0$ has roots p, q and r. Find the value of $p^2qr + pq^2r + pqr^2$.

4 The equation $3x^3 + 2x^2 - x + 5 = 0$ has roots a, b and c. Find the value of:

    a $\dfrac{1}{a} + \dfrac{1}{b} + \dfrac{1}{c}$ **b** $\dfrac{1}{ab} + \dfrac{1}{bc} + \dfrac{1}{ca}$

5 When two resistors of resistances R_1 and R_2 (in suitable units) are connected in series in an electric circuit, the total resistance in the circuit is $R = R_1 + R_2$. When they are connected in parallel, the total resistance satisfies $\dfrac{1}{R} = \dfrac{1}{R_1} + \dfrac{1}{R_2}$.

Two resistors have resistances equal to the two roots of the quadratic equation $3R^2 - 12R + 4 = 0$. Find the total resistance in the circuit if the two resistors are connected:

   a in series   **b** in parallel.

6 The cubic equation $3x^3 - 5x - 3 = 0$ has roots α, β and γ.

   a Write down the value of $\alpha\beta\gamma$.

   b Show that $\alpha + \beta = -\dfrac{1}{\alpha\beta}$.

7 A random number generator can produce four possible values, all of which are equally likely. The four values satisfy the equation $x^4 - 9x^3 + 26x^2 - 29x + 10 = 0$.

If a large number of random values are generated, estimate their mean.

8 The equation $x^4 + bx^3 + cx^2 + dx + e = 0$ has roots p, $2p$, $3p$ and $4p$. Show that $125e = \dfrac{3}{10}b^4$.

9 The equation $x^3 + 2ax^2 + 3a^2x + 2 = 0$, where a is a real constant, has roots p, q and r.

   a Find an expression for $p^2 + q^2 + r^2$ in terms of a.

   b Explain why this implies that the roots are not all real.

 Rewind

Question **9** is an example of proof by contradiction, which you learnt about in A Level Mathematics Student Book 2, Chapter 1.

Section 4: Finding an equation with given roots

The relationships between roots of polynomials and their coefficients can be used to find unknown coefficients in an equation with given roots.

 Rewind

You can already do this by writing down the factors and expanding brackets (see Worked examples 5.6 and 5.7), but this method is more direct.

5 Roots of polynomials

WORKED EXAMPLE 5.13

The quadratic equation $5x^2 + bx + c = 0$ has real coefficients and one of its roots is $4 + 7i$. Find the values of b and c.

The other root is $4 - 7i$. | Complex roots occur in conjugate pairs.

Then
$$(4+7i)+(4-7i) = -\frac{b}{5}$$
$$8 = -\frac{b}{5}$$
$$b = -40$$

Use $p + q = -\frac{b}{a}$.

$$(4+7i)(4-7i) = \frac{c}{5}$$

Use $pq = \frac{c}{a}$.

$$4^2 + 7^2 = \frac{c}{5}$$
$$c = 325$$

Remember that $zz^* = |z|^2$.

WORKED EXAMPLE 5.14

A quartic equation $x^4 + ax^3 + 14x^2 - 18x + b = 0$ has real coefficients and two of its roots are $3i$ and $1 - 2i$. Find the values of a and b.

The four roots are:
$3i, -3i, 1+2i, 1-2i$

As you know two of the complex roots, you can find the other two (their conjugates).

$$(3i)+(-3i)+(1-2i)+(1+2i) = -\frac{a}{1}$$
$$2 = -\frac{a}{1}$$
$$a = -2$$

Use $p + q + r + s = -\frac{x^3 \text{ coefficient}}{x^4 \text{ coefficient}}$. (Be wary of using a, b, c, d, e as shortcuts for the coefficients of x^4, x^3 etc. When those letters are defined differently in a question. Here, a is given as the coefficient of x^3.)

$$(3i)(-3i)(1-2i)(1+2i) = \frac{b}{1}$$

Use $pqrs = \frac{x^0 \text{ coefficient}}{x^4 \text{ coefficient}}$.

$$9(1^2 + 2^2) = b$$
$$b = 45$$

Use $zz^* = |z|^2$.

You can also find a new equation whose roots are related to the roots of a given equation in some way – and you can do this without solving the equation. The strategy is to use the sum and product of roots of the first equation to find the sum and product of roots of the second equation.

WORKED EXAMPLE 5.15

The quadratic equation $3x^2 - 4x + 7 = 0$ has roots p and q. Find a quadratic equation with integer coefficients and roots p^2 and q^2.

$p + q = -\dfrac{-4}{3} = \dfrac{4}{3}$ | You don't need to find p and q, just their sum and product.
$pq = \dfrac{7}{3}$

Let the equation be $ax^2 + bx + c = 0$.

Then

$p^2 + q^2 = -\dfrac{b}{a}$ and $p^2 q^2 = \dfrac{c}{a}$ | Relate the coefficients of the new equation to the roots p^2 and q^2.

Set $a = 1$. | All equations with the required roots are multiples of each other, so you can set $a = 1$.

Then

$b = -(p^2 + q^2)$ and $c = p^2 q^2$

$c = p^2 q^2$
$= (pq)^2$ | You need to relate $p^2 + q^2$ and $p^2 q^2$ to $p + q$ and pq. The second one is easier.

$= \left(\dfrac{7}{3}\right)^2$ | Substitute $pq = \dfrac{7}{3}$.

$= \dfrac{49}{9}$

$(p+q)^2 = p^2 + 2pq + p^2$
$\Rightarrow p^2 + q^2 = (p+q)^2 - 2pq$ | To find $p^2 + q^2$, consider $(p+q)^2$.

$b = -(p^2 + q^2)$
$= -((p+q)^2 - 2pq)$ | Substitute $p + q = \dfrac{4}{3}$ and $pq = \dfrac{7}{3}$.

$= -\left(\left(\dfrac{4}{3}\right)^2 - 2\left(\dfrac{7}{3}\right)\right)$

$= \dfrac{26}{9}$

The equation is

$x^2 + \dfrac{26}{9}x + \dfrac{49}{9} = 0$ | Substitute into $ax^2 + bx + c = 0$.

$\Leftrightarrow 9x^2 + 26x + 49 = 0$ | We want the equation with integer coefficients, so multiply through by 9.

5 Roots of polynomials

WORKED EXAMPLE 5.16

The equation $x^3 - 3x^2 + 2 = 0$ has roots p, q and r. Find a cubic equation with roots $3p$, $3q$ and $3r$.

For the equation $x^3 - 3x^2 + 2 = 0$, $p + q + r = 3$ $pq + qr + rp = 0$ $pqr = -2$	Use the relationship between coefficients and roots (Key point 5.4) for the original equation.
Write the required equation as $x^3 + bx^2 + cx + d = 0$	You can set the coefficient of x^3 to be 1.
If the roots of this equation are $3p$, $3q$ and $3r$ then: $3p + 3q + 3r = -b$	Use the first part of Key point 5.4 for the new equation.
$3(p + q + r) = -b$ $3(3) = -b$ $b = -9$	$p + q + r = 3$ from the first equation.
$(3p)(3q) + (3q)(3r) + (3r)(3p) = c$	Use the second part of Key point 5.4 for the new equation.
$9(pq + qr + rp) = c$ $9(0) = c$ $c = 0$	$pq + qr + rp = 0$
$(3p)(3q)(3r) = -d$	Use the third part of Key point 5.4 for the new equation.
$27pqr = -d$ $27(-2) = -d$ $d = 54$	$pqr = -2$
The equation is: $x^3 - 9x^2 + 54 = 0$	

▶▶ Fast forward

You will see in Section 5 that the equation from the previous example can also be found by using the substitution $u = 3x$.

157

WORKED EXAMPLE 5.17

The equation $3x^3 - 5x^2 + x - 3 = 0$ has roots α, β and γ. Find a cubic equation with roots $\alpha\beta$, $\beta\gamma$ and $\gamma\alpha$.

For the equation $3x^3 - 5x^2 + x - 3 = 0$,
$\alpha + \beta + \gamma = \dfrac{5}{3}$

$\alpha\beta + \beta\gamma + \gamma\alpha = \dfrac{1}{3}$

$\alpha\beta\gamma = \dfrac{3}{3}$

Use the relationship between roots and coefficients (Key point 5.4) for the original equation.

If the equation with roots $\alpha\beta$, $\beta\gamma$ and $\gamma\alpha$ is $x^3 + bx^2 + cx + d = 0$ then

You can take the coefficient of x^3 to be 1.

$\alpha\beta + \beta\gamma + \gamma\alpha = -b$

$b = -\dfrac{1}{3}$

The sum of the roots of the new equation is $-\dfrac{b}{1}$.

$(\alpha\beta)(\beta\gamma) + (\beta\gamma)(\gamma\alpha) + (\gamma\alpha)(\alpha\beta) = c$

Use the second part of Key point 5.4.

$\alpha\beta\gamma(\alpha + \beta + \gamma) = c$

$\left(\dfrac{3}{3}\right)\left(\dfrac{5}{3}\right) = c$

$c = \dfrac{5}{3}$

Factorise to get $\alpha\beta\gamma$ and $(\alpha + \beta + \gamma)$ terms, as you know their values.

$(\alpha\beta)(\beta\gamma)(\gamma\alpha) = -d$

$(\alpha\beta\gamma)^2 = -d$

$\left(\dfrac{3}{3}\right)^2 = -da$

$d = -1$

The product of the roots is $-\dfrac{d}{1}$.

So the equation is

$x^3 - \dfrac{1}{3}x^2 + \dfrac{5}{3}x - 1 = 0$

You can also write this equation as $3x^3 - x^2 + 5x - 3 = 0$.

5 Roots of polynomials

EXERCISE 5E

1 Given the roots of the equations, find the missing coefficients.

    a   **i** $3x^3 - ax^2 - 3x + b = 0$, roots $1, -1, -2$ **ii** $2x^3 + ax^2 + 10x + c = 0$, roots $1, 1, 2$

    b   **i** $x^3 - ax^2 + 4x - b = 0$, roots $3, 2i, -2i$ **ii** $x^3 + bx^2 + 9x + d = 0$, roots $2+i, 2-i, 1$

2 Find the polynomial of the lowest possible order with given roots.

    a   **i** $5 + 2i, 5 - 2i$ **ii** $3 - i, 3 + i$

    b   **i** $1, 3i, -3i$ **ii** $5, i - 1$

    c   **i** $2, -1, 1 + 2i, 1 - 2i$ **ii** $-3, 1, 2 + i, 2 - i$

    d   **i** $-2, 4 + 3i, 4 - 3i$ **ii** $1, -2 + 3i, -2 - 3i$

3 A cubic equation has real coefficients and two of its roots are 2 and $4 - i$.

    a Write down the third root.

    b Find the equation in the form $x^3 + bx^2 + cx + d = 0$.

4 The quartic equation $x^4 - ax^3 + bx^2 - cx + d = 0$ has real coefficients, and two of its roots are $3i$ and $3 - i$.

    a Write down the other two roots.

    b Hence, find the values of a and d.

In questions 5 to 12 you must show detailed reasoning.

5 The equation $x^3 - 3x^2 + 4x + 1 = 0$ has roots p, q and r. Find a cubic equation with roots $3p, 3q$ and $3r$.

6 The equation $4x^3 - 3x + 5 = 0$ has roots α, β and γ. Find a cubic equation with integer coefficients and roots $\alpha - 2, \beta - 2$ and $\gamma - 2$.

7 The quadratic equation $5x^2 - 3x + 2 = 0$ has roots p and q. Find a quadratic equation with roots $\dfrac{1}{p}$ and $\dfrac{1}{q}$.

8 The equation $x^4 - 3x^3 + x + 2 = 0$ has roots a, b, c and d. Find a quartic equation with roots $2a, 2b, 2c$ and $2d$.

9 Let p and q be the roots of the equation $5x^2 - 3x + 2 = 0$.

    a Find the values of pq and $p^2 + q^2$.

    b Hence, find a quadratic equation with integer coefficients and roots p^2 and q^2.

10 The equation $x^3 - 3x^2 + 5 = 0$ has roots α, β and γ.

    a Find the value of $\dfrac{1}{\alpha\beta} + \dfrac{1}{\beta\gamma} + \dfrac{1}{\gamma\alpha}$.

    b Find a cubic equation with roots $\dfrac{1}{\alpha}, \dfrac{1}{\beta}$ and $\dfrac{1}{\gamma}$.

11 The equation $4x^3 - 3x + 7 = 0$ has roots p, q and r. Find a cubic equation with integer coefficients and roots pq, qr and rp.

12 **a** Expand $(\alpha\beta + \beta\gamma + \gamma\alpha)^2$.

    b If α, β and γ are the roots of the equation $x^3 - x^2 + 2x + 6 = 0$, find a cubic equation with roots α^2, β^2 and γ^2.

Section 5: Transforming equations

In the last section you saw how to use relationships between roots and coefficients of a polynomial equation to find another equation with roots related to the roots of the first one.

In some cases, however, there is a quicker way to find this equation, by using a substitution.

Suppose the original equation, with roots p and q, is $5x^2 - 2x + 1 = 0$.

If you set $x = \dfrac{u}{3}$, you get a new equation:

$5\left(\dfrac{u}{3}\right)^2 - 2\left(\dfrac{u}{3}\right) + 1 = 0$

$\Leftrightarrow 5u^2 - 6u + 9 = 0$

Since $u = 3x$, this equation has roots $3p$ and $3q$.

We can formulate the general principle like this.

Key point 5.6

If an equation in x has a root $x = p$, and if we make a substitution $u = \text{f}(x)$, then the resulting equation in u has a root $u = \text{f}(p)$.

WORKED EXAMPLE 5.18

The equation $3x^3 - x^2 + 2x + 5 = 0$ has roots p, q and r.

a Find a cubic equation with roots $p - 2$, $q - 2$ and $r - 2$.
b Hence, find the value of $(p-2)(q-2)(r-2)$.

$u = x - 2$ $\Rightarrow x = u + 2$	When $x = p$, $u = p - 2$ so make the substitution $u = x - 2$.
$3(u+2)^3 - (u+2)^2 + 2(u+2) + 5 = 0$ $3(u^3 + 6u^2 + 12u + 8) - (u^2 + 4u + 4) + 2u + 4 + 5 = 0$ $3u^3 + 17u^2 + 34u + 29 = 0$	Substitute for x.
$\therefore (p-2)(q-2)(r-2) = -\dfrac{29}{3}$	This is the product of the roots of the equation in u.

Tip

Part **b** of this worked example can be answered by also expanding $(p - 2)(q - 2)(r - 2)$ and using the relationships between roots and coefficients of the original equation. You can decide for yourself which method is simpler.

5 Roots of polynomials

WORK IT OUT 5.2

The roots of the quadratic equation $3x^2 - x + 5 = 0$ are p and q. Find a quadratic equation with roots $\dfrac{p}{5}$ and $\dfrac{q}{5}$.

Which is the correct solution? Can you identify the errors made in the incorrect solutions?

Solution 1	Solution 2	Solution 3
From the first equation: $p + q = 1$ and $pq = 5$ So for the second equation: $\dfrac{p}{5} + \dfrac{q}{5} = \dfrac{1}{5}$ and $\dfrac{p}{5} \times \dfrac{q}{5} = \dfrac{5}{25} = \dfrac{1}{5}$ Hence, the new equation is: $x^2 - \dfrac{1}{5}x + \dfrac{1}{5} = 0$ $\Leftrightarrow 5x^2 - x + 1 = 0$	Let $u = \dfrac{x}{5}$; then $\dfrac{p}{5}$ and $\dfrac{q}{5}$ are the roots for u. Make the substitution $x = 5u$: $3(5u)^2 - (5u) + 5 = 0$ $\Leftrightarrow 15u^2 - u + 1 = 0$	Replace x by $\dfrac{x}{5}$: $3\left(\dfrac{x}{5}\right)^2 - \left(\dfrac{x}{5}\right) + 1 = 0$ $\Leftrightarrow 3x^2 - 5x + 25 = 0$

Sometimes the resulting equation in u needs to be rearranged in order to turn it into a polynomial. This happens whenever x is not a linear function of u.

> ⏮ **Rewind**
>
> See Worked example 5.15 for a different method of solving the following problem.

WORKED EXAMPLE 5.19

The equation $7x^2 - 2x + 5 = 0$ has roots p and q.

Find a quadratic equation with roots p^2 and q^2.

$u = x^2$ .... When $x = p$, $u = p^2$, so make the substitution $u = x^2$.
$\Rightarrow x = \sqrt{u}$

$7(\sqrt{u})^2 - 2(\sqrt{u}) + 5 = 0$ .... Substitute for x.
$7u - 2\sqrt{u} + 5 = 0$

$(7u + 5)^2 = (2\sqrt{u})^2$ .... To turn this into a quadratic equation, you need to get rid of the square root, so you need to isolate it and square both sides.
$49u^2 + 70u + 25 = 4u$
$49u^2 + 66u + 25 = 0$

161

You may wish to use technology to solve both equations and check that the relationship between the roots is correct.

A substitution is particularly useful if it transforms a difficult equation into one that can be solved easily.

WORKED EXAMPLE 5.20

Use the substitution $x = u - 1$ to solve the equation $x^4 + 4x^3 + 6x^2 + 4x - 80 = 0$.

$(u-1)^4 + 4(u-1)^3 + 6(u-1)^2 + 4(u-1) - 80 = 0$ — Make the given substitution.

$u^4 - 4u^3 + 6u^2 - 4u + 1$
$ + 4u^3 - 12u^2 + 12u - 4$
$ + 6u^2 - 12u + 6$
$ + 4u - 4 - 80 = 0$

It's a good idea to line up terms when expanding lots of brackets.

$u^4 - 81 = 0$
$(u^2 - 9)(u^2 + 9) = 0$
$u = \pm 3, \pm 3i$

The equation in u can be solved by factorising.

$\therefore x = 2, -4, -1 + 3i, -1 - 3i$ — Use $x = u - 1$.

🔍 Explore

This sort of substitution is the first step in deriving Cardano's formula for solving cubic equations; see what you can find out about it!

EXERCISE 5F

1 Use the given substitution to transform the equation in x into a polynomial equation for u. You may wish to use technology to find roots of both equations and comment on how they are related.

   a   **i** $x^3 - 3x + 1 = 0$, $x = 2u$ **ii** $x^3 + 2x^2 + 5 = 0$, $x = 3u$

   b   **i** $3x^3 - x + 4 = 0$, $x = u - 2$ **ii** $2x^3 + x^2 + 1 = 0$, $x = u + 1$

   c   **i** $5x^3 - 3x^2 + 4x + 15 = 0$, $x = \dfrac{1}{u}$ **ii** $x^3 - 2x^2 - 6x + 10 = 0$, $x = \dfrac{2}{u}$

   d   **i** $3x^2 - x + 3 = 0$, $x = \sqrt{u}$ **ii** $2x^2 + 2x + 1 = 0$, $x = \sqrt{u}$

2 The equation $3x^3 - 4x + 2 = 0$ has roots p, q and r. Use a suitable substitution to find a cubic equation with roots $p - 1$, $q - 1$ and $r - 1$.

3 The equation $2x^4 + 2x + 5 = 0$ has roots a, b, c and d. Find a quartic equation with integer coefficients and roots $\dfrac{a}{2}, \dfrac{b}{2}, \dfrac{c}{2}$ and $\dfrac{d}{2}$.

5 Roots of polynomials

4 a Show that the substitution $x = u - 2$ transforms the equation $x^3 + 6x^2 + 21x + 26 = 0$ into the equation $u^3 + 9u = 0$.

  b Hence, solve the equation $x^3 + 6x^2 + 21x + 26 = 0$.

5 a Find the value of c so that the substitution $x = u + c$ transforms the equation $x^3 - 12x^2 + 45x - 54 = 0$ into the equation $u^3 - 3u^2 = 0$.

  b Hence, find all the solutions of the equation $x^3 - 12x^2 + 45x - 54 = 0$.

6 The equation $3x^3 - x^2 + 5x - 3 = 0$ has roots p, q and r. Use a substitution to find a cubic equation with roots $\dfrac{1}{p}, \dfrac{1}{q}$ and $\dfrac{1}{r}$.

7 The equation $3x^2 - 2x + 5 = 0$ has roots α and β. Using the substitution $x = 3u + 1$, or otherwise, find the value of $\left(\dfrac{\alpha-1}{3}\right)\left(\dfrac{\beta-1}{3}\right)$.

8 The equation $5x^3 - x^2 + 3x + 2 = 0$ has roots a, b and c.

  a Use the substitution $x = \dfrac{1}{u}$ to find a cubic equation for u.

  b Hence, find the value of $\dfrac{1}{ab} + \dfrac{1}{bc} + \dfrac{1}{ca}$.

9 The equation $2x^3 - 5x^2 + 3x + 2 = 0$ has roots p, q and r. Use a suitable substitution to find the value of $\left(\dfrac{1}{p}-1\right)\left(\dfrac{1}{q}-1\right)\left(\dfrac{1}{r}-1\right)$.

10 The equation $x^3 - 2x - 5 = 0$ has roots p, q and r. Use a substitution to find a cubic equation with roots p^2, q^2 and r^2.

11 The equation $3x^2 - 9x + 1 = 0$ has roots α and β. Using a suitable substitution, or otherwise, find an equation with roots α^2 and β^2.

12 The substitution $x = u - k$ transforms the equation $x^4 + 4x^3 + 11x^2 + 14x + 10 = 0$ into an equation of the form $u^4 + bx^2 + c = 0$.

  a Find the value of k.

  b Hence, solve the equation $x^4 + 4x^3 + 11x^2 + 14x + 10 = 0$.

Checklist of learning and understanding

- Complex roots of real polynomials occur in conjugate pairs: if f(z) = 0 then f(z*) = 0. This fact can be used to factorise cubic and quartic polynomials.
- Coefficients of a polynomial can be related to the symmetric functions of its roots.
  - For a quadratic polynomial $ax^2 + bx + c = 0$ with roots p and q:

    $p + q = -\dfrac{b}{a}$

    $pq = \dfrac{c}{a}$
  - For a cubic polynomial $ax^3 + bx^2 + cx + d = 0$ with roots p, q and r:

    $p + q + r = -\dfrac{b}{a}$

    $pq + qr + rp = \dfrac{c}{a}$

    $pqr = -\dfrac{d}{a}$
  - For a quartic polynomial $ax^4 + bx^3 + cx^2 + dx + e = 0$ with roots p, q, r and s:

    $p + q + r + s = -\dfrac{b}{a}$

    $pq + pr + ps + qr + qs + rs = \dfrac{c}{a}$

    $pqr + pqs + prs + qrs = -\dfrac{d}{a}$

    $pqrs = \dfrac{e}{a}$
- These relationships can be used to find:
  - a polynomial with given roots
  - a polynomial with roots related to the roots of another polynomial.
- The second of these problems can sometimes also be solved by making a substitution.

Mixed practice 5

1 Given that $z = 3i$ is one root of the equation $z^3 - 2z^2 + 9z - 18 = 0$, find the other two roots.

2 $f(z) = z^3 + az^2 + bz + c$, where a, b, c are real constants. Two roots of $f(z) = 0$ are $z = 1$ and $z = 1 + 2i$. Find a, b and c.

3 One of the roots of the polynomial $g(x) = x^3 + 3x^2 - 7x + 15$ is $1 + i\sqrt{2}$.

   a Write down another complex root and, hence, find a real quadratic factor of $g(x)$.

   b Solve the equation $g(x) = 0$.

4 Find a quartic equation with real coefficients given that three of its roots are $2i$, -1 and 5.

5 The cubic equation $2x^3 + 3x - 3 = 0$ has roots α, β and γ.

   a Use the substitution $x = u - 1$ to find a cubic equation in u with integer coefficients.

   b Hence find the value of $(\alpha + 1)(\beta + 1)(\gamma + 1)$.

© OCR, AS GCE Further Mathematics, Paper 4725, January 2010
[Question part reference style adapted]

6 Given that $z = 1 + 2i$ is one root of the equation $z^3 + z^2 - z + 15 = 0$, find the other two roots.

7 Two roots of the cubic equation $z^3 + bz^2 + cz + d = 0$ ($b, c, d \in \mathbb{R}$) are -2 and $2 - 3i$.

   a Write down the third root.

   b Find the values of b, c and d.

8 The polynomial $z^3 + az^2 + bz - 65$ has a factor of $(z - 2 - 3i)$. Find the values of the real constants a and b.

9 **a** Show that $\alpha^3 + \beta^3 = (\alpha + \beta)^3 - 3\alpha\beta(\alpha + \beta)$.

   b Let α and β be the roots of the quadratic equation $x^2 + 7x + 2 = 0$. Find a quadratic equation with roots α^3 and β^3.

10 The equation $3x^3 - 4x^2 + 7x + 1 = 0$ has roots p, q and r. Use the substitution $u = x - 3$ to find a cubic equation with roots $p - 3$, $q - 3$ and $r - 3$.

11 The equation $5x^3 - 9x + 4 = 0$ has roots α, β and γ. Use a substitution of the form $u = kx$ to find a cubic equation with roots $\dfrac{\alpha}{2}$, $\dfrac{\beta}{2}$ and $\dfrac{\gamma}{2}$.

12 The quadratic equation $x^2 + 5x + 10 = 0$ has roots α and β.

   a Write down the values of $\alpha + \beta$ and $\alpha\beta$.

   b Show that $\alpha^2 + \beta^2 = 5$.

   c Hence find a quadratic equation that has roots $\dfrac{\alpha}{\beta}$ and $\dfrac{\beta}{\alpha}$.

© OCR, AS GCE Further Mathematics, Paper 4725, January 2007
[Question part reference style adapted]

13 **a** A cubic equation $ax^3 + bx^2 + cx + d = 0$ has roots x_1, x_2 and x_3.

   i Write down the values of $x_1 + x_2 + x_3$ and $x_1 x_2 x_3$ in terms of a, b, c and d.

   ii Show that $x_1 x_2 + x_2 x_3 + x_3 x_1 = \dfrac{c}{a}$.

b The roots α, β and γ of the equation $2x^3 + bx^2 + cx + 16 = 0$ form a geometric sequence.

  i Show that $\beta = -2$.

  ii Show that $c = 2b$.

 Rewind

Geometric series are covered in A Level Mathematics Student Book 2, Chapter 4.

 a Show that:

  i $p^2 + q^2 + r^2 = (p+q+r)^2 - 2(pq+qr+rp)$

  ii $p^2q^2 + q^2r^2 + r^2p^2 = (pq+qr+rp)^2 - 2pqr(p+q+r)$.

b Given that the cubic equation $ax^3 + bx^2 + cx + d = 0$ has roots p, q and r:

  i write down the values of $p+q+r$ and pqr in terms of a, b, c and d

  ii show that $pq + qr + rp = \dfrac{c}{a}$.

c The equation $2x^3 - 5x + 2 = 0$ has roots x_1, x_2 and x_3.

  i Show that $x_1^2 + x_2^2 + x_3^2 = 5$.

  ii Find the values of $x_1^2 x_2^2 + x_2^2 x_3^2 + x_3^2 x_1^2$ and $x_1^2 x_2^2 x_3^2$.

  iii Hence, find a cubic equation with integer coefficients and roots x_1^2, x_2^2 and x_3^2.

6 Mathematical induction

In this chapter you will learn how to:

- use the principle of induction to prove whether patterns continue forever
- apply this principle to matrices
- apply this principle to number theory
- apply this principle to inequalities
- adapt the method to solve problems in a range of other contexts.

Before you start…

GCSE	You should be able to use laws of indices.	1 a Given that $3^n - 7 = A$, express $3^{n+1} - 7$ in terms of A. b Simplify $5^{n+2} - 5^n$.
Chapter 1	You should be able to multiply matrices.	2 Given that $\mathbf{M} = \begin{pmatrix} 1 & a \\ 0 & 2 \end{pmatrix}$ find $\mathbf{M}^3$.
A Level Mathematics Student Book 1, Chapter 9	You should be able to work with factorials.	3 Simplify $26! - 25!$

What is mathematical induction?

In both mathematics and science we are very interested in patterns. In science, we observe patterns and conjecture a general rule; this is called inductive reasoning. There is no way to prove that this rule is correct, and the pattern may not continue forever. In mathematics, you have come across deductive reasoning, where you start from known facts and use logic to derive new results. But sometimes a potential new result is based on observations of a pattern. In such cases, you need a way of proving that the pattern continues indefinitely. One of the most powerful ways of doing this is a method called mathematical induction.

🔍 Explore

Kurt Gödel, 1906–1978, was an Austrian, and later American, logician, mathematician and philosopher. Gödel proved that there are some true mathematical facts that can never be proved! Find out about *Gödel's Incompleteness Theorem*.

Section 1: The principle of mathematical induction

Powers of matrices sometimes follow interesting patterns.
Suppose you want to find the 15th power of the matrix $\mathbf{A} = \begin{pmatrix} 1 & 1 \\ 0 & 1 \end{pmatrix}$.

In general, raising a matrix to a power requires repeated multiplication. But in this case there seems to be a helpful pattern:

$$\mathbf{A}^2 = \begin{pmatrix} 1 & 2 \\ 0 & 1 \end{pmatrix}, \mathbf{A}^3 = \begin{pmatrix} 1 & 3 \\ 0 & 1 \end{pmatrix}, \mathbf{A}^4 = \begin{pmatrix} 1 & 4 \\ 0 & 1 \end{pmatrix}, \mathbf{A}^5 = \begin{pmatrix} 1 & 5 \\ 0 & 1 \end{pmatrix} \ldots$$

It appears that $\mathbf{A}^n = \begin{pmatrix} 1 & n \\ 0 & 1 \end{pmatrix}$ for all integer powers n. But how can you be **certain** that the observed pattern continues?

> **Tip**
>
> Remember that you can use your calculator to find powers of a matrix.

Suppose that you have checked (by repeated multiplication) that the pattern above holds up to $n = 10$; so you know that $\mathbf{A}^{10} = \begin{pmatrix} 1 & 10 \\ 0 & 1 \end{pmatrix}$. To confirm that the pattern continues to $n = 11$, you don't have to start the multiplication from the beginning; you can use the result for $\mathbf{A}^{10}$ that you have already checked:

$$\mathbf{A}^{11} = \mathbf{A}^{10}\mathbf{A}$$

$$= \begin{pmatrix} 1 & 10 \\ 0 & 1 \end{pmatrix}\begin{pmatrix} 1 & 1 \\ 0 & 1 \end{pmatrix}$$

$$= \begin{pmatrix} 1 & 11 \\ 0 & 1 \end{pmatrix}$$

You can then repeat the same procedure to continue the pattern from $n = 11$ to $n = 12$, from $n = 12$ to $n = 13$, and so on up to $n = 15$.

In general, **suppose** that you have checked that the pattern holds up to some $n = k$. This means that $\mathbf{A}^k = \begin{pmatrix} 1 & k \\ 0 & 1 \end{pmatrix}$. You can then **prove** that it continues up to $n = k + 1$, because:

$$\mathbf{A}^{k+1} = \mathbf{A}^k \mathbf{A}$$

$$= \begin{pmatrix} 1 & k \\ 0 & 1 \end{pmatrix}\begin{pmatrix} 1 & 1 \\ 0 & 1 \end{pmatrix}$$

$$= \begin{pmatrix} 1 & k+1 \\ 0 & 1 \end{pmatrix}$$

So $\mathbf{A}^{k+1}$ still has the required form.

Building upon the previous result like this, rather than starting all over again, is called an **inductive step**. In this example it is fairly straightforward, but in other problems this can be more difficult.

You have now found out the following things about the pattern $\mathbf{A}^n = \begin{pmatrix} 1 & n \\ 0 & 1 \end{pmatrix}$:

1. The pattern holds for the first case: when $n = 1$, $\mathbf{A}^1 = \begin{pmatrix} 1 & 1 \\ 0 & 1 \end{pmatrix}$.
2. If you **assume** the pattern up to some power k, you can then **prove** that it also holds for the next power, $k + 1$.

Does this prove that the pattern continues forever? You know that it holds for $n = 1$; because it holds for $n = 1$ it follows that it holds for $n = 2$; because it holds for $n = 2$ it follows that it holds for $n = 3$; and so on.

Key point 6.1

Suppose that you have a statement (or rule) about a positive integer n. If you can show that:
1. the statement is true for $n = 1$, and
2. if you **assume** that the statement is true for $n = k$, then you can **prove** that it is also true for $n = k + 1$

then the statement is true for all positive integers n.

You can continue this process to reach any number n, however large. Therefore, the pattern holds for all positive integers.

The previous example illustrates the **principle of mathematical induction**.

The hardest part is, undoubtedly, step 2. To do this you need to make a link between one proposition and the next – the inductive step. The exact way to do this depends upon the type of problem. In the following sections you will see how to apply the principle of mathematical induction in various contexts.

Section 2: Induction and matrices

As you saw in Section 1, mathematical induction can be used to prove results about powers of matrices. The inductive steps involve relating one power to the next one.

Key point 6.2

When using induction to prove a result about powers of matrices, use:
$$\mathbf{A}^{k+1} = \mathbf{A}^k \mathbf{A}$$

It is very important that your proof is set out clearly, following the steps given in Key point 6.1 and illustrated in Worked example 6.1.

WORKED EXAMPLE 6.1

Use mathematical induction to prove that $\begin{pmatrix} 3 & -4 \\ 1 & -1 \end{pmatrix}^n = \begin{pmatrix} 1+2n & -4n \\ n & 1-2n \end{pmatrix}$ for all integers $n \geq 1$.

Let $\underline{A} = \begin{pmatrix} 3 & -4 \\ 1 & -1 \end{pmatrix}$. We want to prove:

$\underline{A}^n = \begin{pmatrix} 1+2n & -4n \\ n & 1-2n \end{pmatrix}$

⋯ State the result you are trying to prove.

When $n = 1$:

$\underline{A}^1 = \begin{pmatrix} 3 & -4 \\ 1 & -1 \end{pmatrix} = \begin{pmatrix} 1+2\times 1 & -4\times 1 \\ 1 & 1-2\times 1 \end{pmatrix}$

⋯ Check that the result is true for the starting value (in this case, $n = 1$).

Assume that the result is true for some $n = k$. Then:

$\underline{A}^k = \begin{pmatrix} 1+2k & -4k \\ k & 1-2k \end{pmatrix}$

⋯ Assume the result is true for $n = k$. Write down what that means. (You will need to use this result later.)

When $n = k + 1$, we are working towards:

$\underline{A}^{k+1} = \begin{pmatrix} 1+2(k+1) & -4(k+1) \\ k+1 & 1-2(k+1) \end{pmatrix}$

$= \begin{pmatrix} 3+2k & -4k-4 \\ k+1 & -1-2k \end{pmatrix}$

⋯ Write down what you are trying to prove. It will help you in your working, but you **must not** use this result! Remember, you cannot use the result you are trying to prove as part of the reasoning in your proof.

LHS $= \underline{A}^k \underline{A}$

$= \begin{pmatrix} 1+2k & -4k \\ k & 1-2k \end{pmatrix} \begin{pmatrix} 3 & -4 \\ 1 & -1 \end{pmatrix}$

⋯ Make a link between $\underline{A}^{k+1}$ and $\underline{A}^k$. This is where you use the assumption that the statement is true for $n = k$.

$= \begin{pmatrix} 3+6k-4k & -4-8k+4k \\ 3k+1-2k & -4k-1+2k \end{pmatrix}$

⋯ You must show sufficient detail of your calculation.

$= \begin{pmatrix} 3+2k & -4k-4 \\ k+1 & -1-2k \end{pmatrix}$

$=$ RHS, as required.

Hence, the statement is true for $n = k + 1$.

⋯ Write down what you have proved.

The statement $\underline{A}^n = \begin{pmatrix} 1+2n & -4n \\ n & 1-2n \end{pmatrix}$ is true for $n = 1$, and if it is true for some k then it is also true for $k + 1$. Hence, the statement is true for all integers $n \geq 1$ by the principle of mathematical induction.

⋯ Always write a conclusion.

EXERCISE 6A

1 Use mathematical induction to prove that $\begin{pmatrix} 1 & 3 \\ 0 & 1 \end{pmatrix}^n = \begin{pmatrix} 1 & 3n \\ 0 & 1 \end{pmatrix}$ for all positive integers n.

6 Mathematical induction

2 Prove by induction that $\begin{pmatrix} 1 & 0 \\ a & 1 \end{pmatrix}^n = \begin{pmatrix} 1 & 0 \\ na & 1 \end{pmatrix}$ for all $n \in \mathbb{N}$.

> **Tip**
>
> Remember that the symbol $\mathbb{Z}$ is used to denote the set of all integers (whole numbers) and $\mathbb{N}$ the set of positive integers.

3 Use mathematical induction to prove that, for all positive integers n, $\begin{pmatrix} 1 & i \\ 0 & 1 \end{pmatrix}^n = \begin{pmatrix} 1 & ni \\ 0 & 1 \end{pmatrix}$.

4 Let $\mathbf{A} = \begin{pmatrix} 1 & i \\ i & 1 \end{pmatrix}$.

  a Find $\mathbf{A}^4$.

  b Use mathematical induction to show that $\mathbf{A}^{4n} = (-4)^n \mathbf{I}$ for all integers $n \geq 1$.

  c Hence, find $\mathbf{A}^{13}$.

5 Let $\mathbf{A} = \begin{pmatrix} 1 & 1 \\ 1 & 1 \end{pmatrix}$. Use induction to prove that $\mathbf{A}^n = \begin{pmatrix} 2^{n-1} & 2^{n-1} \\ 2^{n-1} & 2^{n-1} \end{pmatrix}$ for all $n \geq 1$.

6 Define $\mathbf{M} = \begin{pmatrix} -2 & 9 \\ -1 & 4 \end{pmatrix}$. Prove by induction that $\mathbf{M}^n = \begin{pmatrix} 1-3n & 9n \\ -n & 1+3n \end{pmatrix}$ for all positive integer powers n.

7 Given that $\mathbf{M} = \begin{pmatrix} 1 & a \\ 0 & 2 \end{pmatrix}$, prove by induction that $\mathbf{M}^n = \begin{pmatrix} 1 & (2^n-1)a \\ 0 & 2^n \end{pmatrix}$ for all $n \geq 1$, $n \in \mathbb{Z}$.

8 Using mathematical induction, show that $\begin{pmatrix} 3 & a \\ 0 & 1 \end{pmatrix}^n = \begin{pmatrix} 3^n & \frac{3^n-1}{2}a \\ 0 & 1 \end{pmatrix}$.

9 Prove by induction that $\begin{pmatrix} 1 & 1 & 1 \\ 1 & 1 & 1 \\ 1 & 1 & 1 \end{pmatrix}^n = \begin{pmatrix} 3^{n-1} & 3^{n-1} & 3^{n-1} \\ 3^{n-1} & 3^{n-1} & 3^{n-1} \\ 3^{n-1} & 3^{n-1} & 3^{n-1} \end{pmatrix}$ for all $n \geq 1$.

10 Matrix $\mathbf{A}$ is given by $\mathbf{A} = \begin{pmatrix} 0 & 1 \\ 0 & 0 \end{pmatrix}$. Let p and q be real numbers.

  a Find the matrix $p\mathbf{I} + q\mathbf{A}$, where $\mathbf{I}$ is the 2×2 identity matrix.

  b Use mathematical induction to prove that $(p\mathbf{I} + q\mathbf{A})^n = \begin{pmatrix} p^n & np^{n-1}q \\ 0 & p^n \end{pmatrix}$.

Section 3: Induction and divisibility

Number theory is an important area of pure mathematics that is concerned with properties of natural numbers. One of the important tasks in number theory is studying divisibility.

Consider the expression $f(n) = 7^n - 1$ for $n = 0, 1, 2, \ldots$ Looking at the first few values of n:

$f(0) = 7^0 - 1 = 0$ $f(1) = 7^1 - 1 = 6$

$f(2) = 7^2 - 1 = 48$ $f(3) = 7^3 - 1 = 342$

> **Tip**
>
> Note that in this example the first value of n is $n = 0$. Induction does not have to start from $n = 1$.

It looks as if $f(n)$ is divisible by 6 for all values of n. You can prove this using the principle of mathematical induction.

171

Key point 6.3

If an expression is divisible by an integer d, you can write it as $A \times d$ for some integer A.

WORKED EXAMPLE 6.2

The expression $f(n)$ is defined by $f(n) = 7^n - 1$ for all integers n. Prove that $f(n)$ is divisible by 6 for all integers $n \geqslant 0$.

Proposition: $f(n) = 7^n - 1$ is divisible by 6.	State what you are trying to prove.
$f(0) = 7^0 - 1 = 0 = 0 \times 6$ So $f(0)$ is divisible by 6.	Prove that the statement is true for $n = 0$. State your conclusion explicitly.
Assume that $f(k)$ is divisible by 6. Then $7^k - 1 = 6A$ for some $A \in \mathbb{Z}$.	Assume that the statement is true for $n = k$ and write down what this means.
When $n = k + 1$ we are working towards: $7^{k+1} - 1 = 6B$, for some $B \in \mathbb{Z}$.	Think about what you are working towards.
LHS $= 7 \times 7^k - 1$	Relate $f(k+1)$ to $f(k)$.
$= 7 \times (6A + 1) - 1$ (using the result for $n = k$)	Use the result for $n = k$, $7^k = 6A + 1$.
$= 42A + 7 - 1$ $= 42A + 6$ $= 6 \times (7A + 1)$ $=$ RHS with $B = 7A + 1 \in \mathbb{Z}$	Simplify, looking at what you are working towards (you want to take out a factor of 6).
So $f(k+1)$ is divisible by 6.	What have you proved?
$f(0)$ is divisible by 6, and if $f(k)$ is divisible by 6, then so is $f(k+1)$. Therefore, $f(n)$ is divisible by 6 for all integers $n \geqslant 0$ by the principle of mathematical induction.	Write a conclusion.

WORKED EXAMPLE 6.3

Use mathematical induction to prove that, for all positive integers n, $9^n - 2^n$ is divisible by 7.

Statement to prove: $9^n - 2^n$ is divisible by 7 for all $n \geqslant 1$.	Write down the statement you need to prove.
When $n = 1$: $9^1 - 2^1 = 7$, which is divisible by 7.	Prove the base case: here, the first value you need to consider is $n = 1$.
Assume that the statement is true for some $n = k$. This means that: $9^k - 2^k = 7A$ for some integer A.	Assume that the statement is true for $n = k$ and write down what this means.

Continues on next page ...

172

6 Mathematical induction

When $n = k+1$ we are working towards:
$9^{k+1} - 2^{k+1} = 7B$ for some integer B.

LHS $= 9 \times 9^k - 2^{k+1}$

$= 9 \times (7A + 2^k) - 2^{k+1}$

$= 63A + 9 \times 2^k - 2^{k+1}$

$= 63A + (9 - 2) \times 2^k$

$= 63A + 7 \times 2^k$

$= 7(9A + 2^k)$

which is divisible by 7.

Hence, the statement is true for $n = k + 1$.

The statement is true for $n = 1$, and if it is true for $n = k$ then it is also true for $n = k + 1$. Hence, the statement is true for all $n \geqslant 1$ by the principle of mathematical induction.

Think about what you are working towards.

You need to relate this to the expression for k. You can use only one of 9^{k+1} and 2^{k+1}.

Use the result for $n = k$:
$9^k - 2^k = 7A$ so $9^k = 7A + 2^k$

The last two terms have a common factor 2^k.

Show explicitly how you can tell that this is a multiple of 7.

What have you proved?

Write a conclusion.

Explore

In number theory there are other methods of proving divisibility. For example, you can use the factor theorem to factorise $a^n - b^n$ as $(a - b)(a^{n-1} + a^{n-2}b + a^{n-3}b^2 + \ldots + b^{n-1})$. Can you see how this immediately gives you the required result in Worked example 6.3?

Deciding whether extremely large numbers are prime needs some very clever tests for divisibility. These are very important in code breaking and there are huge financial rewards for finding large prime numbers. Find out about modular arithmetic and Fermat's Little Theorem.

Did you know?

For a long time it was thought that $1 + 1706n^2$ was never a square number. If you tried the first billion values of n, you would find that none of these are squares. The first example of a square found is when n is 30 693 385 322 765 657 197 397 207. So just trying lots of examples does not work; this is why methods such as proof by induction are so important in mathematics.

EXERCISE 6B

1. Show that $5^n - 1$ is divisible by 4 for all $n \in \mathbb{N}$.

2. Show that $4^n - 1$ is divisible by 3 for all $n \in \mathbb{N}$.

3. Show that $7^n - 3^n$ is divisible by 4 for all $n \in \mathbb{N}$.

4. Use induction to prove that $30^n - 6^n$ is divisible by 12 for all integers $n \geqslant 0$.

5. Show using induction that $n^3 - n$ is divisible by 6 for all integers $n \geqslant 1$.

6. Using the principle of mathematical induction, prove that $n(n^2 + 5)$ is divisible by 6 for all integers $n \geqslant 1$.

7. Use induction to show that $7^n - 4^n - 3n$ is divisible by 12 for all $n \in \mathbb{Z}^+$.

8. Prove, using the principle of mathematical induction, that $3^{2n+2} - 8n - 9$ is divisible by 64 for all positive integers n.

9. Show that the sum of the cubes of any three consecutive integers is divisible by 9.

Section 4: Induction and inequalities

One of the most surprising uses of mathematical induction is in proving inequalities. For example, consider the inequality $2^n > 6n + 1$. Trying the first few integer values of n shows that this inequality is satisfied for $n \geqslant 5$. In fact, by looking at the graphs of $y = 2^n$ and $y = 6n + 1$ you can see that the inequality is satisfied for all **real** numbers n greater than approximately 4.94. Note that the inequality cannot be solved algebraically. However, you can use induction to show that it holds for all **integers** $n \geqslant 5$.

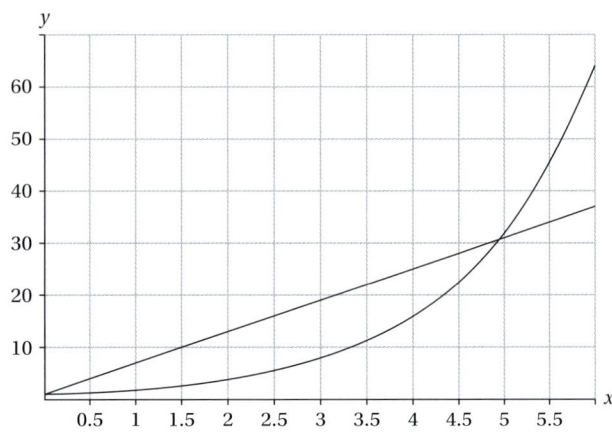

WORKED EXAMPLE 6.4

Use induction to prove that the inequality $2^n > 6n + 1$ holds for all integers $n \geqslant 5$.

For $n = 5$: — Show it is true for the starting value.

LHS $= 2^5 = 32$, RHS $= 6 \times 5 + 1 = 31$

LHS $>$ RHS, so the inequality holds for $n = 5$.
Assume that it holds for $n = k$ ($k \geqslant 5$): — Write down what you are assuming (for some $n = k$).

$2^k > 6k + 1$

Let $n = k + 1$.

Working towards: — Write down what you are trying to prove.

$2^{k+1} > 6k + 7$

LHS $= 2 \times 2^k > 2 \times (6k + 1)$ — Relate to the case $n = k$.

$\quad = 12k + 2$ (using the result for $n = k$)

$\quad = 6k + (6k + 2)$ — Look at what you are working towards – separate the $6k$ term.

$\quad > 6k + 7$

(because $6k + 2 > 7$ for $k \geqslant 5$) — Use the fact that $k \geqslant 5$: then $6k + 2$ is greater than 32, so it is definitely greater than 7.

LHS $>$ RHS, so the inequality holds for $n = k + 1$. — What have you proved?

The inequality holds for $n = 5$, and if it holds for $n = k$, then it also holds for $n = k + 1$. Therefore, it holds for all integers $n \geqslant 5$ by the principle of mathematical induction. — Write a conclusion.

Many interesting inequalities involve the factorial function. For the inductive step you often need to make a link between $n!$ and $(n+1)!$

Key point 6.4

$$(n+1)! = (n+1) \times n!$$

WORKED EXAMPLE 6.5

Prove that $n! > 20n$ for all integers $n \geq 5$.

When $n = 5$:

LHS $= 5! = 120$, RHS $= 20 \times 5 = 100$ — Show that the inequality holds for the starting value (in this case, $n = 5$).

So LHS $>$ RHS; the statement is true when $n = 5$.

Assume it is true for some $n = k$; then: — Assume that the inequality holds for some k. Write down what this means.
$k! > 20k$

When $n = k + 1$ we are working towards:
$(k + 1)! > 20(k + 1) = 20k + 20$ — Write down what you are trying to prove next.

LHS $= (k + 1) \times k!$ — Make a link between $(k+1)!$ and $k!$.

$> (k + 1) \times 20k$ — Use the assumed result for $n = k$.

$= 20k^2 + 20k$ — Look at what you are working towards: there is $20k$ in the required expression.

$> 20 + 20k$ — Use the fact that $k \geq 5$.

(because $k > 1$, so $20k^2 > 20$)

So LHS $>$ RHS and the statement is true for $n = k + 1$. — Write down what you have proved.

The statement is true for $n = 5$, and if it is true for $n = k$ then it is also true for $n = k + 1$. Therefore, it is true for all $n \geq 5$ by the principle of mathematical induction. — Write a conclusion.

EXERCISE 6C

Prove the following inequalities by induction, for the specified values of the integer n.

1. $2^n > 1 + n$ for all $n \geqslant 2$.
2. $2^n > 2n$ for $n \geqslant 3$.
3. $2^n > 11n$ for $n \geqslant 7$.
4. $n! > 2^n$ for all $n \geqslant 4$.
5. $n! > 3^n$ for all $n \geqslant 7$.
6. $2^n > n^2$ for all $n \geqslant 5$.
7. $3^n > n^3$ for all $n \geqslant 4$.
8. a Solve the inequality $n^2 > n + 1$.

   b Prove by induction that $n! > n^2$ for $n \geqslant 4$.
9. Use mathematical induction to prove that $n! > 3n^2 + 2n$ for all integers $n > 4$.

Checklist of learning and understanding

- In mathematics, rules usually can not be proved by trying lots of examples. Mathematical induction provides a logically rigorous way of showing that a pattern will continue forever.
- The steps of a mathematical induction proof are:
  1. State a proposition.
  2. Prove that the initial case is true.
  3. Assume that the kth case is true.
  4. Link the kth case to the $(k+1)$th case.
  5. Show that if the proposition is true for k, it is also true for $k+1$.
  6. Write a conclusion.
- The inductive step depends on the type of problem.

Problem type	Inductive step
Powers of matrices	Use $\mathbf{A}^{k+1} = \mathbf{A}^k \mathbf{A}$.
Divisibility	Algebraic substitution
Inequality	Algebraic substitution
Anything else	There will probably be a hint in the previous part of the question.

Mixed practice 6

> **Tip**
>
> Some questions in this exercise are different from all the previous examples. You need to be able to adapt familiar methods to new contexts!

1. Use mathematical induction to prove that $\begin{pmatrix} 1 & 0 \\ 1 & 1 \end{pmatrix}^n = \begin{pmatrix} 1 & 0 \\ n & 1 \end{pmatrix}$ for all positive integers n.

2. Prove that $3^{2n} + 7$ is divisible by 8 when $n \in \mathbb{N}$.

3. Prove by induction that $3^n > 5n + 2$ for all integers $n \geqslant 3$.

4. Use mathematical induction to prove that $12^n - 1$ is a multiple of 11 for all positive integers n.

5. Prove that $11^{n+2} + 12^{2n+1}$ is divisible by 133 for all integers $n \geqslant 0$.

6. Use the principle of mathematical induction to show that $15^n - 2^n$ is a multiple of 13 for all $n \in \mathbb{N}$.

7. Prove that for all positive integers n, $(1 - \sqrt{5})^n$ has the form $a - b\sqrt{5}$ where a, b are positive integers.

8. The matrix $\mathbf{A}$ is given by $\mathbf{A} = \begin{pmatrix} 2 & 0 \\ 0 & 1 \end{pmatrix}$.

   a. Find $\mathbf{A}^2$ and $\mathbf{A}^3$.

   b. Hence suggest a suitable form for the matrix $\mathbf{A}^n$.

   c. Use induction to prove that your answer to part **b** is correct.

   © OCR, AS GCE Further Mathematics, Paper 4725, June 2006
   [Question part reference style adapted]

9. a. Show that for any two complex numbers z and w, $(zw)^* = z^* w^*$.

   b. Prove by induction that $(z^n)^* = (z^*)^n$ for positive integer n.

10. Prove by induction that, for any matrix $\mathbf{M}$, $\det(\mathbf{M}^n) = (\det \mathbf{M})^n$ for all positive integers n. You may use the result that $\det \mathbf{AB} = \det \mathbf{A} \det \mathbf{B}$ for any two matrices $\mathbf{A}$ and $\mathbf{B}$.

11. Use mathematical induction to prove that
$$\begin{pmatrix} 0 & -1 \\ i & 1+i \end{pmatrix}^n = \frac{1+i}{2} \begin{pmatrix} i^n - i & i^n - 1 \\ i - i^{n+1} & 1 - i^{n+1} \end{pmatrix} \text{ for } n \geqslant 1.$$

12. Use mathematical induction to prove that
$$\begin{pmatrix} -i & -1 \\ 2 & 0 \end{pmatrix}^n = \frac{1}{3} \begin{pmatrix} i^n + 2^{n+1}(-i)^n & i^{n+1} - 2^n(-i)^{n-1} \\ 2i^{n-1} + 2^{n+1}(-i)^n & 2i^n + 2^n(-i)^n \end{pmatrix} \text{ for } n \geqslant 1.$$

FOCUS ON ... PROOF 2

Roots of real polynomials

In this section, you are going to prove that complex roots of real polynomials come in conjugate pairs. You will need to use the following properties of complex conjugates.

Key point 1

$(z \pm w)^* = z^* \pm w^*$

$(zw)^* = z^* w^*$

$\left(\dfrac{z}{w}\right)^* = \dfrac{z^*}{w^*}$

For any integer n:

$(z^n)^* = (z^*)^n$

All these results are proved in a similar way; the next proof shows just one of them.

PROOF 8

Prove that $(zw)^* = z^* w^*$.

Let $z = x + iy$

$w = u + iv$

The best way to describe complex conjugates is to write them in terms of their real and imaginary parts.

Then: $z^* = x - iy$

$w^* = u - iv$

LHS $= (zw)^*$

$= ((x+iy)(u+iv))^*$

$= ((xu - yv) + i(xv + yu))^*$

$= (xu - yv) - i(xv + yu)$

Start with the left-hand side.

RHS $= z^* w^*$

$= (x - iy)(u - iv)$

$= xu - ixv - iyu - yv$

$= (xu - yv) - i(xv + yu)$

If you get stuck, start again on the right-hand side and try to meet in the middle.

Therefore, LHS = RHS.

Every proof needs a conclusion.

You are now ready to prove the main result.

Key point 2

If $f(x)$ is a real polynomial and if $f(z) = 0$, then $f(z^*) = 0$.

Rewind

Remember from Chapter 5 that a **real polynomial** is a polynomial for which all coefficients are real numbers.

Key point 2 says that, if a number z is a root of $f(x)$, then so is its conjugate, z^*.

PROOF 9

Prove that if $f(x)$ is a real polynomial and if $f(z) = 0$, then $f(z^*) = 0$.

Let $f(z) = a_n z^n + a_{n-1} z^{n-1} + \ldots + a_1 z + a_0$

> Write a general form of the polynomial, arranging the terms in decreasing powers. It is helpful if you label the coefficients with subscripts that correspond to the powers.

Then

$(a_k z^k)^* = (a_k)^* (z^k)^*$

> Take the complex conjugate of each term and use the results of Key point 1: $(zw)^* = z^* w^*$.

$= a_k (z^k)^*$

> Since a_k is real, $(a_k)^* = a_k$.

So

$f(z^*) = a_n (z^*)^n + \ldots + a_1 z^* + a_0$

$= (a_n z^n)^* + \ldots + (a_1 z)^* + (a_0)^*$

> Use the result you proved above.
>
> For the last term, remember that a_0 is real.

$= (a_n z^n + \ldots + a_1 z + a_0)^*$

> Use Key point 1 again: $z^* + w^* = (z + w)^*$.

$= (f(z))^*$

$= 0$, as required.

> Remember that you started by assuming that $f(z) = 0$.

Questions

1 Prove the rest of the results in Key point 1.

2 Does the proof of Key point 2 work if z is a real number? What does the result say then?

3 Where in Proof 9 did you use the fact that $f(x)$ is a **real** polynomial? Does the result of Key point 2 still hold if some of the a_k are complex numbers?

4 You already know that you can use the roots of a polynomial to write it as a product of linear factors: if the roots of $f(x)$ are $z_1, z_2, \ldots, z_n$, then $f(x) = a(x - z_1)(x - z_2)\ldots(x - z_n)$. However, some of the z_k may be complex. Key point 2 implies that, once you have found all the roots of a real polynomial, you can write it as a product of **real** linear and quadratic factors. Can you see why this is the case? You may want to start by looking at some examples.

FOCUS ON ... PROBLEM-SOLVING 2

Solving cubic equations

In this section, you will look at a famous historical example of problem-solving. It shows you how mathematicians adapt their definitions and rules in order to be able to solve a wider variety of problems.

The cubic formula

You know that the quadratic equation $ax^2 + bx + c = 0$ can be solved by applying the quadratic formula: $x = \dfrac{-b \pm \sqrt{b^2 - 4ac}}{2a}$. Some quadratic equations have no real solutions. This happens if, and only if, the discriminant $b^2 - 4ac$ is negative.

A similar formula for the solution to the cubic equation was discovered by Cardano and Tartaglia in the 16th century. The formula is rather complicated, and here we consider only the special case of cubic equations with no x^2 term.

The equation $x^3 + px + q = 0$ has solutions given by $x = -\dfrac{p}{3u} + u$, where

$$u = \sqrt[3]{-\dfrac{q}{2} \pm \sqrt{\dfrac{q^2}{4} + \dfrac{p^3}{27}}}.$$

The quantity $\dfrac{q^2}{4} + \dfrac{p^3}{27}$ plays a role similar to the discriminant of a quadratic equation: it tells you how many solutions the equation has.

Unfortunately, as you will see below, there are examples where this discriminant is negative but the equation still has real solutions. This is where mathematicians needed to engage in some serious problem-solving to make the formula work correctly.

> **Explore**
>
> Find out about other methods of solving cubic equations; some involve using trigonometry and the compound angle formula.

Using the formula

Consider the equation $x^3 + 9x - 26 = 0$.

Here $p = 9, q = -26$, so:

$$u = \sqrt[3]{13 \pm \sqrt{196}} = -1 \text{ or } 3$$

When $u = -1$, $x = \dfrac{-9}{-3} - 1 = 2$

When $u = 3$, $x = \dfrac{-9}{9} + 3 = 2$

So in this case, both possible values of u give the same solution for x. Plotting the graph confirms that $x = 2$ is the only real solution of the equation.

Focus on ... Problem-solving 2

The negative discriminant

Now consider the equation $x^3 - 3x = 0$. For this equation, $p = -3$, $q = 0$.
Then:

$$u = \sqrt[3]{0 \pm \sqrt{0 + \frac{-27}{27}}} = \sqrt[3]{\pm\sqrt{-1}}$$

This appears to be a dead end – you are looking for real solutions, so you can't take the square root of -1. However, you can see (by factorising) that there should be three real solutions: 0, $\sqrt{3}$ and $-\sqrt{3}$. Is there any way you can make the formula work to find those three solutions?

Problem-solving often requires perseverance and 'thinking outside the box'. So what happens if you start working with complex numbers and carry on with the calculation?

You now need $u = \sqrt[3]{\pm i}$. There are in fact three different complex numbers for which the cube is i:

$u_1 = -i$, $u_2 = \dfrac{\sqrt{3}}{2} + \dfrac{1}{2}i$ and $u_3 = -\dfrac{\sqrt{3}}{2} + \dfrac{1}{2}i$

When $u = -i$:

$$x = \frac{1}{-i} + (-i) = i - i = 0$$

When $u = \dfrac{\sqrt{3}}{2} + \dfrac{1}{2}i$:

$$= \frac{2(\sqrt{3} - i)}{3 + 1} + \left(\frac{\sqrt{3}}{2} + \frac{1}{2}i\right)$$

$$= \frac{2(\sqrt{3} - i)}{3 + 1} + \left(\frac{\sqrt{3}}{2} + \frac{1}{2}i\right)$$

$$= \frac{\sqrt{3}}{2} - \frac{1}{2}i + \frac{\sqrt{3}}{2} + \frac{1}{2}i = \sqrt{3}$$

When $u = \dfrac{\sqrt{3}}{2} + \dfrac{1}{2}i$: a similar calculation gives the third solution, $x = -\sqrt{3}$.

 Fast forward

In Pure Core Student Book 2 you will learn how to find cube roots of a complex number. For now, you should just check that the three roots given here are correct.

Questions

1. Apply the formula to solve the equation $x^3 + 6x - 20 = 0$.

2. Find the three possible values for $u = \sqrt[3]{-i}$. Confirm that these lead to the same three solutions of the equation $x^3 - 3x = 0$.

3. The fact that this formula uses complex numbers to find real solutions was one of the arguments that persuaded mathematicians to accept complex numbers. Did it change your opinion on whether complex numbers 'exist'?

 Fast forward

In Pure Core Student Book 2 you will also use complex numbers to solve differential equations and prove trigonometric identities.

FOCUS ON ... MODELLING 2

Complex numbers and radios

You may be aware that complex numbers are used in electronics. The building blocks of electronic circuits are resistors, capacitors and inductors. Normally each of these needs to be analysed in a different way using quite tricky differential equations.

- For a resistor: $V = IR$, where V is the voltage, I is the current and R is the resistance. This relationship is a result of Ohm's law.

- For a capacitor, $I = C\dfrac{dV}{dt}$ where C is the capacitance.

- For an inductor, $V = L\dfrac{dI}{dt}$ where L is the inductance.

In a circuit with an alternating voltage, the input voltage varies sinusoidally with time with (angular) frequency ω. The opposition to the flow of current in this type of circuit, called the impedance, Z, depends on the frequency.

Using complex numbers and the concept of impedance, you can treat all three types of component as 'complex' resistors. The impedance of a resistor is R, the impedance of a capacitor is $\dfrac{1}{i\omega C}$ and the impedance of an inductor is $i\omega L$. Then you can use a general version of the Ohm's law relationship, which says that $V = IZ$.

The diagram shown is a model of a simple circuit that can act as a radio.

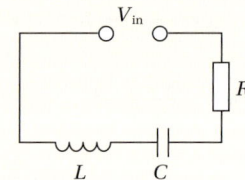

The total impedance for this circuit is:

$$Z = R + i\omega L + \dfrac{1}{i\omega C} = R + i\omega\left(L - \dfrac{1}{\omega^2 C}\right)$$

If the input voltage is V_{in}, then the resulting current is:

$$I = \dfrac{V_{in}}{Z} = \dfrac{V_{in}}{R + i\omega(L - 1/\omega^2 C)} = \dfrac{V_{in}}{R^2 + \omega^2(L - 1/\omega^2 C)^2}\left(R - i\omega\left(L - \dfrac{1}{\omega^2 C}\right)\right)$$

For fixed values of L, C and R, if you plot the modulus of the current against ω, you should get a graph that looks like this.

The current is a maximum when the denominator of the expression above is minimised. This happens when $\omega = \dfrac{1}{\sqrt{LC}}$. Think about what this frequency represents. For particular values of L and C in a circuit, there is a natural frequency that results in a higher current than any other frequency. This phenomenon is called **resonance**. If the frequency of the input voltage is the same as the resonant frequency of the circuit, the circuit will produce a large current that can be used to power a speaker.

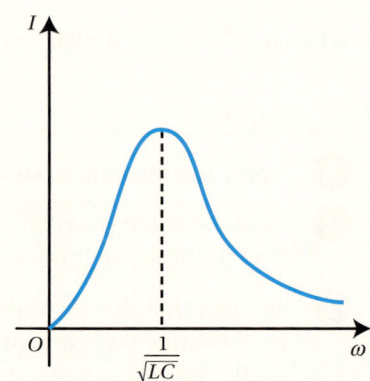

Focus on ... Modelling 2

Questions

1. Radio 1 has a frequency of 98 MHz or 6.15×10^8 in the units required for ω. If an inductor has $L = 10^{-5}$ (a fairly typical value), find the required capacitance for a circuit to 'tune in' to Radio 1.

2. a What is the current in the circuit when it is being driven at the resonant frequency?

   b What would happen if $R = 0$?

   c Why would $R = 0$ be a poor modelling assumption?

3. Use technology to sketch the current against ω. Explore the effect on the graph of changing C while keeping the same resonant frequency. Why might smaller values of C produce a better radio?

4. a The argument of the expression for the current gives the 'phase difference' between the input voltage and the current; this is a measure of the delay between the input and the circuit responding. Find an expression for this phase difference.

   b What is the value of the phase difference when the circuit is at resonance?

CROSS-TOPIC REVIEW EXERCISE 2

1. **In this question you must show detailed reasoning.**
   Find the determinant of $\begin{pmatrix} 2i & -1 \\ 3i & i \end{pmatrix}$.

2. Solve the equation $3z^* - 2i = 2z + 5$, where z is a complex number.

3. The quadratic equation $2x^2 + kx + 5 = 0$ has solutions p and q. Express $p^2 + q^2$ in terms of k.

4. Use mathematical induction to prove that $13^n - 1$ is divisible by 12 for all positive integers n.

5. The complex numbers z and w are given by $z = 5 - 2i$ and $w = 3 + 7i$. Giving your answers in the form $x + iy$ and showing clearly how you obtain them, find

   a $4z - 3w$ b z^*w.

   © OCR, AS GCE Further Mathematics, Paper 4725, June 2009
   [Question part reference style adapted]

6. The cubic equation $x^3 + ax^2 + bx + c = 0$, where a, b and c are real, has roots $(3 + i)$ and 2.

   a Write down the other root of the equation.

   b Find the values of a, b and c.

   © OCR, AS GCE Further Mathematics, Paper 4725, June 2008
   [Question part reference style adapted]

7. Use the substitution $x = u + 2$ to find the exact value of the real root of the equation $x^3 - 6x^2 + 12x - 13 = 0$.

   © OCR, AS GCE Further Mathematics, Paper 4725, January 2006

8. a Given that $z = x + iy$, where $x, y \in \mathbb{R}$, find $|z - i|$ in terms of x and y.

   b Sketch on an Argand diagram the locus of points satisfying $|z - i| = |z + 1|$.

9. a By writing $z = x + iy$, or otherwise, solve the equation $z^2 = i - 1$.

   b Solve the quadratic equation $w^2 + 2iw = i$.

10. Prove, using mathematical induction, that $2^n > 5n$ for all integers $n \geqslant 5$.

11. It is given that $u_n = 13^n + 6^{n-1}$, where n is a positive integer.

    a Show that $u_n + u_{n+1} = 14 \times 13^n + 7 \times 6^{n-1}$.

    b Prove by induction that u_n is a multiple of 7.

    © OCR, AS GCE Further Mathematics, Paper 4725, January 2009
    [Question part reference style adapted]

12. The quadratic equation $x^2 + 2kx + k = 0$, where k is a non-zero constant, has roots α and β. Find a quadratic equation with roots $\dfrac{\alpha + \beta}{\alpha}$ and $\dfrac{\alpha + \beta}{\beta}$.

    © OCR, AS GCE Further Mathematics, Paper 4725, June 2010

13 Let $z = \text{cis}\left(\dfrac{\pi}{3}\right)$ and $w = \text{cis}\left(\dfrac{\pi}{4}\right)$.

   a Find zw in the form $r\,\text{cis}\,\theta$.

   b Find zw in the form $x + iy$, where x and y are expressed in terms of surds.

   c Show zw on an Argand diagram and, hence, find the exact value of $\tan\left(\dfrac{\pi}{12}\right)$.

14 a Show that $(\alpha - \beta)^2 \equiv (\alpha + \beta)^2 - 4\alpha\beta$.

The quadratic equation $x^2 - 6kx + k^2 = 0$, where k is a positive constant, has roots α and β, with $\alpha > \beta$.

   b Show that $\alpha - \beta = 4\sqrt{2}k$.

   c Hence find a quadratic equation with roots $\alpha + 1$ and $\beta - 1$.

© OCR, AS GCE Further Mathematics, Paper 4725, January 2009
[Question part reference style adapted]

15 The complex number z, where $0 < \arg z < \dfrac{1}{2}\pi$, is such that $z^2 = 3 + 4i$.

   a Use an algebraic method to find z.

   b Show that $z^3 = 2 + 11i$.

The complex number w is the root of the equation $w^6 - 4w^3 + 125 = 0$ for which $-\dfrac{1}{2}\pi < \arg w < 0$.

   c Find w.

© OCR, AS GCE Further Mathematics, Paper 4725, June 2010
[Question part reference style adapted]

16 Let z and w be two complex numbers.

   a Show that $(zw)^* = z^*w^*$.

   b Prove by induction that $(z^n)^* = (z^*)^n$ for positive integer n.

17 Use matrix methods to solve the system of equations:
$$\begin{cases} (2+i)z + 3iw = 2i \\ z + (1+i)w = 1 - i \end{cases}$$

18 A polynomial is defined by $f(x) = x^3 + x + 10$.

   a Find an integer root of the equation $f(x) = 0$.

   b Solve the equation $f(x) = 0$.

The integer root of $f(x) = 0$ is p and the complex roots are z_1 and z_2.

   c On an Argand diagram, shade the locus of points z that satisfy $|p| \leqslant |z| < |z_1|$.

   d Calculate $|\arg(z_1) - \arg(z_2)|$.

19 a Let z be a complex number. By writing $z = r(\cos\theta + i\sin\theta)$, or otherwise, prove that $zz^* = |z|$.

Given that z is a complex number with modulus 1, and defined by matrix $\mathbf{A} = \begin{pmatrix} 1 & z \\ z^* & 1 \end{pmatrix}$:

   b Show that $\mathbf{A}^2 = 2\mathbf{A}$.

   c Use mathematical induction to prove that $\mathbf{A}^n = 2^{n-1}\mathbf{A}$ for all positive integers n.

   d Find $\mathbf{A}^{10}$ when $z = \dfrac{1}{2} + \dfrac{\sqrt{3}}{2}i$.

20 a Write down the matrix **C** which represents a stretch, scale factor 2, in the *x*-direction.

   b The matrix **D** is given by $\mathbf{D} = \begin{pmatrix} 1 & 3 \\ 0 & 1 \end{pmatrix}$. Describe fully the geometrical transformation represented by **D**.

   c The matrix **M** represents the combined effect of the transformation represented by **C** followed by the transformation represented by **D**. Show that $\mathbf{M} = \begin{pmatrix} 2 & 3 \\ 0 & 1 \end{pmatrix}$.

   d Prove by induction that $\mathbf{M}^n = \begin{pmatrix} 2^n & 3(2^n - 1) \\ 0 & 1 \end{pmatrix}$, for all positive integers *n*.

   © OCR, AS GCE Further Mathematics, Paper 4725, June 2005
   [Question part reference style adapted]

21 The matrix **M** is given by $\mathbf{M} = \begin{pmatrix} 1 & 2 \\ 0 & 1 \end{pmatrix}$.

   a Find $\mathbf{M}^2$ and $\mathbf{M}^3$.

   b Hence suggest a suitable form for the matrix $\mathbf{M}^n$.

   c Use induction to prove that your answer to part **b** is correct.

   d Describe fully the single geometrical transformation represented by $\mathbf{M}^{10}$.

   © OCR, AS GCE Further Mathematics, Paper 4725, January 2010
   [Question part reference style adapted]

22 The matrix **A** is given by $\mathbf{A} = \begin{pmatrix} 1 & 0 \\ 3 & 1 \end{pmatrix}$.

   a Show that $\mathbf{A}^2 = 2\mathbf{A} - \mathbf{I}$.

   b Prove by induction that $\mathbf{A}^n = n\mathbf{A} - (n-1)\mathbf{I}$.

   c The matrix $\mathbf{A}^5$ represents a linear transformation. The image of the point *P* under this transformation has coordinates $(-25, 12)$. Find the coordinates of *P*.

23 a Prove by induction that, for $\theta \in \mathbb{R}$ and $n \in \mathbb{N}$, $(\sin \theta + i \cos \theta)^n = i^{n-1}(\sin n\theta + i \cos n\theta)$.

   b For which values of *n* does $(\sin \theta + i \cos \theta)^n \equiv \sin n\theta + i \cos n\theta$?

Practice paper

PRACTICE PAPER

Pure Core

Time allowed: 1 hour 10 minutes

Total number of marks: 60

1 In this question you must show detailed reasoning.

Two complex numbers are given by $z = 3 - 2i$ and $w = 2 + i$. Showing your method clearly, calculate the following. Give your answer in the form $x + yi$.

   a $w - z^*$ [2]

   b $\dfrac{z}{w}$ [3]

2 Two vectors are given by $\mathbf{a} = 2\mathbf{i} + (p-1)\mathbf{j} - 2\mathbf{k}$ and $\mathbf{b} = p\mathbf{i} + 2\mathbf{j} + (2p-1)\mathbf{k}$, where $p \in \mathbb{R}$.

   a Show that $\mathbf{a}$ and $\mathbf{b}$ are perpendicular for all values of p. [2]

   b Find the value of p for which $\mathbf{a} + \mathbf{b}$ is parallel to the vector $2\mathbf{j} + 14\mathbf{k}$. [3]

3 In this question you must show detailed reasoning.

The cubic equation $2x^3 - 5x + 6 = 0$ has roots α, β and γ. Find the value of $\dfrac{1}{\alpha} + \dfrac{1}{\beta} + \dfrac{1}{\gamma}$. [5]

4 Show that the lines with Cartesian equations $\dfrac{x-2}{5} = \dfrac{y+1}{-1} = \dfrac{z-1}{1}$ and $\dfrac{x+1}{2} = \dfrac{y-1}{2} = \dfrac{z-2}{7}$ are skew. [5]

5 Consider the matrix $\mathbf{A} = \begin{pmatrix} 3c & c-1 \\ 2 & -3 \end{pmatrix}$.

   a Find the value of c for which $\mathbf{A}$ is a singular matrix. [3]

   b Given that c is such that $\mathbf{A}$ is non-singular, find $\mathbf{A}^{-1}$ in terms of c. [3]

6 The complex number a is given by $a = -\sqrt{3} + i$.

   a Find the modulus and the argument of a. [2]

   b On an Argand diagram, represent the locus of points satisfying the inequalities $|z - a| \leqslant |z - i|$ and $0 < \arg(z - a) < \dfrac{\pi}{4}$. [4]

7 Prove by induction that $11^n - 4^n$ is divisible by 7 for all positive integers n. [7]

8 Consider the equation $x^3 + 9x^2 + 31x + 39 = 0$.

   a Use the substitution $u = x + 3$ to find a cubic equation in u. [2]

   b Hence, find all roots of the equation $x^3 + 9x^2 + 31x + 39 = 0$. [5]

9 A linear transformation is represented by the matrix $\mathbf{M} = \begin{pmatrix} 1 & -2 & 2 \\ 0 & 0 & 3 \\ 1 & 0 & -2 \end{pmatrix}$.

   a Find the determinant of $\mathbf{M}$. [1]

A combined transformation consists of the reflection in the x–y plane followed by the transformation represented by $\mathbf{M}$.

   b Find the matrix representing the combined transformation. [3]

   c Find the image of the point $(-1, 2, 4)$ under the combined transformation. [1]

   d A cube with side length 3 is transformed using the combined transformation described above. Find the volume of the image. [2]

10 Lines l_1 and l_2 have equations $\mathbf{r} = \begin{pmatrix} -2 \\ 2 \\ 7 \end{pmatrix} + \lambda \begin{pmatrix} -1 \\ 0 \\ 2 \end{pmatrix}$ and $\mathbf{r} = \begin{pmatrix} 5 \\ 4 \\ 7 \end{pmatrix} + \mu \begin{pmatrix} 3 \\ 1 \\ 1 \end{pmatrix}$.

The lines intersect at the point Q.

Find the vector equation of the line through Q that is perpendicular to both l_1 and l_2. [7]

FORMULAE

The following formulae will be given on the AS and A Level assessment papers.

Pure Mathematics

Binomial series

$(a+b)^n = a^n + {}^nC_1 a^{n-1}b + {}^nC_2 a^{n-2}b^2 + \ldots + {}^nC_r a^{n-r}b^r + \ldots + b^n \quad (n \in \mathbb{N})$

where ${}^nC_r = \binom{n}{r} = \dfrac{n!}{r!(n-r)!}$

Matrix transformations

Reflection in the line $y = \pm x$: $\begin{pmatrix} 0 & \pm 1 \\ \pm 1 & 0 \end{pmatrix}$

Anticlockwise rotation through θ about O: $\begin{pmatrix} \cos\theta & -\sin\theta \\ \sin\theta & \cos\theta \end{pmatrix}$

Rotations through θ about the coordinate axes. The direction of positive rotation is taken to be anticlockwise when looking towards the origin from the positive side of the axis of rotation.

$\mathbf{R}_x = \begin{pmatrix} 1 & 0 & 0 \\ 0 & \cos\theta & -\sin\theta \\ 0 & \sin\theta & \cos\theta \end{pmatrix}$

$\mathbf{R}_y = \begin{pmatrix} \cos\theta & 0 & \sin\theta \\ 0 & 1 & 0 \\ -\sin\theta & 0 & \cos\theta \end{pmatrix}$

$\mathbf{R}_z = \begin{pmatrix} \cos\theta & -\sin\theta & 0 \\ \sin\theta & \cos\theta & 0 \\ 0 & 0 & 1 \end{pmatrix}$

Differentiation from first principles

$f'(x) = \lim\limits_{h \to 0} \dfrac{f(x+h) - f(x)}{h}$

Complex numbers

Circle: $|z - a| = k$

Half lines: $\arg(z - a) = \alpha$

Lines: $|z - a| = |z - b|$

Vectors and 3-D coordinate geometry

Cartesian equation of the line through the point A with position vector $\mathbf{a} = a_1\mathbf{i} + a_2\mathbf{j} + a_3\mathbf{k}$ in direction $\mathbf{u} = u_1\mathbf{i} + u_2\mathbf{j} + u_3\mathbf{k}$ is $\dfrac{x - a_1}{u_1} = \dfrac{y - a_2}{u_2} = \dfrac{z - a_3}{u_3} (= \lambda)$.

Vector product: $\mathbf{a} \times \mathbf{b} = \begin{pmatrix} a_1 \\ a_2 \\ a_3 \end{pmatrix} \times \begin{pmatrix} b_1 \\ b_2 \\ b_3 \end{pmatrix} = \begin{vmatrix} \mathbf{i} & a_1 & b_1 \\ \mathbf{j} & a_2 & b_2 \\ \mathbf{k} & a_3 & b_3 \end{vmatrix} = \begin{pmatrix} a_2b_3 - a_3b_2 \\ a_3b_1 - a_1b_3 \\ a_1b_2 - a_2b_1 \end{pmatrix}$

Answers

Chapter 1

Before you start…

1 $\begin{pmatrix} 0 \\ 11 \\ 5 \end{pmatrix}$

Exercise 1A

1 a i 2×2 ii 3×2
      iii 2×3 iv 4×3
   b i $\begin{pmatrix} 1 & 1 \\ 2 & 3 \end{pmatrix}$ ii $\begin{pmatrix} 1 & 2 & 1 \\ 5 & 3 & -3 \end{pmatrix}$
      iii $\begin{pmatrix} 2 & 4 \\ 6 & 1 \\ 0 & 0 \end{pmatrix}$ iv $\begin{pmatrix} 1 & 8 & -1 & -5 \\ 2 & -3 & 7 & -2 \\ -4 & 3 & 22 & 0 \end{pmatrix}$

2 a i $\begin{pmatrix} 5 & 4 \\ 7 & -5 \end{pmatrix}$ ii $\begin{pmatrix} 5 & 4 \\ 3 & -6 \end{pmatrix}$ iii $\begin{pmatrix} -3 & 5 \\ 4 & 4 \\ -4 & -4 \end{pmatrix}$
   b i $\begin{pmatrix} 1 & -1 \\ 6 & -6 \end{pmatrix}$ ii Not possible iii $\begin{pmatrix} -2 & -1 \\ 1 & 5 \end{pmatrix}$
   c i $\begin{pmatrix} 2 & 4 \\ 2 & 6 \end{pmatrix}$ ii $\begin{pmatrix} -9 & -9 \\ 0 & 6 \end{pmatrix}$ iii $\begin{pmatrix} 4 & 20 \\ 8 & 12 \\ 4 & -12 \end{pmatrix}$
   d i $\begin{pmatrix} -7 & -5 \\ 2 & 12 \end{pmatrix}$ ii $\begin{pmatrix} 0 & 0 \\ 0 & 0 \end{pmatrix}$ iii $\begin{pmatrix} 7 & 15 \\ 4 & 8 \\ 0 & -10 \end{pmatrix}$

3 a i $\begin{pmatrix} 1 & 4 \\ 5 & 6 \end{pmatrix}$ b ii Not possible
   c i Not possible d ii $\begin{pmatrix} 5 & 0 \\ 1 & 7 \end{pmatrix}$
   e i Not possible f ii $\begin{pmatrix} 10 & -2 & 4 \\ 0 & 2 & 1 \\ 8 & 1 & 7 \end{pmatrix}$

4 a i $\begin{pmatrix} 3 & -1 \\ 7 & -2 \end{pmatrix}$ ii $\begin{pmatrix} 1 & -3 \\ 9 & 4 \end{pmatrix}$
   b i $\begin{pmatrix} 10 & -3 \\ -2 & 19 \end{pmatrix}$ ii $\begin{pmatrix} 6 & -3 \\ 1 & 14 \end{pmatrix}$

5 a i $x=3, y=8$ ii $x=2, y=5$
   b i $x=3, y=-1$ ii No solution

6 a i $\begin{pmatrix} -5 & -3 \\ -5 & 1 \end{pmatrix}$ ii $\begin{pmatrix} 19/3 & -3 \\ 13/3 & 19/3 \end{pmatrix}$
   b i $\begin{pmatrix} 23 & -5 \\ 15 & 18 \end{pmatrix}$ ii $\begin{pmatrix} -1/3 & 5/3 \\ -1/3 & -5/3 \end{pmatrix}$

7 $a=3, b=-1.5, s=2, t=7$

8 $(x, y)=(-1, -4)$ or $(-3, 0)$

9 $a=-\dfrac{2}{7}, b=-\dfrac{1}{7}, c=\dfrac{3}{11}, d=\dfrac{2}{11}$

10 Switching rows for columns before or after addition makes no difference; the same elements are added and the sum ends in the same position either way.

Exercise 1B

1 a i Yes, 2×2 ii Yes, 2×3
   b i No ii No
   c i Yes, 1×2 ii Yes, 1×1
   d i Yes, 2×2 ii Yes, 2×2
   e i Yes, 3×3 ii Yes, 3×3

2 a i $\begin{pmatrix} 12 & 6 \\ 24 & 13 \end{pmatrix}$ ii $\begin{pmatrix} 3 & -1 & 1 \\ 2 & 1 & 3 \end{pmatrix}$
   b i Not possible ii Not possible
   c i $(0 \ \ 0)$ ii (10)
   d i $\begin{pmatrix} 8 & -5 \\ 6 & -3 \end{pmatrix}$ ii $\begin{pmatrix} 0 & 4a \\ 2-2a & 4+4a \end{pmatrix}$
   e i $\begin{pmatrix} 2-a & 1+a^2 & 1+5a \\ 2+2a & 2+2a & 12+a^2 \\ 12 & 1 & 1+5a \end{pmatrix}$
      ii $\begin{pmatrix} -2 & 2 & 6 \\ -1 & 1 & 3 \\ -3 & 3 & 9 \end{pmatrix}$

3 a i No ii Yes
   b i Yes ii Yes
   c i No ii No

4 a i $x=3, y=2$ ii $a=4, b=1$
   b i $x=1, y=5$ ii $p=1, q=-2$

5 a $\begin{pmatrix} 14 & 8 \\ 3 & 21 \end{pmatrix}$ b $\begin{pmatrix} 20 & 15 \\ 5 & 30 \end{pmatrix}$
   c $\begin{pmatrix} 343 & -109 \\ 0 & 125 \end{pmatrix}$

6 a $(1 \ \ 4)$ b (-13) c $\begin{pmatrix} -1 & 7 \\ -5 & 35 \end{pmatrix}$

7 a $\begin{pmatrix} 4 & -3 & 15 \\ 0 & 1 & 12 \\ -12 & 0 & 4 \end{pmatrix}$ b $\begin{pmatrix} -1 & 13 & -7 \\ -2 & 14 & 5 \\ -14 & 6 & 4 \end{pmatrix}$

   c $\begin{pmatrix} 10 & -3 & -3 \\ 5 & 19 & 8 \\ 3 & 6 & 16 \end{pmatrix}$

8 a $\begin{pmatrix} -6a+2 & a+6 \\ 0 & -10 \end{pmatrix}$ b $\begin{pmatrix} a^2+4a & 3a-4 \\ 6a^2-a & -6a-3 \end{pmatrix}$

9 a $(2p-2 \quad 2p+10)$ b $\begin{pmatrix} 3p^2-4 \\ -p \\ -3p-4 \end{pmatrix}$

   c Dimension mismatch

10 $b=-5$

11 Proof

12 $d=1.5c$

13 a $\mathbf{X}=\begin{pmatrix} a_{11}b_{11}+a_{12}b_{21} & a_{11}b_{12}+a_{12}b_{22} \\ a_{21}b_{11}+a_{22}b_{21} & a_{21}b_{12}+a_{22}b_{22} \end{pmatrix}$

   $\mathbf{Y}=\begin{pmatrix} b_{11}c_{11}+b_{12}c_{21} & b_{11}c_{12}+b_{12}c_{22} \\ b_{21}c_{11}+b_{22}c_{21} & b_{21}c_{12}+b_{22}c_{22} \end{pmatrix}$

   b Proof

14 The result always applies for matrices **A** and **B** where the product **AB** exists.

Exercise 1C

1 a i 19   ii 5
   b i 13   ii 11
   c i $-5a$ ii $7a$
   d i $5a^2+6$ ii $2a^2+3$

2 13, 11, 143

3 Proof

Exercise 1D

1 a i $\dfrac{1}{19}\begin{pmatrix} 4 & 1 \\ -7 & 3 \end{pmatrix}$ ii $\dfrac{1}{5}\begin{pmatrix} 2 & -1 \\ 3 & 1 \end{pmatrix}$

   b i $\dfrac{1}{13}\begin{pmatrix} 5 & 3 \\ -1 & 2 \end{pmatrix}$ ii $\dfrac{1}{11}\begin{pmatrix} 3 & 2 \\ -1 & 3 \end{pmatrix}$

   c i $-\dfrac{1}{5a}\begin{pmatrix} -1 & -a \\ -3 & 2a \end{pmatrix}$; $a=0$ ii $\dfrac{1}{7a}\begin{pmatrix} 2a & a \\ -5 & 1 \end{pmatrix}$; $a=0$

   d i $\dfrac{1}{5a^2+6}\begin{pmatrix} 5a & 3 \\ -2 & a \end{pmatrix}$ ii $\dfrac{1}{2a^2+3}\begin{pmatrix} 3 & -2a \\ a & 1 \end{pmatrix}$

2 a i -1.5 ii 0.2
   b i 0 ii 0

   c i ± 0.5 ii ± 2
   d i $0, -2$ ii $0, 0.2$

3 a i $\dfrac{1}{4}\begin{pmatrix} 1 & 4 \\ -5 & 0 \end{pmatrix}$ ii $\dfrac{1}{4}\begin{pmatrix} 2 & -2 \\ 11 & -1 \end{pmatrix}$

   b i $\begin{pmatrix} -1 & 0 \\ -1 & 1 \end{pmatrix}$ ii $\dfrac{1}{5}\begin{pmatrix} -8 & 2 \\ 7 & 7 \end{pmatrix}$

   c i $\begin{pmatrix} 1.25 \\ -0.25 \end{pmatrix}$ ii $(2.2 \quad -0.4)$

4 $\begin{pmatrix} -0.6 & 0.4 \\ -1.4 & 3.6 \end{pmatrix}$

5 a Proof   b $\begin{pmatrix} -0.6 & -0.12 \\ 0.2 & 0.64 \end{pmatrix}$

6 $\begin{pmatrix} 3 \\ -8 \end{pmatrix}$

7 $k=\pm\sqrt{3}$

8 a $|\mathbf{A}|\geqslant 5$ b $\dfrac{1}{5+3c^2}\begin{pmatrix} 1 & -3c \\ c & 5 \end{pmatrix}$

9 $\dfrac{1}{4}\begin{pmatrix} 7 & 9 \\ 15 & 1 \end{pmatrix}$

10 a Proof   b $\dfrac{1}{3}\mathbf{B}^{-1}$

11 $\mathbf{A}^{-1}\mathbf{BA}$

12 a $\mathbf{Q}^{-1}$ b $\dfrac{2}{3}\mathbf{I}$

13 Proof

14 a $\dfrac{1}{\det \mathbf{A}}$ b $\det \mathbf{A}$

   c $(\det \mathbf{A})^n$

Exercise 1E

1 a i -52 ii 0
   b i 12 ii $-5-4d$

2 a i $\dfrac{1}{26}\begin{pmatrix} 0 & 3 & 4 \\ 0 & 5 & -2 \\ 13 & -9 & 1 \end{pmatrix}$

   ii $\dfrac{1}{26}\begin{pmatrix} 52 & -30 & 16 \\ -26 & 19 & -11 \\ 0 & 3 & 1 \end{pmatrix}$

   b i $\dfrac{1}{12}\begin{pmatrix} 6 & 2 & 4 \\ 30 & 22 & 20 \\ 9 & 7 & 8 \end{pmatrix}$

   ii $\dfrac{1}{5+4d}\begin{pmatrix} -1 & -d-2 & 3d+4 \\ 4 & 3 & -1 \\ 4 & 3 & -6-4d \end{pmatrix}$

Answers

3 **a i** $x = 1 \pm \sqrt{5}$ **ii** $x = 0$
  b i $x = -0.5, 1$ **ii** $x = -1, 4$

4 **a i** $X = \begin{pmatrix} -8 & -1 & -6 \\ -9 & -3 & -1 \\ 9 & 2 & 4 \end{pmatrix}$

  ii $X = \begin{pmatrix} -1 & 0 & -1 \\ -61 & -15 & -35 \\ 16 & 4 & 9 \end{pmatrix}$

  b i $X = \begin{pmatrix} 2 & -2 & 15 \\ -4 & 7 & -40 \\ -1 & 5 & -13 \end{pmatrix}$

  ii $X = \begin{pmatrix} -10 & 6 & 23 \\ 2 & -2 & -6 \\ -7 & 5 & 19 \end{pmatrix}$

  c i $X = \begin{pmatrix} -5 \\ -4 \\ 5 \end{pmatrix}$ **ii** $X = (-8 \quad 3 \quad 10)$

5 $x = 3$ or -6

6 $x = \dfrac{-5}{2} \pm \dfrac{1}{2}\sqrt{29}$

7 $X = \begin{pmatrix} 52 & 23 & -32 \\ -30 & -13 & 20 \\ 60 & 27 & -36 \end{pmatrix}$

8 **a** $A^{-1} = \dfrac{1}{6a-6}\begin{pmatrix} -6-4a & 4a & -2a \\ 7+3a & -1-3a & 3a-1 \\ 10 & -4 & 2 \end{pmatrix}$

  b $X = \dfrac{1}{6a-6}\begin{pmatrix} -12-10a & 6+4a & -6-2a \\ 13+9a & -10 & 8 \\ 22 & -10 & 8 \end{pmatrix}$

  c $a = 0.75$

9 **a** $x \neq -1$ **b** $B = \dfrac{1}{4x+4}\begin{pmatrix} x+4 \\ -12 \\ 4+7x \end{pmatrix}$

10 Discussion

11 $A^{-1} = \dfrac{1}{-a-7}\begin{pmatrix} -7 & a & 7a & -3a \\ -1 & -1 & a & 3 \\ 5 & -2-a & -5a & 2a-1 \\ -1 & -1 & -7 & 3 \end{pmatrix}$

Mixed practice 1

1 $\begin{pmatrix} 3p & -p-4 \\ -12 & 8p+4 \end{pmatrix}$

2 $a = \dfrac{4}{3}, b = 6, c = \dfrac{7}{3}, k = -3$

3 **a** Proof
  b For example: $C = \begin{pmatrix} 1 & 0 \\ 0 & 0 \end{pmatrix}, D = \begin{pmatrix} 0 & 0 \\ 1 & 0 \end{pmatrix}$

4 **a** $(7 \quad 23)$
  b $\begin{pmatrix} 6 & -15 \\ 4 & -10 \end{pmatrix}$; singular; $|CB| = 0$

5 $B = \dfrac{1}{4}\begin{pmatrix} 5 & 19 \\ -2 & -10 \end{pmatrix}$

6 **a** $a = -1$
  b $A^{-1} = \dfrac{1}{4(a+1)}\begin{pmatrix} 4 & 2 \\ -2 & a \end{pmatrix}$

7 **a** $\dfrac{1}{2}\begin{pmatrix} 1 & -a \\ 0 & 2 \end{pmatrix}$ **b** $\begin{pmatrix} 1 & 0 \\ 2 & 1-2a \end{pmatrix}$

8 $2a^2 + 6a - 15$

9 $x = -\dfrac{1}{2} \pm \dfrac{\sqrt{7}}{2}$

10 $X = \dfrac{1}{7}\begin{pmatrix} 12 & 17 \\ -2 & -18 \\ -3 & -41 \end{pmatrix}$

11 $x = -0.5, y = 0$

12 **a** Proof
   b For example: $C = \begin{pmatrix} 1 & 2 \\ 2 & 4 \end{pmatrix}, D = \begin{pmatrix} 2 & 6 \\ -1 & -3 \end{pmatrix}$
   Importantly, the second column of **C** must be a multiple k of the first, and the upper row of **D** must be a multiple $-k$ of the lower.

13 **a** Proof
   b For example, $A = \begin{pmatrix} 1 & 2 \\ 3 & 4 \end{pmatrix}$ and $B = \begin{pmatrix} 2 & 0 \\ 1 & 1 \end{pmatrix}$.

Chapter 2

Before you start…

1 **a** $3\mathbf{i} - 5\mathbf{j}$ **b** $\begin{pmatrix} 3 \\ 0 \\ -2 \end{pmatrix}$

2 $a = -1, b = -2$

3 $p = -\dfrac{3}{5}, q = -10$

4 **a** 113.6 and 246.4 **b** 0.644

Work it out 2.1

Solution 3 is correct.

Exercise 2A

1 **a i** $\mathbf{r} = \begin{pmatrix} 4 \\ -1 \end{pmatrix} + \lambda\begin{pmatrix} 1 \\ 4 \end{pmatrix}$ **ii** $\mathbf{r} = \begin{pmatrix} 4 \\ 1 \end{pmatrix} + \lambda\begin{pmatrix} 2 \\ -3 \end{pmatrix}$

191

b i $\mathbf{r} = \begin{pmatrix} 1 \\ 0 \\ 5 \end{pmatrix} + \lambda \begin{pmatrix} 1 \\ 3 \\ -3 \end{pmatrix}$ **ii** $\mathbf{r} = \begin{pmatrix} -1 \\ 1 \\ 5 \end{pmatrix} + \lambda \begin{pmatrix} 3 \\ -2 \\ 2 \end{pmatrix}$

c i $\mathbf{r} = \begin{pmatrix} 4 \\ 0 \\ 0 \end{pmatrix} + \lambda \begin{pmatrix} 2 \\ 3 \\ 3 \end{pmatrix}$ **ii** $\mathbf{r} = \begin{pmatrix} 0 \\ 2 \\ 2 \end{pmatrix} + \lambda \begin{pmatrix} 1 \\ -3 \\ -3 \end{pmatrix}$

d i $\mathbf{r} = \begin{pmatrix} 0 \\ 2 \\ 3 \end{pmatrix} + \lambda \begin{pmatrix} 1 \\ 0 \\ -3 \end{pmatrix}$ **ii** $\mathbf{r} = \begin{pmatrix} 4 \\ -3 \\ 0 \end{pmatrix} + \lambda \begin{pmatrix} 2 \\ 3 \\ -1 \end{pmatrix}$

2 a i $\mathbf{r} = \begin{pmatrix} 4 \\ 1 \end{pmatrix} + \lambda \begin{pmatrix} -3 \\ 1 \end{pmatrix}$ **ii** $\mathbf{r} = \begin{pmatrix} 2 \\ 7 \end{pmatrix} + \lambda \begin{pmatrix} 2 \\ -9 \end{pmatrix}$

b i $\mathbf{r} = \begin{pmatrix} -5 \\ -2 \\ 3 \end{pmatrix} + \lambda \begin{pmatrix} 9 \\ 0 \\ 0 \end{pmatrix}$ **ii** $\mathbf{r} = \begin{pmatrix} 1 \\ 1 \\ 3 \end{pmatrix} + \lambda \begin{pmatrix} 9 \\ -6 \\ -3 \end{pmatrix}$

3 a i Yes **ii** Yes
b i Yes **ii** No
4 a i No **ii** No
b i Yes **ii** Yes
5 a $\mathbf{r} = (3\mathbf{i} - \mathbf{j} + 4\mathbf{k}) + \lambda(5\mathbf{i} - \mathbf{j} + 2\mathbf{k})$
  b Proof
  c $2\sqrt{30}$
6 a $\mathbf{r} = 4\mathbf{i} - \mathbf{j} + 5\mathbf{k} + \lambda(3\mathbf{i} + 8\mathbf{j} - 3\mathbf{k})$ **b** No
7 $\mathbf{r} = \begin{pmatrix} 4 \\ 1 \\ 7 \end{pmatrix} + \lambda \begin{pmatrix} 1 \\ -6 \\ 2 \end{pmatrix}$
8 $\mathbf{r} = (4 + 2\lambda)\mathbf{i} + (-1 - \lambda)\mathbf{j} + (2 + 3\lambda)\mathbf{k}$
9 a Proof **b** $(0, 3, 0)$
10 a $\mathbf{r} = \begin{pmatrix} 7 \\ 1 \\ 2 \end{pmatrix} + \lambda \begin{pmatrix} -4 \\ -2 \\ 3 \end{pmatrix}$
  b $(-5, -5, 11), (19, 7, -7)$
11 a $\mathbf{r} = \begin{pmatrix} 2 \\ 1 \\ 4 \end{pmatrix} + \lambda \begin{pmatrix} 2 \\ -3 \\ 6 \end{pmatrix}$ **b** 7
  c $(-8, 16, -26), (12, -14, 34)$

Exercise 2B

1 a i $4x + 7y = 5$ **ii** $3x - 2y + 13 = 0$
  b i $\dfrac{x-4}{2} = \dfrac{y+1}{-1} = \dfrac{z-5}{7}$
   ii $\dfrac{x-1}{-1} = \dfrac{y-7}{1} = \dfrac{z-2}{2}$

c i $x = -1$, $\dfrac{y-5}{-2} = \dfrac{z}{2}$
 ii $\dfrac{x-3}{7} = y$, $z = 6$

2 a i $\mathbf{r} = \begin{pmatrix} 0 \\ 2 \end{pmatrix} + \lambda \begin{pmatrix} 5 \\ 3 \end{pmatrix}$
 ii $\mathbf{r} = \begin{pmatrix} 0 \\ -1 \end{pmatrix} + \lambda \begin{pmatrix} 3 \\ -4 \end{pmatrix}$
 b i $\mathbf{r} = \begin{pmatrix} 0 \\ -17/5 \end{pmatrix} + \lambda \begin{pmatrix} 5 \\ 3 \end{pmatrix}$
 ii $\mathbf{r} = \begin{pmatrix} 0 \\ -4/3 \end{pmatrix} + \lambda \begin{pmatrix} 3 \\ -2 \end{pmatrix}$

3 a i $\mathbf{r} = \begin{pmatrix} 2 \\ 2 \\ -1 \end{pmatrix} + \lambda \begin{pmatrix} 5 \\ 3 \\ 7 \end{pmatrix}$ **ii** $\mathbf{r} = \begin{pmatrix} -1 \\ 6 \\ 5 \end{pmatrix} + \lambda \begin{pmatrix} 4 \\ -1 \\ 3 \end{pmatrix}$

b i $\mathbf{r} = \begin{pmatrix} -1 \\ 0 \\ 1 \end{pmatrix} + \lambda \begin{pmatrix} 3 \\ -7 \\ -5 \end{pmatrix}$ **ii** $\mathbf{r} = \begin{pmatrix} 3 \\ -1 \\ 0 \end{pmatrix} + \lambda \begin{pmatrix} 2 \\ -4 \\ 5 \end{pmatrix}$

c i $\mathbf{r} = \begin{pmatrix} 11 \\ -1 \\ -2 \end{pmatrix} + \lambda \begin{pmatrix} 3 \\ 6 \\ 0 \end{pmatrix}$ **ii** $\mathbf{r} = \begin{pmatrix} -1 \\ 1 \\ 3 \end{pmatrix} + \lambda \begin{pmatrix} 5 \\ 0 \\ -2 \end{pmatrix}$

4 a Neither **b** Parallel
 c Neither **d** Same line
5 For example, $\mathbf{r} = \begin{pmatrix} 6 \\ 0 \end{pmatrix} + \lambda \begin{pmatrix} 3 \\ -5 \end{pmatrix}$
6 It does not.
7 a $\dfrac{x-1}{3} = \dfrac{4-y}{2} = \dfrac{z+1}{3}$
 b $\dfrac{1}{\sqrt{22}} \begin{pmatrix} 3 \\ -2 \\ 3 \end{pmatrix}$ or $\dfrac{-1}{\sqrt{22}} \begin{pmatrix} 3 \\ -2 \\ 3 \end{pmatrix}$

8 a $p = -4.5, q = -2$
 b $(4, -0.5, -2), (-8, -8.5, -2)$

Exercise 2C

1 a i $(10, -7, -2)$ **ii** $(4.5, 0, 0)$
 b i No intersection **ii** No intersection
 c i $(3, 2, -5)$ **ii** No intersection
2 Proof
3 $(1, -5, 2)$
4 It does not.
5 4.5
6 5.10

Answers

Work it out 2.2
Solution 3 is correct.

Exercise 2D
1. a i 9 ii 2
   b i −3 ii 3
   c i 5 ii −1
2. a i 64.0° ii 66.9°
   b i 107.5° ii 64.9°
   c i 70.3° ii 101.3°
3. a i $\dfrac{9}{2\sqrt{21}}$ ii $-\dfrac{20}{\sqrt{570}}$
   b i $-\dfrac{2}{\sqrt{102}}$ ii $\dfrac{1}{\sqrt{35}}$
   c i 0 ii 0
4. a 61.0°, 74.5°, 44.5°
   b 94.3°, 54.2°, 31.5°
5. a i No ii Yes
   b i Yes ii No
6. a i 44.5° ii 56.5°
   b i 26.6° ii 82.1°
7. 87.7°
8. 40.0°
9. a Proof b 106.8°, 73.2°
   c $\dfrac{5}{4}$
10. a Proof b 41.8°, 48.2°
    c $6\sqrt{5}$
11. $\left(\dfrac{64}{9}, \dfrac{4}{9}, \dfrac{19}{9}\right)$
12. $\sqrt{\dfrac{6}{11}}$
13. 3
14. a $\left(\dfrac{5}{6}, \dfrac{19}{6}, \dfrac{9}{2}\right)$ b 48.5°
    c Proof d $\dfrac{11\sqrt{11}}{6}$ (= 6.08)
    e 4.55
15. a (9, −5, 8) b Proof
    c (3, 4, −1)

Exercise 2E
1. a i $\mathbf{a}\times\mathbf{b} = \begin{pmatrix}19\\-13\\-5\end{pmatrix}, \mathbf{b}\times\mathbf{a} = \begin{pmatrix}-19\\13\\5\end{pmatrix}$

   ii $\mathbf{a}\times\mathbf{b} = \begin{pmatrix}-14\\-5\\-6\end{pmatrix}, \mathbf{b}\times\mathbf{a} = \begin{pmatrix}14\\5\\6\end{pmatrix}$

   b i $\mathbf{a}\times\mathbf{b} = 6\mathbf{i}-8\mathbf{j}-19\mathbf{k}, \mathbf{b}\times\mathbf{a} = -6\mathbf{i}+8\mathbf{j}+19\mathbf{k}$

   ii $\mathbf{a}\times\mathbf{b} = -2\mathbf{i}-2\mathbf{j}-6\mathbf{k}, \mathbf{b}\times\mathbf{a} = 2\mathbf{i}+2\mathbf{j}+6\mathbf{k}$

2. a i $\mathbf{a}\times\mathbf{b} = \begin{pmatrix}1\\-7\\3\end{pmatrix}$ ii $\mathbf{a}\times\mathbf{b} = \begin{pmatrix}16\\1\\5\end{pmatrix}$

   b i $\mathbf{a}\times\mathbf{b} = -15\mathbf{j}-5\mathbf{k}$ ii $\mathbf{a}\times\mathbf{b} = -4\mathbf{i}+11\mathbf{j}+3\mathbf{k}$

3. a i $\dfrac{1}{26}\begin{pmatrix}0 & 3 & 4\\0 & 5 & -2\\13 & -9 & 1\end{pmatrix}$

   ii $\dfrac{1}{26}\begin{pmatrix}52 & -30 & 16\\-26 & 19 & -11\\0 & 3 & 1\end{pmatrix}$

   b i $\dfrac{1}{12}\begin{pmatrix}6 & 2 & 4\\30 & 22 & 20\\9 & 7 & 8\end{pmatrix}$

   ii $\dfrac{1}{5+4d}\begin{pmatrix}-1 & -d-2 & 3d+4\\4 & 3 & -1\\4 & 3 & -6-4d\end{pmatrix}$

4. $\mathbf{a}\times\mathbf{b} = -2\mathbf{i}+9\mathbf{j}+3\mathbf{k}$

5. $\mathbf{r} = \begin{pmatrix}-1\\1\\7\end{pmatrix} + \lambda\begin{pmatrix}0\\1\\0\end{pmatrix}$

6. $\mathbf{r} = \begin{pmatrix}3\\1\\6\end{pmatrix} + \lambda\begin{pmatrix}6\\4\\3\end{pmatrix}$

7. $\dfrac{x-3}{3} = -\dfrac{y-1}{1} = -\dfrac{z-2}{7}$

8. $\dfrac{x+3}{7} = -\dfrac{y-1}{6} = -\dfrac{z-1}{3}$

Mixed practice 2
1. $\mathbf{r} = \begin{pmatrix}7\\0\\3\end{pmatrix} + \lambda\begin{pmatrix}4\\-1\\-1\end{pmatrix}$
2. a (−1, −3, 1) b 60.5°
3. Proof
4. $\mathbf{i}+3\mathbf{k}$
5. 72.0°

6 a $\mathbf{r} = \begin{pmatrix} 1/2 \\ -2 \\ 4/3 \end{pmatrix} + \lambda \begin{pmatrix} 2 \\ 3 \\ -2 \end{pmatrix}$

   b Yes (at $\left(\frac{11}{6}, 0, 0\right)$)   c $61.0°$

7 a $(8, 7, 1)$ b Proof ($\lambda = 1$)

8 There is no intersection (skew lines).

9 $\mathbf{r} = \begin{pmatrix} -1 \\ 0 \\ 3 \end{pmatrix} + v \begin{pmatrix} 3 \\ 7 \\ -4 \end{pmatrix}$

10 a Proof
   b $(2+\sqrt{6}, -1-2\sqrt{6}, 2\sqrt{6}), (2-\sqrt{6}, 2\sqrt{6}-1, -2\sqrt{6})$

11 a $\mathbf{r} = \begin{pmatrix} 4 \\ 4 \\ -6 \end{pmatrix} + \lambda \begin{pmatrix} -1 \\ 2 \\ 3 \end{pmatrix}$ b $\mathbf{r} = \mu \begin{pmatrix} 1 \\ 2 \\ -1 \end{pmatrix}$

   c $(3, 6, -3)$ d $3\sqrt{6}$

12 a $(4, 1, -2)$ b Proof

   c $(1, 1, 2)$ d $\dfrac{5\sqrt{26}}{2}$

Chapter 3

Before you start…

1 $x=1, y=-1$

2 $\mathbf{a} = 5\mathbf{i} + 3\mathbf{j} - 2\mathbf{k}, \mathbf{b} = -\mathbf{j} + \mathbf{k}$

3 a $P'(-2, 1), Q'(-4, 1), R'(-2, 2)$
   b $P'(-2, -1), Q'(-4, -1), R'(-2, -2)$
   c $P'(2, 4), Q'(2, 8), R'(4, 4)$

4 $\theta = 150°$

5 a 30   b $\dfrac{1}{30}\begin{pmatrix} 8 & 3 & 5 \\ -2 & 3 & -5 \\ -8 & 12 & 10 \end{pmatrix}$

6 10

Exercise 3A

1 a i $x=-1, y=2$ ii $x=2.5, y=1.5$
  b i $x=0, y=0.5$ ii $x=-\dfrac{59}{12}, y=\dfrac{5}{3}$
  c i $x=-4, y=-3$ ii $x=-18, y=-13$

2 a i $x=\dfrac{4}{3}, y=-\dfrac{23}{3}, z=-\dfrac{28}{3}$
    ii $x=-1, y=5, z=3$
  b i $x=\dfrac{22}{9}, y=\dfrac{38}{9}, z=\dfrac{122}{9}$
    ii $x=\dfrac{26}{11}, y=\dfrac{3}{11}, z=\dfrac{35}{11}$

3 $a=-0.5$

4 $a \neq -1$

5 a $k=-4$ b $x=\dfrac{5}{k+4}, y=\dfrac{2-2k}{k+4}$

6 a $a \neq -3, 5$
   b $x=\dfrac{2a-7}{a^2-2a-15}, y=\dfrac{a-10}{a^2-2a-15}$

7 a $\begin{pmatrix} 2 & 1 & 1 \\ 1 & 2 & 3 \\ 1 & 1 & 2 \end{pmatrix} \begin{pmatrix} g \\ p \\ y \end{pmatrix} = \begin{pmatrix} 115 \\ 210 \\ 135 \end{pmatrix}$ b 40 g

8 a $\begin{pmatrix} 1 & 1 & 1 \\ 3.5 & 2.8 & 3.1 \\ 0 & 1 & -2 \end{pmatrix} \begin{pmatrix} X \\ Y \\ Z \end{pmatrix} = \begin{pmatrix} 50 \\ 157 \\ 0 \end{pmatrix}$

   b 20 from X, 20 from Y, 10 from Z

9 25

10 a $c \neq 1.5$
   b $x=\dfrac{17c-15}{10c-15}, y=\dfrac{35}{10c-15}, z=\dfrac{11c+15}{10c-15}$

11 a Proof
   b $x=\dfrac{3k}{k^2+3k+8}, y=\dfrac{k-4}{k^2+3k+8}, z=\dfrac{4+3k-k^2}{k^2+3k+8}$

Exercise 3B

1 a i
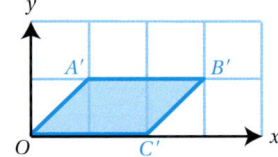

   ii
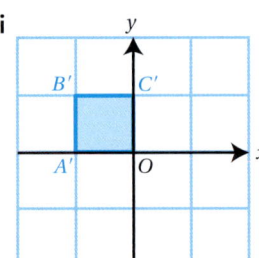

  b i
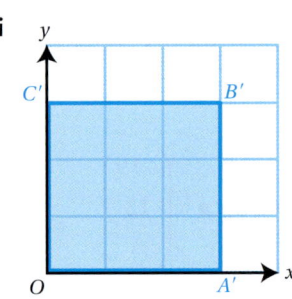

Answers

ii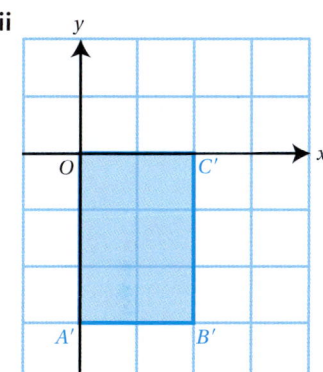

10 a $A'(-3, 1)$, $B'(-4, -2)$, $C'(-3, -2)$

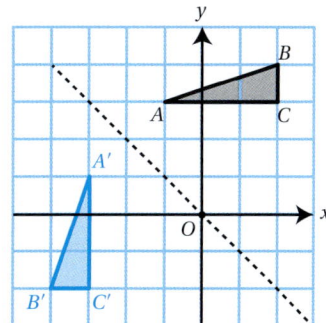

2 a i $\begin{pmatrix} 2 & 1 \\ 0 & 2 \end{pmatrix}$ ii $\begin{pmatrix} 2 & 3 \\ 1 & -1 \end{pmatrix}$

b i $\begin{pmatrix} 1 & -2 \\ -4 & 1 \end{pmatrix}$ ii $\begin{pmatrix} 2 & 1 \\ -1 & 1 \end{pmatrix}$

3 a Reflection, $y = -x$ b Reflection, $y = x$
  c Neither d Reflection, $x = 0$
  e Rotation 180° f Neither

4 a i (5, 3) ii (−3, 5)
  b i (3, 1) ii (1, −3)
  c i (21, 12) ii (−28, 16)
  d i $\left(-2, -\frac{1}{2}\right)$ ii $\left(\frac{4}{3}, -\frac{1}{3}\right)$

5 a i (6, −3) ii (−6, 3)
  b i (7, −2) ii (−2, −7)
  c i $\left(\frac{2}{3}, -\frac{5}{3}\right)$ ii (1, 0.4)
  d i (−2, −6) ii (−2, −6)

6 a $\begin{pmatrix} -1 & 0 \\ 0 & -1 \end{pmatrix}$ b $\begin{pmatrix} 0 & 1 \\ -1 & 0 \end{pmatrix}$

7 a $\begin{pmatrix} 0 & 1 \\ -1 & 0 \end{pmatrix}$, 90° rotation anticlockwise about the origin
  b Rotation of θ_1 followed by rotation of θ_2 is equivalent to a rotation of $(\theta_1 + \theta_2)$.
  c $\begin{pmatrix} 0 & -1 \\ 1 & 0 \end{pmatrix}$, 90° rotation about the y-axis
  d A pair of successive reflections is always equal to a rotation of double the angle between the reflection lines, in the same direction as from the first line to the second. (In part c, $y = x$ to the y-axis is a 45° rotation, so the combination is the same as a 90° rotation.)

8 a Reflection in the same line
  b Rotation 90° clockwise about the origin

9 $P'(-1, 1)$, $Q'(-1, 6)$, $R'(2, 4)$

b Determinant $= -1$

The scale factor of the areas is 1 (i.e. the two triangles have the same area) but the orientations are different.

11 a $T = \begin{pmatrix} 0 & 3 \\ 3 & 0 \end{pmatrix}$ b $P = (-3, 1)$
   c 90

Exercise 3C

1 a 60° b 53.1°
  c 135° d 233°

2 a Shear with the x-axis invariant, mapping (0, 1) to (6, 1)
  b Shear with the y-axis invariant, mapping (1, 0) to (1, 2)
  c Shear with the x-axis invariant, mapping (0, 1) to (−3, 1)
  d Shear with the x-axis invariant, mapping (0, 1) to (−1.5, 1)

3 a $\begin{pmatrix} \frac{1}{2} & -\frac{\sqrt{3}}{2} \\ \frac{\sqrt{3}}{2} & \frac{1}{2} \end{pmatrix}$ b $\begin{pmatrix} 1 & 3 \\ 0 & 1 \end{pmatrix}$

  c $\begin{pmatrix} -1 & 0 \\ 0 & 1 \end{pmatrix}$ d $\begin{pmatrix} 1 & 0 \\ 1/2 & 1 \end{pmatrix}$

  e $\begin{pmatrix} -\frac{\sqrt{3}}{2} & \frac{1}{2} \\ -\frac{1}{2} & -\frac{\sqrt{3}}{2} \end{pmatrix}$ f $\begin{pmatrix} 5 & 0 \\ 0 & 5 \end{pmatrix}$

4 a (1, −3) b $(\sqrt{2}, -2\sqrt{2})$
  c (3, 11) d $\left(\frac{\sqrt{3}-3}{2}, \frac{3\sqrt{3}+1}{2}\right)$
  e (1, −1/3) f (8/3, −1)

195

5 **a** $(2, -1)$ **b** $(2, 1)$
   c $(-0.5, 1)$ **d** $(-1, 4)$
   e $\left(\sqrt{3} - \frac{1}{2}, 1 + \frac{\sqrt{3}}{2}\right)$ **f** $(-2, 2)$

6 $\left(\frac{\sqrt{2}}{2}, \frac{5\sqrt{2}}{2}\right)$

7 **a** $P(1, 1), Q(6, 1), R(-3, -2), S(-8, -2)$
   b 1

8 **a** $\begin{pmatrix} 1 & 0 \\ 1.5 & 1 \end{pmatrix}$ **b** $(0, 0), (1, 1.5), (-3, 5.5)$

Exercise 3D

1 **a** $y = 0$ line of invariant points; $y = 3x$ invariant line
   b $y = 0$ invariant line; $2x - 5y = 0$ invariant line
   c $x - 2y = 0$ invariant line; $x + y = 0$
   d $y = x$ line of invariant points; $2x - y = 0$ invariant line

2 **a** $y = -3x$ line of invariant points; $3y = x$ invariant line
   b None
   c $y = \frac{3 \pm \sqrt{21}}{2} x$
   d Invariant lines $y = \frac{3 \pm \sqrt{21}}{6} x$
   e No invariant lines
   f $x = 0$ line of invariant points; $y = 0$ invariant line

3 **a** $a = -2$ **b** No; **A** is singular
4 **a** $y = -x$ **b** $y = -x$ and $y = -3x$
5 **a** $y = -x$, $9x + 2y = 0$; neither is a line of invariant points
   b $y = -x$, $9x + 2y = 0$
6 $\theta = \tan^{-1}(3)$ or $\tan^{-1}\left(-\frac{1}{3}\right)$
7 **a** $y = -2x$ line of invariant points; $y = 0$ invariant line
   b $b = 1$
8 **a** $a = -2, b = -4$ **b** $y = -x$

Exercise 3E

1 **a** $\begin{pmatrix} 1 & 0 & 0 \\ 0 & 0 & -1 \\ 0 & 1 & 0 \end{pmatrix}$ **b** $\begin{pmatrix} \sqrt{3}/2 & -1/2 & 0 \\ 1/2 & \sqrt{3}/2 & 0 \\ 0 & 0 & 1 \end{pmatrix}$

c $\begin{pmatrix} -1 & 0 & 0 \\ 0 & 1 & 0 \\ 0 & 0 & 1 \end{pmatrix}$ **d** $\begin{pmatrix} 1 & 0 & 0 \\ 0 & -1 & 0 \\ 0 & 0 & 1 \end{pmatrix}$

2 **a** $\left(1 + \frac{\sqrt{3}}{2}, -1, \frac{1}{2} - \sqrt{3}\right)$ **b** $(-2, 1, 1)$
   c $(2, -1, -1)$ **d** $(2, 1, 1)$

3 $(-2, -5, 1)$

4 **a** $\begin{pmatrix} 1 & 0 & 0 \\ 0 & -1 & 0 \\ 0 & 0 & 1 \end{pmatrix}, \begin{pmatrix} 1 & 0 & 0 \\ 0 & -1 & 0 \\ 0 & 0 & -1 \end{pmatrix}$

   b $\begin{pmatrix} 1 & 0 & 0 \\ 0 & 1 & 0 \\ 0 & 0 & -1 \end{pmatrix}$

   c -1; the transformation preserves volume but reverses orientation.

5 $A'(1, 1, -1), B'(1, 1, -3), C'(1, 4, -1)$
6 $A = (-\sqrt{2}, -3\sqrt{2}, -1)$
7 $\left(-\frac{3\sqrt{3}}{2} - \frac{1}{2}, 1, -\frac{3}{2} + \frac{\sqrt{3}}{2}\right)$

8 $\begin{pmatrix} 0 & -1 & 0 \\ 1 & 0 & 0 \\ 0 & 0 & 1 \end{pmatrix}$

9 $\begin{pmatrix} 0 & -1 & 0 \\ 0 & 0 & -1 \\ 1 & 0 & 0 \end{pmatrix}$

10 $(1, -3, 4)$

11 **a** $T = \begin{pmatrix} 0 & 1 & 0 \\ 0 & 0 & -1 \\ -1 & 0 & 0 \end{pmatrix}$ **b** Proof

12 **a** $T = \begin{pmatrix} 1 & 3 & 2 \\ 0 & 1 & 1 \\ 1 & 0 & 2 \end{pmatrix}$

b They must not be collinear. (Equivalently, the triangle with the three points as vertices must have non-zero area).
The position vectors of the points can then form the columns of a non-singular matrix **A**, and the transformation **T** which satisfies **TA** = **B** can be found as **T** = **BA**$^{-1}$.

If the points are collinear then **A** is singular and **T** is not uniquely described.

13 a 15 units^3

b The orientation of the image is reversed.

14 a Stretch with scale factor 4 in y-direction

b Enlargement with scale factor 3

c Enlargement with scale factor -0.5

15 2 units

Mixed practice 3

1 $x=0$

2 a $\begin{pmatrix} 1 & 0 & 0 \\ 0 & 1 & 0 \\ 0 & 0 & -1 \end{pmatrix}$

b Reflection in the plane $z=0$

3 a i $k=\dfrac{35}{3}$

ii $\mathbf{M}^{-1} = \dfrac{1}{3k-35}\begin{pmatrix} k & -5 \\ -7 & 3 \end{pmatrix}$

b $x=53, y=-30$

4 a i Shear, x-axis invariant, $(0, 1)$ mapped to $(5, 1)$

ii Reflection in the line $y=2x$

b $\dfrac{1}{2}\begin{pmatrix} 2 & 0 & 0 \\ 0 & 1 & -\sqrt{3} \\ 0 & \sqrt{3} & 1 \end{pmatrix}$

5 a $y=-3x$ line of invariant points; $y=-9x$ invariant line

b $y=-x$ invariant line

6 a $\mathbf{A}=\begin{pmatrix} 0 & 1 \\ -1 & 0 \end{pmatrix}$, $\mathbf{B}=\begin{pmatrix} 1 & 0 \\ 0 & 3 \end{pmatrix}$ **b** det $\mathbf{C}=0$

7 a $\begin{pmatrix} 1 & 0 \\ 4 & 1 \end{pmatrix}$

b i Rotation 45° clockwise about the origin

ii $|\mathbf{X}|=1$

Area scale factor of this transformation is 1 (i.e. the area of the image is the same as that of the original object).

8 a $a=-3$

b $x=\dfrac{2}{a+3}, y=\dfrac{2-4a}{a+3}, z=\dfrac{7a-1}{a+3}$

9 $a=1$ or -0.5, $b=2$

10 a $\mathbf{T}=\begin{pmatrix} 2 & 3 \\ 0 & 2 \end{pmatrix}$

b i $k=2$

ii Shear, x-axis invariant, $(0, 1)$ mapped to $(1.5, 1)$

11 a i $(0, 5)$ **ii** $P'(2, 1), Q'(30, -25), R'(28, -26)$

b i $x-2y=0$ **ii** $y=-x$

12 a $y=3x; y=(4-3k)x$ **b** $k=1, 2$

c $y=3x$

d $k=1: y=x, k=2: y=-2x$

13 a $a=-1, b=0$

b i $\mathbf{T}=(1-3, k=2\ 0\ 1)$

ii Enlargement with scale factor 2; shear with x-axis invariant mapping $(0, 1)$ to $(-3, 1)$

14 a $s=3, t=4$

b i $k=-16$

ii Enlargement scale factor 2 and rotation 45° about origin

iii $\mathbf{B}^{15} = 16384\begin{pmatrix} \sqrt{2} & \sqrt{2} \\ -\sqrt{2} & \sqrt{2} \end{pmatrix}$

Focus on … Proof 1

1 a Proof   **b** Proof

2 a For example the 2×2 zero matrix

b For example $\begin{pmatrix} 1 & 0 \\ 1 & 0 \end{pmatrix}$ and $\begin{pmatrix} 0 & 0 \\ 1 & 1 \end{pmatrix}$

Focus on … Problem-solving 1

1 a $BM = BA \cos \theta$

b $\cos \theta = \dfrac{(\mathbf{a}-\mathbf{b})\cdot \mathbf{d}}{|\mathbf{d}|}$, where $\mathbf{d}$ is in the direction from B to M.

c Proof

d The shortest distance is $2\sqrt{14}$.

2 i a $\overrightarrow{PQ} = \begin{pmatrix} -\mu - 3\lambda \\ 1+2\mu+\lambda \\ 8+3\mu-\lambda \end{pmatrix}$

b $7 - 2\mu - 11\lambda = 0$, $26 + 14\mu + 2\lambda = 0$

c $\sqrt{6}$

ii Proof and discussion. It is possible to use completing the square, but it is difficult with two variables.

iii a $\mathbf{n} = \begin{pmatrix} -5 \\ -10 \\ 5 \end{pmatrix}$ **b** Proof

Focus on ... Modelling 1

1. **a** 2 paths: $A\text{-}(p)\text{-}A\text{-}(q)\text{-}B, A\text{-}(p)\text{-}A\text{-}(r)\text{-}B$
   b 6 paths: $A\text{-}(p)\text{-}B\text{-}(p)\text{-}A, A\text{-}(q)\text{-}B\text{-}(q)\text{-}A,$
   $A\text{-}(q)\text{-}B\text{-}(r)\text{-}A, A\text{-}(r)\text{-}B\text{-}(q)\text{-}A,$
   $A\text{-}(r)\text{-}B\text{-}(r)\text{-}A, A\text{-}(s)\text{-}C\text{-}(s)\text{-}A$

2. **a** 2 paths: $B\text{-}(q)\text{-}A\text{-}(p)\text{-}A\text{-}(s)\text{-}C, B\text{-}(r)\text{-}A\text{-}(p)\text{-}A\text{-}(s)\text{-}C$
   b 4 paths: $B\text{-}(q)\text{-}A\text{-}(p)\text{-}A\text{-}(q)\text{-}B, B\text{-}(q)\text{-}A\text{-}(p)\text{-}A\text{-}(r)\text{-}B, B\text{-}(r)\text{-}A\text{-}(p)\text{-}A\text{-}(q)\text{-}B, B\text{-}(r)\text{-}A\text{-}(p)\text{-}A\text{-}(r)\text{-}B$

3. **a** 2 **b** 11
4. **a** 80 190 **b** 24
5. **a** 1 **b** 2
   c 2

Cross-topic review exercise 1

1. $-\dfrac{15}{4}$
2. $\mathbf{r}=(3\mathbf{i}+12\mathbf{j}-5\mathbf{k})+t(-4\mathbf{i}-11\mathbf{j}+11\mathbf{k})$
3. **a** -7 **b** 28
4. **a** $45.3°$ **b** 3.54
5. **a** $\mathbf{r}=(2\mathbf{i}-3\mathbf{j}+\mathbf{k})+t(3\mathbf{i}-\mathbf{j}+5\mathbf{k})$
   b Proof
6. **a** $\begin{pmatrix} 24 \\ -11 \\ -28 \end{pmatrix}$ **b** $\mathbf{r}=\begin{pmatrix} -3 \\ 1 \\ 1 \end{pmatrix}+\lambda\begin{pmatrix} 24 \\ -11 \\ -28 \end{pmatrix}$
7. **a** $\begin{pmatrix} 1 & 0 & 0 \\ 0 & -1 & 0 \\ 0 & 0 & 1 \end{pmatrix}$
   b -1; preserves volume but reverses orientation
8. **a** $\begin{pmatrix} 2 & 3 & 3 \\ 4 & 1 & 5 \\ -1 & 1 & 0 \end{pmatrix}\begin{pmatrix} a \\ b \\ c \end{pmatrix}=\begin{pmatrix} 15 \\ 15.2 \\ 1.2 \end{pmatrix}$
   b i apples £1.50
   ii bananas £2.70
   iii carrots £1.30
9. **a** $\mathbf{r}=(3\mathbf{i}-7\mathbf{j}+\mathbf{k})+\lambda(\mathbf{i}+\mathbf{j}+2\mathbf{k})$ **b** -1
10. **a** $70.3°$ **b** 7 units^2
    c 91 units^2
11. Zero matrix
12. Skew
13. **a** $\dfrac{1}{(3a-6)}\begin{pmatrix} 3 & -2 & 4 \\ -3 & a & -2a \\ -3 & a & a-6 \end{pmatrix}$ **b** $\dfrac{1}{3a-6}\begin{pmatrix} 5 \\ 2a-9 \\ 5a-15 \end{pmatrix}$
14. **a** 2 **b** Proof
15. **a** $\begin{pmatrix} 1 & 0 & 0 \\ 0 & 0 & -1 \\ 0 & 1 & 0 \end{pmatrix}$ **b** Proof
16. **a** $35.3°$ **b** $\left(\dfrac{7}{3},\dfrac{5}{3},-\dfrac{1}{3}\right)$ **c** 2.89
17. -30

Chapter 4

Before you start...

1. $x=1\pm\dfrac{\sqrt{3}}{3}$
2. $x=-1, y=3$ or $x=3, y=1$
3. **a** $\dfrac{\pi}{3}$ **b** $\dfrac{5\pi}{6}$ **c** $\dfrac{4\pi}{3}$
4. **a** $\dfrac{\sqrt{2}}{2}$ **b** $\dfrac{\sqrt{3}}{2}$ **c** $\sqrt{3}$
5.

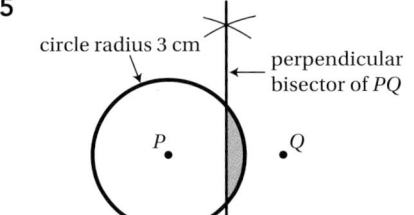

Exercise 4A

1. **a i** 5 **ii** -2
   b i 1 **ii** -1
   c i 2 **ii** 7
   d i 0 **ii** -3
   e i 0 **ii** 0
   f i $a-1$ **ii** $-4-b$
2. **a i** $5\mathbf{i}$ **ii** $-8\mathbf{i}$
   b i -5 **ii** 1
   c i -9 **ii** -16
   d i $-2\mathbf{i}+5$ **ii** $-14+10\mathbf{i}$
3. **a i** $-1+\mathbf{i}$ **ii** $15+6\mathbf{i}$
   b i $5\mathbf{i}$ **ii** $14+23\mathbf{i}$

Answers

    c i $8-i$ ii $16+2i$

    d i $8+6i$ ii $7-24i$

    e i 1 ii 13

4 a i $3+4i$ ii $3-i$

    b i $\frac{1}{2}+\frac{1}{5}i$ ii $-\frac{1}{2}+\frac{1}{8}i$

    c i $\frac{3}{2}+\frac{3}{2}i$ ii $-3+11i$

5 a i $2i$ ii $7i$

    b i $2\sqrt{2}i$ ii $5\sqrt{2}i$

    c i $\frac{4}{3}-2i$ ii $-\frac{1}{3}+\frac{5}{3}i$

    d i $\frac{1}{3}+\frac{1}{2}i$ ii $\frac{5}{4}-\frac{\sqrt{5}}{2}i$

6 a i $x=\pm 3i$ ii $x=\pm 6i$

    b i $x=\pm\sqrt{10}i$ ii $x=\pm\sqrt{13}i$

    c i $x=1\pm 2i$ ii $x=\frac{1}{2}\pm\frac{\sqrt{39}}{2}i$

    d i $x=1\pm\frac{\sqrt{51}}{3}i$ ii $x=-\frac{3}{5}\pm\frac{4}{5}i$

7 a i $-i$ ii 1

    b i 16 ii $125i$

    c i -8 ii $8i$

    d i i ii i

8 a i $a=-\frac{7}{13}, b=\frac{17}{13}$ ii $a=\frac{12}{37}, b=-\frac{2}{37}$

    b i $a=8, b=-18$ ii $a=1, b=0$

    c i $a=1, b=0$ ii $a=-6, b=6$

9 a i $z=\pm(\sqrt{2}-\sqrt{2}i)$

      ii $z=\pm\left(\frac{3\sqrt{2}}{2}+\frac{3\sqrt{2}}{2}i\right)$

    b i $z=\pm(\sqrt{3}+i)$

      ii $z=\pm\left(\sqrt{\frac{\sqrt{26}+5}{2}}+i\sqrt{\frac{\sqrt{26}-5}{2}}\right)$

10 $a=\pm\sqrt{3}, b=\mp\frac{1}{\sqrt{3}}$

11 a $\begin{pmatrix} -1 & 0 \\ 0 & -1 \end{pmatrix}, \begin{pmatrix} 0 & -i \\ -i & 0 \end{pmatrix}$; proof   b $\begin{pmatrix} -1 & 0 \\ 0 & -1 \end{pmatrix}$

12 $9+9i$

13 $a=8, b=1; a=-1, b=10$

14 $z=-\frac{1}{2}+\frac{1}{2}i$

15 a $x=-\frac{1}{5}, y=-\frac{2}{5}$ b $-\frac{3}{5}-\frac{6}{5}i$

16 $1-2i, -1+2i$

17 $z=\pm\left(\frac{1}{\sqrt{2}}+\frac{1}{\sqrt{2}}i\right)$

18 $x=\pm\frac{5\sqrt{2}}{2}, y=\pm\frac{\sqrt{2}}{2}$

Exercise 4B

1 a i $2+3i$ ii $4-4i$

    b i $-i-3$ ii $-3i+2$

    c i $-3i$ ii i

    d i -45 ii 9

2 a i $-\frac{1}{5}-\frac{8}{5}i$ ii $-\frac{10}{17}+\frac{6}{17}i$

    b i $-4i$ ii i

    c i $\frac{15}{17}+\frac{8}{17}i$ ii $\frac{3}{5}-\frac{4}{5}i$

    d i $-1+i$ ii $\frac{2}{5}-\frac{11}{5}i$

3 a $z=\frac{7}{5}-\frac{3}{5}i$ b $z=6-\frac{1}{2}i$

4 a $z=\frac{9}{2}-\frac{9}{2}i, w=-3-\frac{4}{3}i$

    b $z=\frac{3}{10}+\frac{1}{10}i, w=\frac{3}{5}+\frac{1}{5}i$

5 a $z=\frac{1}{2}-2i$ b $z=-\frac{2}{3}-3i$

6 a $z=\frac{2}{3}+7i$ b $z=-\frac{5}{3}+\frac{1}{3}i$

7 a i $z^*=3+x-iy$ ii $z^*=x-2-iy$

    b i $z^*=x+2-i(3y-1)$

      ii $z^*=3-x-i(y+3)$

    c i $z^*=\frac{x(x^2+y^2+1)}{x^2+y^2}-i\frac{y(x^2+y^2-1)}{x^2+y^2}$

      ii $z^*=\frac{x(x^2+y^2-1)}{x^2+y^2}-i\frac{y(x^2+y^2+1)}{x^2+y^2}$

    d i $z^*=i\frac{2xy}{x^2+y^2}$ ii $z^*=\frac{2x^2}{x^2+y^2}$

8 $-\frac{13}{5}-\frac{1}{5}i$

9 a Re: $2x-3y$, Im: $3x-2y$ b $z=-4-4i$

10 $x=6, y=3$

11 Proof

12 $z = -\dfrac{1}{2}\mathrm{i}$

13 No solutions

14 a Proof **b** $z = 2, w = \mathrm{i}$

15 Re: $\dfrac{x(x+1)+y^2}{(x+1)^2+y^2}$, Im: $\dfrac{y}{(x+1)^2+y^2}$

Exercise 4C

1 a i

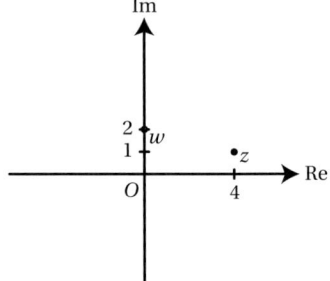

ii

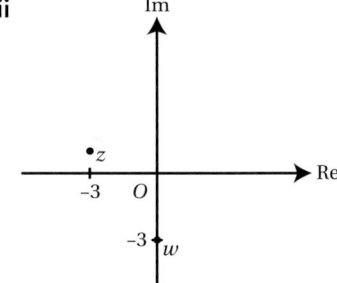

b i

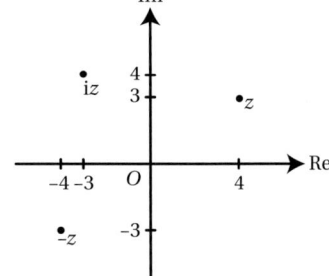

ii

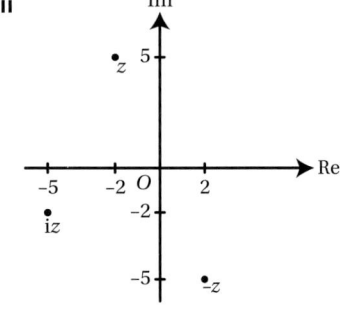

c i

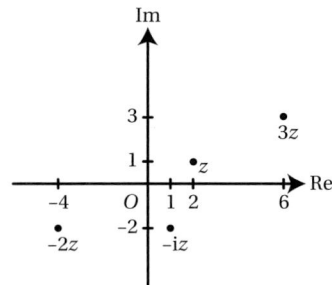

ii

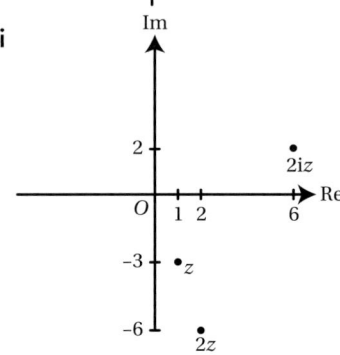

2 a i

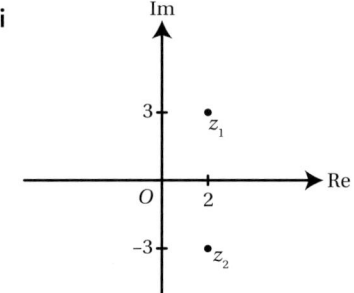

ii

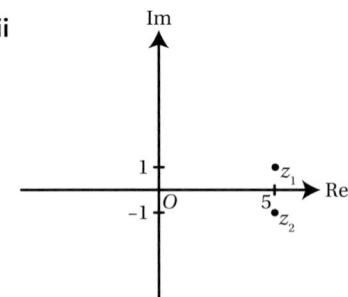

b i

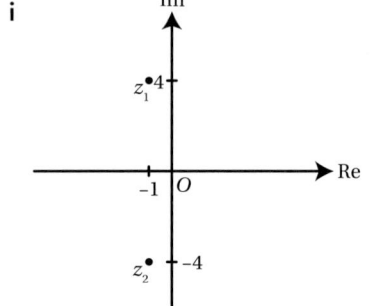

ii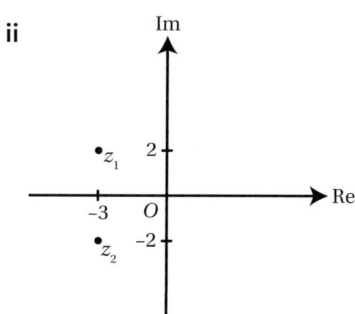

3 a i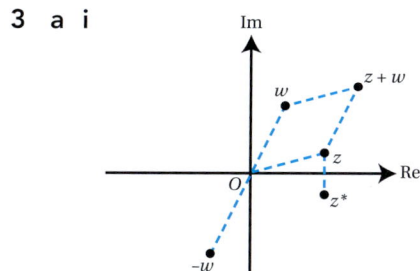

ii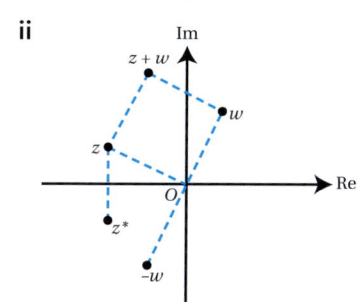

b i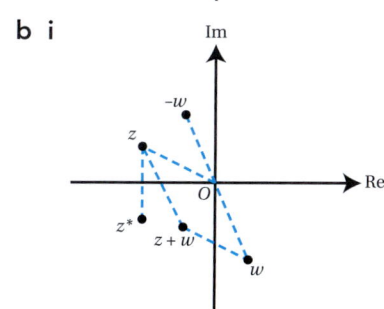

ii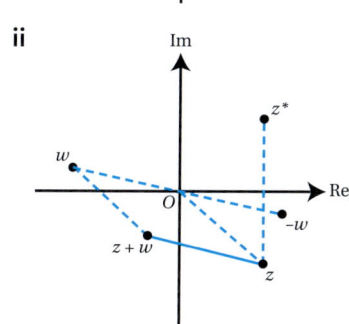

Exercise 4D

1 a i $\dfrac{3\pi}{4}$ ii $\dfrac{\pi}{4}$
   b i $\dfrac{\pi}{2}$ ii $\dfrac{3\pi}{2}$
   c i $\dfrac{2\pi}{3}$ ii $\dfrac{5\pi}{6}$
   d i $\dfrac{5\pi}{18}$ ii $\dfrac{4\pi}{9}$

2 a i 5.585 ii 0.349
   b i 4.712 ii 1.571
   c i 1.134 ii 2.531
   d i 1.745 ii 1.449

3 a i 60° ii 45°
   b i 150° ii 120°
   c i 270° ii 300°
   d i 69.9° ii 265°

Work it out 4.1

Solution 1 is correct.

Exercise 4E

1 a i mod=6, arg=0 ii mod=13, arg=0
   b i mod=3, arg=π ii mod=1.6, arg=π
   c i mod=4, arg=$\dfrac{\pi}{2}$
      ii mod=0.5, arg=$\dfrac{\pi}{2}$
   d i mod=2, arg=$-\dfrac{\pi}{2}$
      ii mod=5, arg=$-\dfrac{\pi}{2}$
   e i mod=$\sqrt{2}$, arg=$\dfrac{\pi}{4}$
      ii mod=$\sqrt{7}$, arg=0.714
   f i mod=2, arg=$-\dfrac{2\pi}{3}$
      ii mod=$4\sqrt{2}$, arg=$-\dfrac{\pi}{4}$

2 a i mod=$2\sqrt{5}$, arg=0.464
      ii mod=5, arg=5.64

b i mod = 2, arg = $\frac{5\pi}{6}$

ii mod = $\sqrt{38}$, arg = 1.34

c i mod = $\sqrt{10}$, arg = 3.46

ii mod = $\sqrt{13}$, arg = 2.55

3 a i $\frac{1}{2} + \frac{\sqrt{3}}{2}i$ **ii** $\frac{-\sqrt{2}}{2} + \frac{\sqrt{2}}{2}i$

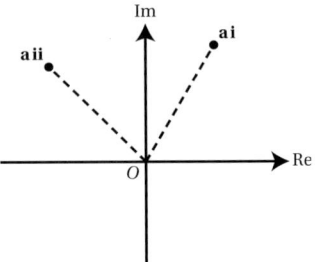

b i 3i **ii** −5i

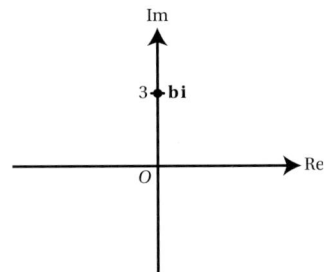

c i 4 **ii** −1

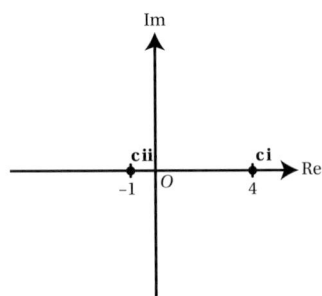

4 a i $2 + 2\sqrt{3}i$ **ii** $1 + i$

b i $-\sqrt{2} + \sqrt{2}i$ **ii** $-1 + \sqrt{3}i$

c i $-3i$ **ii** -4

5 a i $4\operatorname{cis}\left(\frac{\pi}{2}\right)$ **ii** $5\operatorname{cis}(\pi)$

b i $4\operatorname{cis}\left(-\frac{\pi}{3}\right)$ **ii** $\frac{2}{3}\operatorname{cis}\left(\frac{\pi}{6}\right)$

6 a i mod = 4, arg = $\frac{\pi}{3}$

ii mod = $\sqrt{7}$, arg = $\frac{3\pi}{7}$

b i mod = 1, arg = $\frac{\pi}{5}$

ii mod = 1, arg = $-\frac{\pi}{4}$

c i mod = 3, arg = $-\frac{\pi}{8}$

ii mod = 7, arg = $-\frac{4\pi}{5}$

d i mod = 10, arg = $-\frac{2\pi}{3}$

ii mod = 2, arg = $-\frac{5\pi}{6}$

e i mod = 6, arg = $\frac{\pi}{10}$

ii mod = $\frac{1}{2}$, arg = $\frac{\pi}{3}$

7 a $\frac{3\sqrt{2}}{2} - \frac{3\sqrt{2}}{2}i$

b $4\sqrt{2}\operatorname{cis}\left(\frac{3\pi}{4}\right)$

8 a $|z| = 2$, $\arg z = \frac{\pi}{3}$, $|w| = 6$, $\arg w = -\frac{\pi}{6}$

b

c $|zw| = 12$, $\arg(zw) = \frac{\pi}{6}$, $|zw| = |z||w|$, $\arg zw = \arg z + \arg w$

9 a $3\sqrt{3} + 5i$

b $2\sqrt{13}\operatorname{cis} 0.766$

10 a $2r\cos\theta$ **b** r^2

c $\operatorname{cis} 2\theta$

11 Re = 0, Im = $\frac{1 - \cos\theta}{\sin\theta}$ (or $\frac{\sin\theta}{1 + \cos\theta}$)

Answers

Exercise 4F

1 a i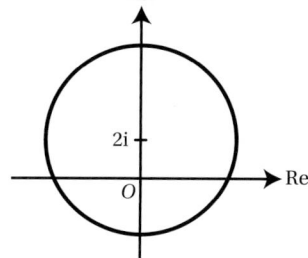

ii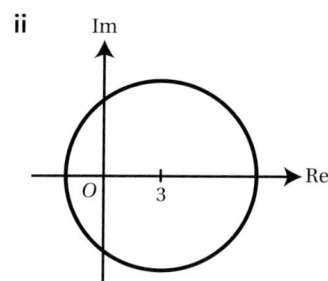

b i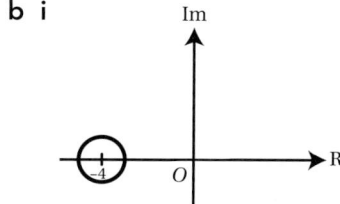

ii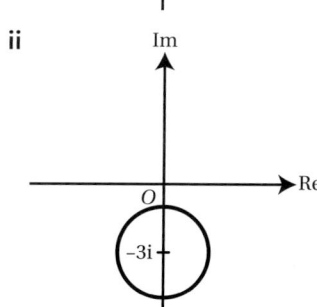

c i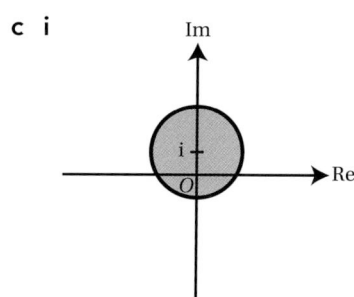

ii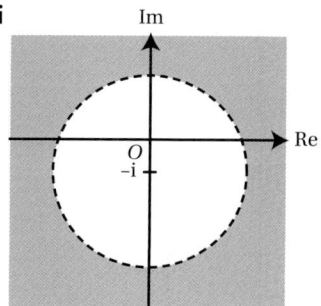

d i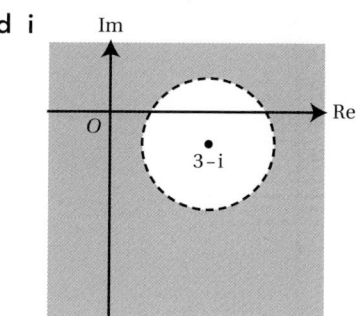

ii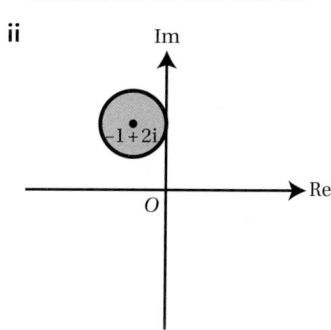

2 a ii $\{x+iy : (x-3)^2 + y^2 = 25\}$

  b i $\{x+iy : (x+4)^2 + y^2 = 1\}$

  ii $\{x+iy : x^2 + (y+3)^2 = 4\}$

  c i $\{x+iy : x^2 + (y-1)^2 \leqslant 4\}$

  ii $\{x+iy : x^2 + (y+1)^2 > 9\}$

  d i $\{x+iy : (x-3)^2 + (y+1)^2 > 4\}$

  ii $\{x+iy : (x+1)^2 + (y-2)^2 \leqslant 1\}$

3 a i

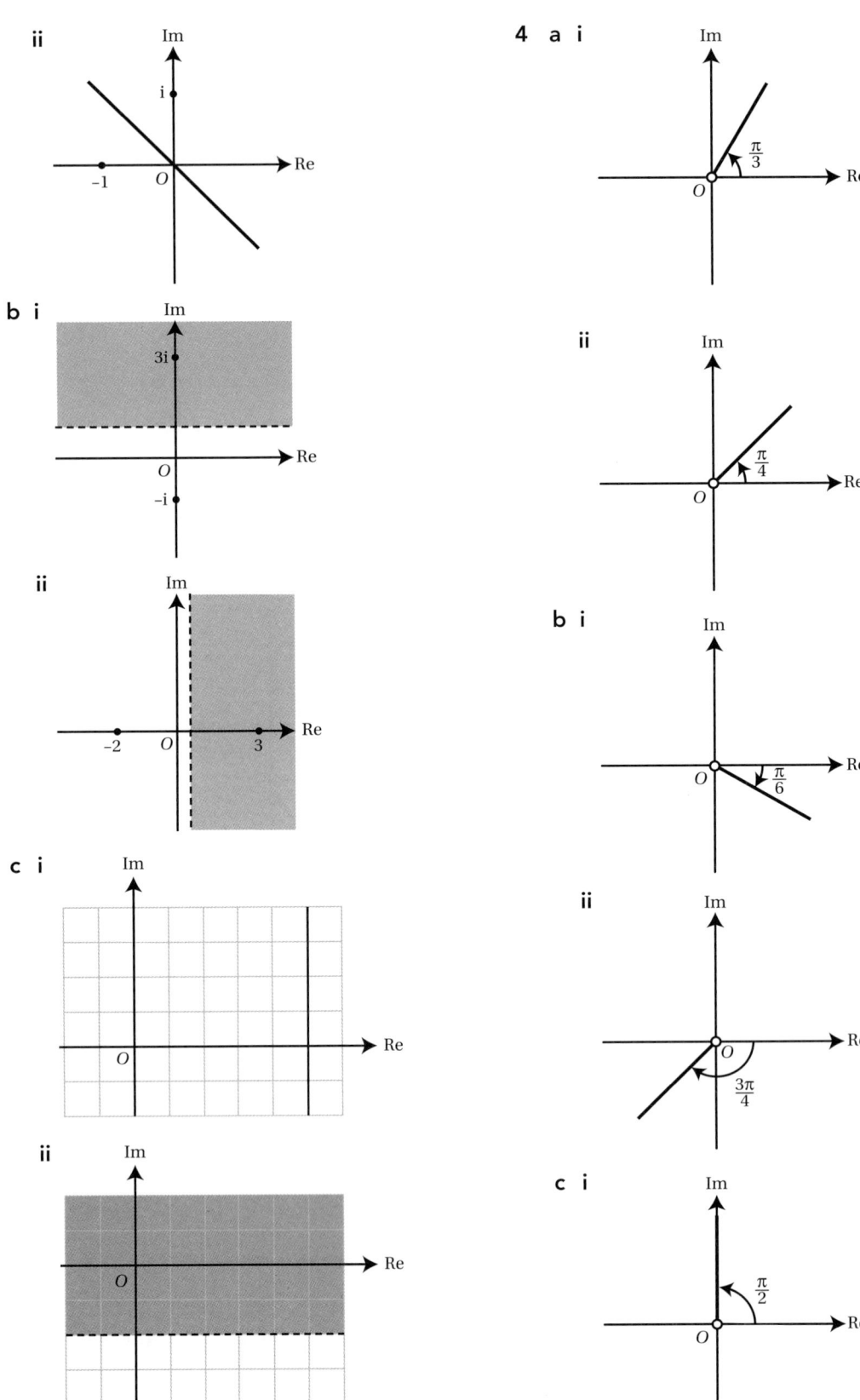

ii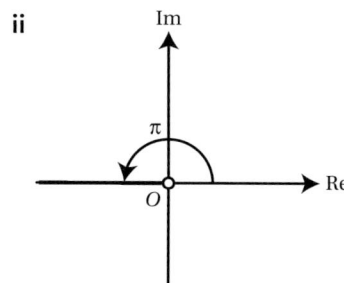

5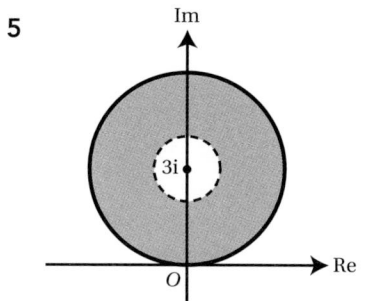

6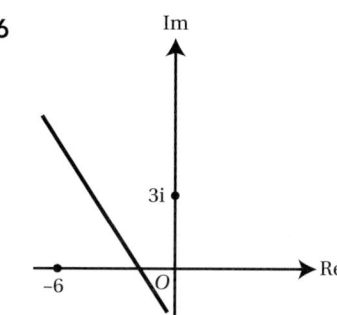

7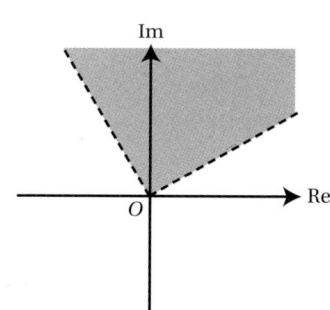

8 a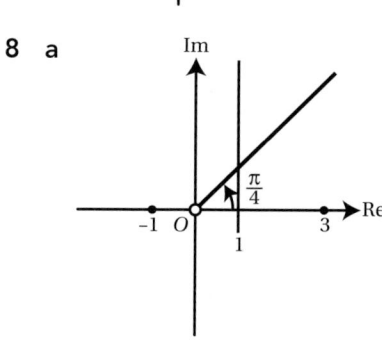

b $z = 1+i$

9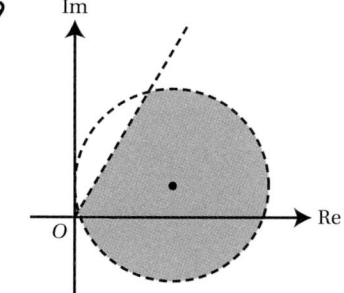

10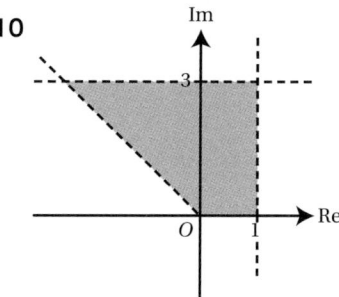

11 $z = 1+i$

12 $\dfrac{\pi}{2}$

Work it out 4.2

Solution 2 is correct.

Exercise 4G

1 a i $21\operatorname{cis}\left(\dfrac{11\pi}{30}\right)$ ii $4\operatorname{cis}\left(\dfrac{2\pi}{9}\right)$

   b i $4\operatorname{cis}4$ ii $3\operatorname{cis}\dfrac{-5\pi}{14}$

2 a i $\cos\left(\dfrac{-11\pi}{12}\right) + i\sin\left(\dfrac{-11\pi}{12}\right)$

     ii $\cos\left(\dfrac{13\pi}{20}\right) + i\sin\left(\dfrac{13\pi}{20}\right)$

   b i $\cos\left(\dfrac{\pi}{12}\right) + i\sin\left(\dfrac{\pi}{12}\right)$

     ii $\cos\left(\dfrac{4\pi}{15}\right) + i\sin\left(\dfrac{4\pi}{15}\right)$

   c i $\cos\left(\dfrac{7\pi}{20}\right) + i\sin\left(\dfrac{7\pi}{20}\right)$

     ii $\cos\left(\dfrac{-5\pi}{12}\right) + i\sin\left(\dfrac{-5\pi}{12}\right)$

   d i $\cos\left(\dfrac{9\pi}{20}\right) + i\sin\left(\dfrac{9\pi}{20}\right)$

     ii $\cos\left(\dfrac{13\pi}{20}\right) + i\sin\left(\dfrac{13\pi}{20}\right)$

3 $3\text{cis}\left(\dfrac{5\pi}{12}\right)$

4 $\sqrt{3}+i$

5 a $\dfrac{\sqrt{2}-\sqrt{6}}{4}+\dfrac{\sqrt{2}+\sqrt{6}}{4}i$ b $-2-\sqrt{3}$

6 a Proof   b Proof

Mixed practice 4

1 a $8+2i$ b $-\dfrac{1}{17}-\dfrac{4}{17}i$

2 $-\dfrac{\sqrt{3}}{2}+\dfrac{7}{2}i$

3 a i $\sqrt{29}$ ii 1.95
   b $\sqrt{29}, -1.95$

4 $a=3, b=2$

5 a $z=-7\pm 2i$
   b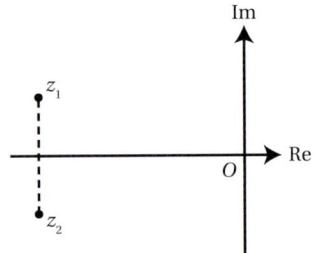

6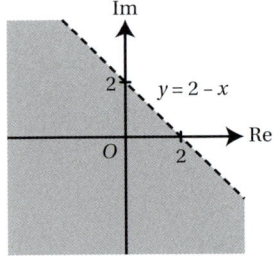

7 $\begin{pmatrix} 2.5 & -1.5i \\ 3i & 2 \end{pmatrix}$

8 $-2-\dfrac{3}{8}i$

9 Proof

10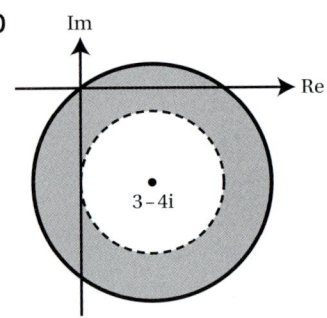

11 a $13, 1.18$ b $-\dfrac{11}{85}-\dfrac{27}{85}i$

12 Proof

13 a $w=iz$ b Proof

14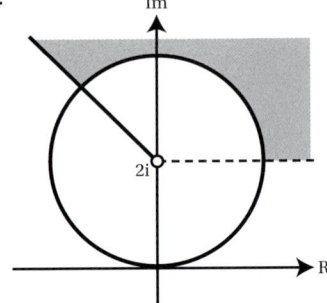

15 a, b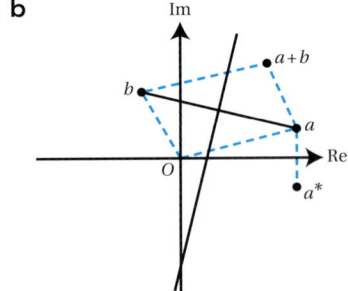

16 a $3\sqrt{2}, -\dfrac{\pi}{4}$

    b, c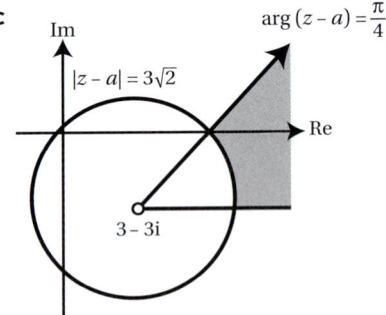

17 $w+2+2i$

18 $\dfrac{1}{2}$

19 Proof

20 $w=5i, z=3+2i$

21 a Proof   b Proof

22 a $\left(\sqrt{6}-\sqrt{2}\right)+i\left(\sqrt{6}-\sqrt{2}\right)$
    b Proof
    c $\cos\left(\dfrac{5\pi}{12}\right)=\dfrac{\sqrt{6}-\sqrt{2}}{4}, \sin\left(\dfrac{5\pi}{12}\right)=\dfrac{\sqrt{6}+\sqrt{2}}{4}$

23 Proof

24 θ

Chapter 5

Before you start...

1. **a** Proof **b** $f(x)=(2x+1)(x-2)(x-3)$
2. **a** $17-7i$ **b** $x=1+2i, 1-2i$
3. **a** 6 **b** 34

Exercise 5A

1. **a** i $(x-(1+i))(x-(1-i))$
   ii $(x-(3+4i))(x-(3-4i))$
   b i $\left(x-\left(-\dfrac{3}{2}+\dfrac{\sqrt{7}}{2}i\right)\right)\left(x-\left(-\dfrac{3}{2}-\dfrac{\sqrt{7}}{2}i\right)\right)$
   ii $(x-(-1+2i))(x-(-1-2i))$
   c i $3\left(x-\left(\dfrac{1}{3}+\dfrac{\sqrt{29}}{3}i\right)\right)\left(x-\left(\dfrac{1}{3}-\dfrac{\sqrt{29}}{3}i\right)\right)$
   ii $5\left(x-\left(-\dfrac{2}{5}+\dfrac{\sqrt{6}}{5}i\right)\right)\left(x-\left(-\dfrac{2}{5}-\dfrac{\sqrt{6}}{5}i\right)\right)$

2. **a** i $(z-2i)(z+2i)$ ii $(z-5i)(z+5i)$
   b i $(2z-7i)(2z+7i)$ ii $(3z-8i)(3z+8i)$
   c i $(z-1)(z+1)(z-i)(z+i)$
   ii $(2z-3)(2z+3)(2z-3i)(2z+3i)$

3. **a** i $(x-2)(x^2+4x+7), x=2, -2\pm i\sqrt{3}$
   ii $(x+1)(x^2+2x+5), x=-1, -1\pm 2i$
   b i $(x+2)(2x^2-4x+3), x=-2, 1\pm\dfrac{\sqrt{2}}{2}i$
   ii $(x-1)(3x^2+2x+2), x=1, -\dfrac{1}{3}\pm\dfrac{\sqrt{5}}{3}i$

4. $x=3, 5\pm i$
5. **a** Proof **b** $(2x+1)(x^2+4x+6)$
6. **a** Proof
   b $x(x-3)(2x+1)(2x+3); x=0, 3, -0.5$ and -1.5
7. **a** Proof
   b $(x+1)(x-2)(x^2+4x+5); x=-1, 2, -2+i, -2-i$
8. $2, -2, 5i, -5i$

Work it out 5.1

Solution 3 is correct.

Exercise 5B

1. **a** i $a=0, b=25$ ii $a=0, b=9$
   b i $a=-6, b=25$ ii $a=-2, b=5$
2. **a** i $(x-5)(x^2-6x+13), x=5, 3\pm 2i$
   ii $(x+3)(x^2-4x+5), x=-3, 2\pm i$
   b i $(x-1)(x^2-2x+5), x=1, 1\pm 2i$
   ii $(x+4)(x^2-6x+10), x=-4, 3\pm i$
3. **a** i $(x^2-2x+10)(x^2+4), x=1\pm 3i, \pm 2i$
   ii $(x^2-6x+10)(x^2+1), x=3\pm i, \pm i$
   b i $(x^2-4x+13)(x^2+2x+3)$, $x=2\pm 3i, -1\pm i\sqrt{2}$
   ii $(x^2-4x+29)(x^2+x+2)$, $x=2\pm 5i, -\dfrac{1}{2}\pm i\dfrac{\sqrt{7}}{2}$
   c i $(x^2+4)(x^2+2x+6), x=\pm 2i, -1\pm i\sqrt{5}$
   ii $(x^2+16)(x^2-4x+5), x=\pm 4i, 2\pm i$
4. $x=-2, 5+i$
5. **a** Proof **b** $x=-3, -4i$
6. **a** $2-5i$ **b** $\pm i$
7. $-2i, 4+i; (x^2+4)(x^2-8x+17)$
8. **a** Proof
   b $(z^2+4)(z^2+z+1)$ **c** $-2i, \dfrac{-1\pm\sqrt{3}i}{2}$
9. $x^4-6x^3+29x^2-96x+208$

Exercise 5C

1. **a** k **b** $4k$
   c k^2-4k **d** $\dfrac{1}{2}$
   e k^3-6k^2 **f** $\dfrac{k-4}{4k}$
2. **a** $-\dfrac{9}{a}$ **b** a^2
   c $\dfrac{9}{a^2}+2a$ **d** $\dfrac{9}{a^2}+4a$

Exercise 5D

1. **a** -2 **b** 3
   c $-\dfrac{8}{3}$ **d** -4
2. **a** $-\dfrac{1}{2}, -\dfrac{3}{2}$ **b** $0, -\dfrac{2}{3}$
   c $0, -\dfrac{8}{5}$

3 $-\dfrac{1}{8}$

4 a $\dfrac{1}{5}$ b $\dfrac{2}{5}$

5 a 4   b $\dfrac{1}{3}$

6 a 1   b Proof

7 $\dfrac{9}{4}$

8 Proof

9 a $-2a^2$

   b $-2a^2 < 0$; but if p, q, r were all real, the sum of their squares would be positive.

Exercise 5E

1 a i $a=-6, b=-6$ ii $a=-8, c=-4$
   b i $a=3, b=12$ ii $b=-5, d=-5$

2 a i $x^2-10x+29$ ii $x^2-6x+10$
   b i x^3-x^2+9x-9
      ii $x^3-3x^2-8x-10$
   c i $x^4-3x^3+5x^2-x-10$
      ii $x^4-2x^3-6x^2+22x-15$
   d i $x^3-6x^2+9x+50$
      ii $x^3+3x^2+9x-13$

3 a $4+i$
   b $x^3-10x^2+33x-34=0$

4 a $-3i, 3+i$ b $a=6, d=90$

5 $x^3-9x^2+36x+27=0$

6 $4x^3+24x^2+45x+31=0$

7 $2x^2-3x+5=0$

8 $x^4-6x^3+8x+32=0$

9 a $\dfrac{2}{5}, -\dfrac{11}{25}$ b $25x^2+11x+4=0$

10 a $-\dfrac{3}{5}$ b $5x^3-3x+1=0$

11 $16x^3+12x^2-49=0$

12 a $(\alpha\beta)^2+(\beta\gamma)^2+(\gamma\alpha)^2+2\alpha\beta\gamma(\alpha+\beta+\gamma)$
   b $x^3+3x^2+16x-36=0$

Work it out 5.2

Solution 2 is correct.

Exercise 5F

1 a i $8u^3-6u+1=0$; roots for u are half of roots for x.
      ii $27u^3+18u^2+5=0$; roots for u are a third of roots for x.
   b i $3u^3-18u^2+35u-18=0$; roots for u are two more than roots for x.
      ii $2u^3+7u^2+8u+4=0$; roots for u are one less than roots for x.
   c i $15u^3+4u^2-3u+5=0$; roots for u are 1/roots for x.
      ii $10u^3-12u^2+8u+8=0$; roots for u are 2/roots for x.
   d i $9u^2-17u+9=0$; roots for u are squares of roots for x.
      ii $4u^2+1=0$; roots for u are squares of roots for x.

2 $3u^3+9u^2+5u+1=0$

3 $32u^4+4u+5=0$

4 a Proof
   b $x=-2, -2\pm 3i$

5 a $c=3$
   b $x=3, 3, 6$

6 $3u^3-5u^2+u-3=0$

7 $\dfrac{2}{9}$

8 a $2u^3+3u^2-u+5=0$
   b $-\dfrac{1}{2}$

9 -1

10 $u^3-4u^2+4u-25=0$

11 $9u^2-75u+1=0$

12 a $k=1$
   b $x=-1\pm i, -1\pm 2i$

Mixed practice 5

1 $-3i, 2$

2 $a=-3, b=7, c=-5$

3 a $1-i\sqrt{2}$; x^2-2x+3 b $-5, 1\pm i\sqrt{2}$

4 $x^4-4x^3-x^2-16x-20=0$

5 a $2u^3-6u^2+9u-8=0$ b 4

Answers

6 $1-2i, -3$
7 a $2+3i$
   b $b=-2, c=5, d=26$
8 $a=-9, b=33$
9 a Proof   b $x^2+301x+8=0$
10 $3u^3+23u^2+64u+67=0$
11 $20u^3-9u+2=0$
12 a $-5, 10$ b Proof
    c $x^2-\dfrac{1}{2}x+1=0$
13 a i $-\dfrac{b}{a}, -\dfrac{d}{a}$ ii Proof
    b i Proof   ii Proof
14 a i Proof   ii Proof
    b i $-\dfrac{b}{a}, -\dfrac{d}{a}$ ii Proof
    c i Proof   ii $\dfrac{25}{4}, 1$
    iii $4x^3-20x^2+25x-4=0$

Chapter 6

Before you start...

1 a $3A+14$
   b 24×5^n
2 $\begin{pmatrix} 1 & 7a \\ 0 & 8 \end{pmatrix}$
3 $25 \times 25!$

Exercise 6A

1 Proof   2 Proof
3 Proof
4 a $\begin{pmatrix} -4 & 0 \\ 0 & -4 \end{pmatrix}$ b Proof   c $\begin{pmatrix} -64 & -64i \\ -64i & -64 \end{pmatrix}$
5 Proof   6 Proof
7 Proof   8 Proof
9 Proof
10 a $\begin{pmatrix} p & q \\ 0 & p \end{pmatrix}$ b Proof

Exercise 6B

1 Proof   7 Proof
3 Proof   9 Proof
2 Proof   6 Proof
4 Proof   8 Proof
5 Proof

Exercise 6C

1 Proof   2 Proof
3 Proof   4 Proof
5 Proof   6 Proof
7 Proof
8 a $n<\dfrac{1}{2}(1-\sqrt{5})$ or $n>\dfrac{1}{2}(1+\sqrt{5})$
    b Proof
9 Proof

Mixed practice 6

1 Proof   2 Proof
3 Proof   4 Proof
5 Proof   6 Proof
7 Proof
8 a $\mathbf{A}^2 = \begin{pmatrix} 2 & 0 \\ 0 & 1 \end{pmatrix}\begin{pmatrix} 2 & 0 \\ 0 & 1 \end{pmatrix} = \begin{pmatrix} 4 & 0 \\ 0 & 1 \end{pmatrix}$,
    $\mathbf{A}^3 = \begin{pmatrix} 4 & 0 \\ 0 & 1 \end{pmatrix}\begin{pmatrix} 2 & 0 \\ 0 & 1 \end{pmatrix} = \begin{pmatrix} 8 & 0 \\ 0 & 1 \end{pmatrix}$
    b $\mathbf{A}^n = \begin{pmatrix} 2^n & 0 \\ 0 & 1 \end{pmatrix}$ c Proof
9 a, b Proof
10 Proof   11 Proof
12 Proof

Focus on ... Proof 2

1 Proof
2 Yes, but it doesn't say anything, since z and z^* are the same number.
3 When we used $(a_k)^* = a_k$. No.
4 Discussion. Consider expanding and simplifying $(x-z)(x-z^*)$

Focus on … Problem-solving 2

1 $x = 2$
2 $u_1 = i, u_2 = -\frac{\sqrt{3}}{2} - \frac{1}{2}i$ and $u_3 = \frac{\sqrt{3}}{2} - \frac{1}{2}i$
3 Discussion

Focus on … Modelling 2

1 2.64×10^{-13}
2 a $\frac{V_{in}}{R}$
   b The resonant current grows without limit.
   c Even the wires will have some resistance.
3 The width of the resonant peak is smaller, so there will be less interference from stations with slightly different frequencies.
4 a $\arctan\left(\dfrac{\omega L - \dfrac{1}{\omega C}}{R}\right)$
   b 0

Cross-topic review exercise 2

1 $-2 + 3i$
2 $5 - \frac{2}{5}i$
3 $\frac{k^2}{4} - 5$
4 Proof
5 a $11 - 29i$ b $1 + 41i$
6 a $3 - i$ b $a = -8, b = 22, c = -20$
7 $2 + \sqrt[3]{5}$
8 a $\sqrt{x^2 + (y-1)^2}$
   b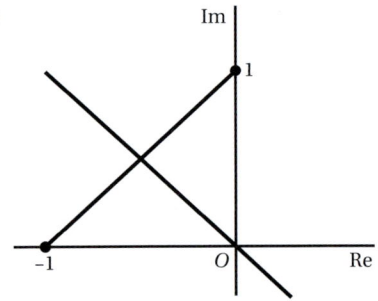

9 a $z = \pm\left(\sqrt{\dfrac{\sqrt{2}-1}{2}} + i\sqrt{\dfrac{\sqrt{2}+1}{2}}\right)$
   b $w = -i \pm \left(\sqrt{\dfrac{\sqrt{2}-1}{2}} + i\sqrt{\dfrac{\sqrt{2}+1}{2}}\right)$
10 Proof
11 a Proof b Proof
12 $x^2 - 4kx + 4k = 0$
13 a $\operatorname{cis}\left(\dfrac{7\pi}{12}\right)$
   b $\dfrac{\sqrt{2}-\sqrt{6}}{4} + i\left(\dfrac{\sqrt{2}+\sqrt{6}}{4}\right)$
   c $2 - \sqrt{3}$

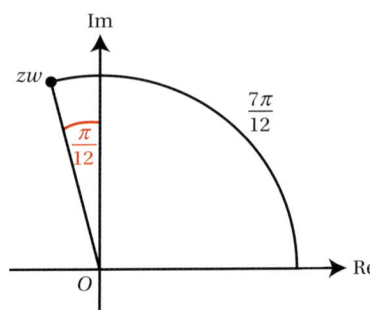

14 a Proof b Proof
   c $x^2 - 6kx + k^2 - (4\sqrt{2})k - 1 = 0$
15 a $2 + i$ b Proof
   c $2 - i$
16 a Proof b Proof
17 $z = -5 - i, w = 3 - 3i$
18 a -2 b $-2, 1 \pm 2i$
   c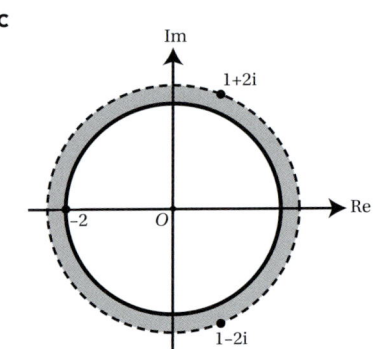
   d 2.21

19 a Proof
  b Proof
  c Proof
  d $\begin{pmatrix} 256 & 256+256\sqrt{3} \\ 256-256\sqrt{3} & 256 \end{pmatrix}$

20 a $\begin{pmatrix} 2 & 0 \\ 0 & 1 \end{pmatrix}$
  b Shear with the x-axis invariant, mapping (0, 1) to (3, 1)
  c Proof **d** Proof

21 a $\begin{pmatrix} 1 & 4 \\ 0 & 1 \end{pmatrix}, \begin{pmatrix} 1 & 6 \\ 0 & 1 \end{pmatrix}$
  b $\begin{pmatrix} 1 & 2n \\ 0 & 1 \end{pmatrix}$
  c Proof
  d Shear with the x-axis invariant, mapping (0, 1) to (20, 1)

22 a Proof **b** Proof
  c (−25, 387)

23 a Proof
  b one more than a multiple of 4 ($n = 4k+1$)

Practice paper

1 a $-1-i$ **b** $\dfrac{4-7i}{5}$

2 a Proof **b** -2

3 $\dfrac{5}{6}$

4 Proof

5 a $\dfrac{2}{11}$ **b** $\dfrac{1}{2-11c}\begin{pmatrix} -3 & 1-c \\ -2 & 3c \end{pmatrix}$

6 a $2, \dfrac{5\pi}{6}$

  b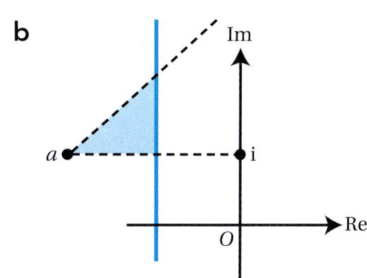

7 Proof

8 a $u^3 + 4u = 0$
  b $-3, -3+2i, -3-2i$

9 a -6 **b** $\begin{pmatrix} 1 & -2 & -2 \\ 0 & 0 & -3 \\ 1 & 0 & 2 \end{pmatrix}$

  c $\begin{pmatrix} -13 \\ -12 \\ 7 \end{pmatrix}$ **d** 162

10 $\mathbf{r} = \begin{pmatrix} -1 \\ 2 \\ 5 \end{pmatrix} + v\begin{pmatrix} 2 \\ -7 \\ 1 \end{pmatrix}$

Glossary

Argand diagram: A diagram used to represent complex numbers geometrically.

Argument: The angle relative to the real axis of a complex number on an Argand diagram.

Associative: A matrix operation is associative if different ways of grouping the matrices give the same answer; for example, $(\mathbf{AB})\mathbf{C} = \mathbf{A}(\mathbf{BC})$.

Axis of rotation: A line about which a rotation takes place in three dimensions.

Cartesian equation: Equation involving x and y.

Cartesian form: A form involving x- and y-coordinates (e.g. the Cartesian form of a complex number is $x + \mathrm{i}y$).

Cofactor: A stage in calculation of an inverse matrix.

Cofactor matrix: A matrix made up of all the cofactors.

Commutative: A matrix operation is commutative when changing the order of the matrices does not change the result; for example, $\mathbf{AB} = \mathbf{BA}$.

Commute: Two numbers (or matrices or transformations) commute if the order of combining them does not matter.

Complex conjugate (z^*): If $z = x + \mathrm{i}y$, then the complex conjugate of z, $z^* = x - \mathrm{i}y$.

Complex number: A number that can be written in the form $x + \mathrm{i}y$, where x and y are real.

Conformable: Two matrices are conformable if they have the correct dimensions for addition or multiplication to be possible.

Conjugate pair: A pair of complex numbers, z and z^*.

Cross product: See **Vector product**.

Determinant: The product of the lead diagonal elements of a matrix minus the product of the reverse diagonal elements.

Direction vector: A vector pointing in the direction of a line.

Dot product: See **Scalar product**.

Identity matrix: A square matrix with ones on the lead diagonal and zeroes everywhere else.

Image: The new shape that results after a transformation has been applied.

Imaginary axis: The axis showing the imaginary part of a complex number on an Argand diagram.

Imaginary part: The number multiplying i in a complex number (e.g. the imaginary part of $2 + 3\mathrm{i}$ is 3).

Inductive step: The part of a proof by induction where the link is made between the statements for $n = k$ and $n = k + 1$.

Invariant line: An invariant line l is a line for which the image of any point on l is also on l.

Invariant point: Any point that is unaffected by a transformation; the origin O is an invariant point for every linear transformation.

Inverse matrix: The inverse of a square matrix $\mathbf{A}$ is denoted $\mathbf{A}^{-1}$ and has the property that $\mathbf{A}\mathbf{A}^{-1} = \mathbf{A}^{-1}\mathbf{A} = \mathbf{I}$.

Line of invariant points: A line on which every point is an invariant point.

Locus: The set of all possible positions of points satisfying a given condition.

Modulus: The distance from the origin of a complex number on an Argand diagram.

Modulus–argument form: Description of a complex number in terms of its modulus and argument; this can be written as $[r, \theta]$.

Non-singular: A matrix with a non-zero determinant.

Null matrix: A matrix in which every element is equal to zero; also called the zero matrix, symbol $\mathbf{Z}$.

Object: The original shape before a transformation is applied.

Plane of reflection: The set of points positioned an equal distance from the object and its reflected image.

Preserves the orientation: A transformation preserves orientation if the vertices of the image occur in the same order as the vertices of the object.

Principle of mathematical induction: Method of proof where the result about one integer is used to prove the result for the next integer.

Radian: The most commonly used unit of angle in advanced mathematics; a full turn measures 2π radians. 1 radian is about $57°$.

Real axis: The axis showing the real part of a complex number on an Argand diagram.

Real part: The part of a complex number that does not contain i; the real part of $x + \mathrm{i}y$ is x.

Glossary

Real polynomial: A polynomial for which all the coefficients are real numbers.

Reverses the orientation: A transformation reverses orientation if the vertices of the image occur in reverse order compared to the vertices of the object.

Scalar product (or dot product): A way of multiplying two vectors so that the answer is a scalar, denoted $\mathbf{a} \cdot \mathbf{b}$.

Shear: A transformation in which points can be moved horizontally or vertically, but in proportion to each point's distance from the origin.

Singular: A matrix $\mathbf{A}$ with det $\mathbf{A} = 0$ is called singular and has no inverse.

Skew lines: Lines that are not parallel but do not intersect.

Square matrix: A matrix that has the same number of rows as columns.

Transpose: The transpose of matrix $\mathbf{A}$ is denoted by $\mathbf{A}^\mathbf{T}$ and is such that the rows of $\mathbf{A}^\mathbf{T}$ are the columns of $\mathbf{A}$.

Unit square: The square with vertices (0, 0), (1, 0), (1, 1), (1, 0).

Vector equation (of a line): Equation in the form $\mathbf{r} = \mathbf{a} + \lambda \mathbf{d}$.

Vector product (or cross product): A way of multiplying two vectors so that the answer is a vector; denoted $\mathbf{a} \times \mathbf{b}$.

Zero matrix: See **Null matrix**.

Index

adjacency matrices   103, 105
angles
    radians   122–3
    between vectors   48–54
Argand diagrams   119–20
    horizontal and vertical lines   133
    loci involving the argument   132–3
    loci involving the modulus   129–31
argument of a complex number   121–2
associativity, matrix multiplication   11

binomial series   188

Cartesian equation of a line   39–43
Cartesian form of a complex number   122
cis θ 125
cofactors of matrix elements   25
commutativity, and matrix multiplication   11
complex conjugates   115–16, 144–7
    proving properties of   178–9
complex numbers   109–11
    Cartesian form   122
    converting between forms   123–5
    division   115–17, 135–6
    in electronics   182
    factorising polynomials   143
    geometric representation   119–20
    given formulae   188
    modulus and argument   121–2
    operations in modulus–argument form   134–6
    and polynomial equations   144–7
    in quadratic equations   111
    in simultaneous equations   117
    solving cubic equations   181
    square roots of   112–13
    and trigonometric functions   125–7
complex plane, loci in   129–33
conformable matrices   3
cross product (vector product)   56–7
    application to inverse matrices   58–9
cubic equations
    finding an equation with given roots   157–8
    roots and coefficients   151, 152–3
    solving   180–1
    see also polynomial equations
cubic formula   180

determinants
    of a 2 × 2 matrix   14–16
    of a 3 × 3 matrix   23–5
    and inverse matrices   18–19
    and simultaneous equations   67–8
    of transformation matrices   73, 91–2
difference of two squares   143
differentiation from first principles   188
direction vectors   34, 35, 39
discriminant, cubic formula   180, 181
divisibility, application of mathematical induction   171–3
dot product (scalar product) of vectors   48–9

electronics, use of complex numbers   182
enlargement matrices   72, 73, 80, 82

factorials, application of mathematical induction   175
formulae given on assessment papers   188

Gödel, Kurt   167

i   110
    see also complex numbers
identity matrices   2, 13–14
    proving properties of   98–9
imaginary numbers   109
    see also complex numbers
imaginary part of a complex number   110
inductive steps   168
    see also mathematical induction
inequalities
    application of mathematical induction   174–5
    involving complex numbers   129–33
intersections of lines   45–7
invariant lines   85–6
invariant points   83–4
inverse matrices
    2 × 2 matrices   17–21
    3 × 3 matrices   25–6
    uses of   19–21
    and the vector product   58–9
inverse transformations   74–5

Index

linear simultaneous equations, matrix method 65–8
lines in three dimensions
    angles and the scalar product 48–54
    intersections of 45–7
    vector equation of 33–7
lines in two dimensions
    Cartesian equation of 39–43
    vector equation of 34, 39–43
loci in the complex plane 129
    involving the argument 132–3
    involving the modulus 129–31

mathematical induction 167
    application to divisibility 171–3
    application to factorials 175
    application to inequalities 174–5
    application to matrices 168–70, 169–70
    principle of 168–9
matrices 1–3
    3×3 23–6
    addition and subtraction 3–4
    application of mathematical induction 168–70
    determinants 14–16, 23–5
    identity matrix 13–14
    inverses 17–21, 25–6, 58–9
    powers of 168–70
    proving properties of 98–9
    representation of networks 103, 105
    scalar multiplication 5
    solving linear simultaneous equations 65–8
matrix multiplication 7–11
    using inverse matrices 19–21
matrix transformations 188
    in 2-D 70–5, 78–82
    in 3-D 88–92
modelling
    complex numbers and radios 182
    counting paths in networks 103–5
modulus of a complex number 121–2

negative numbers 112
network problems 103–5
non-singular matrices 18, 21
null matrix (zero matrix) 2, 14
number theory, divisibility 171–3

parallel lines, vector equations 33, 36
parametric equation of a line 41

path counting, networks 103–5
perpendicular lines
    and the vector product 56–8
    vectors of 51–4
polynomial equations
    complex solutions 144–7
    cubic formula 180–1
    finding an equation with given roots 154–8
    proof involving complex conjugates 178–9
    roots and coefficients 148–53
    transforming equations 160–2
polynomials, factorising 141–3
position vectors 33–4
principle of mathematical induction 168–9
problem-solving
    calculating distances 100–1
    solving cubic equations 180–1
projection 101
proofs
    properties of identity and inverse matrices 98–9
    roots of real polynomials 178–9
    see also mathematical induction

quadratic equations
    finding an equation with given roots 155, 156
    roots and coefficients 148–50
    using complex numbers 111
    see also polynomial equations
quartic equations
    finding an equation with given roots 155
    roots and coefficients 152
    see also polynomial equations

radians 122–3
real part of a complex number 110
real polynomials
    complex solutions 144–7
    proof of complex conjugate roots 178–9
    see also polynomial equations
reflection matrices 71, 72, 73, 78–9, 81, 188
    in 3-D 88–9, 90
resonance 182
'right hand rule' 58
roots of cubic and quartic equations, functions of 151–3
roots of quadratic equations, functions of 148–50
rotation matrices 70, 72, 73, 81, 188
    in 3-D 89–90
    general rotations 78

scalar product (dot product) of vectors   48–9
shears, transformation matrices   80–1, 82
shortest distance from a point to
a line   52–4, 100–1
simultaneous equations   45, 46
    with complex numbers   117
    matrix method   65–8
singular matrices   18
skew lines   46
square matrices   2
stretches, transformation matrices   79–80, 81–2
successive transformations   73–4
    in 3-D   91
    inverses   75

transformation matrices in 2-D   70–3
    determinants   73
    enlargements   80
    invariant points and invariant lines   83–6
    inverse transformations   74–5
    reflections   78–9
    rotations   78
    shears   80–1
    stretches   79
    successive transformations   73–4
    summary   81–2
transformation matrices in   3-D 88
    determinants   91–2
    reflections   88–9, 90
    rotations   89–90
    successive transformations   91
transforming polynomial equations   160–2
transpose of a matrix   2–3

vector equation of a line   33–7
    relationship to Cartesian equation   39–43
vector product (cross product) 56–7
    application to inverse matrices   58–9
vectors
    angles and the scalar product   48–54
    direction vectors   34, 35
    given formulae   188
    intersections of lines   45–7
    of parallel lines   33
    perpendicular lines   51–4, 100–1
    position vectors   33–4

zero matrix (null matrix)   2, 14

Acknowledgements

The authors and publishers acknowledge the following sources of copyright material and are grateful for the permissions granted. While every effort has been made, it has not always been possible to identify the sources of all the material used, or to trace all copyright holders. If any omissions are brought to our notice, we will be happy to include the appropriate acknowledgements on reprinting.

Thanks to the following for permission to reproduce images:

Cover image: David Angel/Getty Images

Back cover: Fabian Oefner www.fabianoefner.com

Petr Tyurin/EyeEm/Getty Images; Robert Decelis Ltd/Getty Images; Photograph by Patrick Murphy/Getty Images; ARUNAS KLUPSAS/Getty Images; claudiodivizia/Getty Images; Auscape/UIG/Getty Images; Alfred Eisenstaedt/The LIFE Picture Collection/Getty Images; Photograph by Vitaliy Piltser/Getty Images